Mounting Pressures on the Rule of Law

This important book offers an original perspective on the rule of law, development, and democracy in Latin America, establishing a new approach in recognizing the realities of political economy as opposed to merely structural and institutional factors.

With contributions from an international team of experts, the book outlines the main challenges that have arisen in the pursuit of a developmental agenda in the region, including subnational variations, state capture by local elites, variations in state capacity, border divergence from centrally designed perspectives, environmental conflicts, uneven access to justice, and the role of international organizations. In doing so, the book explores the democratic and developmental implications of conflicts over the rule of law and its application, uneven enforcement, and state capture.

Whether a reference tool for the seasoned scholar, a guide aiding practitioner's individual expertise, or an introduction to students interested in the complex intersections between the rule of law, development, and democracy, this book is a must-have for any library.

Jacqueline Behrend is Professor of Comparative Politics at the School of Politics and Government of the Universidad Nacional de San Martin in Argentina, where she is also Vice-Dean for Academic Affairs and a tenured Research Fellow at the National Scientific and Technical Research Council (CONICET) in Argentina. She holds a DPhil in Politics from the University of Oxford. Her research focuses on subnational comparative politics. She was president of the *Red Eurolatinoamericana de Gobernabilidad para el Desarrollo* (RedGob) in 2022–2023.

Laurence Whitehead is a senior research fellow at Nuffield College, Oxford, and Chairman of the Board of the Oxford Institute of Energy Studies. He also edits Oxford University Press' book series on Democratization and succeeded Jacqueline Behrend as president of the *Red Eurolatinoamericana de Gobernabilidad para el Desarrollo* (RedGob) for 2023–2024.

Routledge Studies in Latin American Politics

38. The Latin American Military and Politics in the Twenty-First Century
A Cross-National Analysis
Kees Koonings and Dirk Kruijt

39. The Consequences of Brazilian Social Movements in Historical Perspective
Edited by Valesca Lima, Rafaela N. Pannain and Gabriela Pereira Martins

40. Geopolitical Landscapes of Donald Trump
International Politics and Institutional Characteristics of Mexico-Guatemala Relations
Edited by Carlos Heredia-Zubieta

41. Crime, Violence, and Justice in Latin America
Edited by Carlos Solar & Carlos A. Pérez Ricart

42. Dominican Politics in the Twenty First Century
Continuity and Change
Edited by Jacqueline Jiménez Polanco & Ernesto Sagás

43. Mano Dura Policies in Latin America
Sebastián A. Cutrona and Jonathan D. Rosen

44. Latin America in Times of Turbulence
Presidentialism under stress
Mariana Llanos and Leiv Marsteintredet

45. Explaining Support for Populism in Contemporary Latin America
Dinorah Azpuru

46. Mounting Pressures on the Rule of Law
Governability for Development and Democracy in Latin America
Edited by Jacqueline Behrend and Laurence Whitehead

https://www.routledge.com/Routledge-Studies-in-Latin-American-Politics/book-series/RSLAP

Mounting Pressures on the Rule of Law

Governability for Development and Democracy in Latin America

Edited by Jacqueline Behrend and Laurence Whitehead

Routledge
Taylor & Francis Group
NEW YORK AND LONDON

First published 2025
by Routledge
605 Third Avenue, New York, NY 10158

and by Routledge
4 Park Square, Milton Park, Abingdon, Oxon, OX14 4RN

Routledge is an imprint of the Taylor & Francis Group, an informa business

Funding for Open Access has been provided by CAF – banco de desarrollo de América Latina y el Caribe.

Library of Congress Cataloging-in-Publication Data
Names: Behrend, Jacqueline, 1975- editor. | Whitehead, Laurence, editor.
Title: Mounting pressures on the rule of law: governability for development and democracy in Latin America/edited by Jacqueline Behrend and Laurence Whitehead.
Description: Abingdon, Oxon [UK]; New York, NY: Routledge, 2025. |
Series: Routledge studies in Latin American politics | Includes bibliographical references and index. | Summary: "This important book offers an original perspective on the rule of law, development, and democracy in Latin America, establishing a new approach in recognizing the realities of political economy as opposed to merely structural and institutional factors. With contributions from an international team of experts, the book outlines the main challenges that have arisen in the pursuit of a developmental agenda in the region, including subnational variations, state capture by local elites, variations in state capacity, border divergence from centrally designed perspectives, environmental conflicts, uneven access to justice and the role of international organizations. In doing so, the book explores the democratic and developmental implications of conflicts over the rule of law and its application, uneven enforcement, and state capture. Whether a reference tool for the seasoned scholar, a guide aiding practitioner's individual expertise or an introduction to students interested in the complex intersections between the rule of law, development and democracy, this book is a must-have for any library"–Provided by publisher.
Identifiers: LCCN 2024043634 (print) | LCCN 2024043635 (ebook) | ISBN 9781032793542 (hardback) | ISBN 9781032976822 (paperback) | ISBN 9781003519195 (ebook) Subjects: LCSH: Rule of law–Latin America. | Civil rights–Latin America. | Democracy–Latin America.
Classification: LCC KG552 .M68 2025 (print) | LCC KG552 (ebook) | DDC 340/.11–dc23/eng/20240925
LC record available at https://lccn.loc.gov/2024043634
LC ebook record available at https://lccn.loc.gov/2024043635

ISBN: 978-1-032-79354-2 (hbk)
ISBN: 978-1-032-97682-2 (pbk)
ISBN: 978-1-003-51919-5 (ebk)

DOI: 10.4324/9781003519195

Typeset in Times New Roman
by Deanta Global Publishing Services, Chennai, India

Contents

Contributors

Karabekir Akkoyunlu is Lecturer in the Department of Politics and International Studies, SOAS University of London, where he convenes courses on Social Science Research Methods, Introduction to Comparative Politics, and Middle East Politics. His research focuses on the actors and institutions of democratization and autocratization, tutelary hybrid regimes, and civil–military relations, with a particular interest in Turkey, Iran, and Brazil. His forthcoming monograph is *Guardianship and Democracy in Iran and Turkey: Tutelary Consolidation, Popular Contestation* (Edinburgh University Press, 2024).

Susana Berruecos holds a doctorate in Government and an MSc in Public Administration and Public Policy from the London School of Economics and Political Science (LSE), as well as a bachelor's degree in Political Science from the Instituto Tecnológico Autónomo de México (ITAM). She joined the Latin American Centre at the University of Oxford as Academic Visitor in December 2022 and is now Research Associate at Oxford School of Global and Area Studies (OSGA). She is currently Head of Policy and Public Affairs at Canning House. She has been a visiting fellow at LSE and Georgetown University. She has published on judicial politics, democratization, security, and electoral institutions and is co-editor of *Mexico's Struggle for Public Security: Organized Crime and State Responses.*

Jan Boesten is a Deutsche Forschungsgemeinschaft (DFG) postdoctoral researcher at the Institute for Latin American Studies (LAI) at the Freie Universität Berlin, as well as an Associate Member of Nuffield College at the University of Oxford. His work has appeared in the *Latin American Research Review* (LARR), *Colombia Internacional, Precedente,* and several edited volumes. The book, *Constitutional Origin and Norm Creation in Colombia: Discursive Institutionalism and the Empowerment of the Constitutional Court*, based on his PhD research, has been published with Routledge. His current research, funded by a DFG grant, compares peace processes in Colombia in search for institutional caveats of non-state armed order and their ramifications for institutional trajectories. He is a founding member of the Interdisciplinary Research Group on Peace and Conflict (GIFK).

Maxwell A. Cameron is Professor in the Department of Political Science and the School of Public Policy and Global Affairs at the University of British Columbia. His research and teaching focus on the comparative politics of democratization in Latin America. He is Vice President and President-elect of the Latin American Studies Association (LASA), and in 2022, he was awarded the LASA Guillermo O'Donnell Democracy Award and Lectureship.

Lucas G. Christel holds a PhD in Political Science from the National University of San Martín. He is currently Research Assistant at the National Scientific and Technical Research Council (CONICET), Director of the Southern Cone and Brazil Regional Center CALAS, and Director of the BA in Political Science at UNSAM. He is interested in the socio-technical controversies over the risks of extractive industries, collective action dynamics, environmental politics, and issues of climate change, energy transition, and biodiversity.

John Crabtree is Research Associate at the Latin American Centre, University of Oxford. He holds a master's degree from Liverpool University and a doctorate from Oxford Brookes University. His most recent published books include *Business Power and the State in the Central Andes: Bolivia, Ecuador and Peru in Comparison*, co-authored with Francisco Durand and Jonas Wolff (Pittsburgh University Press, 2023). A Spanish version of the book is entitled *Estado y poder empresarial en Bolivia, Ecuador y Perú: un estudio comparativo* (Pontificia Universidad Católica del Perú, Plural and Abya Yala, 2024).

J. Carlos Domínguez Virgen is Full-time Professor at Instituto Mora in Mexico City. He holds a BA in Economics from the Monterrey Institute of Technology (ITESM); a BA in Philosophy from Birkbeck College, UK; and an MPhil and a DPhil in Development Studies from Oxford University, UK. He is a member of the National Research System in México (SNI, Level II). He has published extensively on the politics of large infrastructure projects, planned development, social movements, and democracy in Mexico and other Latin American countries. One of his latest books is *Democracias en vilo. La incertidumbre política en América Latina* (Instituto Mora, 2020), coordinated jointly with Alejandro Monsivais.

Par Engstrom (BA UCL, MSc London, DPhil Oxford) is Associate Professor of Human Rights at the Institute of the Americas and Vice-Dean of Impact and External Engagement at the Faculty of Social and Historical Sciences at University College London. He has been Visiting Professor at the Paris School of International Affairs (PSIA) at Sciences Po, France, and at the University of São Paulo, Brazil.

Ricardo A. Gutiérrez holds a bachelor's degree in Political Science and a master's degree in Social Sciences Research from the University of Buenos Aires and a PhD in Political Science from Johns Hopkins University. He serves as Professor and Dean of the Politics and Government School at the National University of San Martín and as a principal researcher at the National Scientific and Technical Research Council (CONICET). His research agenda addresses the multiple interactions between state, social, and economic actors in the debate on environmental protection in Latin America.

Luis E. Karamaneff holds a PhD in Political Science from the Universidad Nacional de San Martín, Argentina, and a master's degree in Public Policy from the Catholic University of Córdoba-Georgetown University. He is currently a postdoctoral fellow at the National Scientific and Technical Research Council (CONICET) and Professor at the School of Politics and Government (UNSAM). His area of study focuses on subnational political economy. He previously served as Director of Productive Development and Employment and Coordinator of Labor Intermediation in the Province of Tucumán, Argentina.

José Antonio Lima has a PhD in International Relations from the University of São Paulo and is also a journalist. His research agenda is currently dedicated to civil–military relations in Brazil and the international relations of the Middle East.

Daniel Llanos Ramírez is a political scientist specializing in the Latin American region. Currently a research scientist at the Heidelberg Institute for Conflict Research, his work focuses on organized crime and violence in Honduras and El Salvador. He is a founding member of the Interdisciplinary Research Group on Peace and Conflict (GIFK). His research interests focus on peacebuilding, conflict resolution, crime, and the intersection between environmental activism and violence. Daniel has work experience in governmental organizations in the field of international relations and the European Union Affairs Committee in the German Bundestag, the Colombian Embassy in Berlin, and the German development bank KfW.

Edward Perez holds an LLM from the University of Cambridge (United Kingdom), an MPP from Universidad de los Andes (Colombia), and a law degree from Universidad Católica Andrés Bello (Venezuela). He is currently a PhD student at University College London's Faculty of Law (United Kingdom). Prior to his academic pursuits, he worked as an attorney at the Inter-American Court of Human Rights, a senior legal adviser at the Center for Reproductive Rights, and a consultant for other international institutions and NGOs. His current research focuses on structural remedies in cases of human rights violations, specifically those issued by the Inter-American Court, and their legitimacy, potential, and impact.

Aarón Quiñón Cárdenas is a political scientist from the Catholic University (PUCP) in Lima. He is a researcher at the Center for Mining and Sustainability Studies (CEMS) at the University of the Pacific and in the Research Group on State and Society (GIES) at the PUCP. He has also conducted research at the Research Center of the University of the Pacific and the National Jury of Elections (JNE). He has published academic articles and public policy documents on decentralization, political parties, extractive industries, and democracy in Peru and Latin America. Currently, he combines a research agenda on the political economy of artisanal and small-scale mining with political regimes and populism. He is Program Lead Coordinator at the civil association Recambio.

Vinícius G. Rodrigues Vieira is Associate Professor of Economics and International Relations at the Armando Alvares Penteado Foundation (FAAP), Lecturer in International Relations at the Getúlio Vargas Foundation (FGV), Research Professor in Public Policy at the Brazilian Institute of Development, Research, and Education (IDP), and Associate Researcher at the Institute for Advanced Study of the University of São Paulo (IEA-USP). He holds a doctorate from Nuffield College, University of Oxford, and is the author of *Shaping Nations and Markets: Identity Capital, Trade, and the Populist Rage* (Routledge, 2024). Since 2023, he has been serving as the co-chair of the research committee on International Political Economy of the International Political Science Association (IPSA).

Yanina Welp is Research Fellow at the Albert Hirschman Centre on Democracy, Graduate Institute (Geneva). She holds a PhD in Political and Social Sciences from Pompeu Fabra University (Spain) and two bachelor's degrees in Social Communication and Political Science from the University of Buenos Aires (Argentina). Her last book is *The Will of the People: Populism and Citizens Participation in Latin America* (De Gruyter 2022).

Anna Wilson is OSGA Research Associate (Latin American Centre) at the University of Oxford and led the research project "Towards improved formalisation of artisanal and small-scale mining in Peru" at the Oxford Department of International Development. Her research is anthropological, and interests include public policy, infrastructure, and mining. She also has experience in public policymaking in the central UK government.

Preface

Christian Asinelli, Corporate Vice President of Strategic Programming of the CAF-development bank of Latin America and the Caribbean

This publication is the direct outcome of the annual conference of the Euro-Latin American Governability for Development Network (Red Euro-Latinoamericana de Gobernabilidad para el Desarrollo (RedGob)), which took place on the 13th and 14th of July 2023 at the National University of San Martin (UNSAM), Argentina.

The conference was organized by the UNSAM with the support of both the CAF development bank of Latin America and the Caribbean, and the International Institute for Democracy and Electoral Assistance. The meeting brought together specialists, academic authorities, and public policy decision-makers from across the region to discuss the achievements, the limitations, and the institutional windows of opportunity available in relation to ideas such as rule of law and its absence; governability and state capacity; democratic and sustainable development; access to justice; electoral justice; and criminality and corruption; amongst others.

As a direct product of these debates, *Mounting Pressures on the Rule of Law: Governability for Development and Democracy in Latin America* offers our region something of fundamental worth: the promotion, dissemination, and strengthening of our understanding of the idea of "rule of law," and the relationship between this and another key concept – that of "governance for development." From a strictly theoretical perspective, both categories lack a single or predetermined definition, and so their meanings and usages exist in a state of constant transformation shaped by the sociopolitical climate, citizens' demands, and the ethical-judicial codes and equilibriums that prevail at any given historical moment. However, if observed from an institutional political perspective, the link between rule of law and governance for development becomes critically important, determining as it does the balance between public decision-making processes and the application of the law. This is because balancing the shared interests of a democratic society with the need for general stability, promotion of the public good, and the equilibration of competing political forces can clash with the administration of a uniform legal order that is sometimes inconsistent with these prerequisites.

This complicated balancing act creates two key challenges for the governments of Latin America and the Caribbean. On the one hand, promoting sustainable and equitable regional development policies in line with legal agreements that are fair and of equal access to all; and, on the other hand, making sure that these decisions, mechanisms, and balances originate *from* and are designed *for* the same region in which they are to apply, in acknowledgement of the fact that local idiosyncrasies, democratic debates, and systems of political legitimacy are sovereign and non-transferable.

At CAF, we are convinced that Latin American and Caribbean programmes must possess strategic perspectives that take into account all aspects of development. With this in mind, more than 20 years ago, we began opening up spaces in which institutional experiences could be shared, and where regional leaders, public officials, young people, and communal authorities could be given training in "soft" skills and a range of interdisciplinary capabilities. This commitment stems from the fact that knowledge is part of our institutional backbone and sustains our efforts to improve the quality of life in Latin America and the Caribbean. Our work thus focuses on the promotion of skills and knowledge in areas such as governance and public innovation, digital transformation, state capacity, gender equality, diversity and social inclusion, and climate change.

Responsibility for the sustainable development and regional integration of Latin America and the Caribbean lies in our hands, and our success depends on the work of each and every one of us. On that note, special credit must go to the School of Politics and Government of the National University of San Martín, to RedGob, and to all the specialists who shared with us their valuable and original contributions both within the framework of last year's conference and, subsequently, with a view to making this book a reality.

1 The rule of law, development, and democracy in Latin America

Theory and experience

Jacqueline Behrend and Laurence Whitehead

Introduction

This chapter lays the ground for a comparative and theoretical discussion of the multiple challenges and mounting pressures that the rule of law faces in the pursuit of governability for development in contemporary Latin America. It does so by addressing how the rule of law interacts with development and democracy. The rule of law is widely seen by scholars and experts as contributing both to economic development and democratic governance. However, this linkage is not straightforward – it is a contested process where the interests of diverse actors need to be reconciled. Latin America is at a crossroads in which new economic development projects bring to the fore tensions between the interests of various communities and actors, both private and public, that are affected by those projects. At the same time, after the post-Cold War wave of democratization, many Latin American countries reformed their judicial systems to enhance the role of prosecutors, courts, and other state agencies to fight corruption and other misdoings. In some cases, these reforms have served their purpose and given citizens new, powerful tools to contest and advance rights, but in others the new institutions have become entangled with existing practices and failed to deliver justice.

This volume makes three theoretical moves and seeks to contribute to scholarship on the rule of law in areas that are understudied and merit closer attention. The first is how the rule of law is invoked in disputes over competing ideas about development in the region. This is at the heart of developmental, environmental, and social disputes in contemporary Latin America and ought to be studied in greater depth. The second move is the development of an expansive understanding of the rule of law as encompassing much more than the enforcement of rules. It also involves ideas of justice and considerations of what is fair in a given context, how laws are created, contested, become embedded, and are enforced across territory. The third move draws attention to the contrast between idealized views of the rule of law and a behavioural perspective of such matters. The rule of law is not uniform, and there are brown areas (O'Donnell, 1999) where the state and the law don't fully prevail, but instead coexist with entanglements between formal rules and informal structures and practices (Behrend & Whitehead, 2021, 2023). These three conceptual anchors

DOI: 10.4324/9781003519195-1

organize the discussions that follow in this edited collection. The main theoretical implications of this book concern processes whereby governability for development, the rule of law, and democracy become entangled in contemporary Latin America, producing diverse outcomes, and how conflicting views of these arenas and their interrelations shape policy. The book aims to set a new agenda for the study of the rule of law that goes beyond the strictly institutionalist approach of the seminal edited volumes in the field of judicial politics or those that deal with institutional weakness.

Elsewhere, we developed the concept of entanglement to refer to how formal and informal structures and practices are generated, interact, or share proximity in such a way that each cannot be explained independently of the other (Behrend & Whitehead, 2023). One of the main principles of entanglement is "non-separability" (Wendt, 2015: 33). This means that the outcomes that political scientists and comparativists seek to explain cannot be understood as the result of causal processes that flow in only one direction or that can be isolated (Behrend & Whitehead, 2023). In discussions about governability for development, the entanglement of economic development agendas with disputes and demands over how the rule of law is applied generates conflicts that shape policymaking and have effects in different arenas.

In this volume, we adopt an expanded understanding of the rule of law that goes beyond institutions and focuses on its contested nature. Like the concepts of democracy and development, the concept of the rule of law is an "essentially contested" concept (Gallie, 1956). To economic actors concerned with securing their investments, the rule of law is likely to be equated to legal guarantees that protect private property. To citizens concerned with having an equal say in the development projects that are undertaken in their territory, the rule of law is more likely to relate to the activation of dormant constitutional rights and to embedding these rights and making them readily available to local populations (Taylor, 2023). To others, the rule of law is limited to specific outcomes that can be understood and measured objectively. Yet others may equate the rule of law to enforcement. Here, we propose to explore how these contested visions of the rule of law become entangled with governability for development, both directly, in disputes over specific development projects, and indirectly, in conflicts over who governs, what malfeasance is investigated and prosecuted, and who has the monopoly over the use of violence in a society. Several edited volumes in the discipline of comparative politics have dealt with the rule of law, judicial politics, and institutional weakness in Latin America, and this volume engages with some of these discussions.[1] But, as far as we know, none of these collections have linked these agendas to the idea of governability for development. It is this gap in the literature that this book seeks to address.

The rule of law and governability for development

From the governability perspective, much of the mounting pressure on Latin America's current rule of law systems derives from the demands of economic development. With primary exports still a critical source of foreign exchange, legal disputes often concern extractivism in the energy and mining sectors. Commercial agriculture represents another crucial sector of the regional economy that generates intense controversy concerning land titles, water rights, labour conditions, and the protection of nature, all matters that occasion growing litigation. Contraband, money laundering, and related illicit economic activities test the limits of an overstretched and poorly supervised justice system. Acute inequalities of wealth, income, and regional welfare strain the tax systems and challenge the integrity of the public provision of goods and services. In brief, when development plans fall short, the rule of law is brought into contention and conflicts over development projects – be they dams, mining, commercial agriculture, new construction projects, or others – are often judicialized. This becomes a question of political economy, extending beyond the realm of judicial proceduralism.[2]

The often-heard phrase "the law is the law" makes it appear as if the law is something unambiguous, whose interpretation is straightforward and uncontested. Yet many laws are far removed from this idealized notion. It is impossible for a law written in a specific context to foresee all the possible situations in which it may need to be enforced.[3] Thus, the rule of law is necessarily contentious and conflict-ridden (and all the more so for laws regulating developmental issues). The chapters of this book illustrate multiple situations where the law is contested and interpreted in conflicting ways.

The law – and the rule of law – creates arenas of equality for citizens, but this formal equality contrasts with multiple inequalities that arise from social and economic relations, territorial variations, and legal agency – i.e., the capacity to make effective use of the law. Any short- or long-term discussion of policies oriented towards Latin America's development and insertion into the world economy involves taking account of competing views of justice and fairness, as well as competing interests. Moreover, the rule of law is not spread homogeneously across Latin American countries or even within countries. Subnational variation in the rule of law – a phenomenon O'Donnell first signalled in 1996 – remains an important feature of Latin American countries.

When courts rule in disputes over development projects, the rights of communities often conflict with the rights of powerful business interests. In many cases, courts privilege the legal rights of investors over those of indigenous or local communities. However, communities have at times – often with the help of legal mobilization – succeeded in making their rights prevail over those of powerful economic actors in the courts. In Latin American democracies, there is a tension between the formal equality created by the law and the severe social inequalities that tend to make the interests of powerful groups prevail over those of less privileged citizens. Both sides invoke the rule of law, and courts must decide which party will prevail. In these disputes, both national and international courts can play an important role.

The "governability for development" agenda was launched in 2001 in reaction to then-prevailing ideas about Latin America's policy options. The "Washington Consensus" was then in vogue, together with the Miami Process of regional convergence around a Free Trade Area of the Americas (FTAA), reinforced by Bretton Woods guidance and conditionality. But this dominant policy template rested on a technical and depoliticized set of prescriptions that downplayed such strategic obstacles as the requirements of coalition-building (in Hirschman's parlance, "reform-mongering" (Hirschman, 1965)), and the generation of popular consent for development projects in emerging democracies. If such issues of governability were not adequately taken into account, policy implementation was liable to be derailed by unanticipated reactions and unexpected forms of resistance.[4] Latin America remained a haven of political democracy but fell behind in social and economic achievements. Indeed, in more recent years as pink tide experiments also floundered and refugee flows increased, the subcontinent's inventory of social imbalances and policy failures accumulated, with the pandemic and the upsurges in criminal violence as further markers of stress. The need to incorporate political and social variables into economic policy prescriptions is more apparent now than ever.

An expansive understanding of the rule of law

The rule of law is often taken to be the fair and even application of the law, whatever it happens to be in a specific country (O'Donnell, 1999). As such, it is linked to the fair and impartial functioning of institutions and norms. Ferejohn and Pasquino (2003) posit that the rule of law involves the notion that government should work its will through general legislation and not by arbitrary decrees or measures, and that public officials themselves are also bound by this legislation. This means that people are able to foresee the legal consequences of their actions. Accountability and law-abidingness appear in most definitions of the rule of law. Other scholars stress the importance of the state in ensuring a democratic rule of law. Ungar (2002) claims that the rule of law requires a law-abiding state, and O'Donnell points to the importance of the state as a "legal system that enacts and backs the rights and freedoms" sanctioned by democratic regimes (O´Donnell, 2010: 7). State agencies have the responsibility to carry out the law and rights, but, at the same time, the rule of law is the basis of state action (Ungar, 2002).

Yet the rule of law encompasses much more than the application of rules. It involves ideas of justice and considerations of what is fair in a given context, and how laws are created, contested, and enforced across territory. It also involves how societal actors mobilize to defend competing conceptions of justice, and how these competing views are negotiated in a given society. Moreover, it involves making choices between the legitimacy of competing claims by diverse rights-holders, and this process can either reinforce existing social or economic inequalities, or it can redress and compensate them.

The law is often seen as an autonomous and limited domain with clear boundaries. When seen from this perspective, what matters most is fair and impartial enforcement, or lack thereof. But laws cannot possibly contemplate all the situations they may be applied to, and they thus require interpretation. In order to enforce the law, judges need to interpret, construct, and expand the contents of rights enshrined in laws (Ansolabehere et al., 2022). Two important dimensions to the rule of law stand out: the first is how the rule of law is understood and interpreted in given contexts both by social actors and by those in charge of imparting justice; the second is how the law may be used to contest and challenge existing understandings by societal actors.

The rule of law is a concept that can be narrowly construed, with all the attention focused on law enforcement. That is certainly a prime feature to consider. But when examining where the rule of law fits in the context of governability for development, a broader conceptualization is required. To elicit social trust and voluntary compliance, the reasons for legal provisions must be explained, and the operations of the justice system must be made acceptable to the affected public. As democratization and development progress, access to justice can no longer be confined to an educated urban minority serviced by costly private legal intermediaries. As individual and group rights to constitutional protections gain wider currency, traditional rule of law procedures require extension and updating. Demands for equitable treatment of previously neglected social categories (indigenous communities, pensioners, urban precariat, vulnerable women, etc.) stretch the capacities of always imperfect justice systems. New sources of legal challenges, such as international drug cartels, mass refugee migrations, pandemics, and environmental crises, pile extra pressures on established formal rule of law providers.

Inherited practices of enforcement outsourcing (whereby informal procedures of dispute resolution substitute for unavailable official arbitrations in some communities and concerning some secondary policy areas) may be expanded to meet such mounting pressures (e.g., private security forces that displace public policing in gated communities). But this can risk diluting or undermining the intelligibility and cohesion of the formal provision by the state. In Latin America, alegal, and even illegal, means of settlement have always operated side by side with formal rule of law systems, but under contemporary conditions, the imbalances between these alternatives can intensify. O'Donnell (1999) referred to this as the rule of law/unrule of law. These realities demand a broad conceptualization that goes beyond questions of direct law enforcement to encompass issues of systemic trust and legitimation, and the structural adaptability of rule of law provisions across the sub-hemisphere. For the avoidance of doubt, all these challenges and mounting strains interact with a long-established and robustly entrenched tradition of constitutional legality throughout the region.

After the transitions to democracy, the rule of law was often invoked as a crucial element of democracy and democratic governance. The transitions to democracy in Latin America in the 1980s and 1990s occurred in parallel to other political and economic transformations. On the economic front, the debt crisis and the neoliberal agenda of the Washington Consensus produced transformations in the role of the state in the economy, in the policy options available to, and promoted by, Latin American governments, and decentralized the provision of key services such as health and education to subnational governments. These economic transformations created new policy disputes and interpretations about the rule of law that were often resolved by the courts. The judicialization of politics became an important feature of public policy in many Latin American countries. On the political front, the rule of law began to be increasingly invoked first by human rights movements and then by other social movements, including indigenous peoples, environmental movements, and other active citizen groups who saw in legal mobilization a new opportunity to fulfil constitutional rights. These were either new rights enshrined in constitutional reforms or existing rights that were not being duly enforced. Kapiszewski refers to this transformation as a legal transition, which transformed the role of courts, leading the judicial arena to become a locus of politics. Courts became involved in settling political conflicts and economic governance disputes to a greater degree than before (Kapiszewski, 2012).

Enforcement and institutional weakness

Scholars of Latin America have pointed to institutional weakness and uneven enforcement of the rule of law. Yet laws that are never enforced are not something new or unique to Latin America or recently democratized countries. Legal anthropologist Fernanda Pirie points out that throughout history, many rules that were never applied were written out on parchment or stone. Societies have written down rules as a means to make goals explicit, as a way of creating conceptual order, and these practices can be a powerful symbol of justice (Pirie 2021). Laws symbolize the societies that lawmakers want to bring about (Pirie 2021) and, eventually, dormant laws can be activated by new social movements, prosecutors, or courts. Brinks, Levitsky, and Murillo (2019) theorize about institutional weakness in Latin America by focusing on whether institutions achieve their statutory goals. They argue that institutional weakness can be due to the insignificance of an institution, or to non-compliance with rules or instability (i.e., when institutions and rules are changed so frequently that they fail to take hold). Non-compliance can be due to non-enforcement, non-punitive enforcement, or weak state capacity. In addition, the authors claim that political actors sometimes purposefully design weak institutions. There are certainly many examples of all these situations in the chapters of this book, but there are also examples of how the rule of law can become embedded, activated, or can help empower citizens as agents. The literature on enforcement emphasizes how some laws are approved without ever having the intention of actually applying them, how they often serve as "window dressing," or how they may have been approved to comply with international requirements. But Levitsky and Murillo (2013) and Brinks et al. (2019) also argue that weak or dormant rules can be activated. Social mobilization or judicial interpretation can help enforce laws that were previously ignored. Moreover, enforcement (or lack thereof) is heterogeneous, as is state capacity, both across Latin American countries, territorially within countries, and even across different state agencies within a single country. State apparatuses in Latin America are not homogeneously politicized or ineffective, and neither is the rule of law. In many countries, there are pockets of institutional strength for policymaking and implementation (González-Ocantos et al., 2023).

Enforcement is important for legitimacy, but it is not the only source of legitimacy. How conflicts and disputed claims are resolved can also be a source of legitimacy. As the chapters of this book show, the law – including constitutional provisions and the Inter-American Human Rights system – may at times help environmental activists and indigenous peoples achieve their aims. But it may also become entangled with illiberal structures and practices. Prosecutors may investigate with zeal in notorious corruption cases (González-Ocantos et al., 2023), but they may fail to investigate other corruption cases or use their position to persecute private enemies, as in Mexico (Berruecos and Whitehead in this book). In this regard, the chapters in this volume are concerned with identifying the drivers of rule of law heterogeneity rather than only identifying its failures. In the end, the fact that laws exist on paper means that, eventually, they can be invoked. The rule of law can be achieved incrementally through mobilization, legal activism, Supreme Court rulings, changing contexts, or waves of reforms.

Our perspective on the rule of law deviates from narrow accounts that dichotomize between weak and strong laws, or enforcement and non-enforcement. Instead, we focus on the tensions and conflicts that arise both at the level of designing and agreeing on sets of rules, as well as on how these rules are then applied. We focus on rules, actors, and processes, and on the inherent tensions and conflicts that the rule of law implies and which cannot be avoided because there is no law enforcement without interpretation and no law writing without conflict, tension, and negotiation.

A democratic rule of law or the rule of law as a promise

Our concern is with the *democratic* rule of law. Hence, the rule of law in abstract needs to be distinguished from the democratic rule of law in particular. The former can refer to authoritarian and even totalitarian regimes where a uniform legal order is administered to all subjects. For example, the rule of law can exist in institutionalized authoritarian regimes that restrict political citizenship, but a democratic rule of law implies that citizens are construed as agents (O'Donnell, 2010). It is citizens as agents who can mobilize to activate or embed new or dormant rights and who can contest established understandings about what is fair and just in each society. This means that in a democracy, there is an intrinsic relationship between the rule of law, the state, and citizen agency.

Our focus is on contemporary Latin America where – at least in principle – the law is supposed to apply equally to all, including the lawgivers, and to be subject to democratic review as new issues arise or old rules seem to the society to be no longer appropriate. Laws can be too rigid and oppressive, as well as too fanciful and unobtainable. Social struggles over the rule (and unrule) of law are not just about granting access to entitlements that were previously hard to acquire; it can also be about softening the burden of disproportionate and unreasonable rulings.

The idea of the rule of law also functions as a promise of more equitable development and greater democracy. Laws hold the promise of justice and order, and they also express social ambitions. Of course, there is then the question of to what extent these promises are realized. Over the 4,000 years of lawmaking that Pirie (2021) documents, constitutions and laws have been aspirational documents more than practical ones. But this does not mean that they are less important, cynical, or merely window-dressing documents. Once laws and constitutions are written down, they become a powerful tool for citizens, and they can take on a life of their own. Citizens can turn to these rules to seek justice and resist the arbitrary exercise of power. Laws obviously do not eliminate power asymmetries, and some citizens always have greater access to the law and courts than others. But laws create certain arenas of equality and, even when judicial outcomes reinforce existing inequalities, unfair rulings can be measured against the notions of justice espoused in-laws. Human rights movements, environmental activists, and indigenous peoples have in many cases succeeded in using the law to bring human rights violators to trial, stop contamination, or prevent development projects that threatened their livelihoods. Both national law and the Inter-American Human Rights System play an important role in this respect.

But because the law is both operational and also aspirational, its application, the rule of law, is contested and subject to interpretation, confrontation, advances, and setbacks. Competing views of the rule of law give rise to debates and clashes of opinion. They also stimulate collective mobilization of activists who may bring pressure to bear and can seek to overawe their opponents through displays of support. It is through performative gestures and contestations as much as by force of argument that claims to rights are forged, and rival ideas about legitimacy are defined. The starting point for such controversies is often some existing constitutional or legal provision or procedural rule, but what converts such formal provisions into lived realities is a contested process of learning how to apply them, where they can be made enforceable, and within what limits. It is by pressure and experimentation from below that theoretical entitlements may become socially embedded. Judges, courts, and legal practitioners adjust their understandings of the prevailing legal order not just in response to decrees from the established authorities but also in the light of emerging collective expectations. It is through such processes that new constitutional rights provisions can become meaningful in everyday life, moving from parchment promises to constraining institutions – or can be rolled back. Taylor argues that constitutional embedding occurs through legal mobilization, and it is through this kind of mobilization that rights can become real and come to have social and legal meaning. Embedding is understood as the process whereby, following the adoption of new constitutions that recognize a wide set of rights, citizens gradually come to learn about these rights, and they begin to take some of the problems in their lives to the formal legal system, experimentally (Taylor, 2023).

Bottom-up challenges and alternative understandings of the rule of law

Some of the chapters in this volume draw attention to the interactive and contested nature of much regional understanding of legitimate order. Beyond the "top down" official rules that structure judicial processes, there are also powerful "bottom-up" challenges and alternative understandings. Some of these challenges seek to expand rights, but other challenges distort and refract the rule of law. Effective social order arises from the matching of these potentially divergent positions. But given their discrepant origins and dynamics, these two levels of deliberation and adjudication are frequently incongruent. If so, then tacit bargaining and selective mutual adjustment will be needed to generate an agreed rule of law outcome. Not all legal rulings are enforced with equal vigour and consistency, and informal processes of dispute resolution may be at variance with official scripts when societal veto groups exert sufficient blocking pressure. Consequently, in practical terms, Latin American law and order outcomes are not infrequently contested, inconsistent, unstable, and "unruly."

In the conventional model of the rule of law ideal (which underlies much legal theory), there would be a harmonious set of formal rules and procedures enforced by the legal authorities, and these would mesh seamlessly with popular understandings of the people's rights and obligations. Although Costa Rica's legal order may roughly approximate the first of these models, and the counterpart in Guatemala may come fairly close to the polar opposite, the realities prevailing across most of the subcontinent are far more entangled, contested, and unstable than either of these images. Within the legal profession, rival cohorts and specialisms jostle for control, and each faction draws strength in part from opinion formers and pressure groups located outside that closed circle. Property law may trend in one direction, family law in another, with penal rules operating at variance with human rights provisions, and so on. Moreover, contestants for ascendancy in the court of public opinion tend to make tactical advances followed by partial retreats, rather than achieve irreversible systemic victories. The new constitutionalism of recent pink tide administrations provides a contemporary illustration – their legal innovations often sparked backlash or generated new points of contestation. Sometimes public opinion may have run ahead of the prevailing legal consensus, but it is also possible for judicial progressivism to outstrip popular acceptance.

Since the whole of Latin America has been formally governed by constitutional principles for up to two centuries, and since a specialized and relatively insulated judicial system has been in operation across the subcontinent for even longer, this "mode of existence" (Latour, 2012) has considerable authority. In Weberian terms, it derives its legitimacy from both traditional and rational-legal sources. Indeed, it is even possible to find examples of charismatic judicial legitimation (e.g., Brazilian Judge Sergio Moro acquired the status of a crusader in his *Lava Jato* prosecution of then former President Luiz Inácio "Lula" da Silva). It provides the default solution to recurrent challenges over entitlements to rule. Not only do rival contestants for political power generally dress up their claims in legal garb, but most citizen consent is also filtered through constitutional justifications. The resilience of such rule-of-law processes of legitimation derives partly from the weight of history. But equally, it rests on loose and informal tacit understandings of how the literal language of governing charters can be stretched and selectively interpreted in order to maintain an appearance of stability while also absorbing discordant realities. In contemporary Latin America, the resilience of these practices is reinforced by the prevalence of elections, and the proliferation of multiple forms of both representative and direct democracy procedures. Credible claims to legitimate authority rest on extensive rule of law foundations.

However, as we have seen, it is artificial to derive claims to legitimate political authority solely from such constitutional/juridical sources.[5] For example, most South American populations have experienced state-directed violence by military regimes that were subsequently assessed to have been illegitimate (although today's voters sometimes endorse candidates who claim otherwise). Former Presidents of Bolivia, Brazil, Honduras, Panama, and Peru currently face trial for abuse of power when in office, even though the relevant judicial authorities upheld the legitimacy of their conduct when in office. Survey evidence indicates divided opinions on the conduct of both past and present rulers with variable – but often substantial – support for those most prone to disregard inconvenient laws.

The evidence presented in this volume reinforces these arguments and adds a further dimension. Weber's stress on the monopoly on physical force within a given territory has always posed big challenges – which territory, with what boundaries, how consensually established, etc. In contemporary Latin America, while inherited state boundaries are mostly long-established and relatively well-demarcated, the same cannot be said for the physical distribution of effective means of coercion. Smuggling, arms and people trafficking, and refugee flows are all endemic practices across many state frontiers. In addition, regionalist, localist, closed community, blockaded, and "no-go" areas criss-cross officially unitary political demarcations throughout the subcontinent. Not only subnational but also supranational expressions of coercive power (bases, corporate enclaves, blockades, economic sanctions, electronic monitoring, etc.) may also qualify as national sovereignty. While some of these limits on state power may be legitimized by treaties or legal agreements, a substantial portion are directly unauthorized and outside the law. In between lies a broad swath of informal and even extra-legal practices.

Outline of the book

This book brings together a group of scholars to make a novel contribution to the study of the rule of law by focusing on the relationship between the rule of law, development, and democracy. It deepens our understanding of the rule of law as a contested process of social construction of the rules that order a given society and, as such, involves disputes about justice, fairness, democracy, and equitable development. Both democracy and development are essentially contested concepts, and so is the rule of law. This volume focuses on one key structural challenge – the rule of law matters, and although its coverage is patchy and unreliable, mounting societal demands for justice are often able to rely on the law and legal mobilization to achieve justice.

Over the last decades, there has been huge progress in Latin America in the sanctioning of new rights, including environmental rights, social rights, women's rights, indigenous rights, reproductive rights, etc. New constitutions were drafted in many countries, and mobilization has often succeeded in activating dormant rights. But there are important variations across and within countries with regard to effective access to justice, the role of local elites in regional development, and conflicts about who benefits and at what cost to local communities. Reconciling the need to construct coalitions of support with effective decision-making is at the heart of governability for development.

The chapters in this volume address several important questions about the complex interactions between the rule of law, development, and democracy. For example, how is the rule of law invoked in conflicts about competing interests in development projects? What challenges do policymakers face when seeking to reconcile diverse and often opposing legal claims? How do new constitutional rights become meaningful? How do courts rule when the legitimacy of rules is contested? How does the judiciary intervene with regard to military intervention? What role do development banks and supranational institutions play in such processes?

There is no smooth or assured development process in contemporary Latin America. Despite all the energies and expertise directed to this goal in recent decades, results are still uneven, contested, and non-cumulative. Progress on some fronts has been offset by regression elsewhere, with the pandemic and climate change adding to the sense of discouragement. One- size-fits-all technical prescriptions keep producing undesired "side effects." Chapter 2 by Crabtree, Wilson, and Quiñón Cárdenas, and Chapters 3 and 5 by Karamaneff and Domínguez, respectively, illustrate some of the challenges faced by new development projects and national policies that seek to stimulate local development. In the case of Peru, the expansion of the mining sector poses challenges for the formalization of workers and involves reconciling the pressures from informal workers with the requirements of large-scale mining. The chapter evidences the complexity and heterogeneity of the mining sector and how conflicting views of the rule of law can privilege the interests of some mining actors over others. Karamaneff's chapter shows how the implementation of development projects in subnational districts in Argentina that lack adequate bureaucracy and state capacity may require a temporary departure from formal procedures and established regulations. However, establishing adequate control mechanisms and strengthening local state capacity is fundamental for ensuring the sustainability of such projects in the long run, and this requires finding a balance between flexibility and effective compliance with the rule of law. Domínguez's chapter points to the challenges that infrastructure megaprojects in Mexico pose for policymaking and the difficulties of reconciling basic technical and financial concerns with democratic aspirations and the desire for socio-environmental justice. A multiplicity of actors is involved in such projects, but, at the same time, there is a wide margin for discretionary decision-making.

The rule of law is a long-established and foundational feature of Latin American social organization and regional self-understanding. But its nature is neither stable, nor straightforward, nor uniform. It should be understood as both an attractive ideal and a problematic social construct. In highly stratified and loosely integrated communities and populations, the weight of the law can bear down very unequally on the various groups it is supposed to govern. It may be felt as highly prescriptive and inflexible for some sectors and issues, but hardly relevant or restraining for others. However, social movements in Latin America have often used legal mobilization to advance their claims with great success. This is most evident in human rights, environmental movements, and, more recently, women's activism. Christel and Gutiérrez show how the rule of law's promises can be invoked and become effective in environmental conflicts. The authors focus on the relevance of contentious and institutional forms of participation in environmental governance in two cases: forest protection and open-pit mining. They see the rule of law as not only a pending challenge but also an opportunity in environmental disputes over development projects.

Subnational research has highlighted the importance of understanding the variation that can exist within countries in macro-political processes like democratization, economic development, and enforcement of the rule of law. However, we still know little about how these processes become entangled in subnational political systems. Informal political dynasties are frequently entrenched in power at the subnational level, not only in peripheral jurisdictions but also in economically developed jurisdictions. Economic elites are often concentrated in particular regions and entangled with local political actors and judicial institutions. Consequently, the rule of law enforcement may depend disproportionately on oversight by the Supreme Court, an institution that intervenes episodically and in the face of major conflicts. This leaves considerable space for extra-legal activities, excesses, or connivance from local courts in some jurisdictions. Behrend's chapter (Chapter 6) provides illustrations of these subnational rule of law variations on variations in the case of Argentina. It shows the entanglements between subnational political dynasties, economic interests, and the rule of law. The legitimacy of rules can be contested when governors seek to remain in office for longer than the constitution mandates, and the Supreme Court has often intervened and been authoritative in these cases, but it has also applied the law more strictly in some districts than in others. Boesten and Llanos' chapter (Chapter 7) on the oligarchic tensions of the core-periphery divide in Colombia, in turn, shows how the rule of law can be contested by warring and civil oligarchs who operate at the margins of legality. The Colombian case evidences relatively robust democratic institutions with a high level of violence and draws on an apparent core/periphery divide: violence is mostly concentrated in the latter, while the former may enjoy boom cycles at the same time. Behind this apparent core/periphery divide lie subnational institutions that have very little in common with the democratic promises of the country's constitution.

Although civilian constitutional government has become much more secure in the region over the past generation, this does not entirely offset underlying currents of nostalgia for past periods of military rule, nor contemporary impulses to bypass the rules in order to achieve hopeful quick victories over the forces of disorder. As a result, these subterranean authoritarian currents can still crystallize around campaigns to re-empower the military and the security forces, reinterpreting the past to whitewash previous episodes of human rights abuse and opening the way to what Akkoyunlu and Lima have effectively identified as "stealth militarization" (effectively abridging the rule of law while ostensibly upholding it).[6]

Although the rule of law system in Latin America may rest on somewhat contested and even unstable foundations – and currently faces mounting pressures – it is also deeply entrenched and contains the potential for adaptation and upgrading. In some countries, and on some matters, it already shows considerable promise. Where it flounders, it should be possible to bring in best practices from elsewhere, or at least to suggest avenues for upgrading. Such "reform-mongering" (Hirschman, 1965) is all the more vital because the alternative of growing lawlessness is clearly looming and threatens vital interests in many jurisdictions. However dissatisfied with the current provision the public may be, most citizens remain wedded to the "myth of legality" as a guiding source of stability and can summon up images of how the rule of law ought to operate in principle, in contrast to what they actually confront.

Multiple sources of reform can be cited. Recent years have displayed a strong drive to replace antiquated written procedures with more agile and timely digital processes, and oral hearings. Environmental rights enshrined in new constitutions have proven to be powerful tools for environmental activists, as noted above. Access to justice has been extended in accordance with the demands of decentralization and democratic inclusiveness (although much more remains to be done in this respect).[7] The range of intermediary institutions contributing to rule of law outcomes (*defensorías*, auditor's offices, NGOs, journalistic consortia, etc.) has blossomed. Mechanisms of direct democracy (including recall elections) have attempted to bridge the gap between unresponsive parties and legislatures and citizen demands for officeholder accountability in some countries.[8] Yet these mechanisms are not always successful. Welp's chapter (Chapter 9) illustrates how mechanisms of direct democracy have been used in disputes over natural resources and finds that in most of the cases she analyzes these mechanisms have not served as an effective way of resolving conflicts. Poorly designed rules of the game are often the cause that limits the effectiveness of mechanisms of direct democracy.

At the international level, there has also been a great expansion of measures intended to reinforce and coordinate rule of law standards across the subhemisphere. This is evidenced in the role that the Inter-American Human Rights System has started to play in defending the rights of local and indigenous populations, and ruling in conflicts that arise in the context of new development projects, as Engstrom and Pérez's chapter (Chapter 12) documents. Likewise, Rodrigues Vieira's chapter (Chapter 13) shows that development banks have increasingly included the United Nations' Sustainable Development Goals in their agendas. The chapter documents the diverse approaches to subnational spheres of authority – including those comprising indigenous peoples – of the sustainable development policies enacted by different development banks operating in Latin America. In summary, as pressures on the rule of law have mounted, the supply of advice and support has also increased.

Social perceptions tend to be Janus-faced. Although the underprivileged majorities may feel relatively unprotected by an inaccessible and inflexible formal provision of official justice (and may often resort to informal and even extralegal sources of dispute resolution), they are also periodically hopeful that their theoretical entitlements might eventually be more effectively realized. Likewise, the minorities that most benefit from legal privilege are also prone to some ambivalence – not only might they lose out to more powerful competitors from above, but if the rule of law becomes more inclusive, their relative advantages could also be eroded. In brief, then, the existing unevenness of justice provision also renders the system unstable over time and generates mixed emotions rather than unqualified trust. In this context, the region's public prosecutors, who have been gaining authority and autonomy over the past decade, are confronting massive challenges to their reputations and capacities as the region's rule of law "gatekeepers." Whitehead and Berruecos sketch a map of the region's prosecutorial agencies, showing both the common features shared across the region and also the major dimensions of institutional variation from country to country. These are large bureaucratic agencies with a high degree of discretion that are critical to the overall functioning of the rule of law. As shown elsewhere in this volume, there is a multiplicity of challenges pressing in on these agencies, which are also under stress from their difficulties of internal organization. Moreover, in many countries, they become entangled in high political scandals that further jeopardize the trust they need from society. In addition to this overview chapter, Berruecos and Whitehead also provide a more detailed account of a critical case when they examine the difficulties of the reform process in contemporary Mexico in Chapter 10.

Important proportions of the subject population in many countries find themselves required to navigate between official, extra-official, and even outright criminal de facto powers, and may be caught between clashing centres of control – perhaps governed differently by day and by night, or across rival domains of activity. Idler and Whitehead's chapter (Chapter 14) draws attention to this reality under the illuminating rubric of "shadow" citizenship. When rules are issued from multiple and incompatible sources of authority, and when compliance is fragmented and subject to frequent renegotiation, the abstract idea of a unitary rule of law may give way to a cloudier pattern of theoretical laws loosely meshed with socially accepted but unstable norms and practices.

Such rule of law issues arise in many parts of the world, even in those with greater socio-economic and developmental stability, but they are particularly visible and acute in Latin America with its long tradition of ambitious and partially enforced constitutionalism, which provides resources for innovation and reform, even as it also generates successive sources of challenge.

Notes

1 See, for example, Botero, Brinks, and González-Ocantos (2022); Ingram and Kapiszewski (2018); Brinks, Levitsy, and Murillo (2020); Maravall and Przeworski (2003), Méndez, O'Donnell, and Pinheiro (1999).

2 Claudio Couto and Rogerio Arantes (2022) document the region's recent expansion of constitutional provisions to include such public policy matters as employment and healthcare provision. Brazil's 1988 constitution led the way here. But they are unable to determine whether this is positive or negative for democracy and development. For cautiously positive assessments, see the chapters by Diana Rodríguez-Franco and César Rodríguez-Garavito on strategic litigation, and Alicia Ely Yamin on the right to health (notably in Colombia) in Hübner Mendes, Gargarella, and Guidi (2022).

3 See Hart (1961).
4 Thus, for example, Argentina's celebrated Convertibility Plan ended in the spectacular failure of 2001/2002; Venezuela's liberalization drive provoked the Chavista backlash; Brazil's real plan was followed by the heterodoxies of Lula's PT administration, and a series of "pink tide" elections followed. On the external front, International Monetary Fund (IMF) conditionality was shunned as soon as foreign exchange reserves could be rebuilt; the Miami Process foundered in 2005; the global financial crisis of 2008 undermined consensus mantras even in Washington; and the redistribution of economic leadership from Europe and North America towards China and Asia shifted the burden of proof from western orthodoxies towards alternative development models.
5 As David Beetham (2013) has pointed out, any sound analysis of the legitimation of power needs to explain why the people may accept the established order at one time but not another (as with the collapse of the Soviet bloc). Beyond collective beliefs (which are often contested, confused, and unstable), there are other tests of legitimacy to consider, such as the legal validity of the acquisition and exercise of power; the justifiability of the rules invoked to regulate a power relationship; and the legitimation conferred by such acts of "consent" as voting, petitioning and tax-paying. (Beetham, 2013). In view of the variety, subjectivity, and contextual specificity of all these tests, he argues that legitimation involves a multidimensional and graduated process, always concerning "legitimacy-in-context" rather than some universalized abstraction. On this view, the instability and erosion of legitimacy is of as much interest as infrequent episodes of outright collapse. Latin America well illustrates this viewpoint.
6 For the resilience of the Brazilian legal order despite the Bolsonaro episode, see Vilhena Vieira (2024).
7 Luciana Gross Cunha (2022) takes a pessimistic view of results so far

> access to justice is restricted to the judiciary, and all changes in in the legislation and in the Justice model have occurred as means of strengthening the role of the State and increasing the power and autonomy of public and private legal careers. This scenario, in turn, has promoted an explosion in the number of new cases, resulting in the collapse of the Judiciary, which, in Latin America, has an extremely high cost.
>
> Instead, she advocates "a new approach to access to justice that considers the importance of the administrative management of institutions, the legitimacy of other forms of conflict resolution" (Gross Cunha, 2022: 469).

8 González-Ocantos (2016) has highlighted the internal pressures for system improvements within the judiciary arising from the emergence of new generations of legal innovators. Couso (2023) makes a contrast between progressive and radical variants of the region's new constitutionalism. The first type favours judicial activism of the kind studied by González-Ocantos, whereas the radical variant adds detailed rights provisions to the charter while requiring judges to apply the law literally, thus restricting judicial interpretations.

References

Ansolabehere, Karina Mariela, Sandra Botero, and Ezequiel González Ocantos. 2022. "Conceptualizar y medir la cultura legal: evidencia a partir de una encuesta a jueces federales mexicanos". *Política y Gobierno* 29: 1–30.

Beetham, David. 2013. *The Legitimation of Power* (2nd Edition). Basingstoke: Palgrave Macmillan.

Behrend, Jacqueline, and Laurence Whitehead. 2023. "Dynasties, Double-Dealings, and Delinquencies: Some Entangled Features of Subnational Politics in Mexico". In Mariana Llanos and Leiv Marsteintredet, eds. *Latin America in Times of Turbulence: Presidentialism under Stress*. New York: Routledge.

Behrend, Jacqueline, and Laurence Whitehead. 2021. "Mixed Messages about Democratization in the Many Mexicos". *Latin American Policy* 12: 1–16.

Botero, Sandra, Daniel M. Brinks, and Ezequiel A. González Ocantos. 2022. *The Limits of Judicialization: From Progress to Backlash in Latin America*. New York: Cambridge University Press.

Brinks, Daniel, Steven Levitsky, and María Victoria Murillo. 2019. *Understanding Institutional Weakness: Power and Design in Latin American Institutions*. New York: Cambridge University Press.

Brinks, Daniel, Steven Levitsky, and María Victoria Murillo, eds. 2020. *The Politics of Institutional Weakness in Latin America*. New York: Cambridge University Press.

Couso, Javier. 2022. "Latin American New Constitutionalism". In Conrad Hubner Mendes, Roberto Gargarella, and Sebastian Guidi, eds. *The Oxford Handbook on Constitutional Law in Latin America*. Oxford: Oxford University Press.

Couto, Claudio, and Rogerio Arantes. 2022. "Constitutions and Public Policies". In Conrad Hubner Mendes, Roberto Gargarella, and Sebastian Guidi, eds. *The Oxford Handbook on Constitutional Law in Latin America*. Oxford: Oxford University Press.

Ferejohn, John, and Pasquale Pasquino. 2003. "Rule of Democracy and Rule of Law". In José María Maravall and Adam Przeworski, eds. *Democracy and the Rule of Law*. Cambridge: Cambridge University Press.

Gallie, W. B. 1956. "Essentially Contested Concepts". *Proceedings of the Aristotelian Society* 56: 167–198.

González-Ocantos, Ezequiel. 2016. *Shifting Legal Visions: Judicial Change and Human Rights Trials in Latin America*. New York: Cambridge University Press.

González-Ocantos, Ezequiel A., Paula Muñoz, Nara Pavao, and Viviana Baraybar Hidalgo. 2023. *Prosecutors, Voters, and the Criminalisation of Corruption in Latin America*. Cambridge: Cambridge University Press.

Gross Cunha, Luciana. 2022. "Access to Justice". In Conrado Hübner Mendes, Roberto Gargarella, and Sebastián Guidi, eds. *The Oxford Handbook on Constitutional Law in Latin America*. Oxford: Oxford University Press.

Hart, H. A. L. 1961. *The Concept of Law*. Oxford: Clarendon Press.

Hübner Mendes, Conrado, Roberto Gargarella, and Sebastián Guidi. 2022. *The Oxford Handbook of Constitutional Law in Latin America*. Oxford: Oxford University Press.

Kapiszewski, Diana. 2012. *High Courts and Economic Governance in Argentina and Brazil*. New York: Cambridge University Press.

Hirschman, Albert O. 1965. *Journeys Toward Progress*. New York: Doubleday.

Ingram, Matthew and Diana Kapiszewski, eds. 2018. *Beyond High Courts: The Justice Complex in Latin America*. Notre Dame, IN: University of Notre Dame Press.

Latour, Bruno. 2012. *An Inquiry into Modes of Existence*. Cambridge, MA: Harvard University Press.

Levitsky, Steven, and María Victoria Murillo. 2013. "Building Institutions on Weak Foundations: Lessons from Latin America". *Journal of Democracy* 24: 93–107.

Maravall, José María, and Adam Przeworski. 2003. *Democracy and the Rule of Law*. Cambridge: Cambridge University Press.

O'Donnell, Guillermo. 2010. *Democracy, Agency, and the State: Theory with Comparative Intent*. Oxford: Oxford University Press.

O'Donnell, Guillermo. 1999. "Polyarchies and the (Un)Rule of Law in Latin America: A Partial Conclusion". In Juan E. Méndez, Guillermo O'Donnell and Paulo Sérgio Pinheiro, eds. *The (Un)Rule of Law and the Underprivileged in Latin America*. Notre Dame, IN: Notre Dame University Press.

Pirie, Fernanda. 2021. *The Rule of Laws: A 4,000-Year Quest to Order the World*. London: Profile Books.

Taylor, Whitney K. 2023. *The Social Constitution: Embedding Social Rights through Legal Mobilization*. New York: Cambridge University Press.

Ungar, Mark. 2002. *Elusive Reform: Democracy and the Rule of Law in Latin America*. Boulder, CO: Lynne Rienner.

Vilhena Vieira, Oscar. 2024. *Estado de direito e populismo autoritário*. Rio de Janeiro: Fundaçao Getúlio Vargas.

Wendt, Alexander. 2015. *Quantum Mind and Social Science: Unifying Physical and Social Ontology*. Cambridge: Cambridge University Press.

2 Extending legal security in the Peruvian mining sector

The formalization of informal miners

John Crabtree, Anna Wilson, and Aaron Quiñón Cárdenas

Introduction

The Andean region has long been a major geological resource, supplying the world with a range of minerals. As the energy transition gathers pace, it is likely to be an important supplier of critical minerals[1] such as copper and lithium, as well as other primary products. But such resources are usually located in difficult terrain where the resident population has many unmet basic needs, and the record of exploitative extractivism is either still remembered or actively experienced. Three types of production vie with one another in the Andes: state mining companies, foreign private mining corporations, and artisanal/small-scale production (ASM), sometimes organized as cooperatives (as in Bolivia) or companies, but frequently constituting part of the informal sector in terms of labour rights. Relations between these sectors are often conflicted and unstable, and it is challenging to design tax and regulatory rules that balance the interests of all parties. It can be even more difficult for remote national bureaucracies to oversee fair and legitimate processes of dispute resolution. Even in countries where mining has been outlawed, the problems associated with artisanal and small-scale mining (ASM) remain (Spalding, 2023). With a focus on Peru, this chapter seeks to identify some of the main obstacles to the provision of legal certainty in ways that uphold the rights and obligations of different interests in the mining sector, highlighting the challenges to policymakers in encouraging the formalization of informal mining.

While the analysis is based on the Peruvian experience, there are communalities between this and the experiences of other countries both within the Andean region and, indeed, further afield.[2] Within Peru, informal mining, concentrated in the gold sector, is widespread and represents a significant part of the economy.[3] The literature on mining and mining conflicts has tended to focus on larger-scale mining, specifically the effects of the "resource curse," while ASM mining and other contentious areas have received much less attention (Arce 2015). We examine some constructive policy options that have been proffered which – if implemented – would serve to reinforce legal certainty within this troubled field, not just in Peru but elsewhere.[4] We believe that these proposals, and the obstacles they face in implementation, are germane to the discussion surrounding

DOI: 10.4324/9781003519195-2

the persistence of informality, the extension of legal protection to vulnerable workers, the attempt to tackle serious environmental and social issues that typify mining, and, more generally, to the extension of state competences to a sector that has long worked at the margins of the law. In short, they concern the building of the "rule of law" in areas where this has traditionally been weak or absent.

The paper begins with a consideration of informality as a concept, along with some reflections on definitional and measurement problems. It then moves into a discussion of the context in which the Peruvian authorities, both in the executive and legislature, put forward detailed schemes designed to encourage informal mining workers to sign up for administrative procedures previously put in place to enable informal miners to register themselves as "formal." Then, from field research in the Arequipa region (where informal gold mining is particularly common), it seeks to analyze the obstacles to formalization in practice. Finally, in the concluding section, we make some observations as to the conditions that would enable such obstacles to be overcome. We hope that these will prove useful for the discussion surrounding the formalization of informal mining in other countries in Latin America and beyond.

Informality and its persistence

Far from diminishing over time, the informal sector has remained a conspicuous characteristic of the labour market in Latin America. Although it contracted somewhat as a consequence of the commodity super-cycle in the early years of the new millennium (ILO, 2018), the reduction in growth rates since around 2013 has seen it growing once again (ECLAC 2023). This trend has become particularly clear since 2020 as a lasting consequence of the Covid-19 pandemic. Peru has long been one of the countries with the largest informal sectors in the region. It was also a country particularly hard hit by Covid. Informality grew substantially as a result of the economic dislocations of the late 1980s, but it never returned to previous levels when the economy stabilized in the 1990s. Indeed, the free-market policies of the Fujimori years (1990–2000) saw formal sector employment contract as a result of privatization and deregulation. Chacaltana (2001) discredits the business view that the answer to informalization is to "deformalize" the formal sector by eliminating labour rights.

The scale of informality in Peru and its relationship to legality and state structures gave rise to some of the foundational works on the subject. Matos Mar (1986), the Peruvian anthropologist, wrote about how the rise of informality risked overwhelming state capacities to respond and how a new informal institutionality was developing. This also gave rise to the work of Hernando de Soto, whose *Otro Sendero* (1987) stressed the entrepreneurial capacities of the informal sector, for whom the lack of property rights was seen as the key to unleashing this potential source of economic dynamism. Although De Soto's work has attracted strong criticism, his focus on the legal constraints on the informal sector is an important insight when it comes to thinking about formalization in the mining sector.

Informal gold mining is concentrated in areas of high mineral deposits, especially in the Andean highlands and parts of lowland Amazonia. It is estimated to include some 300,000 miners. If we include family members, we are perhaps talking of a population of well over one million. The sector also contributes significantly to the economy. It accounts for at least a quarter of the country's gold production but possibly much more, gold being Peru's second largest commodity export.[5] It is, however, a sector that deviates somewhat from commonly accepted characteristics of informality: it is not typically an urban phenomenon since most mining settlements are located far from the main centres of population in remote areas in the Andes or lowland Amazonia; nor are informal miners necessarily poor. Some small-scale producers have benefitted from high prices to become wealthy entrepreneurs capable of purchasing costly machinery and vehicles.

In establishing some sort of working definition of mining informality, we should perhaps highlight the concept of precarious employment that is, both in law and in practice, beyond the realm of existing labour legislation, income taxation, social protection, and entitlement to such employment benefits as sick pay, holiday pay, or pensions. Such lack of entitlements is characteristic of informal miners as well as workers in the informal economy more broadly. The sector is highly heterogeneous, with the many living in conditions of poverty in makeshift housing that once typified the development of urban informality. At the extremes of poverty are the *pallaqueras,* women who make a precarious living picking over the tailings of gold mining operations (Orozco, 2017).

The legal definition of ASM includes two sub-sectors: artisanal operations producing up to 25 tonnes of rock a day, and small-scale units which extract up to 350 tonnes. The amount of gold they produce varies widely according to ore grades, but the average for ASM producers in Peru as a whole is 1.92 ounces per tonne. Our study does not engage with what are considered "illegal" operations, in which miners have not complied with the government's initial registration process enabling formalization to begin (as we go on to describe in the next section). Illegal mining can also vary widely, from organized operations at scale with significant social and environmental impacts to small, unregistered operations.

However, the demarcation between what is "informal" and what is "illegal" mining remains a grey area. In the Amazonian region of Madre de Dios, for example, there is a mixture of illegal operations and those ASM that have initiated the registration process and are thereby classified as seeking formalization. The ASM, who are the subject of this paper, are located in the highland areas of Arequipa, extracting hard rock through subterranean mining, as opposed to those who use alluvial mining methods in the Amazon lowlands. Hard rock gold extraction operations are to be found across much of Andean Peru, but such activities are concentrated in areas such as Puno and Arequipa regions (in the south) and in La Libertad (in the north).

Towards a new approach in Peru

Despite the extensive literature on informality in Peru and its persistence, public policy has failed in recent decades to produce credible responses. Probably the main advocate has been De Soto who, indeed, has worked with mining communities in discussing ways forward. However, despite his prominence among policy advisors at various points since 1990, his views do not appear to have had a major impact on policymaking. The neoliberal approaches that have prevailed in Peru for much of the last 30 years, with which De Soto is associated, have had negative impacts on boosting labour protections. A common business response to informality has been to argue that the solution to informality is to make labour legislation more flexible and to reduce the protections enjoyed by workers in the formal sector, thereby encouraging employers to take on more employees. This is an argument backed up by organizations like the OECD (OECD, 2023). But this approach has encountered strong resistance from trade unions which, despite their declining influence since the 1980s, have managed to protect employment rights and labour stability.

The first policies in Peru to initiate the formalization of ASM began in 2002; however, these were unsuccessful, and in 2012 the Humala administration (2011–2016) introduced what it termed "an extraordinary process." In their analysis of state policy up until this point, Dargent and Urteaga (2016) saw the agenda driven primarily by exogenous (international and domestic) pressures, and they questioned the sustainability of state responses given a lack of state actors capable of driving policy forward. Here we seek to take up this question and see how policy has evolved since then and to what effect. In 2017, the Kuczynski administration (2016–2018) launched what it called the "integral mining formalisation process." This aimed to make compliance with the rules easier: informal miners were invited to register themselves with state authorities if they wished to avoid being classified as "illegal." Importantly, a distinction was thus drawn between informal ASM and illegal mining. While illegal activity has been the subject of repeated state repression, especially during the Humala government, lasting success has been elusive since, in large part, the state has lacked the resources to control it.

As of early 2024, few of the ASM had managed to fulfil the complex and often costly procedures involved in registration. They were allowed to come within the law by complying with the necessary registration procedures, known as Reinfo (the Registro Integral de Formalización Minera), without necessarily complying with all the subsequent conditions attached to the process of formalization. As we shall see below in the case of Arequipa, of the numbers registering for Reinfo, only a very small proportion completed the process. Moreover, the time limit for registration was repeatedly extended, raising the possibility that ASM can simply stay on the Reinfo without having to comply with the often challenging and burdensome requirements for formalization. At the time of writing, the Reinfo scheme was due to expire at the end of 2024. If and when the scheme expires, those who have failed to meet its conditions face the threat of being cast back into being considered "illegal."

So why have successive governments sought to take the initiative in seeking to push ahead with formalization in the mining sector? A number of reasons suggest themselves:

1. The scale of the sector. The numbers involved in informal (and illegal) mining have grown rapidly in recent years with the rise in world gold prices and the relative lack of dynamism in other sectors of the economy. Large numbers in impoverished rural areas have found mining to be a profitable, albeit precarious, activity. Although the problem of informal mining is hard to tackle, the size of the sector makes it difficult to ignore.
2. The negative environmental impacts of mining. These have become better understood at the policymaking level, and with it the need to introduce regulations to control their more egregious negative effects. The scale of deforestation and environmental degradation in the Madre de Dios region stands out as an example of the harmful effects of unregulated mining. However, the negative impacts of small-scale mining are notable elsewhere, especially the poisoning of rivers through the use of mercury. Peru is under international pressure to improve its environmental standards. The creation of an environment ministry (Minam) under the García government represented an important milestone in this respect, as was the 2013 Minamata Convention which sought to restrict the use of mercury to purify gold. Many ASM operators continue to use mercury for lack of alternative technologies.
3. The salience of conflict within the mining sector. As well as often violent conflicts between peasant and indigenous communities in recent years, there have been many conflicts between informal miners and the holders of official mining concessions. The extension of mining concessions increased rapidly after 2000 (especially under the García government) as part of attempts to increase private sector investment in the mining industry. Often these concessions were granted in areas where mining was already conducted by ASM producers whose rights were frequently not recognized. Conflicts have resulted in several deaths in recent years.
4. Concerns about growing levels of contraband trade, especially with Bolivia. It was often repeated in our interviews that most explosives are imported illegally from Bolivia, while Bolivia has also become known as a major illegal export conduit for ASM gold producers whose ability to export is otherwise limited. Bolivia has rapidly become a major exporter of gold in recent years, much of it thought to originate in Peru. Bolivia has also been

identified as the source of the illicit fuel used in mining (especially in areas close to the border) since government subsidies in Bolivia make it cheaper to acquire.

5. The potential tax gains. Informal ASM producers do not contribute in direct taxation to the Treasury. The increase in their earnings has contributed little to the government's tax income, although it may contribute in other ways (e.g., through taxes on consumption).[6] Peru is under pressure from the IMF and World Bank to increase its tax take which, traditionally, has been among the lowest in Latin America. Some ASM operations (but by no means all) can make large profits.[7]
6. The political power of ASM. Due to their number and their ability to use buoyant incomes to support their cause, some of the larger-scale informal miners have been able to wield significant influence both at the regional and national levels. Workers' organizations have enthusiastically backed the formalization process, seeing it as a way to secure greater legal and social stability for their members and to resolve pending issues over the recognition of land rights as against those of concession holders. The confederation of informal miners (the Confederación Nacional de Pequeña Minería y Minería Artesanal del Perú, Cofemin) used its political muscle in Congress to elaborate a bill to fully legalize informal mining.
7. Political shifts since 2021. The 2021 elections brought to office a government (that of Pedro Castillo) that was widely voted for in areas where ASM workers and firms base their operations. Although the policy of formalization began well before the 2021 elections, it received a boost with the election of a president more responsive to political pressures from his supporters. Cofemin gained more scope to lobby for its objectives. Castillo's removal from office in December 2022 represented a setback, and his supporters were among those who rallied against the new government of Dina Boluarte by blocking roads and engaging in other protests.

In general terms, these concerns are related to one another and pertain to the building of a more democratic state in areas where this is largely absent, as well as reinforcing the rule of law in such areas.

Policy paradigms

Traditionally, the Ministry of Energy and Mines (Minem) has focused its attention on attracting investment in the medium and large-scale mining sectors; by comparison, the ASM sector has received scant attention. However, this has changed significantly in recent years for the reasons outlined above. In 2012, during the Humala administration, the scheme for registering and regulating ASM producers was reformed. Subsequently, a specific department was created within Minem, the Dirección General de Formalización Minera (DGFM), to oversee policy to this end. Two other institutions at the central government level are also involved in the oversight of small-scale mining: Osinergmin (Organismo Supervisor de la Inversión en Energía y Minería), which comes under the Prime Minister's Office, and OEFA (Organismo de Evaluación y Fiscalización Ambiental), which comes under the aegis of the Ministry of the Environment (Minam). However, the implementation of formalization is left in the hands of decentralized authorities. A World Bank report, published in 2015, while praising Peru's system of mining concessions, suggested that the formalization of ASM operations and its harmonization with other sectors was failing to meet expectations. The study focused on the Apurímac region, detecting major shortcomings attributable to "technical" and "administrative" shortcomings (2015, 13).

Indeed, the efficacy of the system introduced by the Humala administration and subsequently adapted under Kuczynski has been hobbled by shortcomings, which we will analyze in the next section of this chapter, taking Arequipa as our case study. Here, we outline two major attempts to formulate a more coherent approach to the problem of ASM formalization. The first of these was a detailed policy paper written by the Minem and published in 2022. The second was a draft bill written in close communication with a variety of stakeholders, including the Confemin, which was presented to the Congressional Commission on Mining on 15 June 2022. Both documents cover a wide range of policy choices and whilst overall these appear complementary, they contain some key differences with regard to concession rights, formalization processes, and tax requirements. These differences reflect the positions of DGFM, which wrote the policy, and the ASM lobby, which was core to drafting the bill. Despite such differences, taken together, these policy documents represented a major advance in discussion at the level of central government about the future of the ASM sector and how it could be brought within the ambit of formalization and legality. For the first time, the problem was being debated and the complexities involved in formalization openly acknowledged.

The Minem report (2022) is a lengthy and detailed document by the DGFM, intended to provide a policy blueprint. It was the result of extensive consideration and sought to look at some of the broader implications of formalization in the mining sector, providing a list of priority actions. As well as tackling short-term administrative difficulties, the report sets out an agenda for reducing labour precariousness in the mining sector through greater social protection and improved technical assistance. It linked the development of ASM mining to the improvement of social and environmental conditions in mining areas and the promotion of human and legal rights. It stressed the need for adequate financial support for small-scale mining and for strengthening state capacities at the local, regional, and national levels, as well as providing improved coordination between state institutions at the local level. It pointed to the importance of state-building in areas where state presence is conspicuous by its absence.

The document thus represented a new approach for ASM with measures seeking to increase the attractiveness of formalization while tackling some of the negative consequences derived from the past. Whilst interviewees from the public offices in Lima broadly welcomed the general policy direction, ASM producers and some regional bureaucrats were sceptical about the effects of this policy. In general, there was concern about whether the policy would address the needs of miners to access state support whilst enhancing their legal rights. The policy's success would depend on a much more supportive relationship between various levels of public administration – national, regional, and local – overcoming legacies of extreme administrative centralization. It would also depend on ASM miners being able to organise themselves more effectively and to pressure for implementation. Although there are national-level organizations that purport to represent ASM interests, these wield far less influence than established sectoral organizations such as the Sociedad Nacional de Minería, Petróleo y Energía (SNMPE) which represents medium and large-scale mining interests. Organization among the smallest mining enterprises is fragmentary at best, let alone those of individuals and families.

The draft ASM law, the "Ley de la Minería a Pequeña Escala – MAPE," was formally submitted to Congress on 23 November 2022, only days before the government of Pedro Castillo came to an abrupt end.[8] It set out in general terms what the ASM sector consisted of – adding to the list of ASM producers a separate classification of what it called "traditional producers." This referred to those miners whose production was under 5 tons/day, including *pallaqueras*, which together represent the majority of those working in the ASM sector. It established new responsibilities on the part of the state, providing a legal framework for what it called "the sustainable, and efficient development of activities within the sector," and for its "promotion and protection" (Congreso de la República, 2022). Although the Minem was to play a central role in the operation of the new law, the bill sought to create mechanisms to overcome the large number of institutions involved with the sector and integrate them into the processes of planning and implementation.

The draft law looked to establish a tax regime for MAPE miners. It sought to deal with areas of major contention in the sector such as state mediation in conflicts between ASM miners and the holders of concessions. It also sought to tackle problems like the acquisition of explosives and the management of chemical inputs such as mercury and cyanide. However, while the law addressed many of the issues that afflict small-scale miners, it was essentially broad-brush; its implementation would hinge on the detailed regulations that would follow promulgation and be imposed by government decree. The law would imply a substantial increase in state responsibilities – "state building" – in terms of the registration, oversight, and regulation of the activities of ASM.

The text of the draft law owed much to the lobbying of the ASM mineworkers themselves, specifically to the Confemin, which was expected to play a significant role in planning and implementation along with a variety of state actors. The confederation worked closely with members in Congress in the elaboration of the legislation, working also with specialist advisors. When it seemed in August 2022 that the moves to legislate were being thwarted by the disinterest of the then minister of energy and mines, the confederation put 1,000 miners on to the streets of Lima, persuading President Castillo to accelerate the promotion of the law by forming a technical commission to discuss and resolve pending issues.[9]

However, advances came to a sudden halt in December 2022 with the overthrow of Castillo and his replacement by Dina Boluarte, whose government was much closer to the interests of large-scale mining and whose overriding priority was to attract foreign investment into the large-scale mining industry. The channels for communication with the new administration were further blocked by the anti-government protests in which ASM miners took an active part. As of the end of 2023, the legislation proposed remained stuck in Congress, with the political impetus to see it approved clearly diminished.

Obstacles to formalization, the evidence from Arequipa

As a region, Arequipa has one of the largest concentrations of ASM miners in Peru. Though the exact number is unknown – one of the Minem policy recommendations was the holding of a nationwide census of small-scale miners to determine how many there are – it is thought to total 60,000–70,000, with some 3,500 *pallaqueras*. Much ASM mining is concentrated in the north-western part of the region in the provinces of Caravelí, Condesuyos, and Camaná. Almost all producers mine gold, though some also extract copper. Much of this terrain is arid and mountainous, with mining taking place at altitudes ranging as high as 4,000 metres above sea level. As opposed to alluvial gold production in the Amazon region, in Arequipa mining is hard-rock and subterranean, demanding the use of explosives. While ore grades in the region vary, generally they are considerably lower (around 2 ounces per ton of rock extracted) than in northern Peru, but slightly above the national average (1.9 ounces per ton). Mining settlements tend to be precariously built and exposed to landslides that can erase whole communities.[10] While incomes vary widely according to the scale of mining and where it takes place, a majority of miners (possibly as much as two-thirds) are very small operations conducted by individuals and/or their families. As with informality more broadly, the mining sector is highly heterogeneous.

ASM mining in Arequipa has received scant official attention until recently, long considered a "problem sector." Public policy has focused on the promotion and development of large-scale mining, given its significance in terms of private investment and exports. As we have seen, this has been changing in recent years, largely because of increased recognition in official circles that small-scale mining accounts for a substantial proportion of overall gold production, while the rise in world prices has increased incentives and led to its rapid expansion with all its attendant problems.

As it stands, the Reinfo system of registration is ad hoc and far from fit for purpose. Of those who have initiated the process, few in Arequipa have completed the formalization process, leading critics to conclude that they have managed to "legalize" their operations without complying with the standards officially required for formalization. According to one official, no more than 3% of the 17,000 miners registered in the Reinfo have concluded the process satisfactorily. The rest are in a sort of "limbo" status. As the termination date for registration has repeatedly been extended – at the time of writing it was to expire in 2024 – the number of applicants who have yet to fulfil the criteria for formalization has grown.

In order to complete formalization, miners are expected to comply with a complex series of bureaucratic requirements that usually involve them having to contract the use of consultants whose charges can be excessive and whose services tend to be far from ideal.[11] The costs of registration are therefore high and, in the case of the smallest-scale miners, prohibitively so.[12] These reports are often needlessly long and, to quote one official, "full of unnecessary garbage." The system in place does not allow easy tracking by applicants of the progress of applications to help them identify bottlenecks. It is also slow and cumbersome, involving long delays in processing applications. This is due to the lack of staffing, with the number of unprocessed applications building up over time. In Arequipa, the backlog is of 2–3 years, with some applicants starting the process as far back as 2011.

There are two institutions in Arequipa charged with the processing of applications, ARMA (Autoridad Regional Ambiental de Arequipa) and GREM (Gerencia Regional de Energía y Minas), the former coming under the aegis of the environment ministry (Minam) and charged with the assessment of environmental issues, the latter forming part of the regional government. Neither has the staffing to keep abreast of Reinfo applications. They receive an annual transfer under an arrangement with Minem in Lima known as the *convenio especial,* which is divided proportionally between regional governments based on the number of applications and other criteria. But the allocation is not assessed by identifiable need but by simply dividing up the budget available at the national level. This is wholly insufficient for the task in hand.[13] While officials in Lima remain anxious to maintain a tight control over how the funds are used – aware that corruption is commonplace – inadequate resourcing levels and cumbersome administrative systems lead to long delays in disbursing funds. Officials at the local level say that they are starved of resources for substantial parts of the year, forcing them to dismiss available staff for lack of funds.

Bureaucratic problems apart, probably the biggest obstacle to advancing the process has been in formalizing mining activities on land officially granted in concessions. As the World Bank document (2015) showed, a high proportion of concessions in Peru remain unworked by those who hold them, and many hold concessions more for speculative reasons than genuine intentions to develop their mining potential. Also, in many cases, concessions have been granted with no consideration of the informal mining activities already taking place in these areas, sometimes for generations. Among the documents required for formalization is a written agreement (*contrato de explotación*) on the part of those holding concessions that allows ASM activities to continue. Often such agreement is not forthcoming.

The relationship between ASM miners and concession holders is frequently exploitative, reflecting the power asymmetries between the two. Small-scale miners often have no alternative but to pay a royalty to the concession holders and/or to sell minerals directly to them. Where a contract exists, the concession holder can charge 10–15%, rising in extreme cases to 40%. The GREM advises that the maximum should be 10% for high ore grade and 5% for low ore grade. One official described 40% as "daylight robbery." Conflicts with concession holders are common in Arequipa, with at least 20 instances in recent years. In such circumstances, concession holders look for assistance from the police to uphold their interests and to frighten ASM producers into leaving their concession. The problem of violence is less in Arequipa than in La Libertad, where higher ore grades foment conflict[14]; however, it is still common.

As the World Bank study acknowledged, changes are required to encourage concession holders to develop their concessions and to shorten their duration where no mining activity takes place. Concessions can last as long as 30 years.[15] Changes to the system of concessions allowing others to mine them when the concession owner fails to do so are likely to run into opposition from the large-scale miners' lobby groups. Hitherto, at least, the government in Lima has done little to improve the way in which concessions are regulated. It remains unclear what happens to ASM miners once a concession ends and the *contrato de exploración* expires.

Problems with the owners of subsoil concessions can be exacerbated where peasant communities have formal or informal titles to the surface. The "triangular" relationship between the community, concession holder, and informal miners can foster conflict.[16] Although some miners may be members of peasant communities, the increase in gold prices has brought a rush of outsiders seeking remunerative employment in community territories. In Ispacas in Condesuyos province, the local community sought to restrict (unsuccessfully) mining activity to local people and to exclude migrants from elsewhere. As well as permission from the concession holder, the formalized miner needs to have permission to operate from the community.[17] The community receives little or nothing from mining activity carried out on its land, except what is called *servidumbre,* or the right to use community roads, etc. Still, some community members have accumulated significant wealth from informal mining, and mining has tended to eclipse traditional agricultural activities. It has also challenged established structures of local community power and reciprocity, undermining collective decision-making.

Closely connected with the lack of recognition for informal miners has been their resort to illegal mechanisms to acquire the essential inputs to conduct mining activity: explosives and chemical inputs for the separation of ore from rock, usually mercury.[18] This has limited legal use as Peru is a signatory of the Minamata Convention. ASM miners find it impracticable, costly, or often impossible to acquire these inputs from legal sources, leading them to do so on illicit markets.

Most of the mercury used in Arequipa is thought to come in the form of contraband from Bolivia. Although we cannot be sure that this is the case, some regional officials say that the Peruvian police play a significant role in this trade, casting a blind eye to acquisitions in return for the payment of bribes, thus (amongst other things) adding to the costs of production and further undermining the rule of law.[19] Attempts to wean small-scale miners off the use of mercury have produced scant results as most miners prefer to employ known technologies over unfamiliar alternative methods. The use of gravimetric concentrators has the added disadvantage of using copious amounts of usually scarce water. Still, many hard rock miners sell at least a proportion of their production to processing plants, avoiding the use of mercury.

Similarly, small-scale producers find themselves forced onto the black market to acquire explosives. The official procedures for acquiring explosives are complex and costly.[20] Acquiring explosives through official channels and then obtaining authorization for their use involve substantial payments. Although the Minem policy document and the bill before Congress address these difficulties, miners are meanwhile sucked into illicit arrangements with black market dealers. As with mercury, the explosives illegally obtained and used in mining in Arequipa are said to originate in Bolivia, which has also become an important informal transit route for illegally exported gold.

The relationship between processing plants also creates challenges to formalization.[21] Selling to processors means that the producers receive a sometimes heavily discounted price, whereas exporting illegally can be far more profitable. The smallest ASM producers are most disadvantaged by the commodity chain, having to trade through the greatest number of intermediaries. Since gold export requirements are extremely complex, adding to other related responsibilities such as tax compliance, most ASM miners are effectively blocked from directly exporting gold themselves. This leaves selling unprocessed or part-processed ores directly to processors or indirectly via intermediaries who collect minerals (*acopiadores*) as the only legally viable routes. Processors too face challenges in purchasing from small-scale producers, since within the legal trade of which they are a part of, they must maintain records of the provenance and legality of production, which can be complex when dealing with large numbers of small producers and intermediaries. Disagreements can arise with processors over the methods used to evaluate the purity of their ores, but many utilize testing regimes to try to minimize potential disagreements.

Compliance with the system as currently construed is thus challenging for ASM miners, with small-scale producers often deferring at least part of their trade to illicit arrangements because of the difficulties and increased costs they face in complying with legal trading requirements for essential inputs, processing, and onward sales. Many of these factors contribute to the common narrative that small-scale producers are viewed as being beyond the pale of legality, an image that is hard to dispel in the public mind and a key reason why policy reform is difficult to achieve.

Finally, and linked to the previous obstacles to formalization, is that of taxation. Formalization implies small-scale miners coming within the scope of the tax authorities, paying the appropriate level of tax in accordance with the size and scope of their operations – as any formal or legal business does. Although, as consumers, informal miners contribute to government tax income through VAT, they effectively pay no income tax. Given the large profits made by many small-scale miners due to high world gold prices, SUNAT, the Peruvian tax authority, is keen to add these potential tax earnings to Treasury tax receipts. Also, as the customs authority, SUNAT has a keen interest in reducing flows of contraband across Peru's land frontier with Bolivia, whether in the form of explosives, mercury, or gold exports.

Our study confirmed that most ASM miners are prepared to pay a tax on the profits they make if – in return – the state is able to guarantee the provision of social benefits, facilitate legal access to production inputs, and resolve problems arising from concession rights. Legal purchases within Peru could always be offset against tax. Although collecting tax due might cause problems for the tax authorities, only the larger producers would be susceptible to taxation if, as the proposed legislation implies, the smaller ones are effectively exempt. This was one of the reasons for the proposed legislation adding a category of "tradicionales" within the range of ASM producers whose modest earnings would remain untaxed.

Conclusions: Paving the way towards formalization

The Minem policy paper and the draft legislation on formalization represent significant advances in thinking about what needs to be done to enable this agenda to move forward. In the very short term, however, they appear to have been placed firmly on the back burner by a government less amenable to pressures from informal workers and more interested in meeting the requirements of large-scale mining. For the time being, the formalization of informal miners no longer seems a priority. It has also encountered significant opposition. Sooner or later, however, the needs of such workers and the effects of ASM (e.g., socio-economic and environmental) will have to be attended to, and recent work done in producing policy blueprints will regain salience.

The legislative proposals and the Minem policy document go some way towards addressing the defects previously posed by formalization policy. They represent an advance in policy thinking and design and (to some extent) as to how such policies might be implemented. This is a significant advance on what Dargent and Urteaga (2016) observed in 2015 at the time of the Humala administration. The Minem document points towards a more holistic approach to the problem that goes well beyond the simple remit of the registration process as it currently exists, pointing to the need for politicians and the wider society to re-evaluate the role played by small-scale miners who have so far been marginalized from major sectoral decision-making. The document also emphasizes the need to bring these miners within the framework of recognized worker rights and provide them with the tools to reduce their dependence on illegal practices.

However, realizing this agenda will be neither easy nor rapid. It will depend on an exercise of state building and the extension of the rule of law in areas where state institutions are practically absent. It will depend on the careful management of legal rights and, crucially, on the ability of small-scale miners and other actors (such as communities) to negotiate and defend those rights. It will involve the building of active citizenship amongst those traditionally at the margins of society. Policy implementation would require significant public funding, both in the short term as well as in the longer run. This is not impossible, but it would require a change in the way in which the available funding is currently allocated and managed. It will require overcoming resistance from opponents such as some of Peru's larger mining interests. Ultimately, any change will depend on the political will and leadership to make it happen.

Notes

1 The definition of "critical minerals" differs; the EU 2023 list includes copper due to high demand, whereas the USA list considers it "near critical."

2 For a comparison of approaches between Peru, Bolivia, and Colombia, see Baraybar Hidalgo and Dargent (2020). The authors contrast the differing social and political actors in determining government responses.

3 Peru was the seventh-largest gold producer worldwide in 2022 according to the World Gold Council, with production of 125.7 tonnes. https://www.gold.org/goldhub/data/gold-production-by-country. Accessed 2 January 2024. Exact estimates for gold exported are difficult to calculate due to the scale of contraband exports, chiefly to Bolivia.

4 The findings of this chapter are based on a study completed in February 2024, authored jointly by the Department for International Development at the University of Oxford and the Centro de Estudios sobre Mineria y Sostenibilidad (CEMS) at the Universidad del Pacífico, Lima. See Wilson, Quiñón, Sánchez-Ancochea (2023). The research in Arequipa was greatly assisted by Lucas Zegarra, to whom the authors would like to express their thanks.

5 According to one industry source, Peru exports around 180 tons of gold per annum, of which 100 tons are produced by ASM producers who mostly sell their production to processing plants.

6 It should be stressed that such profits can be offset by the often high cost of living in informal mining settlements, with inflated demand creating supply bottlenecks for specific goods.

7 According to one observer, an ASM producer with an output of 20 tons/day and an ore grade of 0.8% would be making US$8,500 a day at 2022 prices, or US$259,000 a month. If taxed at 18%, that would fall to over US$200,000, which would be used to cover costs, reinvestments, and profits divided between interested parties.

8 On December 7, Castillo was ousted from office by the Congress through impeachment. This followed his thwarted attempt to close down Congress and the judiciary. He was followed in office by his vice-president, Dina Boluarte, whose government quickly moved in a decidedly more conservative direction.

9 The "*grupo tecnico*" brought together officials from various ministries, the tax authority (SUNAT), and the Superintendency of Banks and Insurance (SBS) along with delegates from the confederation. The miners demanded the resignation of the then minister of energy and mines.

10 A major landslide in February 2023 caused widespread loss of life and destruction of housing and infrastructure in the key informal mining centre of Secocha in Camaná province.

11 In our interviews, we repeatedly heard the claim that consultants simply copy and paste previous applications without even changing the names and coordinates of the areas registered in previous applications.

12 These can cost at least 10,000 soles (US$2,550) according to some estimates, roughly twice what they should cost. The price depends on a negotiation between the producer and the consultant. In many cases, it can be as much as 30,000 soles. Producers usually lack the information to negotiate prices more to their advantage.

13 In 2022, the total budget distributed by Minem was 7 million soles (around US$1.8 million). This was subsequently doubled in 2023 to 14 million soles.

14 Killings at Pataz in La Libertad at the end of 2023 caused mining lobbyists to call on the government to close down the Reinfo scheme. Such demands continued subsequently following similar incidents there.

15 As of 2017, the length of concessions was increased from 15 to 30 years, but incremental penalties were introduced in cases where a concession was not used within 15 years.

16 Research on this has been sporadic and mainly focused on the Amazon region. In the Andes, some studies point to informal negotiations between peasants and informal miners in which access is traded for economic benefits, with some communities linking up mining and agriculture as part of a development strategy. See Bobadilla and Tarazona (2008) and Toledo and Veiga (2018).

17 There is nothing in the rules that insists on a process of prior consultation with peasant or indigenous communities in the case of ASM. But those ASM who wish to formalize themselves need to ask permission from the regional government to work in indigenous territories. In practice, this means negotiating with the community (which often has surface land rights), whether miners are from the locality or from outside.

18 While responsibility for environmental compliance lies with the Environment Ministry and the OEFA in the case of large-scale mining, it lies with regional governments in that of ASM. These normally lack the resources to fulfil this function, and informal practices (including corruption) prevail.

19 ASM producers in Arequipa can pay up to US$5,000 to acquire 4 kilos of mercury. While prices remain high, producers are prepared to pay such costs to ensure the supplies they require.

20 They involve acquiring an *expediente técnico*, which lasts six months and involves paying a consultant and possibly also officials at the regional government to acceler-

ate the process. Also required is the authorization to use explosives which, along with the necessary inspections, involves further costs.

21 There are numerous such plants in the Arequipa region, many concentrated around the town of Chala in Caravelí province, which sits on the Panamerican Highway.

References

Arce, Moisés, 2015. 'Resource Extraction, Political Fragmentation and Subnational Protest in Peru' in EU-LAC *Social Protests and Democratic Responsiveness: Assessing Realities in Latin American and the Caribbean and the European Union*. Hamburg: EU-LAC Foundation.

Baraybar Hidalgo, Viviana, and Eduardo Dargent, 2020. 'State Responses to the Gold Rush in the Andes (2004–08): the Politics of State Action (and Inaction)' *Studies in Comparative International Development* 55, 516–537.

Bobadilla, Percy, and David Tarazona, 2008. *Nosotros hacemos los pueblos. El empoderamiento en la Minería Artesanal: los casos de algunas localidades en Arequipa, Ayacucho y Puno*. Lima: Pontificia Universidad Católica del Perú.

Chacaltana, Juan, 2001. 'Reforma en la contratación y despido en el Perú' *Economía* 24(48), 133–151.

Congreso de la República, 2022. *'Proyecto de ley: Ley de la minería a pequeña escala – MAPE'*. Lima: Congreso de la República.

Dargent, Eduardo, and Madai Urteaga, 2016. 'Respuesta estatal por presiones externas: los determinantes del fortalecimiento estatal frente al boom del oro en el Perú (2004–15)' *Revista de Ciencia Política* 36(3), 655–677.

De Soto, Hernando, 1987. *El otro sendero: la revolución informal*. Lima: Instituto Libertad y Democracia.

Economic Commission for Latin America and the Caribbean (ECLAC), 2023, *Social Panorama of Latin America and the Caribbean, 2002*. Santiago: ECLAC.

International Labour Organization, 2018, *Women and Men in the Informal Economy: a Statistical Picture*. Geneva: ILO.

Matos Mar, José, 1986. *Desborde popular y crisis del estado: el nuevo rostro del Perú en la decada de 1980*. Lima: Instituto de Estudios Peruanos. Third edition.

Ministerio de Minería y Energía, 2022. *Política nacional sectorial para la pequeña minería y minería artesanal al 2030*. Lima: Minem.

OECD, 2023. *Estudios económicos de la OCDE: Perú*. Paris: OECD

Orozco, Olinda, 2017. *Pallaqueras: entre piedras y oro*. Lima: Solidaridad

Spalding, Rose J., 2023. *Breaking Ground: From Extraction Booms to Mining Bans in Latin America*. Oxford: Oxford University Press.

Toledo, Zaraí, and Marcello Veiga, 2018. 'Locals' Attitudes toward Artisanal and Large-scale Mining. A case study of Tambogrande, Peru'. *Extractive Industries and Society* 5(2), 327–334.

Wilson, Anna, Aaron Quiñón, and Diego Sánchez-Ancochea, 2023. *Hacia una mejor formalización de la minería artesanal y de pequeña escala (MAPE) en el Perú: explorando obstáculos y opciones de política pública en el Perú*. Centro de Estudios sobreMinería y Sostenibilidad de la Universidad del Pacífico and the Department for International Development, University of Oxford.

World Bank Group, 2015. *República del Perú: Sistema de Otorgamiento de concesiones mineras: problemática de la pequeña minería y la minería artesanal*. Lima: Banco Mundial.

3 Bureaucratic bypass as a strategy in the implementation of public policies

The case of industrial promotion in Argentina (1982–92)

Luis E. Karamaneff

Introduction

Living conditions and development opportunities for the inhabitants of Latin America vary considerably depending on the province or region in which they live. Many of the public policies designed to address these disparities pose a dilemma for researchers, given their tendency to view Weber's classical bureaucratic model as the only way to achieve efficient implementation. But carrying out industrial policy in ways that are considered correct and within the rule of law in the nations of the Global North often clashes with what is perceived as fair and viable in parts of the Global South. One such difference lies in the nature of the non-governmental actors that subnational governments rely on when trying to build confidence in the private sector, attract investment, strengthen state capabilities, and reduce territorial inequality.

A prime example of these regional disparities can be seen in the federally constituted Republic of Argentina, which, among Latin America's five largest countries, suffers from the highest levels of inter-provincial inequality. So great is this disparity that the province with the lowest product in the country has a GDP per capita almost ten times smaller than that of the richest (González and Del Tredici, 2019). As a result of a variety of agreements with varying emphases reached between provincial and national governments over the years, the state has offered incentives in terms of tariffs, financial arrangements, and taxes to try to at least lessen these ostensible territorial inequalities. These benefits were channelled through a regional industrial promotion scheme, which offered subsidies to capital in the hope that the establishment of new productive enterprises in the less-developed provinces could be achieved by increasing the internal rates of return on investment projects in these areas.

Through the regional industrial promotion scheme, a policy of productive decentralization was implemented in order to improve employment and reduce concentration trends in four economically underdeveloped provinces: Catamarca, La Rioja, San Juan, and San Luis.[1] Although the promotion of industry had important effects in all provinces, in San Luis the changes were so great that the productive structure of the province was completely transformed, with the industrial sector producing more than 50% of its GGP by 1990, which was

DOI: 10.4324/9781003519195-3

double the average rate both at the national level and in the other provinces where these policies were implemented. Between 1983 and 1991, the economy of San Luis grew by 227%, tripling the province's contribution to the national economy and surpassing average national per capita output (CEPAL, 2001).[2]

The literature highlights two important conditions required for the implementation of policies promoting economic development to be effective. First, it has been demonstrated that bureaucracies with highly selective, meritocratic hiring policies that offer long-term career rewards can foster commitment and a sense of corporate coherence, thereby decisively influencing the economic growth of states (Johnson, 1982; Nordlinger, 1987; Amsden, 1989; and Kohli, 2004). Secondly, the idea of "embeddedness" (Evans, 2012) posits that the links between the bureaucracy and the private sector facilitate the flow of information and allow for the establishment of credible commitments between the two.

The concept of "embedded autonomy" synthesizes, on the one hand, the necessity of the state being able to set goals and mobilize resources, and, on the other hand, the role of the private sector in organizing the productive process. However, none of the numerous studies that have been conducted with the aim of investigating the general effects of industrial promotion have provided evidence of the existence of a Weberian bureaucracy in the regions where such policies have been implemented, far less in the province of San Luis.[3] On the contrary, these studies have found that control over the organization of the state was concentrated in the hands of a small group of individuals linked together by personal relationships, while bureaucratic personnel were neither hired meritocratically nor enjoyed predictable professional careers.

Taking these findings as a starting point, this chapter seeks to answer the following questions: how does a state that lacks both qualified bureaucratic resources and a relationship of embeddedness with the private sector manage to transform its productive structure? Are there significant differences in the actions that provincial governments implement in order to attract capital? And, finally, what political and/or bureaucratic factors do entrepreneurs consider when moving or relocating their assets? These issues pose a double challenge for any analysis of the implications of the rule of law outside of the Global North: on the one hand, that of rethinking and relaxing traditional notions of how industrial policy is carried out at the subnational level in Latin America; and, on the other hand, that of attempting to resolve the legal loopholes inherent in policy implementation in federal nations suffering from significant regional inequalities.

To this end, we propose the following hypothesis: that states with low bureaucratic capacity and embeddedness with the private sector can transform their economies by bypassing the public administration. This is because the resources and social capital enjoyed by the agents of this bypass provide the business sector with security when it comes to the granting and realization of the fiscal benefits offered by industrial policy. This form of government–business sector interaction improves the processes of defining interests and objectives, as well as the efforts of the state to satisfy them. In this sense, the relational component that the bypass offers the state can help it solve coordination problems and manage conflicts of interest, facilitating the delivery of investments to a particular region.

With the aim of answering the questions noted above, as well as clearly outlining how bureaucratic bypass functions within the context of a concrete public policy, this chapter considers how bypass was implemented as part of Argentina's regional industrial promotion scheme. To this end, the chapter is organized as follows: in the first section, "The Concept of Bureaucratic Bypass," the concept of bureaucratic bypass is established. The second section, "Regional Industrial Promotion in Argentina," analyzes regional industrial promotion policies in Argentina. The third section, "Bureaucratic Bypass as an Alternative," looks at bureaucratic bypass as an alternative means of promoting industry, while the fourth section, "The Case of San Luis," focuses on its implementation in the case of San Luis. Finally, the fifth section, "Conclusions," presents the chapter's overall conclusions.

The concept of bureaucratic bypass

Bureaucratic bypass consists of the informal delegation of official competencies to an external agent charged with performing tasks that the state apparatus lacks the intention or the capacity to carry out (Karamaneff, 2021). This is because in the absence of a coherent and self-oriented administrative structure, the personal ties that link together non-bureaucratic agents can constitute a source of cohesion that allows them to reduce the information and transaction costs implicit in the fulfilment of certain objectives. Thus, when a bureaucratic structure is incapable of establishing regular connections with the private sector, the government instead encourages the informal interaction of these agents with the business community via personal channels.

In a context of widespread political instability, the fragmentation of business communities, and a growing distrust of state intervention (Evans, 2012), strategies to attract investment must be agile and well-timed. This is due to the volatility of institutional conditions, where any competitive advantage must be seized quickly. In this context, states without "embedded autonomy" – and which therefore cannot rely on the prompt formation of Weberian bureaucracies – may instead resort to strategies such as bureaucratic bypass. This state of affairs appears paradoxical to certain authors who stress the importance of the formality of institutions (Levitsky and Helmke 2012; Levitsky and Murillo 2009; Murillo, Levitsky, and Brinks, 2021), because informal mechanisms like bureaucratic bypass facilitate the generation of resources and social capital, which in turn strengthens a state's formal capacity to solve coordination problems and conflicts of interest.

This is because through their possession of resources that make them relevant and reliable actors for the business community, agents of bypass can act in the public sphere – and throughout the investment attraction cycle – in favour of government sectors that are not in a position to do so for themselves. Through bypass, then, non-state actors can, in the context of economic and institutional adversity, use their personal and professional networks to help carry out operations designed by the state. In this sense, bypass agents strengthen state capacities as a consequence of their actions, rather than this being their motive. But governments and other political authorities can exploit this collateral effect of the actions of the agents of bypass.

Given that states may not possess the elements needed for efficient public administration, the direction of the process is provided by the governing elite, which, lacking a highly skilled and embedded bureaucracy, finds an alternative in the form of private sector intermediaries. These intermediaries – generally a mix of lawyers, economists, accountants, and finance specialists – have higher levels of training than bureaucrats and enjoy close links with one another (as members of the same professional networks) and with political leaders (who are often drawn from the same elites), allowing them to coordinate their actions with high levels of fluidity. Government leaders turn to these intermediaries in order to coordinate assets (such as information and contacts), to influence the actions of businesses, and to facilitate agreements between the two sectors. Together they come to constitute informal networks of professionals who, at least initially, help to connect small groups of high-level provincial officials with the owners and managers of atomized companies.

The operators of these networks are able to use their close links with the business world to make the process of relocation to a less-developed province more reliable and predictable and provide minimum guarantees of competence and commitment, which make such a move appear less risky. These networks are concurrently political and operational: they influence the decisions of the business community as to the location of their companies; shape government decisions regarding the sectors and/or entrepreneurs to be encouraged to relocate; and, at the same time, provide material support and information on the economic, political, and/or productive conditions of the state. This does not mean the state can entirely dispense with the formation of a Weberian bureaucracy, but rather that certain, specific functions of the latter are temporarily substituted in the absence of the relevant bureaucratic capacities.

Subsequently, as the state confronts the necessity of meeting new demands on the part of the established business community, it increases some of its capacities – through administrative reorganization and the creation of a specialized bureaucracy – in order to streamline procedures and provide the process of productive transformation with the infrastructure and institutional framework it depends on. Thus, bureaucratic bypass may not be particularly long-lasting; instead, it functions as an efficient short-term tool for boosting industrial capital accumulation, before transforming itself in order to address the new problems and opportunities its own operative success has generated.

However, the lack of adherence to formal rules and procedures implicit in the process of bypass can also pose risks due to a lack of controls, which can lead to possible abuses, irregularities, and the absence of transparency when it comes to attracting investments. Bypass, therefore, allows provincial administrations to evade controls during the early implementation of regional industrial policy because, by operating in an informal space, local courts adjust to provincial government needs to avoid unduly prejudicing the policy implementation process. This exposes the existence of loopholes implicit in policy implementation in federal countries with large regional inequalities because, as Cao (2018) points out, it is national courts that truly function as enforcers of accountability.

Finally, the absence of a Weberian bureaucracy does not mean that bypass operates in a vacuum, but rather within public administrations that lack embeddedness with the same private sector they are trying to attract to their regions. This indicates that the state continues to play a key role in processes of development, strengthening its own capacities in order to respond to the broader socio-political context within which it exists. Were it not to function in this way, a predatory logic would prevail in the absence of the construction of state capacities, with the state failing to provide collective goods, and private agents responding by switching from productive activities to mere rent-seeking.

Regional industrial promotion in Argentina

In 1973, the last federal administration of President Juan D. Perón signed the "Historical Reparation Act," which established that "the national State assumes an irrevocable commitment with the provinces of Catamarca, La Rioja and San Luis to broker the measures necessary to promote their growth as a historical reparation for their contribution to the country's formation.[4] Within this same framework, Law 22.021 of 1979 was passed a few years later, granting a series of tax benefits to anyone who carried out economic activities in the Province of La Rioja. In 1982, Law 22.702 extended the same promotional benefits to companies that established themselves in Catamarca and San Luis, helping to consolidate on the ground the lofty proposals of 1973's Historical Reparation Act. Finally, in November 1983, the military regime passed Law 22.973, which extended identical benefits to San Juan.

Although it was subject to later adjustments and modifications, the general system of tax benefits applying to the four provinces offered the following incentives:

- Income tax deductions and/or exemptions;
- Exemption of taxes on a company's capital and the assets making up its patrimony;
- Relief (on a decreasing scale) from value-added tax (VAT) on sales made to the domestic market;

- Relief (on a decreasing scale) from VAT for suppliers of raw materials, inputs, or goods on sales made to companies benefiting from the scheme;
- Exemption from the payment of duties and other import taxes on purchases of capital goods, tools, and components of such goods;
- The possibility of investors in beneficiary companies deducting the value of these investments from their taxable income or deferring the payment of these taxes (although this benefit was later discontinued).

Originally, those companies that invested in the four provinces could be exempted from taxes entirely, but the granting of such tax benefits was the sole province of the national government's Ministry of the Economy (see Figure 3.1). As Macón (1985) shows, bureaucratic struggles between two sectors of the Ministry – namely, the industrialists who enthusiastically supported the tax incentives, and the agencies responsible for financial supervision – helped to keep the system of promotional incentives under control. However, in 1979, 1982, and 1983 the national government delegated its authority to grant tax breaks to the governments of the four provinces (see Figure 3.2).

In conceding to the four provincial governments the power to directly authorize investment projects with values below a certain minimum figure

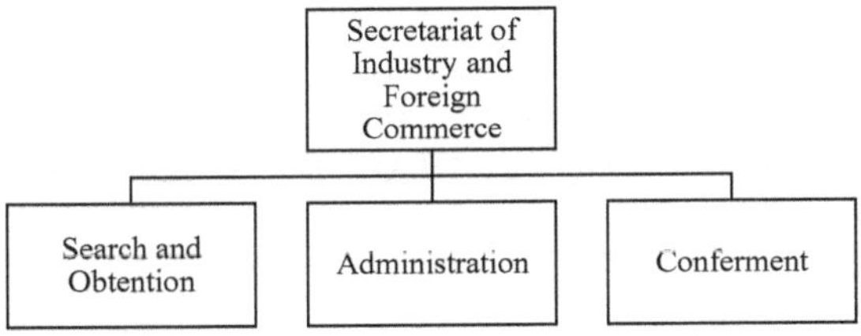

Figure 3.1 Diagram of organizational structure of central government bodies with implementation.al authority.

Source: Author's own elaboration.

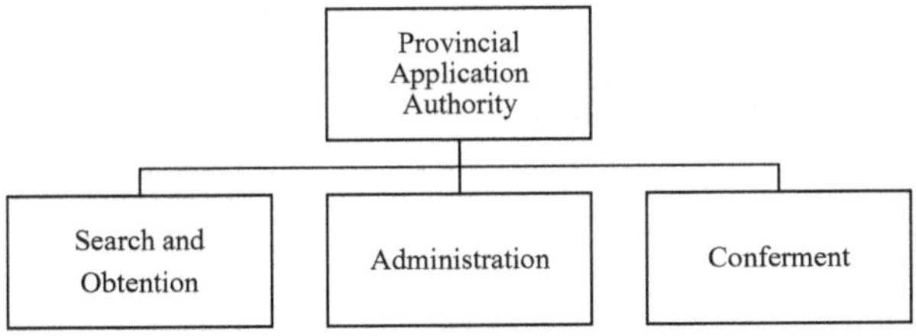

Figure 3.2 Diagram of organizational structure with delegated implementational authority.

Source: Author's own elaboration.

Table 3.1 Promoted provinces compared to the rest of the country's provinces in terms of their share of the total theoretical cost of the regional fiscal incentive system, 1980–88 (in percentages)

Province	*1980*	*1981*	*1982*	*1983*	*1984*	*1985*	*1986*	*1987*	*1988*
Four promoted provinces	1.0	3.9	12.0	10.9	30.0	58.5	63.6	79.5	98.0
Remaining provinces	99.0	96.1	88.0	89.1	70.0	41.5	36.4	20.5	2.0
Total	100	100	100	100	100	100	100	100	100

Source: Secretariats of Industry and Finance, reproduced in the "Diario de Sesiones de la Honorable Cámara de Diputados de la Nación," 17 May 1988, p 272.

(approximately one million dollars), the national government delegated the following powers to the provinces:

1. Evaluation of the projects and petitions submitted to them.
2. Regulation of the procedures to be observed when carrying out such evaluations.
3. Granting or rejecting the benefits requested.
4. Control over the exercise of the rights granted and over the fulfilment of the obligations assumed by the beneficiaries.
5. Interpretation, on a mandatory and general basis, of the rules governing financial incentives.
6. Modification, termination, or lapsing of agreed benefits.
7. Sanctioning powers.

The enforcement authority enjoyed by the governments of the four provinces allowed them to massively expand the granting of financial incentives to private companies. Handing out national tax breaks helped them to promote industries, provide employment, and increase their own tax revenues at the expense of both other provinces and the central government itself. As the 1980s progressed, the tax breaks granted by the four provinces gradually eclipsed those granted by the national government for investment in all of Argentina's other provinces combined (see Table 3.1).

Bureaucratic bypass as an alternative

Despite the incentives, however, neither the regional benefits laws nor the delegation of authority could, by themselves, successfully achieve the economic development of the provinces. A company's decision to move assets and relocate to another province could not be made solely on the basis of the incentives or compensation that the government could offer. Relocating an industry is never a knee-jerk reaction to fiscal stimulus. There is a certain level of planning involved: from finding a piece of land with basic services on which to construct a factory, to hiring the personnel needed to get it running. Incentives might be able to generate some interest among entrepreneurs, but, given longstanding traditions of such sweeteners, the latter did not represent much of a novelty either.

It was to the governments of the promoted provinces that such policies offered a genuinely historic opportunity because it gave them control over the approval and granting of benefits. This gave them a chance to transform their economies or, at the very least, achieve an increase in investments in their territories. Consequently, regional industrial policy became a field of competence in attracting industries already established in the country by persuading entrepreneurs of the advantages of relocating their operations to these new locations.

But it was not enough for provincial governments to have been delegated enforcement authority alone; this had to be complemented not only by the relentless task of spreading awareness of incentives but also by advertizing the benefits of the province in question. This also meant that certain problems had to be confronted, such as the lack of support from, or active opposition by, organizations within the public administration, and changes in import tariffs or the exchange rate linked to macroeconomic instability. The implementation of the regional promotion scheme therefore also rested on the capacity of local actors to attract entrepreneurs and investors through the use of these incentives; that is, on their ability to broadcast to potential investors and critics the benefits of both the promotional legislation and of the province itself, and to try to correct over time the undesirable effects of bad publicity concerning local conditions.[5]

Thus, in the eyes of businessmen, other state agencies, and the public opposition, provincial governments constituted the visible face of the policy being promoted. This being the case, the transfer of real responsibilities highlighted the insufficiency of subnational actors' capacity to attract investments via linkages with the private sector. This was due not only to a lack of contact networks tying local public administrations to the business community in the country's productive centres (ie., potential investors), but also to a lack of expertise on the part of the former when it came to establishing interactions with market actors.

Industrial promotion did not result in the emergence of new productive agents but rather encouraged existing companies to expand or decentralize. The objective, then, was to look for industries that could relocate; promote the potential advantages of the province; negotiate the requirements of a relocation – which ranged from providing the basic infrastructure to get a factory up and running, to ensuring local schools had space for the children of those who moved – and, finally, broker the quick approval of the projects. This involved getting to know potential stakeholders, establishing links that would guarantee that the requirements implicit in any relocation would be met, and then coordinating its

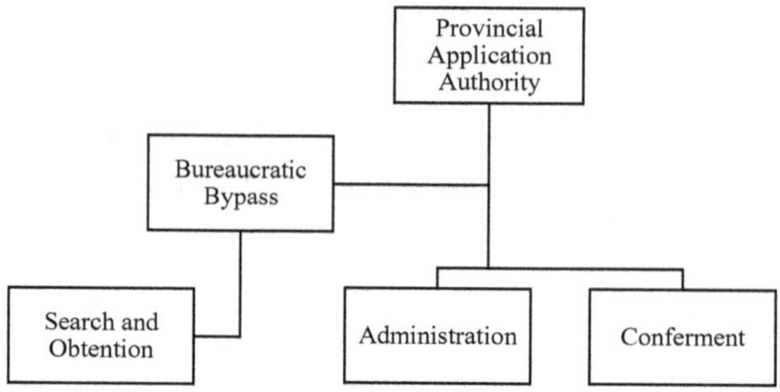

Figure 3.3 Diagram of organizational structure with bureaucratic bypass.
Source: Author's own elaboration.

implementation. In the absence of bureaucracies that possessed these networks and skill sets, the option was to bypass the public administration and turn instead to intermediaries who *did* have these capabilities.

In the face of the new window of opportunity that industrial promotion opened up for them, provincial governments that lacked the administrative resources with which to attract resources instead allowed or encouraged private sector intermediaries to seek out and manage new investments. This prompted a mobilization of private resources that provincial governments endorsed or promoted with the aim of attracting capital. At this stage, there was coordination between entrepreneurs – the potential investors – and provincial governments, which was managed by intermediaries who would gain an immediate economic benefit from a relocation (ie., they were paid by the companies to draw up plans for the move) and/or subsequent advantages (ie., they gained new clients who would later pay them for accounting and legal services).

This brokering work was made possible by the tax benefits that intermediaries used as a lure, and by the absence of a Weberian bureaucracy, which ensured lax controls – unlike the well-known, rigorous controls of the National Secretariat of Industry – applied to the approval of relocations. Thus, the intermediaries not only offered tax benefits but also ensured that they were obtained and applied in a quick and effective manner.

The intermediaries, mostly accountants, lawyers, and other professionals with expertise in the formulation of projects designed to secure subsidies, had wider experience with the national government's regional or sectorial industrial policies. Some of them had studied these types of policies for large consulting firms based in Buenos Aires, while others were natives of the beneficiary provinces themselves and had experience and/or links both with local governments and businessmen from other regions. Either way, they moved with great agility in the context of industrial promotion, taking advantage of all the opportunities presented by the tax benefit schemes.

The remarkable success of industrial promotion in San Luis, explored in detail in the next section, can be largely attributed to the provincial government's strategy of implementing bureaucratic bypass. This allowed a range of intermediaries to maximize the opportunities offered by the industrial promotion programme. In contrast, the varying strategies employed in other provinces attained only relative success. In the case of La Rioja, a similar strategy to that of San Luis was initially implemented but was later moderated by the local bureaucracy, while Catamarca and San Juan adopted alternative policies that failed to even remotely attain the successes achieved by San Luis.[6]

The case of San Luis

The data on the fiscal cost of regional industrial promotion show that the four promoted provinces concentrated 98.0% of the regional incentives granted in the country as a whole and that, of the four, San Luis managed to capture almost 70% of those benefits (see Table 3.2). Prior to the introduction of tax incentives, the economy of San Luis was characterized by the clear predominance of primary activities (agriculture and livestock), and, within these, of cattle raising in particular. Meanwhile, local industry was little diversified in terms of the subsectors that accounted for the bulk of employment and production. Before the implementation of the industrial promotion scheme, the manufacturing industry represented less than 15% of the province's GGP and, within that, the production of food, beverages, tobacco, and non-metallic minerals accounted for 50% of premises, 70% of employment, and 85% of production value. The rest of

Table 3.2 Provincial shares of the theoretical financial cost of the regional fiscal incentive system 1980–88 (in percentages)

Province	*1980*	*1981*	*1982*	*1983*	*1984*	*1985*	*1986*	*1987*	*1988*
Catamarca				0.2	2	6.5	7.3	6.7	8.7
La Rioja	1	3.9	12	10.1	15.6	11.7	9.4	7.7	10
San Juan					0.4	4.3	7.5	5.8	9.9
San Luis				0.6	12	36	39.4	59.3	69.4
Four promoted provinces	1	3.9	12	10.9	30	58.5	63.6	79.5	98
Remaining provinces	99	96.1	88	89.1	70	41.5	36.4	20.5	2
Total	100	100	100	100	100	100	100	100	100

Source: Secretariats of Industry and Finance, reproduced in the "Diario de Sesiones de la Honorable Cámara de Diputados de la Nación," 17 May 1988, p 272.

Table 3.3 Evolution of gross geographic product (GGP) in San Luis, 1980–90

Sectors	*GGP by sector*	
Year	**1980**	**1990**
Agriculture and cattle	25.1	4.4
Mining	11.2	2.1
Industry	14.7	63.7
Public services (water, gas, and electricity)	1.6	0.9
Construction	11.1	3.5
Commerce	13.4	4.5
Transport and communications	3.2	2.4
Financial services	0.2	9.4
Public administration	19.5	9.2
Total	**100**	**100**

Source: Federal Investment Council, Directorate of Statistics and Censes, Province of San Luis. Statistical Information Booklet Number 9, 1995.

the region's industrial subsectors scarcely registered, rounding off a provincial industrial structure that appeared rigid and barely diversified (see Table 3.3).

The scale of the impact of industrial relocations in San Luis was such that the province increased its share of the national economy by a factor of three and surpassed the national average per capita product.[7] This translated into a radical transformation of the province's economic structure, with the secondary sector climbing from a share of 27.4% of GGP in 1980 to one of 68.1% in 1990 (see Table 3.4). This stark transformation was matched by the overhaul of the local labour market, as San Luis quadrupled its industrial employment rate while the other three provinces attained more modest results (see Table 3.5). Finally, given that the arrival of no single branch of industry was promoted more than any other, the relocalizations resulted in an increase in every industry, with particularly significant growth in chemicals and textiles and a slight decline in the food industry's share of the total sector (see Table 3.6).

Table 3.4 Percentage of sectors within total GGP, 1980–90

Year	*1980*	*1990*
Primary	36.4	6.49
Secondary	27.4	68.1
Tertiary	36.3	25.4
Total	100	100

Source: Federal Investment Council, Directorate of Statistics and Censes, Province of San Luis. Statistical Information Booklet Number 9, 1995.

Table 3.5 Industrial employment and employment by promoted companies during the first stage of the regional industrial promotion scheme, 1973–93 (in number of employees)

Province	*Industrial employment*			
	1973	*1993*	*Difference*	*Employment generated by promoted projects*
Catamarca	1994	6525	4531	5430
La Rioja	1750	6611	4861	6117
San Luis	4661	22658	17997	22218
San Juan	8388	12727	4339	5448
Regional total	16793	48521	31728	39213
Remaining urban areas	1525221	1007909	−517312	

Source: "Impacto económico de los regímenes de promoción de las provincias de San Juan, La Rioja, San Luis y Catamarca." Consejo Empresario Mendocino, 1999.

Table 3.6 Different industries located in San Luis (by branch, in absolute terms and percentages)

Branches	*1985*	*%*	*1994*	*%*
Metallurgy	147	18.2	333	21.7
Textiles	80	9.9	238	15.5
Food	252	31.3	288	18.8
Chemicals	42	5.2	221	14.4
Non-metallic Mining	136	16.8	157	10.2
Paper	28	3.4	73	4.7
Base metals	S/D	S/D	74	4.8
Wood	112	13.9	133	8.6
Others	8	0.9	14	0.9
Total	805	100	1531	100

Source: Censo nacional económico, 1985 y "La industria en la Provincia de San Luis," 1994.

In December 1982, although the de facto government of San Luis already possessed the authority to implement industrial relocalization projects, the military authorities of the province adopted a conservative strategy in the hope that tax benefits would be sufficient to win industrialists over to the idea of establishing themselves in the province. The project approval process included the participation of an evaluation committee that, in the words of its members, replicated the criteria of the national government's Secretariat of Industry, "making everything much slower" and delaying the delivery of relocation decrees.[8] This situation would only change in December 1983, with the transition to democracy and the decision of the newly elected governor of the province, Adolfo Rodríguez Saá,[9] to informally outsource the search for investors and at the same time centralize political authority over the approval of projects.

This was quickly reflected in the number of new projects in San Luis: 54 new industries during the last year of the military government, and 266 in the first year of the Rodríguez Saá administration (Morina, 1989). The number of projects authorized in 1984 amounted to one per working day throughout the entire year, which attests to both the interest of businesses in the regional promotion scheme and the ease with which provincial government approval could be obtained. This was due, as mentioned above, to the fact that their possession of implementation authority granted provincial governments sufficient autonomy to negotiate directly with entrepreneurs, create bonds of trust between them, and take on the commitments necessary to secure the establishment of new industries in their territories. To this end, the government of San Luis resorted to the extra-bureaucratic services of private operators in order to take advantage of their links with the business sector.

In this sense, while theory holds that capitalist growth can only take place after a state with embedded autonomy has managed to develop its economy, the case of San Luis shows that the absence of these conditions can be temporarily overcome via bureaucratic bypass. The state capacities required to maintain and enhance development can then be subsequently built on the foundations provided by this mechanism. This is because there are different ways of creating embeddedness with the private sector. This differentiation is especially important for the set of middle-tier states that cannot depend on the existence of autonomous Weberian bureaucracies in the immediate future, but which could still reap some of the benefits of embeddedness.

Conclusions

Regional industrial promotion in Argentina was a productive decentralization policy that represented a golden opportunity to transform the productive structures of Catamarca, La Rioja, San Juan, and San Luis or, at least, to achieve an increase in investments in their territories. These provinces granted financial incentives to private companies and received the full benefit of investment incentives, whose cost was absorbed by the remaining provincial governments and the national government. Through the concession of national tax breaks, they were able to develop regional industry, provide local employment, and boost their own tax revenue.

In this way, regional industrial promotion became a competition for the relocation of the country's pre-existing industries, centred around persuading entrepreneurs that it was possible to establish themselves in a new territory. However, despite the similar conditions prevailing in each province, the ways in which their public sectors were organized varied from one to another, as did the nature of the links that each one established with the private sector. The same policy therefore achieved different results in each of the four provinces.

This chapter showed that bureaucratic capacity and embeddedness can be substituted – albeit temporarily – by bypassing the public administration. This is because the resources and social capital that bypass agents enjoy can provide the juridical security needed for processes of attracting and establishing investment stimulated by the implementation of industrial policy. This novel form of government–business sector interaction improves the processes of defining interests and objectives, as well as the way in which the state acts to satisfy these. In this sense, the component of relational capacity that the bypass offers the state allows it to solve coordination problems and manage conflicts of interest, facilitating the entry of investments into the territory.

In addition to the concept of bureaucratic bypass, this work makes several other related contributions. The first has to do with the importance of non-state actors in the implementation of state industrial policy. Here, the results highlight an approach to governance in which the state is not the only responsible actor, but instead involves a system of decision-making and public policy implementation that also includes non-governmental social actors. The latter intervene in the processes of defining interests and objectives, and in deciding what should be done to satisfy them, giving rise to a form of government–society interaction that helps to make the economic process sustainable. At any level of government, even at the subnational level, the central idea is the same: no model of economic development is viable in the long term without a coalition or political framework to sustain it and defend it from its opponents.

The second contribution arising from the concept of bypass, which is also linked to the first, is that of supplementing principal/agent theories in which governing authorities are a principal that depends on the bureaucracy as an agent to solve information problems and implement public policies (Przweroski, 2015). What the concept of bypass adds to this is the idea that while politicians need agents to implement their public policy decisions, these agents are not always found within the state bureaucracy. Instead, what this research shows is that there may be "functional equivalents" to the latter, which, although outside of the state, solve political authorities' problems in terms of information and capacity constraints.

While other authors (Scharpf 1993; Mayntz 2006, Kooiman 2003; Kickert, Klijn, and Koppenjan1997) have also pointed out that the state bureaucracy can be replaced as an agent of government by civil society bureaucracies – for example, by non-governmental organizations (NGOs) – the bypass argument posits another alternative: that intermediaries can replace the bureaucracy in an informal manner. In turn, this finding is linked to the third contribution of this chapter regarding the utility of informal institutions.

While the literature on institutional weakness (Levitsky and Helmke 2012; Levitsky and Murillo 2009; Murillo, Levitsky, and Brinks 2021) holds that informality tends to undermine state capacity, in the case of San Luis, the strategy of bypass helped to achieve the industrialization and economic development of a peripheral province. Therefore, the concept of bureaucratic bypass contributes to a better appreciation of the potential of informal institutions. This is particularly true in cases where real institutional weakness lies not so much in the informality of its agents, but rather in a lack of state capacity to ensure economic development. In San Luis, the alternative was to turn to informality as a mechanism through which to overcome difficulties and/or take advantage of opportunities to mobilize resources in the province's favour. This presents us with the paradox of certain informal practices actually helping to expand state capacity, which in turn contributes to our understanding of the potential of using and regulating informal institutions.

Something that emerges from this last point is the importance of strengthening state capacities in order to make the economic development process sustainable. Although this study highlights the use of informal networks, this does not imply that these inter-organizational networks are truly autonomous from the state, but rather that, on the contrary, the state itself fosters them in order to later formally integrate them into its own structure. In the case of bureaucratic bypass, for example, governments assume the roles of policy-makers, decision-makers, and funders of policies; conclude agreements with their agents regarding performance standards; and evaluate the products and results of their actions. In this sense, although industries, business organizations and intermediaries combine their resources, mobilize their capacities, and connect themselves together, the government plays an active role in centralizing and coordinating the decisions that make this process sustainable.

Furthermore, the particularities of the case highlight the disparities between the proposals of Global North countries for how industrial policies should be implemented and the manner in which this implementation actually takes place in the nations of the Global South. These differences spring from the fact that implementation mechanisms like bureaucratic bypass violate various Weberian principles of "good" bureaucracy, while at the same time harnessing and regulating the powerful incentives of informality in order to alleviate the administrative constraints and lack of embeddedness suffered by subnational states in middle-income countries. In public administration, measuring the quality of a bureaucracy solely by Weberian standards means that all the deviations found in developing countries are seen as defects to be quickly eradicated and replaced by Weberian best practices. However, numerous studies (Riggs 1964; Rodrik 2008; Andrews 2013) show that in developing countries such practices often backfire, creating a stubborn discord between formal standards and on-the-ground practices.

Finally, the importance of the relationship between the rule of law and governance for development lies in the need for strong and transparent institutions that promote investor confidence and ensure long-term political and economic stability. This means that despite making adjustments in order to overcome the limitations of public administration, the fundamental principles of justice, equity, and legality must be respected. The principal tension created by the implementation of strategies such as bureaucratic bypass is that their use implies a temporary departure from formal procedures and established regulations.

In this respect, the results of this research indicate that, given its effectiveness, bureaucratic bypass should not be prohibited, but rather that its operation should be overseen by local control mechanisms such as tribunals or courts of auditors. These bodies could be responsible for reviewing the actions carried out within the framework of bypass, thus ensuring transparency, accountability, and compliance with relevant laws and regulations. In addition, they would have the authority to impose sanctions in cases where irregularities or abuses were detected in the investment attraction process. In this way, a balance could be established between the need for flexibility and agility in government management, and the need for effective compliance with the rule of law.

Notes

1 The general system of financial incentives was instituted in the early 1980s in the provinces of La Rioja (Ley N. 22.021/79), San Luis, Catamarca (Ley N. 22.702/82), and San Juan (Ley N. 22.973/83).
2 Even years after the end of this promotion scheme, the province continues to show a considerable level of diversification that extends from the processing of agricultural products to high-tech industrial manufacturing, with industrial salary levels far higher than those of the country's main urban centres (Karamaneff and Salvia 2019).
3 See Azpiazu 1989; Cepal 2001; Consejo Empresario Mendocino 1999; Eaton 2003; Bezchinsky et al. 1988; Borello 1989; Sawers and Massacane 2001; Schvarzer 1987; for the case of San Luis in particular, see Behrend 2011; Bianchi 2013; Chávez 2003; Gervasoni 2009; Giraudy 2010; Guiñazú 2003; Mera 2016; Niedwiezcki 2016; Karamaneff and Salvia 2019; Samper 2006; Trocello 2008.
4 Juan Domingo Perón (1895–74), three times president of Argentina, is a central figure in the political and economic history of the country. His focus on the protection of national industry and the creation of a robust internal market significantly influenced Argentina's economic and political development.
5 Between investors, negative comments regarding certain characteristics of the provinces were common and often concerned the absence of infrastructure, the idiosyncrasies of local people, and the lack of recreational activities and entertainment.
6 Para un estudio pormenorizado de cada uno de los casos, ver Karamaneff, L. E. (2022). ¿Desarrollo económico sin capacidades estatales? El caso de la promoción industrial en Argentina (1982–92). Disponible en: https://ri.unsam.edu.ar/handle/123456789/2160
7 This data was obtained from the "Dinámica productiva provincial a fines de los años noventa" by Francisco Gatto and Oscar Cetrángolo. CEPAL, 2003.
8 Interview with a member of the Evaluation Committee during the de facto government and – after the transition to democracy – subsequent officials of the Ministry of Industry.

9 Served five consecutive terms as governor of San Luis between 1983 and 2001, a position he left upon being chosen by the Legislative Assembly as interim president of the republic.

Bibliography

Amsden, A. H. (1989). *Asia's next giant: South Korea and late industrialization*. Oxford University Press.

Andrews, M. (2013). *The limits of institutional reform in development: Changing rules for realistic solutions*. Cambridge University Press.

Azpiazu, D. (1989). La promoción de la inversión industrial en la Argentina. Efectos sobre la estructura industrial. En B. Kosacoff y D. Azpiazu, *La industria argentina: desarrollo y cambios estructurales* (pp. 35–98). Centro Editor de América Latina.

Behrend, J. (2011). The unevenness of democracy at the subnational level: Provincial closed games in Argentina. *Latin American Research Review*, *46*(1), 150–176. http://doi.org/10.1353/lar.2011.0013

Bezchinsky, G., Gatto, F., Gutman, G. E., and Yoguel, G. (1988). Reestructuración industrial en la Argentina y sus efectos regionales: 1973–1984.

Bianchi, M. F. (2013). *The political economy of sub-national democracy: Fiscal rentierism and geography in Argentina* [Doctoral thesis]. Institut d'Études Politiques de Paris.

Borello, J. A. (1989). Posibilidades y limitaciones de una vieja herramienta de desarrollo regional: el caso de la promoción industrial en la provincia de La Rioja; 1980–1987: informe final.

Canitrot, A. (1980). La disciplina como objetivo de la política económica. Un ensayo sobre el programa económico del gobierno argentino desde 1976. *Desarrollo Económico, 19*(76), 453–475.

Cao, H. (2008, November). La administración pública argentina: nación, provincias y municipios. In *ponencia presentada en el XIII Congreso Internacional del Centro Latinoamericano de Administración para el Desarrollo (CLAD) sobre la Reforma del Estado y de la Administración Pública, Buenos Aires* (pp. 4–7).

Cao, H. (2018). *Política, Estado y administración pública en las provincias argentinas (1976–2015)*. Vol. 2. Prometeo.

Censo Nacional Económico. (1985) Instituto Nacional de Estadística y Censos (INDEC). (1985). Censo Nacional de Población y Vivienda 1985: Resultados generales del total del país [National Population and Housing Census 1985: General results for the entire country]. Retrieved from https://biblioteca.indec.gob.ar/bases/minde/1c1985x8_2.pdf.

Chávez, R. B. (2003). The construction of the rule of law in Argentina. A tale of two provinces. *Comparative Politics*, *35*(4), 417–437. https://doi.org/10.2307/4150188

Consejo Empresario Mendocino. (1999). *Impacto económico de los regímenes de promoción de las provincias de San Juan, La Rioja, San Luis y Catamarca*. CEM.

Consejo Federal de Inversiones, Dirección de Estadísticas y Censos, provincia de San Luis. Cuaderno de Información Estadística N.° 9, 1995.

CEPAL. (2001). Panorama Económico Provincial. www.eclac.cl/argentina

de Diputados, C. (1988). Diario de Sesiones de la Honorable Cámara de Diputados de la Nación.

Dirección de Estadísticas y Censos, provincia de San Luis. (1995). Cuaderno de Información Estadística N.° 9.

Eaton, K. (2003). La lógica de la delegación de poderes legislativos: la reforma de la promoción regional en la Argentina. *Desarrollo Económico*, *42*(168), 499–518.

Evans, P. B. (2012). Embedded autonomy: States and industrial transformation. In P. B. Evans (Ed.), *Embedded autonomy*. Princeton University Press.

Gatto, F. and Cetrángolo, O. (2003). *Dinámica productiva provincial a fines de los años noventa*. Serie Estudios y perspectivas, 14. Naciones Unidas. https://repositorio.cepal.org/server/api/core/bitstreams/102e045f-e4ab-495e-9f7b-41fa19e9e0c3/content

Gervasoni, C. (2009). ¿Cuán democráticas son las provincias argentinas? Estrategias objetivas y subjetivas de inferencia descriptiva. *Boletín de Política Comparada, 1*.

Giraudy, A. (2010). Varieties of subnational undemocratic regimes: Evidence from Argentina and Mexico. In *Studies in comparative international development* (Vol. 4, Issue 2). Springer. http://doi.org/10.1007/s12116-012-9117-4

González, L. and Del Tredici, R. (2019). Al amigo, todo. *Página 12*. https://www.pagina12.com.ar/191629-al-amigo-todo

Guiñazú, M. C. (2003). *The subnational politics of structured adjustment in Argentina: The case of San Luis* [Doctoral thesis]. Massachusetts Institute of Technology.

Helmke, G. and Levitsky, S. (2012). *Informal institutions and comparative politics: A research agenda*. Edward Elgar Publishing.

Johnson, C. (1982). *MITI and the Japanese miracle: The growth of industrial policy, 1925–1975*. Stanford University Press.

Karamaneff, L. E. (2022). *¿Desarrollo económico sin capacidades estatales? El caso de la promoción industrial en Argentina (1982–1992)* -[Doctoral thesis]. Universidad Nacional de San Martín. https://ri.unsam.edu.ar/handle/123456789/2160

Karamaneff, L. E. (2021). Un *bypass* a la administración pública. *Revista Estudios de Políticas Públicas*, *7*(2), 50–63.

Karamaneff, L. and Salvia, A. (2019). ¿Se van o se quedan? El fin de la promoción industrial y sus efectos en los mercados de trabajo provinciales. Los casos de Catamarca, La Rioja, San Juan y San Luis (2005–2017). *Estado Abierto. Revista sobre el Estado, la administración y las políticas públicas*, *3*(3), 71–93. INAP Argentina. https://publicaciones.inap.gob.ar/index.php/EA/article/view/120

Kickert, W. J. M., Koppenjan, J. F. M. and Klijn, E. H. (1997). Managing complex networks: Strategies for the public sector. Sage.

Kohli, A. (2004). *State-directed development: Political power and industrialization in the global periphery*. Cambridge University Press.

Kooiman, J. (2003). *Societal governance* (pp. 229–250). VS Verlag für Sozialwissenschaften.

Levitsky, S. and Murillo, M. V. (2009). Variation in institutional strength. *Annual Review of Political Science*, *12,* 115–133. https://doi.org/10.1146/annurev.polisci.11.091106.121756

Macon, J. (1985). *Las finanzas públicas argentinas, 1950–1980*. Buenos Aires, Macchi.

Mayntz, R. (2006). Governance en el Estado moderno. *PostData*, *11*, 103–120.

Mendocino, C. E. (1999). *Impacto económico de los regímenes de promoción de las provincias de San Juan*. San Luis y Catamarca.

Mera, M. E. (2016). *National democracies, local autocracies: The uneven democratization of subnational governments in Argentina and Brazil*. Georgetown University.
Morina, J. O. (1989). *Características e impacto de la promoción industrial en la provincia de San Luis* [Undergraduate thesis]. Universidad Nacional de Buenos Aires. http://repositorio.filo.uba.ar/handle/filodigital/1241
Murillo, V., Levitsky, S. and Brinks, D. (2021). *La ley y la trampa en América Latina: Por qué optar por el debilitamiento institucional puede ser una estrategia política*. Siglo XXI Editores.
Niedzwiecki, S. (2016). Social policies, attribution of responsibility, and political alignments: A subnational analysis of Argentina and Brazil. *Comparative Political Studies*, *49*(4), 457–498.
Nordlinger, E. (1987). Taking the state seriously. In M. Weiner & S. P. Huntington (Eds.), *Understanding political development* (pp. 353–390). Waveland Pr Inc.
Przeworski, A. (2015). Acerca del diseño del Estado: una perspectiva principal-agente. El valor estratégico de la gestión pública. In *Trece textos para comprenderla, editado por la Corporación Andina de Fomento (CAF)* (pp. 399–438).
Riggs, F. W. (1964). Administration in developing countries: The theory of prismatic society. (No Title).
Rodrik, D. (2008). One economics, many recipes: Globalization, institutions, and economic growth. In D. Rodrik (Ed.), *One economics, many recipes*. Princeton University Press.
Samper, J. (2006). *San Luis: Entre el atraso y el autoritarismo*. Dunken.
Sawers, L. and Massacane, R. (2001). Structural reform and industrial promotion in Argentina. *Journal of Latin American Studies*, *33*(1), 101–132.
Scharpf, F. W. (1993). *Games in hierarchies and networks: Analytical and empirical approaches to the study of governance institutions*. Campus Verlag.
Schneider, B. R. (2015). The developmental state in Brazil: Comparative and historical perspectives. *Brazilian Journal of Political Economy*, *35*, 114–132.
Schvarzer, J. (1987). *Promoción industrial en Argentina: características, evolución y resultados* (Vol. 90). Centro de Investigaciones Sociales sobre el Estado y la Administración.
Trocello, M. G. (2008). *Régimen político neopatrimonialista. La cultura política particularista y la producción de "ciudadanos siervos"* (Doctoral dissertation). Universidad Pablo de Olavide.

4 Environmental governance and participation

Mining and forest protection in Argentina

Lucas G. Christel and Ricardo A. Gutiérrez

Introduction

In Latin America and the Caribbean, environmental issues are central to political life. A large part of the world's natural resources is found in the region, including about a quarter of the planet's arable land and just over a fifth of its forest area, as well as considerable fossil fuel reserves. Since the 1980s, the region has undergone three parallel processes: (1) the expansion of extractive and primary industries, (2) a growing social mobilization over environmental issues, and (3) the emergence of new state regulations on environmental protection (Christel and Gutiérrez, 2023). The greatest opportunities and challenges faced by the region in recent decades have been shaped by the regulation of natural resources and environmental conflict (Alcañiz and Gutiérrez, 2022).

The growing political prominence of environmental issues was accompanied by an increasing public and scholarly interest in environmental governance as a way of dealing with the multi-level and multi-actor nature of environmental conflicts and policies. As part of this process, the region has also experienced a growing process of social mobilization and disputes over environmental issues (Christel and Gutiérrez, 2023). But, while most governance arrangements focus on institutional participation, environmental participation in the region is mostly contentious.

Institutional participation in Argentine environmental policymaking has been rather inchoate, while the involvement of citizens and organizations in social protests and judicial litigations appears to be more effective or productive. We do not imply that institutional participation is not important in advancing environmental protection but rather that contentious participation is equally – or more – productive in putting environmental issues on the public agenda and – sometimes – in changing or steering the course of decision-making in favour of environmental protection.

In our view, both governance and participation are related to the rule of law because they require clarity and predictability of procedural channels for good governance and rights and freedoms for environmental participation. In turn, environmental rights and legislation usually come alive through different governance arrangements and participation channels (Christel and Gutiérrez, 2017).

DOI: 10.4324/9781003519195-4

In this chapter, we discuss the tension between governance and participation by analyzing two relevant areas: open-pit mining and forest protection. We use both experiences to show that environmental governance approaches focused on institutional participation fail to grasp the complexity of environmental conflicts and the real impact of participation on decision-making. Therefore, we maintain a twofold argument. On the one hand, an expanded approach to environmental participation is more appropriate for understanding environmental governance in the region. On the other hand, the enforcement of the rule of law can act as a key tool in building more robust and transparent environmental governance, broader environmental participation, and higher levels of environmental protection.

Building on our previous studies on environmental participation (Christel & Gutiérrez 2017, 2021, 2023), we pay special attention to the connection between contentious and institutional modes of participation. For instance, social protest can be effective in establishing linkages between public officials and social contenders, and the latter can take advantage of newly opened participation channels, thereby favouring the connection between social actors and engaged individuals within the state (Keck and Sikkink, 1998; Lemos and Looye, 2003; Tarrow, 2011; Amengual 2013). The resources derived from these types of linkages and connections can be mobilized either to block policies that are considered detrimental by social contenders and state actors – like open-pit mining – or to advance any particular policy they advocate for – like forest protection (Hochstetler and Keck, 2007; Spalding, 2023).

The broad notion of participation we propose entails a plurality of social and state actors that (either individually or in blocks) usually resort to and combine different modes of participation (either institutional or contentious). Over the last decades, institutional participation in environmental policymaking has begun to develop in Argentina without implying the weakening of environmental contention. Moreover, in a challenging context in which environmental rights are highly disputed, both modes of participation have been necessary to embody constitutional rights in concrete policies and practices (Christel and Gutiérrez, 2017).

By analyzing two significant environmental areas in Argentina (forest protection and mining), we show how contention modes intertwine with institutional participation, and how participation (broadly understood) has specific legislative and administrative effects. We will see that while the state embraces different actors with opposing interests and goals, social action does not circumscribe to protest (as a standard social movement theory would expect), and social contenders resort to the aggregation of contentious and institutional modes of action. We will also see that, while the process is usually started by contentious actions, the advancing of environmental rights also depends on the opening and use of mechanisms of institutional participation.

Environmental governance, participation, and the rule of law

In this section, we propose a dialogue between the literature on environmental governance, participation, and the rule of law. First, we recapitulate key aspects from studies of environmental governance and then make some connections to institutional participation in environmental disputes. In the following, we discuss those connections in light of our expanded view on environmental participation and highlight the relevance of contentious modes of participation. Finally, we argue why it is important to analyze environmental conflicts in Latin America from a rule of law perspective.

Governance theories focus on complex scenarios where the boundaries between institutions, sectors, and regulations are blurred and demand interconnection among different rationalities, procedures, and strategies for solving public problems (Sørensen and Torfing, 2007). Governance becomes relevant in contexts where civil society demands greater possibilities for participation and intervention in public affairs (Kooiman 2005, Aguilar, 2007). However, governance schemes do not by themselves guarantee a positive resolution of public issues. On the contrary, the functioning of governance depends on the capacity and will of the actors involved, the existence of common spaces and/or institutional channels for the definition of joint objectives, and the concrete forms of accountability and legitimation of decisions (Ruano de la Fuente, 2002). Governance can be understood in two dimensions (Christel and Möhle, 2022): a horizontal one, as interactions occur at the frontier between the state, market, and civil society (Kooiman, 2005), and a vertical one, as an instrument to theorize and manage a complex political game that occurs at multiple levels (Noferini, 2012; Schmitter, 2004).

The management of natural resources was not indifferent to these theories, and the environmental area was the object of different governance initiatives (Castro et al., 2015, p. 18). Environmental governance, in a broad sense, refers to the set of mechanisms, formal and informal institutions, and practices through which a social order is (re)produced in relation to the environment and natural resources (Christel and Möhle, 2022).

Without limiting the importance of the various aspects of governance theories, participation is a key element of governance. In explicit terms, no governance scheme is possible without concrete interactions between the state, civil society, and economic actors. However, environmental governance approaches in Latin America have almost exclusively focused on institutional participation. One of the most important critiques to environmental governance initiatives is that they usually hide the unequal power relations involved in environmental conflicts and that, in many cases, these conflicts reflect incompatible worldviews that can be hardly bridged through institutional channels (Bridge & Perreault, 2009, Svampa, 2008). This point is crucial for two reasons. First, a large part of current environmental conflicts arises in a context of power relations that allow access and decision power over natural resources to certain actors while excluding others (Alimonda, 2011). Second, environmental participation in the region has specific characteristics and is usually much more complex than institutional patterns alone (Christel and Gutiérrez, 2017; Alcañiz and Gutiérrez, 2022).

Thus, we first present some basic considerations of institutional participation and its role in environmental issues, and later we argue why an expanded approach to environmental participation is much more appropriate for dealing with the complexities of natural resource disputes in Latin America.

The notion of institutional participation refers to the institutional or administrative channels through which lay citizens and social actors participate in policymaking. Institutional participation can be defined as the modes of participation that come from the transformation of voluntary civil society action into forms of permanent political organization based upon the interaction between social and state actors (Avritzer, 2009). These institutions are created with the specific goal of fostering "the participation of social actors in deliberation and decision-making" (Avritzer, 2002, p. 136).

Like other authors, Hiskes (2009, pp. 133–134) stresses the importance of institutional participation in environmental decision-making, arguing that the establishment of environmental justice depends on participatory democracy. The effective access to information and the opportunity to participate in decision-making processes through administrative procedures are crucial to the consolidation of environmental citizenship. Participation has also become a key mechanism through which constitutionally enshrined environmental rights become effective (Gellers, 2015; Epp, 2008) and environmental protection is secured. The enforcement and enjoyment of constitutional rights and their enabling legislation are contingent on administrative and judicial procedures, the implementation of which is closely tied to participation, i.e. the "right to know, participate, and claim" (May, 2013). And, in effect, it is at this point that institutional participation becomes important.

Despite this importance, we argue that institutional participation is not sufficient for the enforcement of environmental rights and the resolution of environmental claims. The social demands and actions related to the environmental crisis cannot be fully comprehended within the terms of participatory policymaking mechanisms. More specifically, we argue that the embodiment of constitutional environmental rights – as well as environmental concerns – in concrete policies and practices is propelled by the combination of institutional and contentious modes of participation. Unlike other approaches, we do not see institutional and contentious participation as separate or antagonistic modes of action but rather as different tactics or tools that people use and combine to advance their grievances. Also, as we mentioned earlier, the broad notion of participation that we propose involves a plurality of social and governmental actors (either individually or in coalition) and is not limited to civil society actors.

Based upon Pasquino's (2009) general definition of participation, we understand participation as a set of actions and behaviours aimed to influence (in either institutionalized or contentious forms) state decisions regarding the regulation of interactions between humans and their environment (Christel and Gutiérrez, 2017). As we will see in the Argentine case, the mobilization of those who form the environmental field goes beyond administrative procedures and institutional modes of participation. An expanded approach allows us to pay particular attention to the different ways in which both contentious and institutional modes of participation are key to understanding environmental conflicts and policymaking.

Our understanding of contention starts with a basic definition of it as the "common action that bears directly on the interests of some other acting group" (Tilly, 1986, pp. 381–382). Two elements are central to the notion of contention: the expression of grievances and claims, and the confrontation of groups with opposing interests (McAdam, Tarrow, and Tilly, 2001; Tarrow, 2011).

We distinguish three modes of contention that are relevant to environmental issues: social protest, judicial litigation, and expert controversy (Christel and Gutiérrez, 2017). Protest and litigation are considered as modes of contention because both include the basic idea of confrontation of interests. We add expert controversy as a mode of environmental contention in like manner. Expert knowledge is especially relevant in the setting and discussion of environmental issues. As far as environmental issues are highly controversial, it is expected that scientists take positions and confront (through their ideas, evidence, and public debates) on different issues.

Behind our distinction between institutional and contentious participation lies the fact that environmental participation is, at least in Latin America, inherently conflictive. On the one hand, institutional participation rights are usually limited by the so-called implementation gaps (Martínez Espinoza, 2015), i.e., the distance between formal and substantive law. On the other hand, the lack of regular access to institutions maximizes contentious modalities and, moreover, the Latin American region is particularly risky for environmental leaders (Global Witness, 2021).

So, this expanded approach allows us to grasp a complex scenario in which there are not only disputes regarding the application of environmental rights and laws – and their enforcement across territory – but there also exist contrasting ideas about what is fair and desirable in the relationship between society and nature. Therefore, environmental participation often expresses conflicting and unequal views of the rule of law and the public good, which governance arrangements cannot easily address. We understand that there is a direct link between participation and the rule of law. The rule of law is not limited to the mere application of rules. It also encompasses concepts of justice and fairness in a particular context, the process of creating, contesting, and enforcing laws across a region. It also involves how different groups within a society advocate for their own interpretations of justice and negotiate with one another to reach a consensus.

Compliance with the rule of law is essential for any modern society. Indeed, as O'Donnell (2001) points out, the rule of law is one of the essential pillars upon which any quality democracy rests. Without entering into an in-depth discussion of the various works on the rule of law, we decide to highlight two specific characteristics: citizenship political equality and predictability. On the one hand, the rule of law implies equality among citizens (O'Donnell, 2001). We emphasize the importance of equality with respect to the right to associate in political organization, to participate in public affairs, and to enjoy a corpus of adequate rights and guarantees for social organization and the exercise of vertical societal accountability. On the other hand, the rule of law involves predictability. The government is ruled by and subject to the law, but the creation of law is also regulated by law. Thus, it is implied that the whole legal system, as well as the overall social order that it entails, "brings definition, specificity, clarity, and thus predictability into human interactions" (O'Donnell, 2001, p. 35).

The growing literature on the rule of law includes environmental aspects. A minimalist definition of environmental rule of law conceptualizes it as a "legal framework of procedural and substantive rights and obligations that incorporates the principles of environmentally sustainable development into the rule of law" (UNEP, 2016, p. 3). Through this perspective, environmental needs are integrated with the essential elements of the rule of law, providing the basis for improving environmental governance and increasing the participation of individuals and communities around the world. Thus, the rule of law and the enforcement of legal rights and obligations in the environmental field are essential. Otherwise, environmental governance can be "arbitrary, discretionary, subjective and unpredictable" (UNEP, 2016, p. 3).

The reinforcement of the rule of law becomes essential for environmental participation. The strength of state institutions enhances institutional participation and promotes accountability of all environmental actors and decision-makers (UNEP, 2016). Environmental rule of law protects human rights related to the environment and creates the conditions for safer and more productive environmental participation. If, as Chen (2017) points out, environmental regulation is a victim of any deterioration in the rule of law, a strong environmental rule of law propels a solid environmental governance. Thus, a solid governance scheme increases the sense of ownership of different stakeholders and gives more legitimacy to environmental policies.

Forest protection in Argentina

The 1994 Argentinian constitutional reform introduced a series of new rights to the original 1853 constitution, including the right to live in a healthy environment. The new Article 41 establishes, among other things, that the national government is in charge of dictating the norms to provide minimum protection on issues such as the rational utilization of natural resources, environmental conservation, preservation of natural and cultural patrimony, and the necessary information for environmental education. Therefore, although the reformed constitution maintains the original domain of natural resources in the hands of provinces, it also gives power to the national state to dictate the laws on minimum protection that are mandatory throughout the national territory. Under these circumstances, it obliges both national and provincial governments to guarantee a healthy environment.

The General Law for the Environment (Law N° 25.675 from 2002) defined the concept of minimum environmental protection. The law includes policy and management instruments such as territorial ordering (*ordenamiento territorial*), environmental impact assessment, a control system for the development of anthropic activities, and so on. In particular, it establishes mechanisms for the participation of citizens in environmental impact assessment and territorial ordering procedures.

Finally, the General Law for the Environment creates the Federal Environmental System, appointing the pre-existing Federal Council for the Environment (COFEMA) as its maximum authority. In this way, the law for the environment generated a complex arrangement of public organizations (both national and provincial) in charge of protecting the right to a healthy environment and implementing environmental policies.

The passing of the Law for the Protection of Native Forests in 2007 was part of a process of environmental law-making based on the General Law for the Environment that began in 2002. Yet, unlike minimum environmental protection laws passed previously, the Native Forests Law was the subject of a broad public debate among social, state, and economic actors, with significant impact on the news media (Gutiérrez and Isuani, 2014; Figueroa and Gutiérrez, 2018).

In December 2002, the Forest Directorate of the National Secretariat for the Environment and Sustainable Development (SAyDS) published the First National Inventory of Native Forests, according to which the total hectares of native forests amounted, in 1998, to just over 33 million. The media replicated this information, highlighting that this extension meant a significant reduction compared to the little more than 100 million hectares of native forests that, according to estimates, existed around 1914–1915. Successive SAyDS reports would confirm the growing loss of native forests and point to the expansion of the agricultural frontier as the main cause of deforestation (Dirección de Bosques, 2005; SAyDS, 2006).

The data generated by SAyDS would be collected by the news media and by social organizations that demanded an end to deforestation. Various environmental organizations, led by Greenpeace Argentina, began to pressure for a law to be passed to protect the remaining native forests. The actions of these organizations included a variety of tactics (such as public campaigns, harassment (*escraches*) of officials, reports, and entry into lands in danger of clearing) that had an impact on the news media and resonated in the political decision-making arenas.

In this context, the issue entered the legislative agenda towards the end of 2004 when national Deputy Miguel Bonasso (at the time close to President Néstor Kirchner) presented a draft declaration requesting the National Executive Branch to suspend all clearings until a territorial planning law was approved. The approval of that declaration in May 2005 gave rise to the debate around a bill for the protection of native forests. Throughout this debate, legislators, businesspeople, members of environmental organizations, representatives of the provincial executive powers, and national officials would express (inside and outside Congress) their divergent positions on the need and scope of a law to protect native forests.

Bonasso himself presented a forest protection bill on 30 May 2006. Environmental organizations and national environmental officials supported his project, while it seemed that the majority of the ruling Front for Victory bloc would approve it. On the opposite side, legislators from the so-called forest provinces (mainly Salta, Formosa, and Misiones) opposed Bonasso's project, alleging that it violated provincial autonomy in matters of natural resources. Finally, the bill was approved in the Natural Resources and Environmental Conservation Committee in September and passed to the floor in November, where it was approved in general after two days of sessions. In the meantime, environmental organizations led by Greenpeace carried out different campaigns to demand the approval of the law, while logging businesspeople expressed their opposition to the law through the media and Bonasso accused the "soybean lobby" of pressuring legislators from the northwest to vote against the law.

The itemized vote on the law (in which legislators from forest provinces hoped to be able to change the articles they considered most harmful) was set for December 7 but could only take place in March 2007, after an agreement between Bonasso and the president of the Front for Victory bloc (Agustín Rossi). Environmental organizations and national environmental officials blamed the legislators from the forest provinces for preventing the itemized discussion of the bill.

The project was approved in particular on 14 March 2007 and then sent to the Senate. Once in the Senate, the bill was sent to six committees, thus delaying its treatment. Those who supported the law once again blamed the legislators from the forest provinces and the lobby of businesspeople in the soybean sector for the delay. Meanwhile, environmental organizations continued with their campaigns in favour of the law, and the SAyDS disseminated media information about the forest crisis and reinforced the importance of enacting the law. Finally, a sub-committee was created with representatives of the six committees to which the project had been sent with the goal of preparing a single opinion that would later be sent to the floor. In order to mitigate some resistance, the joint opinion included a couple of important modifications to the project issued by the Lower

House: the creation of a fund to compensate the provinces and the land tenants that complied with the provisions of the law and the exclusion from the application of the law to owners of 10 hectares or less. Based on that opinion, the project was approved by the Senate on November 21. A week later, the project returned to the Lower House where, with 133 votes in favour and 3 abstentions, it was approved with the modifications introduced in the Upper House.

Among all environmental protection laws, the Native Forests Law is the only minimum protection law that systematically applies and combines territorial ordering and citizen participation mechanisms. Furthermore, it incorporates the ecosystem services concept and the scheme for the payment of those services (Laterra et al., 2017). Thus, it can be stated that it is the first and only law that establishes an environmental governance arrangement for the whole country (Aguiar et al., 2018).

When analyzed in terms of governance, the Native Forests Law and its regulation distribute competences and responsibilities between COFEMA, the national states, and the provinces. This governance scheme also entails the participation of social organizations, economic actors, and experts in two specific instances at the provincial level. According to the Native Forests Law, participation mechanisms are mandatory for the formulation of the Territorial Ordering of Native Forests (OTBNs), which each province must approve by law, and for the granting of clearing permits.

If we centre on the processes that led to the formulation of the Territorial Orderings of Native Forests (OTBNs) in the provinces, the application of the Native Forests Law has worked as a space for the participation and confrontation of social and community organizations, small and large economic actors, public officials, and experts from different disciplines and institutions. Studies conducted in different provinces show that the content of the approved OTBNs and their subsequent regulations can be explained as the result of struggles between production- and protection-oriented actors within and outside institutional participation spaces (Figueroa and Gutiérrez, 2018).

Three different scenarios can be identified as regards participation in the formulation of OTBNs. In a few provinces (e.g., Mendoza), the OTBN was approved without the working of any noticeable participation mechanisms, and the issue was not on the agenda of environmental organizations. In others (e.g., Formosa), the formulation of the OTBN was channelled through the formal participation venues opened by the provincial government without major conflicts. Lastly, in several provinces (e.g., Córdoba, Salta, and Tierra del Fuego), formal participation venues (commissions, fora, etc.) became the arena of fierce debates between productionist and protectionist actors, and the latter resorted to different contentious tactics when they considered that their demands were shut out in those venues.

Most OTBNs did not fully satisfy social actors, and they were also resisted by production-oriented groups. Moreover, in some provinces, protectionist actors mobilized against OTBN projects that they did not consider adequate from their points of view. Sometimes social mobilization was effective in changing OTBN bills (like in Tierra del Fuego) or their regulations (like in Córdoba and Salta).

The discussion on forest protection in Argentina gives some interesting insights into the links between participation, governance, and the rule of law. This case shows that institutional environmental governance by itself cannot comprehend the different forms of participation involved in the discussion and governing of forest protection issues. Formal institutional participation does not leave aside the contentious participation of civil society; quite the contrary, it seems to strengthen and complement it.

As we have seen, the approval of the Native Forests Law at the national level and its enforcement at the provincial level were driven by different forms and degrees of institutional and contentious participation. We can state that the Native Forests Law suffers from a series of limitations that go beyond citizen participation mechanisms and are related to the enforcement of the rule of law. Still, official data show that the deforestation rate has been reduced notoriously in Argentina after the implementation and as a consequence of this law (Figueroa and Gutiérrez, 2018; Alcañiz and Gutiérrez, 2020). This means that the law has generated positive results despite its limitations and, to a certain extent, thanks to the institutional and contentious participation of multiple actors.

Open-pit mining in Mendoza

In the Andean province of Mendoza, the alliance of social, economic, and political actors was successful in restricting the installation of open-pit mining. Mendoza is a representative case of the mining conflict in Argentina for three main reasons. First, because it shows the multi-stakeholder nature of environmental participation and the combination of contentious and institutional modalities. Second, because it is a conflict that persists over time, with moments of conflict and latency from 2004 to the present. Third, because the strong mining potential makes the provincial restrictions on its development highly emblematic.

The first signs of resistance to mining activities appeared in San Carlos in 2003. Later, by the end of 2005, the conflict escalated when a mining company announced its plans to extract gold and copper near the Laguna del Diamante reservoir. As social concerns grew, the Diamante Front was formed. This broad coalition included neighbourhood associations, rural associations, municipal council members, religious organizations, tourism entrepreneurs, professionals, and teachers. At the same time, a grassroots group (San Carlos Self-convened Neighbors) emerged in San Carlos with an assembly based structure and a preference for contentious participation over the Diamante Front's more institutional approach. Despite their differences, both groups worked together throughout the process.

In 2004, the National Atomic Energy Commission (CNEA) announced its intention to resume uranium mining in the Sierra Pintada (located in San Rafael) without having remediated the environmental liability of previous operations. This initiative provoked a new conflict in Southern Mendoza. The local opposition to CNEA's plans united in the Southern Multisectoral for Sustainable Development, a network formed with the participation of rural producers and non-governmental organizations.

The Southern Multisectoral hired expert lawyers and filed a legal action to stop the reopening of Sierra Pintada. They based their claim on Article 41 and the General Environmental Law (Multisectorial del Sur ND), which protects the environment and human health. The Federal Court of San Rafael issued a preventive order that prevented the CNEA from resuming any activity in the mine. After a long legal battle, the Federal Appeals Court of Mendoza upheld the order and directed the CNEA to clean up all the environmental damage caused by the previous mining operations before restarting the mine. The Supreme Court of Justice confirmed this ruling in 2010.

In 2006, the town of General Alvear, near San Rafael, began a new cycle of protests against mining when the granting of new mining permits became public. Neighbours and organizations in General Alvear expressed concern about the impact of mining on the quality of water, a scarce resource essential to the development of the department's traditional rural and tourism activities. The campaign against open-pit mining was led by the General Alvear Multisectoral, a coalition of around 40 non-governmental, business, labour, political, and educational organizations. Through the activities of San Rafael and General Alvear Multisectorals, Southern Mendoza became the main bastion of resistance to open-pit mining in the province by 2006.

By the end of 2006, the conflict over mining was growing and spreading throughout Mendoza. Self-convened assemblies and other institutionalized groups formed Mendoza Assemblies for Pure Water (AMPAP, by its Spanish acronym) with the main goal of working on the approval of a provincial law to forbid metal and uranium mining. In 2006, law 7627/06 precautionarily suspended metal mining permits, explorations, and exploitations. Yet, law 7627/06 was vetoed by Governor Julio Cobos.

The veto of law 7627/06 had the unexpected effect of multiplying anti-mining resistance in several cities and departments. Municipal acts rejecting open-pit mining combined with strong mobilizations demanding the restitution of law 7627/06. Given this growing state–society resistance, a new bill was presented in the provincial legislature, this time to forbid metal mining. After an open debate process with the participation of grassroots organizations, anti-mining networks, and other social organizations, together with a sustained social mobilization, particularly in General Alvear and San Carlos, law 7722/07 was passed in June 2007 and later promulgated by Governor Julio Cobos. Law 7722/07 prohibits the use of certain chemical substances in mining activities. The regulation contains a list of substances classified as toxic or hazardous (cyanide, xanthates, acids, etc.) that cannot be used in any phase of exploration, prospecting, or mining. Technically, the activity is not prohibited, as this would be unconstitutional, but the law does not allow the use of essential substances for leaching the mineral, a key element of open-pit mining.

Following the enactment of Law 7722/07, social challengers became more involved in institutional forms of participation. Environmental lawsuits became more important, while local and grassroots groups, like the Greater Mendoza Popular Assembly for Water and the General Alvear Multisectoral, established closer ties with state agencies, especially by joining the Provincial Environmental Council. However, these groups did not abandon contentious methods.

After the approval of the law, various business groups and mining stakeholders asked the Provincial Court to overturn Law 7722/07, claiming that it violated the National Mining Code and the constitutional right to work. This new phase of the process involved legal battles, social demonstrations, and expert debates. To counter the unconstitutionality claims, grassroots groups again used mobilization and protest strategies throughout the years until the Superior Tribunal of Justice of Mendoza ruled on the issue. Finally, in December 2015, the provincial Superior Tribunal of Justice denied the unconstitutionality requests and ratified the validity of Law 7722/07.

Social organizations' representatives were also highly active in two environmental impact assessment (EIA) procedures of great importance: Rio Colorado Potassium Project's Environmental Impact Declaration and San Jorge Copper Project's EIA. A member from the Greater Mendoza Popular Assembly for Water was appointed to represent the Provincial Environmental Council before the interdisciplinary commission invested with the responsibility of assessing the Rio Colorado Project. In September 2009, the provincial government approved the project's environmental impact declaration in spite of over 100 observations made by the interdisciplinary commission, and the Provincial Environmental Council's refusal to accept the environmental impact declaration.

The role and impact of social organizations were more determinant in the case of the San Jorge EIA. One hundred and eighty-five people enroled to speak in the public hearing scheduled for 26 October 2010; 143 of them expressed their opposition to the project. Social rejection of the project was carried out with a high level of technical and environmental knowledge (Segura, 2010). The public hearing, as is common in the public discussion of environmental issues, became a remarkable arena of expert controversy. Along with the constitutionality and applicability of law 7722/07, two major issues were at stake: the quality of the water course to be intervened by the project (Tigre brook) and the toxicity of xanthate. While a geologist hired by the mining company reported that the Tigre brook's water was not drinkable, environmentalists rejected such a diagnosis on the basis of reports showing that the water was apt for human and animal consumption. Likewise, while the mining company's representatives argued that xanthate, the substance proposed to lixiviate the mineral, was not toxic and therefore its use did not imply a violation of law 7722/07, assembly actors resorted to different classifications in which xanthate was listed as a toxic substance.

The San Jorge public hearing was not binding. The final decision was to be made by the provincial legislature in the context of an electoral campaign. Social resistance to the project increased after the public hearing and reached the legislature. The main opposition candidate for governor (Peronist Francisco Pérez), who would later become the new governor, requested his party's legislators to vote against the project. The San Jorge Project's EIA was rejected by the provincial legislature in August 2010.

The Mendoza case shows that the alliance of social, economic, and state actors was crucial for the advancement of environmental rights. Such achievements as the expansion of the Laguna del Diamante reserve, the passing and ratification of law 7722/07, and the rejection of San Jorge Project's EIA were possible due to the effective combination of different modes of contentious and institutional participation, which on many occasions were undertaken by the same actors. The persistence of social protest throughout the process went hand-in-hand with the importance and effectiveness of litigation, expert controversy, and institutional participation at different stages. Finally, it is worth highlighting that despite the combination of modes of participation, contentious action continues to be a fundamental tool in the defence of the environment. In December 2019, after Rodolfo Suárez (UCR) took office as the new governor, a modification of the emblematic Law 7722/07 was approved. The new regulation (N° 9.209) allowed the use of chemicals such as cyanide and sulfuric acid in metal mining. Instantly, Mendoza's society organized massive marches, rallies in front of the government building, and multiple expressions of rejection of the new law. In a climate of growing social pressure, the government repealed the new law and kept in force the 2007 law that restricts open-pit mining throughout the provincial territory.

The case of Mendoza reveals three elements of interest for understanding the links between participation, governance, and the rule of law. First, it illustrates the productivity of the combination of contentious and institutional modalities in environmental matters. Second, it shows that governance schemes are not properly institutionalized and that social actors only gain access to them when the conflict escalates and is sustained over time. Third, it shows that when the rule of law's predictability is threatened, this can reinforce the contentious nature of social actors' response.

Conclusions

In the previous pages, we analyzed the experiences of forest protection and mining in Argentina and explored the links between environmental governance, participation, and the rule of law. We have shown that environmental disputes are eminently conflictive, that they express competing visions of the rule of law, and that governance schemes almost exclusively involve institutional modalities.

The two cases analyzed present two common points of interest. First, they show that the combination of institutional and contentious modes of participation can be quite efficient in achieving legislative regulations and environmental administrative practices. Both experiences show how institutional participation in environmental policymaking has shyly begun to develop in Argentina without implying the weakening of environmental contention. Both modes of participation have been necessary to embody constitutional rights in concrete policies and practices, especially in a challenging context in which environmental rights are highly disputed. Second, both cases reflect the absence of consolidated governance mechanisms that can respond quickly to the escalation of an environmental conflict. In the case of forest protection, the wording of the national law promoted formal participation. However, the different subnational experiences showed that in the absence of consolidated instruments to promote the involvement of different stakeholders, institutional participation was weak and quickly complemented by contentious participation.

In addition to the two cases analyzed here, other experiences of environmental disputes in Argentina, as well as in Latin America (Alcañiz & Gutiérrez, 2022), show that the combination of institutional and contentious participation does not necessarily translate into the achievement of environmentalists' objectives and environmental progress. Given this, we understand that the rule of law can act as a key tool in building more robust and transparent environmental governance, broader environmental participation, and thus higher levels of environmental protection.

First, the strengthening of the rule of law can bring legal certainty and predictability to state–society interactions on environmental issues by clearly setting the boundaries between legal and illegal activities and by legitimizing decision-making procedures. This is important because, as Ebbesson (2010) points out, there is a tension between the legal certainty provided by the rule of law and the flexibility and uncertainty needed to deal with environmental disputes. Of course, this tension does not mean that legal uncertainty is a better basis for sustainable governance. A balance should be found between stable and predictable laws, and the flexibility and adaptability for decision-making processes and civil society engagement in natural resource management. Second, as we have seen, the rule of law includes a sense of equality of citizenship. Thus, an egalitarian rule of law across the entire national territory, without discrimination between citizens or minorities, is a key element in reducing – or erasing – implementation gaps and reducing the distance between formal and substantive rights. Third, a solid rule of law can be a fundamental element in strengthening participation, association, and information rights, especially in guaranteeing the physical integrity and safety of contenders in environmental conflicts. Thus, as we analyze here, the strengthening of the rule of law appears as both a pending challenge and an opportunity to improve governance processes and modes of environmental participation in Argentina and Latin America.

References

Aguiar, S., Mastrangelo, M.E., García Collazo, M.A., et al (2018) ¿Cuál es la situación de la Ley de Bosques en la Región Chaqueña a diez años de su sanción? Revisar su pasado para discutir su futuro. *Ecología Austral,* 28, 400–417.

Aguilar, L.F. (2007). El aporte de la Política Pública y de la Nueva Gestión Pública a la gobernanza. Revista del CLAD. *Reforma y Democracia*, 39, 5–32.

Alcañiz, I., and Gutiérrez, R.A. (2020). Gender, Land Distribution, and Who Gets State Funds to Stop Deforestation in Argentina. *Journal of Environmental Management* 272: 111060. https://doi.org/10.1016/j.jenvman.2020.111060

Alcañiz, I., and Gutiérrez, R.A. (2022). *The Distributive Politics of Environmental Protection in Latin America and the Caribbean*. New York: Cambridge University Press.

Alimonda, H. (2011). La colonialidad de la naturaleza Una aproximación a la Ecología Política latinoamericana. *La Naturaleza Colonizada. Ecología política y minería en América Latina*. CLACSO.

Amengual, M. (2013). Pollution in the Garden of the Argentine Republic: Building State Capacity to Escape from Chaotic Regulation. *Politics & Society*, 41(4), 527–560. https://doi.org/10.1177/0032329213507551

Avritzer, L. (2002). *Democracy and the Public Space*. Oxfordshire, England: Princeton University Press.

Avritzer, L. (2009). *Participatory Institutions in Democratic Brazil*. Washington, DC: Woodrow Wilson Center Press.

Bridge, G., and Perreault, T. (2009). *'Environmental Governance'. Environmental Governance. A Companion to Environmental Geography*. Malden: Wiley-Blackwell.

Castro, F., Hogenboom, B., and Baud, M. (2015) Introducción. In F. de Castro, B. Hogenboom, and M. Baud (Eds.), *Gobernanza ambiental en América Latina*. CLACSO: Buenos Aires, 13–38.

Chen, M. (2017). Environmental Governance: Disentangling the Relationship between Economic Growth and Rule of Law on Environmental Policy Stringency. *Letters in Spatial and Resource Sciences,* 10, 253–275. https://doi.org/10.1007/s12076-017-0186-x

Christel, L.G., and Mohle, E. (2022). Divergent Valuation Languages, Sustainability and Environmental Governance: Lessons from a Mining Conflict in Catamarca, Argentina. *The Bulletin of Latin American Research (BLAR),* 41(4), 525–540. https://doi.org/10.1111/blar.13372

Christel, L.G., and Gutiérrez, R.A. (2017). Making Rights Come Alive: Environmental Rights and Modes of Participation in Argentina. *Journal of Environmental & Development,* 26(3), 322–347. https://doi.org/10.1177/1070496517701248

Christel, L.G., and Gutiérrez, R.A. (2021). The Political Impact of Environmental Mobilization: A Theoretical Discussion in the Light of the Argentine Case. *Canadian*

Journal of Latin American and Caribbean Studies (CJLACS), 46(1), 57–76. https://doi.org/10.1080/08263663.2021.1855874

Christel, L., and Gutiérrez, R.A. (2023). "Beyond the Lenses of Social Movements: Environmental Mobilization in Latin America". In F. Rossi (Ed.), *The Oxford Handbook of Latin American Social Movements*. Oxford: Oxford University Press.

Dirección de Bosques. (2005). *Primer Inventario Nacional de Bosques Nativos – Proyecto Bosques Nativos y Áreas Protegidas Préstamo BIRF 4085-AR - Informe Nacional* (p. 126). Dirección de Bosques, Secretaría de Ambiente y Desarrollo Sustentable, Argentina.

Ebbesson, J. (2010). The Rule of Law in Governance of Complex Socio-Ecological Changes. *Global Environmental Change,* 20, 414–422. https://doi.org/10.1016/j.gloenvcha.2009.10.009

Epp, C. (2008). Implementing the Rights Revolution: Repeat Players and the Interpretation of Diffuse Legal Messages. *Law and Contemporary Problems*, 71(4), 41–52.

Figueroa, L.M., and Gutiérrez, R.A. (2018). Enfrentados por el ambiente: incidencia de las coaliciones sociedad-estado en la protección de bosques nativos. In R. A. Gutiérrez (Ed.), *Construir el ambiente: sociedad, estado y políticas ambientales en Argentina* (pp. 103–166). Buenos Aires: Teseo.

Gellers, J. (2015). Environmental Constitutionalism in South Asia: Analyzing the Experiences of Nepal and Sri Lanka. *Transnational Environmental Law*, 4(2), 395–423.

Global Witness. (2021). LAST LINE OF DEFENCE The Industries Causing the Climate Crisis and Attacks against Land and Environmental Defenders. September. https://www.globalwitness.org/en/campaigns/environmental-activists/last-line-defence/

Gutiérrez, R.A., and Isuani, F.J. (2014). La emergencia del ambientalismo estatal y social en Argentina. *Revista de Administração Pública*, 48(2), 295–322.

Hiskes, R.P. (2009). *The Human Right to a Green Future*. Cambridge: Cambridge University Press.

Hochstetler, K., and Keck, M.E. (2007). *Greening Brazil: Environmental activism in state and society*. Durham, NC: Duke University Press.

Keck, M., and Sikkink, K. (1998). *Activists beyond Borders: Advocacy Networks in International Politics*. Ithaca, NY: Cornell University Press.

Kooiman, J. (2005). Gobernar en Gobernanza. In A. Cerrillo (Ed.), *La gobernanza hoy: 10 textos de referencia* (p. 25). España: Instituto Nacional de Administración Pública.

Laterra, P., Martín-López, B., Mastrangelo, M., and Garibaldi, L.A. (2017). Servicios ecosistémicos en Latinoamérica: de la investigación a la acción. *Ecología Austral,* 27, 94–98.

Lemos, M.C., and Looye, J. (2003). Looking for Sustainability: Environmental Coalitions across the State-Society Divide. *Bulletin of Latin American Research*, 22(3), 350–370.

Martínez Espinoza, M.I. (2015). Reconocimiento sin implementación: Un balance sobre los derechos de los pueblos indígenas en América Latina. *Revista Mexicana de Ciencias Políticas y Sociales,* 60(224), 251–277. https://doi.org/10.1016/S0185-1918(15)30010-6

May, J. (2013). Constitutional Directions in Procedural Environmental Rights. *Journal of Environmental Law & Litigation*, 28, 27–51.

McAdams, D., Tarrow, S., and Tilly, C. (2001). *Dynamics of Contention*. Cambridge, England: Cambridge University Press.

Noferini, A. (2012). The Participation of Subnational Governments in the Council of the EU: Some Evidence from Spain. *Regional & Federal Studies*, 22(4), 361–385. https://doi.org/10.1080/13597566.2012.677138
O'Donnell, G. (2001). Accountability horizontal. La institucionalización legal de la desconfianza política. *Isonomía*, 14, 7–31.
Pasquino, G. (2009). *Nuovo Corso di Scienza Politica*. Bologna, Italy: Il Mulino.
Ruano de la Fuente, J. (2002). *La gobernanza como forma de acción pública y como concepto analítico*. Trabajo presentado en VII Congreso Internacional del CLAD sobre la Reforma del Estado y de la Administración Pública, Lisboa, Portugal.
SAYDS. (2006). *GEO Argentina 2004*. Secretaría de Ambiente y Desarrollo Sustentable, Argentina.
Schmitter, P.C. (2004). Neo-neofunctionalism. In A. Wiener and T. Diez (Eds.), *European Integration Theory*. Oxford: Oxford University Press.
Segura, E. (2010). If You Don't Understand I Explain It with a Drawing. http://www.mdzol.com/nota/252650
Spalding, R. (2023). *Breaking Ground: From Extraction Booms to Mining Bans in Latin America*. New York. NY: Oxford University Press.
Sørensen, E., and Torfing, J. (2007) *Theories of Democratic Network Governance*. London: Palgrave Macmillan.
Svampa, M. (2008). La disputa por el desarrollo: Territorio, movimientos de carácter socio-ambiental y discursos dominantes. Cambio de época. *Movimientos sociales y poder político*, 1–31.
Tilly, C. (1986). *The Contentious French*. Cambridge, England: The Belknap Press of Harvard University Press.
Tarrow, S. (2011). *Power in movement: Social Movements and contentious politics*. Cambridge, England: Cambridge University Press.
UNEP. (2016) Human Rights and the Environmental Rule of Law. https://wedocs.unep.org/bitstream/handle/20.500.11822/35408/SDG16.pdf

5 "Old wine in new bottles"

Technopopulism and the challenges of infrastructure provision in Latin America

J. Carlos Domínguez Virgen

Introduction

The magnitude and complexity of certain infrastructure megaprojects pose enormous challenges for public policy processes in democratic regimes that, as is the case for Mexico and many other Latin American countries, exist in a state of constant transformation. The design and implementation of these initiatives bring forth inevitable tensions between technical arguments and political considerations, pitting basic technical and financial concerns against democratic aspirations and the desire for socio-environmental justice. These kinds of projects involve a multiplicity of actors from both government and civil society, while at the same time they offer the executive branch a wide margin for making discretionary decisions (Domínguez, 2015, 2016a).

This paper shines a light on such dynamics by briefly reviewing how infrastructure and development have been affected by recent shifts in Mexico, including the National Regeneration Movement (MORENA) taking the reins of the federal government in 2018, and the implementation of three emblematic projects that have dominated the public policy agenda during MORENA's six-year term: the Felipe Ángeles International Airport (AIFA); the Olmeca Refinery in Dos Bocas, Tabasco; and the Tren Maya ("Mayan Train").

The AIFA project consists of the reconfiguration of a military airport in the Santa Lucia area, north of Mexico City, to convert it into a facility that complements the city's pre-existing Benito Juarez International Airport. This decision has been controversial for three reasons. First, because the decision to build the AIFA was made in the context of the cancellation of another airport project in Texcoco, which had been promoted by the previous National Action Party (PAN) and Institutional Revolutionary Party (PRI) federal administrations, and which was already more than 50% complete.[1] Second, because various experts have argued that the AIFA poses problems in terms of air traffic and security, and has only a limited ability to constitute a long-term (50 years or more) solution.[2] And, finally, because the project is the latest in a long line of controversies, delays, and failures when it comes to attempts to solve Mexico City's growing air saturation problems (Domínguez, 2015; Ríos, 2022).

DOI: 10.4324/9781003519195-5

Meanwhile, the importance of the Dos Bocas refinery lies in its status as the first facility of its kind to be built in Mexico since the 1979 construction of a refinery near Salina Cruz, Oaxaca. The project aims to increase national gasoline and diesel production by around 300,000 barrels a day (SENER, 2022), reducing the deficit Mexico faces in this area and thus its need to import refined products. The construction of this type of project is controversial for a number of reasons. These include its environmental impacts, its high cost, which could reach a total of up to 16 billion dollars (Nava, 2023); and its location directly on the shores of the Gulf of Mexico, which entails high logistical costs and makes it potentially vulnerable to extreme weather events.[3]

Finally, the Tren Maya has been proposed as an infrastructure project that will kickstart the development of the southeast of Mexico, historically one of the country's most socially and economically backward regions. The project forms part of the regional integration objectives of the states of Chiapas, Tabasco, Campeche, Yucatan, and Quintana Roo, and has two components: the railway network itself, which will span approximately 1,500 km; and the secondary routes and tourist activities that will grow up around each of its component train stations. In addition to the difficulties of negotiating the acquisition of the land on which to construct all of this, the project has been criticized for its impacts on the local environment, particularly on the nearby *cenotes* (subterranean bodies of water), as well as the danger it poses to local species such as the jaguar.

Based on an analysis of these projects and their implementation, this paper's main argument is that the new regime headed by the leftist president, Andrés Manuel López Obrador (often known as AMLO) between 2018 and 2024, has not provided opportunities for the adoption of new public policy practices and values in an environment of democratic deepening. Instead, his government has preferred to employ uncompromising forms of "technopopulism," which involve the suspension of wider debates and support for a state of exception when it comes to these projects.

Some conceptual coordinates

For the purposes of this paper, we will define "technopolitics" as the selective use of technical arguments in order to justify public policy projects and decisions which also serve political and even ideological interests. In contrast, we will define "technopopulism" as a type of technopolitics that, in addition to being selective in its use of technical arguments, openly appeals to an ideological discourse as a way of completely neutralizing possible controversies (Esmark, 2021; Ríos, 2022).

If we go by these definitions, technopolitical (or sociotechnical) controversies are in reality inevitable, since tensions between technical issues and political beliefs are usually resolved via debates that result in the interweaving of both evaluative spheres. In other words, the political is technologized and the technical is politicized in an attempt to justify and promote a particular solution within the public policy agenda (Sabatier, 1988, 1999; Sabatier and Jenkins-Smith, 1993).

Argumentative and discursive processes of technification/politicization can occur in any area of public decision-making. On the one hand, the social assistance programmes designed in Mexico during the era of technocratic neo-liberalism under PRI and PAN rule integrated highly sophisticated technical considerations, especially in terms of how they measured poverty. But this did not exempt them from also incorporating obvious political considerations and partisan objectives. On the other hand, although the strengthening of independent government bodies can help to isolate some technical discussions from partisan politicking, there is evidence that such institutions can also be captured by technocratic elites who use their image as experts to promote positions that are in themselves political (in that they determine what happens to who, when, and where).[4]

These issues become particularly interesting when we talk about areas that are supposedly "more difficult," in which technical issues are therefore assumed (at least in theory) to be the most important. These include those sectors and subsystems of public policy that involve large investments,[5] a large number of evaluative variables, and high levels of technical complexity. Although these areas are supposed to be shielded from outside discussions and interventions (constituting Baumgartner and Jones' so-called "public policy monopolies" (1991, 1993)), some nuances also necessarily apply.

In fact, t is the magnitude and complexity of the initiatives in question that may contribute to the existence of a very wide margin of uncertainty about them in the context of relatively democratic environments (Domínguez, 2011), given that such environments can enable debates about a variety of issues, including the roots of the problems, the hierarchy occupied by the different values and parameters that need to be considered, and the specific details of each solution, as well as allowing for comparisons to be made between the different solutions. This enables the participation of a wider range of actors, from distinct fields of expertise, and opens the door to the issue that we have mentioned in previous paragraphs: that is, the technification of the political and the politicization of the technical.

Because of their scale and complexity, so-called planned development megaprojects always fall within the scope of technopolitical discussions. Likewise, because of their material visibility, it is not unusual to find them also surrounded by a technopopulist aura, since it is common for governments to conceive of them as opportunities to "leave a historical legacy," which charges them with heavy symbolism. This aspect opens the door for representatives of the executive branch to succumb to the temptation of overriding or minimizing technical discussions in order to fulfil their aspirations of "political transcendence," even if this means jeopardizing the actual viability and soundness of the initiative in question.

One good example is the case of Line 12 of the Mexico City subway. As various authors have argued (among others, Arellano and Dussauge, 2018; Ugalde, 2018), this case exemplifies the juggling and corruption in which political elites are willing to engage in order to inaugurate a given project before the end of their administration's term in government. After all, the possibility of capitalizing on a project's "symbolic charge" begins with the inauguration ritual itself. Unfortunately, this had catastrophic consequences in the case of Line 12, which was affected by structural problems shortly after its inauguration (documented as of 2014), eventually leading to the collapse of an elevated section, killing 25 and leaving 79 injured.

In this case, technical discussions were not completely discarded,[6] but there were critical points in the design process where political goals and sentiments were privileged over the feasibility and soundness of the engineering. This is because technopopulism is relative, i.e., it is not a matter of dichotomies, but rather of degrees. There is always jostling between civil society groups, between different levels of government, within the world of business, between a diversity of interest groups, and, above all, between actors who participate inside and outside the sphere of government as "experts."

In fact, as Ríos (2022) argues in his doctoral thesis, which focuses on the decisions taken over the last two decades – and particularly during the presidency of AMLO – concerning the New Mexico City International Airport (NAICM) planned for Texcoco,[7] the category of "expert" becomes highly problematic in the context of socio-technical (or technopolitical) controversies. This category confers upon those who belong to it, without any further or more rigorous conditions attached, the licence to speak about and cast judgement on any subject, even if it goes beyond the boundaries of the expert's own discipline, as if they were a kind of "philosopher king."

In other words, enjoying a reputation as an expert bestows credibility upon that person, in a manner that can be easily twisted and used to engage in myriad different disputes. Thus, the legal expert starts talking about the layout of runways at an airport, while the biologist launches forth on soil mechanics. This type of situation makes it difficult to resolve technopolitical disputes, bogging down debates and delaying the adoption of particular public policy solutions. In the case of the NAICM, Ríos himself (2022, 102) highlights five "micro disputes" in which different experts exchanged "crossfire," associated with "five areas of specialized knowledge: aeronautical, environmental, territorial, hydrogeological-geotechnical and economic-financial."

Politicians always prefer to shy away from controversy, given that its consequences can include indefinite delays and budget overruns. Controversies can even completely block the materialization of projects considered to be emblematic. The critical question, then, is what strategies are adopted to confront, to partially neutralize, or even to take advantage of controversies, in order to fortify the public policy being promoted?[8] And in this sense, and in the case of Mexico, it is worth asking ourselves: which of these paths has the MORENA federal administration opted for at the federal level?

This paper argues that we have witnessed a growing aspiration on the part of AMLO's government to build an absolutist technopopulism, based on the mythopoetic discourse of the so-called "Fourth Transformation" (4T).[9] One important feature of this is that claims are valued far more on the basis of their contribution to justifying a particular development discourse than they are for their technical content. In this context, it is common for actors to come up against what seems to be one of AMLO's key maxims: "you're either with me or against me." This Manichaeism narrows the debate, limits public policy options, impoverishes democratic life and, above all, puts the very viability of Mexico's infrastructure sector at risk.

Rupture and continuity: What has changed?

In previous works, we have outlined the usefulness of the multi-strand, "windows of opportunity" model (Kingdon, 1984) for understanding the different stages through which initiatives proposed to solve Mexico City's airport capacity problems have gone since the late 1960s.[10] Without going into further detail, the model can be summarized as follows:

1) There are three relatively autonomous strands within decision-making processes – problems, public policy solutions, and political contexts – each of which moves through time.
2) The public policy solutions strand is for the most part dominated by "not very visible" actors with high levels of technical expertise (academics, consultants, lower-ranking public officials), while the political contexts strand is dominated by visible actors (the Executive Branch, heads of government ministries, state governors, congressmen, etc.).
3) When the three strands coincide in time, what John Kingdon defines as a "window of opportunity" is opened.
4) In this context, the existence of a "policy entrepreneur" – someone willing to promote one of the policy solutions that is available on the agenda, meets the basic parameters of feasibility, and aligns with the values predominating at a given time (such as fiscal discipline, environmental justice, and social justice) – may enable such a proposal to be implemented, leading to an abrupt change in public policy in a particular sector.

This basic model had worked convincingly to explain the results of the political processes surrounding the design and implementation of certain megaprojects, particularly in the case of the NAICM. Although the infrastructure sector has been seen as a semi-ordered system, whose shortcomings may even have been in the process of consolidation, the technopolitical discussions concerning the

NAICM occurred in such a way that the "tug-of-war" between the political and the technical was not completely dominated by either of these two spheres. In this sense, it was always possible that the project's technical aspects would be weighed up against its political objectives, sometimes in the context of "big" decisions and sometimes in more marginal areas.

The entire history of the NAICM, with its respective episodes, clearly attests to this. The project endured six PRI presidencies and nearly four decades without being implemented, before it was finally approved by the PAN's President Vicente Fox (2000–2006), and then cancelled during that same administration. Its cancellation was upheld during the six-year term of his successor, President Felipe Calderón Hinojosa (2006–2012), before the subsequent administration of President Enrique Peña Nieto (2012–2018) rescued the project and finally began construction. All these episodes can be explained in terms of the opening and closing of specific windows of opportunity, within restrictions determined by a relatively functional political regime that was, however, still in the process of democratic transition, in which spaces and slots existed for technical considerations to play a relevant role vis-á-vis political decisions.[11] These dynamics of resolution between the political and the technical are not only relevant to the case of the NAICM, but also to other large-scale projects.[12]

Decisions regarding large-scale planned development initiatives have always had a vertical component, with a leading role played by the executive branch (specifically the office of the president). However, the executive's privileged position never completely eliminated the extremely complex web of actors and policy venues whose interactions could stabilize or destabilize the decision-making process. This game of stabilization/destabilization, which could originate in any of the three strands of decision-making – but in particular, those of public policy solutions and political contexts – had almost always occurred without breaking a set of accepted rules and dynamics.

Even within a disadvantageous and unproductive context, consultants and technical experts could launch arguments in the hope of positively influencing the final outcome of public policy in one direction or another. For example, in the case of the NAICM, the option of the current Benito Juarez International Airport continuing to operate in conjunction with a second airport to the north of Mexico City had, on the basis of specialized airspace studies and the opinions of aeronautical experts, been systematically discarded. Likewise, the option of closing the Benito Juarez International Airport and building a single, large airport in Tizayuca (instead of Texcoco) was discarded in light of a range of analyses of the logistical costs of connecting this new infrastructure with the centre of demand.[13] Although a state of push and pull between the technical and the political always existed in the context of the different controversies documented by Domínguez (2015) and more recently by Ríos (2022), there was also a margin for the technical to exercise significant influence, especially when the feasibility and viability of problem-solving initiatives were at stake.

However, since MORENA came to power in 2018, the 4T discourse on development has shifted towards a much more confrontational, top-down, and "flowery" (for want of a better word) rhetoric, which has helped to almost completely displace other public policy concerns. Some elements worth highlighting in MORENA's developmentalist discourse are: the notion of social justice as a historical debt that must be settled with the participation of those principally affected ("the Mexican people in all their wisdom"); the construction of alternative forms of development ostensibly opposed to previously implemented models, in particular the so-called neoliberal model; nationalist discursive elements that privilege collective goals and general welfare over individual interests; and "republican austerity," celebrated as an ethical form of good governance and a way of combating corruption.

In some cases, this discursive construction has been accompanied by rituals of enunciation and symbolic formulations (if not acrobatics), aimed at neutralizing any possibility of technical or political opposition at the national level. A paradigmatic example is the ceremony that was held in 2018 in Palenque to ask Mother Earth for permission to build the Tren Maya.[14] As De Tavira (2022, p. 112–114) suggests, the event was not designed to theatricalize the political through a ceremony that reaffirmed already-established values, but was rather a ritual that inaugurated a new social order. That is to say, it was not a mere act of proselytization, but an announcement of great symbolic violence: that the Tren Maya can no longer be turned back, for it is an act that has been sanctioned on the metaphysical plane, in some region of the quasi-divine.

In this way, the 4T's developmental discourse, which proclaims the necessity of repairing historical injustices within the southeast region of Mexico, defines what is and what is not a valid action in a given territory. The great paradox is that this does not mean that the needs of local populations are actually attended to, or that processes of displacement are carried out within a framework of social justice, or that environmental norms are respected so as to conserve flora and fauna. On the contrary, although it has been framed in a way that privileges the idea of national and collective interests over those of the individual, the Tren Maya has in fact deprived many of those affected of the right to meaningfully participate in processes of consultation and negotiation.

But let us not fool ourselves. Development discourses have always been used as a strategy to justify the implementation of large physical infrastructure projects (for example, with arguments about their public utility and contributions to general welfare; see Domínguez, 2016a). Beyond such rhetoric, however, in practice and in the context of concrete decisions, rather different methods of nurturing and qualifying such discourse used to be employed, based on much broader considerations.

In the past, technical considerations were sought out for their utility in debating or neutralizing political considerations or in defining the hierarchy between different values (for example, between social justice, environmental justice, and fiscal discipline) in order to achieve balance, reach a middle ground, and find ways of incorporating multiple considerations into a single analytical framework that would make them more manageable. There was no need to converse with divine entities when debates could be had with flesh-and-blood actors, even if these poor mortals were themselves fierce opponents of a given public policy proposal.

It is true that rational-administrative tools (Dryzek, 1997), such as cost-benefit analysis, impact assessment, or Environmental Impact Assessment (EIA), functioned as tools with which to exercise power based on a certain notion of development. Even public consultations could be simulations that sought to help legitimize decisions about physical infrastructure. However, the participation of a complex network of actors, institutions, and levels of government opened paths, even if they were very narrow, for some of these tools to expand debates about the feasibility and convenience of the initiatives in question.

In contrast, the MORENA federal administration has been much more forceful in its privileging of political considerations, with a strong populist content, as the key variables in shaping the survival and implementation of infrastructure projects. The cancellation of the NAICM in Texcoco is the most powerful – we might even say "foundational" – example of this new way of doing politics in the infrastructure sector. Rather than being cancelled in response to the usual combination of technopolitical arguments, the project was scrapped on the basis of a citizen consultation held in October 2018, which was intended to gather the opinion of "the people in all their wisdom" based on a multiple-choice question: which option do you think is better for the country?

1) To refurbish the pre-existing Mexico City and Toluca airports and build two runways at the Santa Lucia air base.
2) To continue with the construction of the new airport in Texcoco and stop using the current Mexico City International Airport.

The result was the cancellation of a project that, regardless of how much progress had actually been made on the ground, was already significantly advanced with regard to contractual commitments. This forced the government to renegotiate these obligations. In some cases, contracts were successfully cancelled or exchanged for alternative infrastructure deals, but others were subject to long-term deferral. In financial terms, a more detailed analysis would have to be made to determine whether the cancellation of the NAICM did not result in a sort of MORENA-overseen FOBAPROA scandal.[15] But beyond these implications, the technical solution that was adopted is striking: the construction – or, in reality, adaptation – of the Santa Lucia military airport as a complementary facility to Mexico City's pre-existing Benito Juarez International Airport, despite logistical problems, a lack of interest from airlines and a significant segment of airport service users, and, most importantly, the fact that it constitutes a complicated solution to current airspace issues, which is both inefficient and also insufficient to meet long-term demand.

The episode is a watershed whose symbolic weight transcends the infrastructure sector and is relevant to the history of Mexican public policy in general. Like the consultation of Mother Earth in the case of the Tren Maya, the cancellation of the NAICM symbolizes a change in the rules of the game, rather than changes *within* the rules of the game (as had happened during previous presidencies). In short, the announcement of this decision constituted, at the time, an early, strong, and unequivocal signal that the shape of public policy would change drastically over the coming years: the era of raw, unadulterated technopopulism had begun. Beyond the technical considerations or the logistical and financial costs, the cancellation signalled a new *ethos*: we are willing to do whatever it takes to meet the objectives of the 4T and there are only two possibilities: you are either for it or you are against it.

As mentioned above, this type of technopopulism not only cherry-picks *ad hoc* technical arguments in order to promote a particular vision of development, but it also disregards as *de facto* invalid any technical argument that does not help to justify it. For this to take place, it is necessary to reduce as far as possible the number of actors, both visible and non-visible, who meaningfully participate in the decision-making process. It is necessary to "shrink" the spaces in which technopolitical tensions are expressed, and gradually filter out and discard opposing arguments, contrasting visions, and alternative proposals.

For example, in coming to a decision on the NAICM, insufficient weight was given to the opinions of international aeronautical experts, of the Mexican College of Aviator Pilots, or of the airlines themselves. The opinion of the "people in all their wisdom" was of more concern. But there is also a "small" detail that we cannot omit: the Mexican Army is in charge of the construction and operation of the NAICM and other emblematic projects.

To this, we must add two further issues: first, the nature of the decrees by which these projects are declared national security initiatives, which significantly limits transparency and access to information about them; and second, the active presence of the military in other areas of the infrastructure sector, which has been promoted by the executive branch itself under the pretext of combating drug trafficking and organized crime more generally. Are these not clear signs of the narrowing and verticalization of the physical infrastructure sector, in line with new rules that aspire to technopopulism? Do these issues not suggest the existence of a kind of state of exception in the infrastructure sector?

The case of the refinery now under construction in Dos Bocas, Tabasco, provides another good example of these dynamics. Beyond the debate over whether or not it makes sense to build this type of facility in contemporary Mexico (see Domínguez, 2016b), the evaluation of the current project apparently failed to take into account the studies carried out by PEMEX's technical departments during previous federal administrations, which warned of the disadvantages of locating a new refinery directly on the shores of the Gulf of Mexico. Two of these are worth mentioning in particular: one, the risks derived from extreme weather phenomena, possibly aggravated by climate change; and two, the logistical cost of transporting refined products to the region with the greatest fuel deficit (the centre of the country) instead of transporting crude oil closer to the centres of demand (idem) and refining it there.

We must not forget that these dynamics, the new "rules" shaping "public" decision-making processes, are part of a broader trend characteristic of AMLO's government: an attack on autonomous institutions (those public policy sites *par excellence* where distinct opinions that contrast with official positions are generated), and a constant disqualification of civil society actors including international NGOs, academia (through the judicial persecution of prominent members of this community), and members of the business and journalistic communities, just to mention a few.

Rupture and continuity: What remains the same?

It has not taken long for the same contradictions and dilemmas inherent to official discourses on development, which have also been manifested during past administrations, to appear during the MORENA federal administration: that is, projects that are framed as pursuing macro-level benefits, but which have extremely negative consequences at the local level; projects that are justified via the discourse of "fiscal discipline," but which in reality incur huge cost overruns; or projects whose legitimacy rests on their ability to solve specific problems, without taking into account the possibility of their causing unforeseen and often undesired effects (Domínguez, 2016a).

The case of the Tren Maya is the clearest example of this, because although it is presented as an initiative whose primary objectives are regional integration and the development of tourism in order to generate jobs and combat poverty, in reality, the project has generated numerous controversies in the realm of environmental and social justice, from the time of its announcement through the various stages of its implementation. Indeed, uncertainty has been a constant for some of the communities affected by the initiative. In some cases, concrete information has not been made available with regard to the specific layout of the project or the forms of compensation accessible to communities whose diversity and idiosyncrasies are not taken into account. As De Tavira (2022) explains,

> the discourse of sovereignty awards [governments] the power to organize territory, which sometimes means displacing, imposing or expropriating territories, that is, deterritorializing in the name of the "common good" or for [reasons of] "public utility"...[however]...despite the predominance of this discourse, in reality there are diverse territorialities within the national

territory, which develop alongside or in contrast with the extensive territoriality of the State.

This creates a dilemma whose outcomes are worth watching in the short term. On the one hand, AMLO's populist discourse continues to appeal to broad sectors of the population, particularly by invoking the social inequalities that still prevail across the country. In this sense, his emblematic projects (the Tren Maya, the AIFA airport at Santa Lucia, and the Dos Bocas Refinery) represent key elements of the 4T's legitimacy both in the immediate present and for the post-AMLO era. This explains the hurry to complete them as soon as possible.

But this does not mean that the contradictions surrounding these development projects can be easily dissipated. While it is true that the grandiloquent discourse of the 4T has served to divert attention from the basic technical problems affecting these projects (flooding at the site proposed for the construction of the refinery, airspace risks in the case of the AIFA, and the financial viability and environmental impacts of the Tren Maya, just to mention a few), it remains uncertain how much longer it will be before the technical "imperfections" generate problems on a larger scale, with attendant political costs for either the current or subsequent MORENA federal administrations.

It is one thing to promote initiatives with relatively solid technical and financial justifications, even if they generate contradictions in the areas of social and environmental justice. It is quite another to promote projects that, in addition to these contradictions, also lack solid foundations in technical, engineering, or financial terms. What are the medium-term scenarios for these initiatives? Everything indicates that AMLO's administration will manage to complete all of them just in time, presenting them as resounding triumphs and key elements of the 4T project, leaving his successor to face all of the technical problems they will inherit.

As mentioned above, this has already happened in the case of Mexico City, where a section of the Metro's new Line 12, constructed and completed under pressure during Marcelo Ebrard's term as head of the city government, collapsed with catastrophic consequences. Judging by the minimal impact that this affair had on the 2024 presidential aspirations of Ebrard, and his successors Miguel Mancera and, above all, Claudia Sheinbaum, it seems likely that MORENA's technopopulism will triumph and that Mexican politics will offer us exactly what the title of this paper suggests: old wine in new bottles.

Some final reflections

The arguments presented in previous sections have been based, above all, on the information and analysis available with regard to the three emblematic projects of the AMLO administration (the Tren Maya, the AIFA, and the Dos Bocas Refinery). However, in the interest of a balanced analysis, a few nuances are also worth mentioning here. Firstly, AMLO's unabashed technopopulism has clearly manifested itself in the cases described above; but as a way of doing politics, it remains an *aspiration*, rather than an overwhelming reality that shapes every area of the infrastructure sector (and far less every area of public policy, considering the number of legislative initiatives that the Supreme Court of Justice has suspended). One clear setback can be seen in the case of the Tesla car factory. In this case, AMLO's attempt to influence the specific site chosen for its location was immediately rejected by Tesla's CEO, publicly exposing the limitations of the technopopulist discourse characteristic of the current administration.

Other technopopulist initiatives, however, could be seen as successes. Such is the case of the modifications made to the Mining Law and some aspects of the Energy Reform, which have in both cases aimed to ensure these activities fit better within the broad parameters of social justice, particularly regarding the negotiations necessary to obtain territorial concessions and the terms in which mining concessions are expressed. The same applies to the proposal to form a public company for the purpose of exploiting and commercializing the country's lithium reserves. The effects of each of these cases, though, can only be evaluated in the long term.

In conclusion, the Mexican example can serve as a basis for reflecting on other experiences in Latin America. Despite the MORENA administration's aspirations to construct a hard and fast technopopulism in contemporary Mexico, we should not lose sight of the fact that both technopopulism in particular, and technopolitical controversies more generally, are best understood as existing on a sliding scale. It is worth asking ourselves whether other leftist administrations, such as that of Gustavo Petro in Colombia or Gabriel Boric in Chile, will also succumb to the temptation to exercise this form of government, despite the terrible contradictions that it entails; or whether Brazil's President Lula will now try to moderate the same technopopulist impulses that helped to whip up the political storm that previously resulted in his resignation and eventual imprisonment.

Notes

1 This was the official figure published by the Secretaría de Comunicaciones y Transportes (SCT, 2019). However, several experts who participated in the implementation of the Texcoco airport maintained, in the context of informal conversations, that contractual commitments had reached nearly 70% at the moment of its cancellation.
2 For a broader discussion about the sociotechnical controversy surrounding the AIFA and the previous airport project at Texcoco, see Ríos (2022).
3 For a more detailed look at debates concerning the suitability (or not) of the parameters used for the evaluation of other projects, see Domínguez (2016b).
4 For more details see Ballinas (2011).
5 The parameter set by authors, such as Bent Flyvbjerg (2007, also cited in Domínguez, 2015, 19), is those projects whose costs surpass $1 billion USD or those whose scale

and impacts are disproportionate with respect to the physical area in which they are located.

6 For example, it's difficult to argue against Line 12 being a project that hugely increases mobility within a specific area of Mexico City. In this sense, it cannot be regarded as a project that is merely a political whim with ideological overtones. However, according to specialists in the subject, only the section between Mixcoac and Atlalilco (9 out of the 20 stations constructed) makes sense as a technically and financially feasible solution. For the other 11 stations, complications in the process of obtaining the corresponding rights of way which impacted the financial viability of the project (Ugalde, 2018). Moreover, the insistence on extending the line all the way to Tláhuac station was due to a debt that Marcelo Ebrard assumed on a personal level after the lynching of various police officers that took place in that area in 2004, when he was in charge of the Federal District's public security. For more information about the lynchings, see Gutiérrez (2021).

7 It's significant that the three administrations preceding AMLO's term used the acronym NAICM, which visibilized the project's status as a solution to a problem specific to Mexico City; meanwhile, the acronym most commonly used by the AMLO administration is the "NAIM" (New International Airport of Mexico), emphasizing its status as an emblematic national-level project.

8 Regarding the possibility of a controversy feeding a technopolitical debate and boosting the argument for a particular proposal, it's worth looking at the English-language literature on interest groups, which proposes that certain groups external to the government may – precisely because they are *not* involved in a particular sector – be able to provide a political administration with knowledge to which it would otherwise lack access.

9 The Fourth Transformation situates itself within a historical perspective according to which Mexico has experienced three progressive revolutions (the War of Independence, the Reform of the nineteenth century, and the Mexican Revolution), with the coming to power of MORENA at the federal level constituting a fourth such transformation.

10 In particular, it's worth looking at Domínguez (2011, 2015, 2019)

11 See again the aforementioned works by Domínguez.

12 An example is the debate surrounding the construction of a new refinery in Tula, Hidalgo, during the presidential administration of Felipe Calderón. Although this project was abandoned, it's worth mentioning one particular episode in which technical considerations triumphed over political aims. As we have previously explained (Domínguez, 2016b), Calderón had proposed the refinery's construction as a "sweetener" to win support for his energy reform bill in Congress. However, the president insisted throughout most of the debate that the refinery should be located in Salamanca, in the state of Guanajuato, then controlled by his own PAN party. As various interviewees who took part in the process attest, PEMEX demonstrated to the president that the refinery would be more feasible and convenient in Tula. Eventually, the technical considerations put on the table by PEMEX engineers won out over the intentions of the president himself, at least in this particular case.

13 The Tizayuca option was promoted by the state government of Hidalgo during the 1990s, and although its location would have been distinct from that of the AIFA, the debates over airspace and other technical variables that were considered at that time still remain relevant to the case of the AIFA.

14 According to the Federal Government, the Tren Maya constitutes:

> a project that aims to boost tourism's contribution to the economy of the Yucatán Peninsula, create jobs, promote sustainable development, protect the environ-

ment of the zone by undermining activities such as illegal logging and species trafficking, and favour the better territorial organization of the region. The local population will be involved in and benefit from the works; any rights of way that have not yet been obtained will be negotiated via agreements with the relevant landowners.

(Gobierno de México, 2019, para. 277; cited by De Tavira, 2022, 82)

15 The Savings Protection Banking Fund (FOBAPROA) was a contingency fund created during the 1990s. Particularly during the crisis of 1995, it allowed for the "saving" of banks affected by the crisis in the contemporary Mexican financial system, but in the long term, it also caused a substantial increase in the national debt.

References

Arellano, David and Mauricio Dussauge, 2018, 'Eventos complejos y desastres político-administrativos: La experiencia de la línea 12 del Metro de la Ciudad de México. Introducción al número temático,' *Gestión y Política Pública*, 27(3), Mexico City, July/December.

Ballinas, Cristopher, 2011, *Political Struggles and the Forging of Autonomous Government Agencies*, Springer, London.

Baumgartner, F. and B. Jones, 1991, 'Agenda Dynamics and Policy Subsystems,' *The Journal of Politics*, 53(4), Washington, DC, pp. 1044–1074.

Baumgartner, F. and B. Jones, 1993, *Agendas and Instability in American Politics*, The University of Chicago Press, Chicago.

De Tavira, Federico, 2022, '*Territorialidad y discurso en la producción espacial del desarrollo: el proceso regional del megaproyecto Tren Maya y la experiencia local de Kimbilá, Yucatán*,' Unpublished Masters Thesis in Estudios Regionales, Instituto Mora, Mexico City.

Domínguez, J. Carlos, 2011, 'Ventanas de oportunidad y coaliciones de política pública: el caso del proyecto para un Nuevo Aeropuerto en la Ciudad de México desde una perspectiva histórica,' *Secuencia. Revista de Historia y Ciencias Sociales*, 79, January–April, Mexico.

Domínguez, J. Carlos, 2015, *Megaproyectos fallidos en Latinoamérica. Sociología histórica y política comparada,* Instituto Mora, Mexico City.

Domínguez, J. Carlos, 2016a, 'Introducción: los megaproyectos en las discusiones sobre el desarrollo,' in J. Carlos Domínguez and Claudia Corona, *Megaproyectos y los Dilemas del Desarrollo en Latinoamérica*, Instituto Mora, Mexico City.

Domínguez, J. Carlos, 2016b, 'Megaproyectos como instrumentos de legitimidad política en México: el caso del proyecto para una nueva refinería en Tula (2009–2010),' in J. Carlos Domínguez and Claudia Corona, *Megaproyectos y los Dilemas del Desarrollo en Latinoamérica*, Instituto Mora, Mexico City.

Domínguez, J. Carlos, 2019, 'La oposición al nuevo aeropuerto en la Ciudad de México en los años 2001–2002 versus una década después: ¿qué cambió?' in Berenice Ortega Bayona and Kristina Pirker, *Dilemas de la acción colectiva en América Latina: Entre la incidencia institucional y la protesta social*, Instituto Mora, Mexico City.

Domínguez, J. Carlos, 2023, 'La democracia en América Latina: ¿Madurez o crisis de los cuarenta?' *Letras Libres*, Online Edition, https://letraslibres.com/politica/carlos

-dominguez-virgen-balance-democracia-america-latina/ [last consulted: 21 March 2024]

Domínguez, J. Carlos and A. Monsivais, 2020, *Democracias en vilo. La incertidumbre política en América Latina*, Instituto Mora, Mexico City.

Dryzek, J. S., 1997, *The Politics of the Earth. Environmental Discourses*, Oxford University Press, Oxford.

Esmark, A., 2021, 'How Does Crisis Affect the Conflict between Technocracy and Populism? Lessons from the COVID-19 Pandemic,' *Politics*, https://doi.org/10.1177/02633957211049965 [last consulted: 11 July 2023].

Flyvbjerg, B., 2007, *Mega Delusional: The Curse of the Megaproject*, Aalborg University, <http://flyvbjerg.plan.aau.dk/whatisamegaproject.php>. [last consulted: 15 May 2007].

Gutiérrez, Agustín, 2021, 'Ebrard: Tercera Caída en Tláhuac,' *Milenio*, 6 May 2021, https://www.milenio.com/opinion/agustin-gutierrez-canet/sin-ataduras/ebrard-tercera-caida-en-tlahuac, [last consulted: 11 July 2023].

Kingdon, J., (1984), *Agendas, Alternatives, and Public Policies*, Little, Brown and Company, Boston.

Nava, Diana, 2023, '¿Cuánto ha costado la refinería de Dos Bocas? Rocío Nahle responde,' 11 November 2023, < https://expansion.mx/empresas/2023/11/11/cuanto-ha-costado-dos-bocas-rocio-nahle>, [last consulted: 28 February 2024].

Ríos, Israel, 2022, '*La participación del conocimiento experto en las decisiones sobre el Nuevo Aeropuerto de la Ciudad de México: un caso de controversia sociotécnica*,' Unpublished Doctoral Thesis, Centro de Estudios Urbanos y Ambientales, Colegio de México.

Sabatier, P., 1988, 'Political Science and Public Policy,' *Political Science and Politics*, 24(2), Cambridge, 144–147.

Sabatier, P., 1999, *Theories of the Policy Process*, Westview Press, Boulder.

Sabatier, P. and H. C. Jenkins-Smith, 1993, *Policy Change and Learning*, Westview Press, Boulder.

Secretaría de Comunicaciones y Transportes (SCT), 2019, 'Razones para la Cancelación del Nuevo Aeropuerto en Texcoco,' 26 April 2019, https://www.gob.mx/sct/articulos/razones-para-la-cancelacion-del-proyecto-del-nuevo-aeropuerto-en-texcoco, [last consulted: 28 February 2024].

Secretaría de Energía (SENER), 2022, 'La Refinería Olmeca en Dos Bocas hoy hace historia y se suma al Sistema Nacional de Refinación para asegurar la autosuficiencia energética,' 1 July 2022, <https://www.gob.mx/sener/articulos/la-refineria-olmeca-en-dos-bocas-hoy-hace-historia-y-se-suma-al-sistema-nacional-de-refinacion-para-asegurar-la-autosuficiencia-energetica>, [last consulted: 28 February de 2024].

Ugalde, Vicente, 2018, 'La línea 12 en la mira de la sociología de las élites delincuentes,' *Gestión y Política Pública*, 27(3), Mexico City July/December.

6 Subnational variations and the rule of law in Argentina

Political dynasties, elite turnover, and Supreme Court oversight

Jacqueline Behrend

Introduction

Macro-political and social processes like democratization, elite turnover, economic development, and enforcement of the rule of law can vary enormously within countries to the extent that this variation may be as sharp as the variation across countries. Recent research has shown important variations in political competition and subnational elites, the enforcement of the rule of law, and economic development. Each of these domains of subnational politics is usually studied relatively autonomously from each other. Yet subnational political systems are best understood as entangled processes in which formal and informal structures and practices combine to produce distinct outcomes. In this context, who governs subnational entities and how lawfully they govern can mark important differences. This chapter is about how formal institutions and informal practices come together to enable or inhibit the creation and perpetuation of subnational political elites. It argues that there are two different strategies through which subnational political elites seek to remain in control of provincial politics. One is the creation of subnational political dynasties, where power passes democratically from one relative to another, thus remaining in the family. This allows members of the family to retain control of executive office through democratic means. The other involves governors' attempts to seek reelection beyond the term limits imposed by the provincial constitution through dubious interpretations of provincial constitutional rules. When attempting this strategy, incumbents are usually assisted by local high court rulings. However, these rulings have generally been overturned by the Supreme Court. The chapter therefore explores the links between political elites and the judicialization of politics. Some of the questions it seeks to address are: what strategies do provincial governors use to remain in office or maintain control of their subnational bastions? When are conflicts over who governs judicialized? What role do local courts play and how does the Supreme Court exercise oversight?

Subnational political elites make decisions about policymaking in their districts, and these decisions can have important developmental and governance effects. Therefore, who governs is as important at the subnational level as it is at the national level. However, the effects that political dynasties or governors who

DOI: 10.4324/9781003519195-6

seek to remain in office beyond their constitutional mandates have on regional development are not linear. Continuity in office may aid developmental projects in some cases, but it may give rise to capture in others. Developmental elites may be elected in districts that are pluralistic and have political alternation, but elites in districts with less alternation and pluralism may also pursue developmental policies. Such an assessment is beyond the aims of this chapter, but at the end of the next section, I draw some insights into the diverse effects that elite continuity can have on subnational development.

This chapter makes three main contributions to the study of subnational democratization, political elites, and the rule of law. First, building on my previous work on political dynasties, it provides an overview of the political dynasties that have governed Argentine provinces since re-democratization. Second, it provides an empirical analysis of how governors have sought to perpetuate their power by bypassing bans on their reelection with the help of local courts, and how the Supreme Court has exercised oversight in each case. Finally, it provides some insights into the links between political dynasties and subnational economic development.

Political dynasties are informal structures that arise in democracy and become entangled with formal democratic institutions. This is a complex and under-studied topic that is essential to understanding who governs at the subnational level and how this affects subnational governance. The judicialization of politics and the role of the Supreme Court allow us to see how conflicts over who governs and how many terms they can govern are resolved. Although provinces have a substantial degree of autonomy to design their institutions and electoral norms, the Supreme Court has intervened to settle disputes over conflicting interpretations of local constitutions regarding incumbent governors' reelection. The role of courts at different levels of government varies greatly. While provincial high courts have usually ruled in favour of incumbent governors, even when the constitution clearly banned their reelection, the Supreme Court has usually exercised oversight in cases where the constitutionality of a governor's reelection was in doubt. In these cases, its rulings were authoritative and usually uncontested.

Argentina has created a steady electoral democracy and reasonably functioning democratic institutions. However, at the subnational level, there is enormous variation in political competition, economic development, and in the enforcement of the rule of law. Subnational governments have the power to implement regional economic development strategies, and their capacity to do so is increasingly shaped by subnational actors and conflicts (Eaton, 2017). Informal practices can strongly affect major policy areas of critical importance to the electorate, and they are key to understanding why some provinces are able to deliver a higher quality of democracy and to undertake development projects that improve the lives of their citizens, while others are not. The subnational level has received considerable attention in recent years through studies that show how large-scale processes such as democratization, economic development, or political competition vary within countries as much as between countries (Behrend, 2011; Behrend & Whitehead, 2016a, 2016b; Giraudy, Moncada & Snyder, 2019). Scaling down to the subnational level (Snyder, 2001) is relevant because it shows that aggregate measures do not accurately reflect how important processes unfold within countries and how heterogeneity within countries can have various political and economic effects at the national level. In many countries across the world, the combined processes of democratization and decentralization allowed local political elites to capture the provincial state (Kenawas, 2015). But even if they capture political office, some political dynasties can also promote subnational development. The link between the two – capturing political office and state capture – is neither unilinear nor straightforward and requires careful assessment in each case.

Argentine provinces can be seen as a laboratory of how diverse political institutions and economic structures can produce varying outcomes within a single democratic country. Argentina has 24 autonomous subnational units – 23 provinces and the autonomous City of Buenos Aires. Although the national Constitution has preeminence and all provincial constitutions must abide by the republican form of government, there is significant institutional variation and a notable degree of subnational autonomy in policymaking. In this context, the Supreme Court intervenes regularly and substantively to guarantee the rule of law.

The chapter proceeds as follows. In the first section, I observe the variation in the types of political elites that arose in different provinces after democratization. I focus particularly on family links and the existence of political dynasties in subnational executives. I put forth some ideas about the importance of subnational political elites for the promotion of subnational economic development but highlight that there is no evidence of a causal link between political dynasties and the type of development policies pursued. In the following section, I focus on how the Supreme Court has exercised oversight in subnational electoral conflicts. The final section concludes.

Subnational political dynasties and democracy in contemporary Argentina

Democratization in Argentina did not put an end to political dynasties. As in many other countries within Latin America and other world regions, the evidence presented in this chapter shows that democracy sometimes aids the establishment of new subnational political dynasties. The geographic extension of dynasties to so many countries and regions across the world casts doubt on the assumption that political families and dynasties develop in weakly institutionalized or economically underdeveloped settings alone (Kurtz 1989, 2001). Moreover, families are not merely present in recent or developing democracies but also in established and long-standing ones.[1] Political families can slant the electoral playing field and make it more difficult for political actors who are not part of a family network to compete in elections. They can also capture the state. But they may also pursue policies that improve citizens' well-being.

Political dynasties matter in a democracy for several reasons. In the first place, the question of "who governs" (Dahl, 1961) and who gets elected is central because it indicates how plural and permeable to different interests a political system is. The existence of political dynasties in a democracy could be attributed to the fact that politicians' offspring, like the offspring of doctors, lawyers, or other professions, wish to follow their parents' paths (Smith, 2018). But democratic dynasties could also be a symptom that the democratic process is being captured by a closed political elite that pursues narrow interests, and this could have effects on the policies that are enacted and on possibilities for economic and social development (Behrend, 2011; Smith, 2018). In the second place, subnational political families and dynasties are important for democracy because, in some cases, they are linked to the interests of economic groups that operate in the district, or they may use their positions in office to promote their personal or family business interests. Political dynasties are evidence of the heterogeneity and political variation that can exist within a single democratic country, and this heterogeneity poses diverse developmental challenges.

Political dynasties point to the problem of succession. Why do politicians seek to pass on power to a family member instead of another party member? The main arguments found in the literature indicate that politicians develop political dynasties to perpetuate their power, to achieve power for its own sake, and to reap economic benefits (Dal Bó et al., 2009). In some cases, politicians designate family members as candidates when they cannot run for reelection. A family member can be an insurance against investigation or prosecution by political opponents. In other cases, political dynasties are formed because individuals who grew up in a political family have a genuine interest in politics and pursue the same career as their family members. Another possibility is that a family member is chosen as a successor when political parties are weak, and surnames replace party labels as a form of identification.

As outlined in my previous work (Behrend, 2021a, 2021b), the term political dynasty refers to family succession in a single elected position. A political dynasty exists when an elected public official is succeeded *in the same position*, either immediately or in a subsequent period, by a family relation. These relations can be based on marital links, lineage, or extended family. Political dynasties must be distinguished from political families, where relatives hold elective office simultaneously, previously, or subsequently, but they do not hold the *same elective office*. Political dynasties also need to be distinguished from the concept of nepotism. Nepotism involves designating family members in unelected positions. Political dynasties often incur nepotism, and nepotism may be central to capturing the local state. But, unlike nepotism, the concept of political dynasty refers to electoral politics, which is the focus of this study.

Most governors in Argentina are related to other elected politicians by blood or by marriage. They belong to political families that are elected to the national Congress, subnational legislatures, mayors' offices, etc. Governors with blood or marital links to other elected politicians governed in 21 out of 24 provinces (87.5% of provinces), since the transition to democracy in 1983, as Figure 6.1 shows. In provinces like Catamarca, Córdoba, Corrientes, or Santa Cruz, most governors were related to other elected authorities, that is, they belonged to a political family or dynasty. Only in three provinces, Chubut, La Pampa, and Santa Fe, none of the governors belonged to a political family or dynasty.

Political dynasties are, however, a different phenomenon. The existence of political dynasties in executive office means that power is transferred from one relative to another. Dynasties imply continuity in office even if the transfer of power to a relative is not immediate. At a minimum, they are a symptom of limited political competition. At a maximum, they could be a symptom that the political process is captured by a reduced oligarchy (Behrend, 2011; Smith, 2018).

In Argentina, 12 out of 24 provinces were governed by political dynasties since the transition to democracy in 1983 (50% of provinces), as Figure 6.2 shows. Three provinces were governed by two different dynasties after re-democratization. Eight provinces were governed by dynasties for more than a decade, and three provinces were governed by dynasties for close to or over 30 years, as Figure 6.3 shows. The provinces of Catamarca, Corrientes, San Luis, and Santiago del Estero are among the most salient cases. But Santa Cruz,

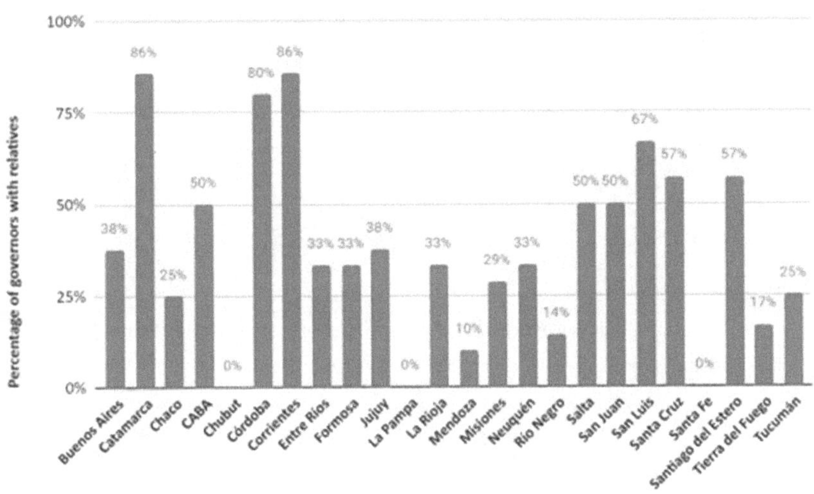

Figure 6.1 Percentage of governors with relatives in Argentina, 1983–2024.

Source: Database of Argentine political families and dynasties (Behrend, 2024).

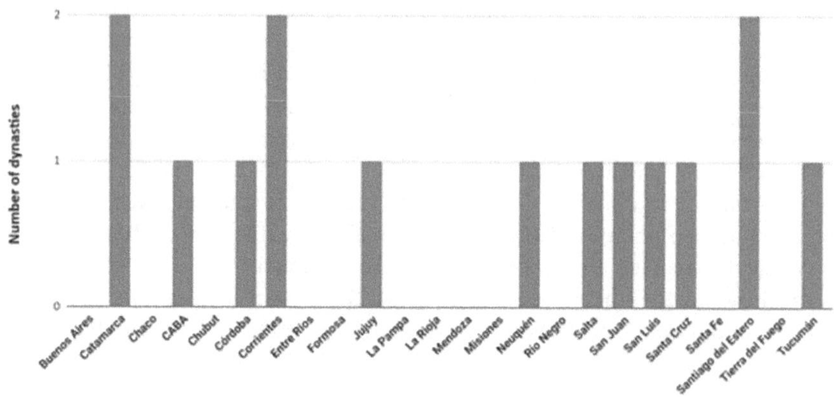

Figure 6.2 Political dynasties by province in Argentina, 1983–2024.

Source: Database of Argentine political families and dynasties (Behrend, 2024).

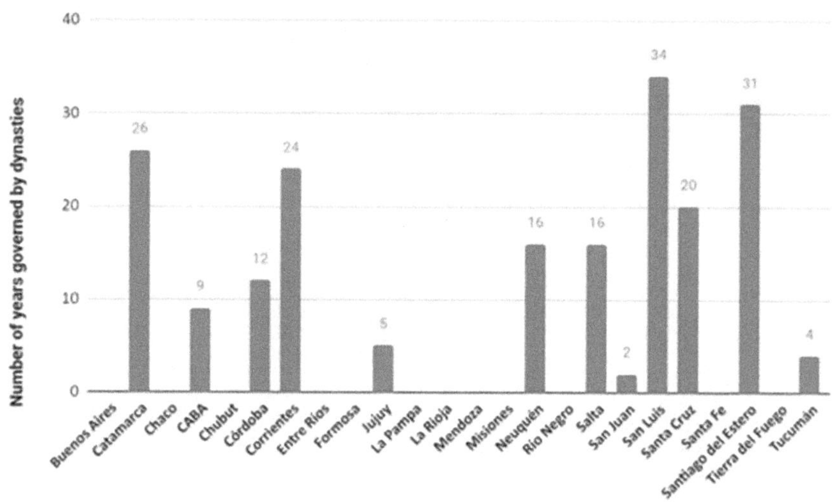

Figure 6.3 Number of years governed by dynasties per province in Argentina, 1983–2024.

Source: Database of Argentine political families and dynasties (Behrend, 2024).

Neuquén, Salta, and Córdoba were also governed by governors from a political dynasty for over a decade.[2] Figure 6.3 shows the number of years governed by political dynasties. In provinces like San Luis, Catamarca, Santiago del Estero, and Corrientes, political dynasties have governed for an extraordinary number of years.

Political dynasties exist across political parties: they are present in the Peronist Party, in the Radical Party,[3] in the Pro Party, and in provincial parties. In some cases, the political party in office changed, but the dynasty persisted.[4] This highlights the contrast between political dynasties as informal arrangements and political parties as formal structures. In other cases, a dynasty was replaced by another dynasty from a different political party.[5] Dynasties exist in provinces with a less developed economic structure, like Santiago del Estero, in provinces that are less developed but have experienced party turnover, like Corrientes and Catamarca; in provinces that are economically more developed, like Córdoba; or with enclave economies, like Neuquén; and, more recently, in the autonomous City of Buenos Aires, which is by far the most developed and pluralistic district in Argentina. The province of Buenos Aires, which is the largest and most diverse district and has a highly developed economic structure, as well as political pluralism, has never been governed by a political dynasty, although there are many dynasties at the municipal level. The two provinces that have an explicit ban on political dynasties in their constitutions – Río Negro and Mendoza – have never had a political dynasty. The existence of political dynasties across parties, diverse economic structures, and provinces that have experienced party alternation as well as provinces that haven't makes it hard to find single, unilinear causes that explain their rise and persistence. The effects of political dynasties on subnational development are also not linear.

Of the 12 districts where subnational political dynasties developed after the transition to democracy, two of the most developed and diversified districts in Argentina are included: Córdoba and the City of Buenos Aires. These two districts, however, have been governed for a shorter period by political dynasties. The provinces of Catamarca, Corrientes, Neuquén, San Luis, and Santiago del Estero have been governed by political dynasties for over 16 years. The province of San Luis was governed by the Rodríguez Saá brothers for 33 years and experienced a dramatic transformation of its economic structure through a developmentalist industrialization programme based on national tax exemptions (Behrend, 2011; Karamaneff in this volume). Unlike other provinces that benefited from the same industrialization policy, the San Luis government built highways and infrastructure to attract businesses to the province. In San Luis, dynastic politics resulted in unprecedented growth and development in the province. In the province of Neuquén, which is one of the most important producers of oil and gas in Argentina, the dynasties that governed the province strongly defended and promoted this industry, which provides employment directly and indirectly to an important part of the population. But in other provinces, political dynasties have not promoted economic development with such zeal. Corrientes and Santiago del Estero, for example, have remained peripheral, and their local economies are unspecialized and not diversified (Behrend & Bianchi, 2017). In these two provinces, there have been limited attempts to implement policies to promote regional development. Catamarca, which is another dynastic province, has an enclave economy devoted to gold and copper mining, but mining only accounts for 5.5% of registered private employment in the province, that is, a total of 1,844 workers are employed in mining (Secretaría de Minería, 2022). Other than mining, its economy is unspecialized and not diversified, and there have been few policies to promote regional development, even though until the early 1990s it benefited from a federal industrial promotion law (Karamaneff, 2022).

These examples illustrate that political dynasties can promote developmentalist policies in some cases but can fail to do so in others. There is no fixed outcome in this regard, and the developmental consequences of political dynasties need to be investigated in each case.

Enforcing the rule of law: Reelection and Supreme Court oversight of subnational politics

Provincial governors may wish to remain in executive office beyond the number of periods allowed by the provincial constitution for a variety of reasons. They may have a genuine vocation to continue in executive office, they may wish to continue developmental projects, they may feel that there are no suitable candidates, they may wish to remain in office for a lust of power itself, they may fear prosecution once they leave office, or, in some cases, incumbent governors may have an economic interest in remaining in office. In developing countries, the economic benefits and rents from political office are powerful incentives that encourage the expansion of political families into different types of elected office (Chandra, 2016). Politicians' salaries may be more attractive than those of other professions (Smith, 2018), and public office can allow politicians to develop business interests linked to, or protected by, the state (Behrend, 2011; Sidel, 2014).

Any of these reasons might lead incumbent governors to try to interpret reelection norms in ways that benefit them, or to nominate a relative as a candidate to succeed them in office. In previous work, I used the concept of a "closed game" (Behrend, 2011) to refer to subnational political elites that controlled key aspects of provincial political systems, including access to business opportunities. Provincial governors, like most politicians, have diverse origins. Some come from a career in liberal professions, others may have developed a career solely in the public sector, and yet others come from the private sector and own businesses.

In 1983, when Argentina's democracy was re-established, the reelection of governors was banned in all provinces. But in the mid-1980s and 1990s, many provinces reformed their constitutions and enabled reelection. After this wave of constitutional reforms, only two provinces – Mendoza and Santa Fe – continued to ban the reelection of governors. Some provinces allow the reelection of governors for one consecutive period, others for two, and others allow the indefinite reelection of governors.[6] Although provincial constitutions are clear about how many terms an incumbent governor can aspire to govern, over the years, conflicts have arisen over the wording and interpretation of the articles of provincial constitutions that regulate reelection. In most cases where conflicts have arisen, local courts – usually the provincial electoral court and the high court (*Superior Tribunal de Justicia*) – have tended to rule in favour of incumbent governors' reelection bids. In such conflicts, the national Supreme Court has the final say and exercises oversight over the interpretation of subnational norms. Local oppositions therefore usually appeal to the Supreme Court after the provincial high court has issued a ruling.

In this section, I focus on cases in which governors sought to transgress the limits to their reelection, on the demands subsequently filed by subnational oppositions before the Supreme Court, and on cases where the opposition preventively asked the Supreme Court to rule on whether an incumbent governor was eligible to run. In most cases, provincial high courts ruled in favour of the governor's reelection. Attempting reelection in dubious cases can be a dangerous move for outgoing governors. Even if they can manage a favourable ruling by the provincial electoral court or high court, the local opposition will very likely take the case to the Supreme Court, which has usually ruled against incumbent governors. An adverse ruling by the Supreme Court entails an additional risk for governors – they may have to come up with an alternative candidate only a few weeks or even days before the election. In some cases, after a court ruling that banned an incumbent governor from running, a relative was nominated to run instead. But relatives need to win elections, and this is not guaranteed, especially in a short period of time. The same may also be true for other unrelated candidates nominated at the last moment. Although in many cases these new candidates won the elections, in a few cases the governor's wager turned against them and their political parties lost the election. Stretching the limits of the law is therefore a dangerous venture for governors.

In federal countries, subnational units have guaranteed realms of authority, but notably in Argentina, the Supreme Court plays a major role in enforcing the rule of law and making sure that provinces do not use their autonomy to install forms of government that are contradictory to democracy. Formally, the Supreme Court exercises oversight and is the final arbiter and regulator in subnational conflicts. In my previous work with Whitehead (Whitehead & Behrend, 2016; Behrend & Whitehead, 2016b) we discussed the mechanism of control/conditionality as a pathway toward subnational democratization. Here, I focus on one of these mechanisms of control: rulings by the Supreme Court with regard to electoral conflicts and disputes over who is eligible to run for governor. Supreme Court rulings are part of ordinary forms of control in a federal democracy, but the Supreme Court does not automatically admit challenges. Those filing the challenge must either have exhausted all previous instances or they must demonstrate that the Court has original jurisdiction in this matter. The Court, therefore, exercises its oversight in subnational elections only in specific cases that cannot be resolved by local authorities. Taking cases to the Supreme Court is a fundamental aspect of democratic normality, but in recent years there has been a process of judicialization of politics and political parties have significantly increased the use of legal mechanisms to resolve political disputes (Berruecos García Travesí & Whitehead, 2021). The judicial arena became a locus of politics, and it drew courts into political conflicts to a greater extent than before. Citizens, civil society groups, and members of the opposition increasingly turned to courts to vindicate rights and contest policy (Kapiszewski, 2012).

Table 6.1 summarizes the cases filed before the Supreme Court in conflicts over gubernatorial candidates' eligibility to run and the rulings issued by

Table 6.1 Supreme Court rulings on the reelection of governors, 1983–2023

Date	*Ruling no.*	*Province*	*Court ruling*	*Article*
6 October 1994	317:1195	Santa Fe	Confirmed that the governor could not be reelected.	Article 64, provincial constitution.
12 September 2003	326:3448	Jujuy	Declared that the Supreme Court did not have competence to rule.	Article 127, provincial constitution.
5 November 2013	336:2148/ 336:1756	Santiago del Estero	Banned the governor's reelection.	Article 152, provincial constitution.
8 April 2015	338:231	Salta	Declared that the Supreme Court did not have competence to rule.	Article 140, provincial constitution.
22 March 2019	342:343/ 342:171	La Rioja	Banned the governor's reelection.	Amendment of Articles 120 and 171, provincial constitution.
12 March 2019	342:235/ 342:287	Río Negro	Banned the governor's reelection.	Article 175, provincial constitution.
9 May 2023	CSJ 561/2023	San Juan	Banned the governor's reelection.	Article 175, provincial constitution.
16 May 2023	CSJ 687/2023	Tucumán	Banned the governor's reelection.	Article 90, provincial constitution.
11 July 2023	CSJ 1300/2023	City of Buenos Aires	Declared that the Supreme Court did not have competence to rule.	Article 97 of the city's constitution.

Source: Own elaboration on data from the Supreme Court.

the Court. It includes a total of nine rulings issued by the Court in this period (1983–2023). Before 2013, only two cases were filed before the Supreme Court to resolve a conflict over the election of a governor. After 2013, cases where the Court had to determine a candidate's eligibility to run became more frequent, and the Court ruled in seven further cases to establish the legitimacy of provincial governors' bids for reelection. Except for one, the cases filed before the Supreme Court usually involved interpretations of provincial constitutional restrictions for incumbent governors, particularly after constitutional reforms enabling reelection, or in situations that gave rise to conflicting interpretations about which period counted as the first term in office.

The first case was filed in 1994 by the Peronist Party of Santa Fe, which claimed that the article banning the immediate reelection of the governor was unconstitutional and restricted the rights of individuals to be elected.[7] The Supreme Court ruled that the republican form of government did not necessarily mean that governors had the right to be reelected if the provincial constitution banned reelection.[8] The Court's ruling was authoritative, and no governors have since attempted reelection in Santa Fe.

In 2003, the Libertad y Democracia Party in Jujuy filed a claim before the Supreme Court asking it to determine whether Governor Eduardo Fellner could stand for reelection. Fellner had been designated interim governor by the provincial legislature after the death of Governor Guillermo Snopek and the resignation of his deputy governor in November 1998 until December 1999 to complete Snopek's mandate. In 1999, Fellner was elected governor for a full period and in 2003, he ran for reelection. The constitution of Jujuy allows only one consecutive reelection, and the claim filed by the opposition party aimed at determining whether his period as interim governor counted as his first period in office. The Court ruled that it had no jurisdiction and returned the case to the provincial high court, which ruled that his year as interim governor did not count and what counted as his first term in office was his first elected period in 1999. Fellner was therefore allowed to run for reelection in 2003.

In 2013, the Radical Party (UCR) of Santiago del Estero filed a case before the Supreme Court, asking it to determine whether Governor Gerardo Zamora could run for a third consecutive term. The province of Santiago del Estero had reformed its constitution to enable the reelection of the governor for one consecutive period. In 2013, a local court ruled that since the provincial constitution had been reformed during his first term as governor (2005–2009), his second term (2009–2013) should be considered his first under the new constitution, and he could therefore run for a third term in 2013. This ruling contradicted the provincial constitution, which explicitly stated that the mandate of the governor in office when the new constitution was sanctioned should be considered his first term in office.[9] Five days ahead of the election, the Supreme Court ruled that Zamora was not eligible to run and suspended the elections. A few days later, Zamora announced that his wife, Claudia Ledesma Abdala, who up to then had not held elective office, would run for governor instead. Ledesma Abdala was elected in December 2013 with 64.7% of votes, thus initiating a political dynasty. Her election marked the beginning of a successful political career. After her term ended, her husband was once again elected governor, and she continued her career as a national deputy (2017–2019) and then as a national senator (2019–2025). As senator, she was named provisional president of the Senate (2019–2023) and became second in the presidential line of succession, after the vice president.

In April 2015, the opposition Frente Grande in Salta filed a case before the Supreme Court requesting that it put an end to the uncertainty regarding the interpretation of Article 140 of the provincial constitution and declare that Governor Juan Manuel Urtubey was not eligible to run for a fourth consecutive term in office. The provincial constitution allows three consecutive terms in office, and there were rumours that Urtubey might seek a fourth. However, the Court dismissed the case, arguing that it had no jurisdiction to rule because the governor had not officialized his candidacy and the case was hypothetical. In the end, Urtubey did not run for reelection.

In March 2019, two conflicts regarding the reelection of governors in the provinces of Río Negro and La Rioja were filed before the Supreme Court within days of each other. In Río Negro, Governor Alberto Weretilneck had been elected deputy governor in 2011 but had become governor when his running mate, Carlos Soria, was killed three weeks after being sworn in.[10] In 2015, he ran for reelection, and in 2019, the provincial high court ruled that he was eligible to run for a third term in office, overriding a ruling against Weretilneck's candidacy by the provincial electoral court. The high court argued that in his first term he had merely replaced his running mate, Carlos Soria, and therefore that term should not count as his first term as governor. The opposition Frente para la Victoria (Peronists) took the case to the Supreme Court, and the Court ruled that he was not eligible to run because Article 175 of the provincial constitution states that governors and deputy governors can be reelected or reciprocally succeed each other for only one term.[11] If they wish to be reelected again, they must let one term pass. This meant that even if his first term as governor did not count, because he had been elected deputy governor and was part of the executive, he could not run again at the time. The Court issued its ruling two weeks before the elections but did not suspend them. Weretilneck's running mate, Arabela Carreras, ran for governor instead and won the elections.

In La Rioja, Peronist Governor Sergio Casas ran a plebiscite in January 2019 to ask voters whether the article in the provincial constitution that banned the governor from running for reelection if he had previously been elected deputy governor should be reformed. Although there was a high level of abstention and blank ballots (voter turnout was only 44%), the result was in favour of modifying Article 120 of the provincial constitution. The opposition Radical Party took the case to the Supreme Court, and one month before the elections, the Court ruled that the constitutional reform that enabled the governor's reelection was illegal. After the provincial elections were suspended,[12] the governor designated Ricardo Quintela as his candidate. A new date for the elections was set, which coincided with the presidential elections of October 2019. Quintela won the election, and the Peronist Party retained the province.

In 2023, in the run-up to the presidential elections, most provinces elected governors, and a new round of cases was filed before the Supreme Court to establish the legitimacy of incumbent governors' bids for reelection. In May 2023, the Supreme Court issued two rulings within a week of each other that suspended the elections for governor in the provinces of San Juan and Tucumán. Unlike previous cases, the Court did not intervene to review a prior ruling by the provincial high courts, but as a case of original jurisdiction.[13]

In San Juan, the opposition filed a claim before the Supreme Court asking it to determine whether incumbent Governor Sergio Uñac could run for a third term in office, given that he had been deputy governor of the province in the period before his election as governor (2011–2015). The constitution of San Juan allows governors to run for two consecutive reelections – a total of three consecutive periods. But like in many other provincial constitutions, if the governor was previously deputy governor, this period counts as his first. Despite this constitutional provision, when consulted, the provincial high court ruled in Uñac's favour and determined that he could run. The Supreme Court suspended the election and ruled that his period as deputy governor counted as his first period in executive office and that he was not eligible to run for a third period as governor. Uñac postponed the elections for governor until the Supreme Court's ruling was confirmed and named his brother Rubén Uñac as the candidate for governor. Unlike the case of Santiago del Estero, where the governor's wife won the election, Uñac's brother did not win, and the Peronist Party lost the province to the opposition. This was a failed attempt at creating a political dynasty and shows that even if governors seek to maintain executive office in the hands of a family member, getting a relative elected is not a simple or automatic process, and the consequences can be negative for the ruling party.

In Tucumán, the situation was similar, although in this case, Peronist Governor Juan Manzur, who had served as deputy governor (2011–2015) and twice as governor (2015–2019 and 2019–2023), had previously asked the provincial high court to determine whether he was eligible to run for deputy governor in 2023. The high court ruled that he could run, and after this ruling, the opposition went straight to the Supreme Court, without first filing a case before the provincial high court. The Supreme Court ruled against Manzur on the same day it ruled against Uñac's reelection in San Juan. Manzur did not postpone the elections and instead stepped down as a candidate. A new candidate for deputy governor, Miguel Acevedo, was designated on the ticket headed by Osvaldo Jaldo. In the elections, Jaldo and Acevedo won by a landslide, and the ruling Peronist Party did not lose the province.

In 2023, the opposition in the province of Formosa filed a claim before the Supreme Court, alleging that the provincial constitution contradicted the principle of the republican form of government enshrined in the national Constitution because it allowed provincial governors to be reelected indefinitely. The governor of Formosa, Gildo Insfrán, had been in office since 1995 and had previously been deputy governor from 1987 to 1995. The province of Formosa presented its case before the Court and argued that in this case, the Supreme Court did not have jurisdiction to intervene because there was no ambiguity in the interpretation of the provincial constitution, which clearly did not establish any limits to the reelection of governors. The Supreme Court refrained from issuing a ruling and neither dismissed nor validated the opposition's claim. It allowed the provincial elections to go ahead as scheduled, and Peronist Governor Gildo Insfrán was reelected for an eighth consecutive term.

In July 2023, the Supreme Court ruled in a case about the eligibility of a candidate to run for head of government (governor) of the autonomous City of Buenos Aires.[14] For all purposes, the city of Buenos Aires has the same autonomy as a province, but it only gained this status after the 1994 constitutional reform. The City of Buenos Aires is considered one of the most plural districts, and three different parties have governed the district since it became autonomous. In 1996, the city elected its first head of government, Fernando de la Rúa, from the Radical Party. In 2000, Aníbal Ibarra, from the Frepaso centre-left alliance, was elected and reelected in 2003. In 2007, Mauricio Macri, from the centre-right Pro Party, won the elections and was reelected in 2011. From this point onwards, the Pro Party won all elections for head of government in the city. In 2023, Jorge Macri, Mauricio Macri's cousin, was nominated to run by the Pro Party (part of the Juntos por el Cambio coalition). His nomination was contested because he did not fulfil the residency requirements established in Article 97 of the autonomous city's constitution, which states that candidates "must be natives of the city or have had regular or permanent residence in it for no less than five years prior to the election date"[15] (author's translation). Jorge Macri fulfilled neither of these criteria. Until a month before his nomination, he had been mayor of the district of Vicente López in the province of Buenos Aires. He was born in the city of Tandil, province of Buenos Aires, and had resided in that same province during his tenure as mayor of Vicente López between 2011 and 2023. Furthermore, between 2005 and 2011 he had been a provincial deputy in the Buenos Aires province Legislature.

The left-wing Parido Obrero (Workers Party) filed a claim before the city's electoral court, claiming that Jorge Macri was not eligible to run for head of government. The electoral court ruled that the residency requirements had been fulfilled when the candidate resided in the city of Buenos Aires between 1987 and 1999,[16] although the constitution is explicit when it says that the residency requirements must be fulfilled "in the five years prior to the election." The electoral court's decision was controversial because it ignored the precedent of a similar case in 2010, when national Deputy Adrián Pérez (Coalición Cívica Party) asked the City of Buenos Aires high court to determine whether he could run for head of government in the 2011 elections. Pérez had been elected deputy for the province of Buenos Aires, and he claimed that his residency was split between the two districts. On that occasion, the high court ruled that he did not fulfil the residency requirements and was therefore not eligible to run. With regard to Jorge Macri's candidacy, the electoral court stated in its ruling that this precedent did not constitute a "majoritarian juridical rule" that could be applied to this case.[17] In parallel, the opposition party took the case to the Supreme Court. The Court ruled that it did not have original jurisdiction – that is, that it could only intervene through appellate jurisdiction – because there was no federal matter at stake and that the City of Buenos Aires high court should determine Jorge Macri's eligibility to run.[18] A few days later, the City of Buenos Aires high court ruled that any objections to a candidate should have been taken up with his political party's electoral board before filing a case with the electoral court and that it therefore had no jurisdiction to issue a ruling.[19] The opposition then appealed to the Supreme Court, but the Court did not issue a ruling before the elections and allowed them to go ahead.

In the end, Jorge Macri ran for head of government and won the elections. His election meant the creation of a political dynasty in the City of Buenos Aires. This case is significant because it illustrates that the democratic deficits examined in this chapter, which include the development of political dynasties and the propensity of local courts to rule in favour of incumbents or ruling parties, are not limited to peripheral provinces but are also present in the nation's most developed and pluralistic district. The case raises important questions about how the rule of law is applied at the subnational level and about the close links between local courts and subnational ruling elites. In many of the cases analyzed in this section, provincial high courts ruled in favour of the incumbent governor and enabled them to run for office even when the provincial constitution clearly stated that they were not eligible. These situations occurred in subnational districts governed by different political parties and in both peripheral and central districts like the City of Buenos Aires. It evidences a lack of independence between the judiciary and the executive in many subnational districts. Local judicial authorities have too often interpreted the provincial constitution to favour incumbent governors or parties, although they knew that it was likely that the Supreme Court would then overrule their decision.

The Supreme Court has played a key role since the transition to democracy, exercising oversight and acting as a regulator in conflicts over who is eligible to run for executive office at the subnational level. Several of the cases that reached the Supreme Court required the interpretation of articles stating that if an incumbent governor had previously been deputy governor, or if the incumbent governor ran for deputy governor, this period was included in the count of how many consecutive periods an individual could run for executive office.

Provincial constitutions make this provision to prevent an incumbent governor from being elected deputy governor and then assuming another period as governor if their running mate resigns. The Supreme Court has been consistent in its interpretation that both the governor and deputy governor are part of the executive. Other cases referred to the period that counted as the first period in office after a constitutional reform. The case of the City of Buenos Aires was the first case in which the Court was asked to determine whether a candidate fulfilled the residency requirements established by the local constitution, and it ruled that it had no jurisdiction.

Conclusions

Political competition varies greatly within Argentina. While some provinces exhibit frequent turnover for executive office and respect reelection norms, other provinces have developed political dynasties, alternate power among dynasties, and governors have sought to remain in office longer than the constitution mandated, often with the complicity of local courts. However, the Supreme Court has exercised oversight of subnational politics in electoral conflicts such as those described in this chapter, and its decisions have been authoritative.[20]

Political leaders' reluctance to give up office or lose control of their districts tests the limits of democracy and the rule of law. This chapter explores two ways in which this occurs at the subnational level: political dynasties in subnational executives, and governors' attempts to seek reelection beyond constitutional term limits. The first dimension belongs to the realm of informal structures and practices, while the second refers to the role of formal institutions and how the rule of law is enforced in subnational politics. Supreme Court oversight is key to preventing incumbent governors from being reelected beyond the number of terms stipulated by provincial constitutions. But the Court has little power to regulate informal structures and practices such as political dynasties because political dynasties develop within the rules of the game of democracy. In two of the cases analyzed in this chapter, a political dynasty arose after a Supreme Court ruling, while in a third case, the dynastic candidate failed to be elected. In the case of Santiago del Estero described in the previous section, after the Supreme Court ruled that the incumbent governor was not eligible to run for a third consecutive term in office, his wife was designated as the candidate and won the elections, thus creating a political dynasty. The Court was able to prevent an unconstitutional interpretation of reelection norms, but the unintended consequence of this ruling was the creation of a new political dynasty in the province. In the case of the City of Buenos Aires, the Supreme Court ruled that it did not have jurisdiction to determine a candidate's eligibility to run, and the ruling by the local electoral court and high court enabled the development of the autonomous city's first political dynasty. The case of San Juan illustrates that dynastic candidates cannot rely solely on name recognition to win elections and that the decision to name a relative as a candidate can prove to be a bad strategy.

Although the Supreme Court is authoritative, the timing of its rulings has at times been questioned. Democracy requires an electoral calendar that is respected, and the timing of elections can have diverse effects. The Supreme Court has, on occasion, waited until the last minute to issue rulings declaring that a candidate was not eligible to run or to postpone elections, as some of the cases described in this chapter show. This can affect the Court's credibility and perceptions of impartiality.

In the cases analyzed in this chapter, local high courts usually ruled in favour of incumbents, even when they knew that their rulings would be scrutinized by the Supreme Court. This shows an important degree of complicity between local courts and subnational executives. The cases highlight the difficulty of achieving effective checks and balances at the subnational level and point to the complex interactions between courts and executives, and between different levels of government, regardless of whether the province in question is developed or peripheral, more plural or less plural.

Subnational political elites engage in diverse strategies to remain in office or to maintain their power. Political dynasties are one way of ensuring dominion over a subnational entity, but this says nothing about how these dynasties govern and what policy preferences they pursue. Further work is needed to determine the causal links between political dynasties and development in specific cases, but the overview of the cases surveyed in this chapter provides some initial insights. As noted, some political dynasties of both developed and peripheral provinces have promoted developmentalist policies, while others have not. Governors of both developed and peripheral provinces, and of different political parties, have sought to maintain their hold on power beyond their term limits in diverse ways. The two dimensions of subnational politics analyzed in this chapter and the case studies sketched out in the analysis show that subnational politics is best understood as an entangled process in which formal and informal institutions, structures, and practices coexist and mutually reinforce each other. This chapter provides examples of such subnational entanglements.

Notes

1 See Dal Bó et al. (2009); Brian Feinstein (2010); Kurtz (1989); Smith (2018); Asako et al. (2015); van Coppenolle (2017); Chandra & Umaira (2011); Chhibber (2011); Chandra (2016); Camp (1982); Vilas (1992); Rossi (2014); Querubin (2011); Cruz et al. (2017); Mendoza et al. (2012); Amundsen (2013).

2 In the case of Córdoba, the founder of the dynasty was Governor José Manuel de la Sota's father-in-law, who was elected in 1958, so only one member of the dynasty governed after the transition to democracy.

3 During part of the period, the Radical Party was part of the Cambiemos and then Juntos por el Cambio label, as was the Pro Party. Here, I consider the governor's party affiliation.
4 In Corrientes, the Romero/Romero Feris dynasty included governors from the Peronist Party in the 1970s, from the Autonomista Party in the 1980s, and from the Partido Nuevo in the 1990s.
5 This was the case in Corrientes, Santiago del Estero, and Catamarca, for example.
6 At present, only two provinces allow the indefinite reelection of governors – Formosa and Catamarca – but in the 1990s, several provinces had no term limits at all for governors.
7 As noted, Santa Fe and Mendoza are the only provinces that do not allow the governor's reelection.
8 Supreme Court ruling 317:1195, Partido Justicialista vs. Santa Fe Province, 6 October 1994.
9 See Transitory Clause No. 6, Constitution of Santiago del Estero. Available at: chrome-extension://efaidnbmnnnibpcajpcglclefindmkaj/https://www.argentina.gob.ar/sites/default/files/constitucion_de_la_provincia_de_santiago_del_estero.pdf. Accessed on 9 May 2024.
10 Weretilneck belongs to the provincial party Juntos Somos Río Negro.
11 See Constitution of Río Negro. Available at: chrome-extension://efaidnbmnnnibpcajpcglclefindmkaj/https://www.congreso.gob.ar/constituciones/RIO-NEGRO.pdf. Accessed on 9 May 2024.
12 They had originally been scheduled for 27 May 2019.
13 The Supreme Court has both original and appellate jurisdiction. Original jurisdiction means that the Court is the first and only court to hear a case. Original jurisdiction is normally limited to a few cases. Appellate jurisdiction means that the Court has jurisdiction to review the decisions of lower courts (in these cases, the provincial high courts). Oversight over subnational elections is usually exercised through appellate jurisdiction, as was the case in the other cases mentioned in this section.
14 The autonomous City of Buenos Aires has the same competences as a province, but its executive office is head of government instead of governor. For all purposes, they have the same responsibilities, autonomy, and competences.
15 See Constitution of the Autonomous City of Buenos Aires. Available at: chrome-extension://efaidnbmnnnibpcajpcglclefindmkaj/https://www.argentina.gob.ar/sites/default/files/constitucion-caba.pdf. Accessed on 28 May 2024.
16 See Electoral Court ruling ELE 74159/2023-0, available at: chrome-extension://efaidnbmnnnibpcajpcglclefindmkaj/https://electoralcaba.gob.ar/uploads/resoluciones/SE_RESUELVE_IMPUGNACION_JORGE_MACRI.pdf. Accessed on 28 May 2024.
17 See Electoral Court ruling ELE 74159/2023-0, op. cit.
18 See Supreme Court ruling CSJ 1300/2023, available at: chrome-extension://efaidnbmnnnibpcajpcglclefindmkaj/file:///Users/Jacqueline/Downloads/57661.pdf. Accessed on 29 May 2024.
19 See City of Buenos Aires High Court ruling INC 74159/2023-1, available at: https://drive.google.com/file/d/1Jt6qiCKvhjvLeQxFeHXIf0Xlj1Hc3d1e/view. Accessed on 29 29 2024.
20 Another – more extreme – form of control of subnational politics, which I discuss elsewhere, is federal intervention, which involves the removal of elected authorities by the national executive. See Behrend (2016).

References

Amundsen, I. (2013). Democratic Dynasties? Internal Party Democracy in Bangladesh. *Party Politics* 22(1), 1–10. https://doi.org/10.1177/1354068813511378

Asako, Y., Iida, T., Matsubayashi, T. & Ueda, M. (2015). Dynastic Politicians: Theory and Evidence from Japan. *Japanese Journal of Political Science* 16(1), 5–32. https://doi.org/10.1017/S146810991400036X

Behrend, J. (2011). The Unevenness of Democracy at the Subnational Level: Provincial Closed Games in Argentina. *Latin American Research Review* 46(1), 150–176. https://doi.org/10.1353/lar.2011.0013

Behrend, J. (2016). Federal Intervention and Subnational Democratization in Argentina: A Comparative Perspective. In Behrend, J. & Whitehead, L., eds. *Illiberal Practices: Territorial Variance within Large Federal Democracies*. Johns Hopkins University Press.

Behrend, J. (2021a). Political Dynasties and Democracy in Contemporary Mexico. *Latin American Policy* 12(2), 385–404. https://doi.org/10.1111/lamp.12237

Behrend, J. (2021b). Dinastías políticas y democracia: una propuesta conceptual. *Revista Agenda Política*. 9(3), 174–189. https://doi.org/10.31990/agenda.2021.3.6

Behrend, J. (2024). *Database of Argentine political families and dynasties*. Unpublished.

Behrend, J. & Bianchi M. (2017). Estructura económica y política subnacional en Argentina. *Caderno CRH* 30(80), 217–235. https://doi.org/10.1590/S0103-49792017000200002

Behrend, J. & Whitehead, L. (2016a). Setting the Comparative Agenda: Territorially Uneven Democratization Processes in Large Federations. In Behrend, J. & Whitehead, L., eds. *Illiberal Practices: Territorial Variance within Large Federal Democracies*. Johns Hopkins University Press.

Behrend, J. & Whitehead, L. (2016b). The Struggle for Subnational Democracy. *Journal of Democracy* 27(2), 155–169. https://doi.org/10.1353/jod.2016.0023

Berruecos García Travesí, S. & Whitehead, L. (2021). Constitutional controversies in the subnational democratization of Mexico, 1994–2021. *Latin American Policy* 12(2), 405–423. https://doi.org/10.1111/lamp.12229

Camp, R. A. (1982). Family Relationships in Mexican Politics: A Preliminary View. *The Journal of Politics* 44(3), 848–862. https://doi.org/10.2307/2130521

Chandra, K. (2016). Democratic Dynasties: State, Party, and Family in Contemporary Indian Politics. In Chandra K., ed. *Democratic Dynasties: State, Party, and Family in Contemporary Indian Politics*. Cambridge University Press.

Chandra, K. & Umaira, W. (2011). India's Democratic Dynasties. *Seminar* 622: 14–21. Available at: https://www.india-seminar.com/2011/622/622_kanchan_&_wamiq.htm

Chhibber, P. (2011). Dynastic Parties: Organization, Finance and Impact. *Party Politics* 19(2), 277–295. https://doi.org/10.1177/1354068811406995

Constitución de la Ciudad Autónoma dc Buenos Aires. Available at: chrome-extension://efaidnbmnnnibpcajpcglclefindmkaj/https://www.argentina.gob.ar/sites/default/files/constitucion-caba.pdf

Constitución de la provincia de Santiago del Estero. Available at: chrome-extension://efaidnbmnnnibpcajpcglclefindmkaj/https://www.argentina.gob.ar/sites/default/files/constitucion_de_la_provincia_de_santiago_del_estero.pdf Accessed on May 9th, 2024.

Constitución de la provincia de Río Negro. Available at: chrome-extension://efaidnbmnnnibpcajpcglclefindmkaj/https://www.congreso.gob.ar/constituciones/RIO-NEGRO.pdf. Accessed on May 9th, 2024.

Cruz, C., Labonne, J. & Querubin, P. (2017). Politician Family Networks and Electoral Outcomes: Evidence from the Philippines. *American Economic Review* 107(10), 3006–3037. https://doi.org/10.1257/aer.20150343

Dahl, R. A. (1961). *Who Governs? Democracy and Power in an American City*. Yale University Press.

Dal Bó, E., Dal Bó, P. & Snyder, J. (2009). Political Dynasties. *The Review of Economic Studies* 76(1), 115–142. https://doi.org/10.1111/j.1467-937X.2008.00519.x

Eaton, K. (2017). *Territory and Ideology in Latin America: Policy Conflicts between National and Subnational Governments*. Oxford University Press.

Feinstein, B. (2010). The Dynasty Advantage: Family Ties in Congressional Elections. *Legislative Studies Quarterly* 35(4), 571–597. https://doi.org/10.3162/036298010793322366

Giraudy, A., Moncada, E. & Snyder, R., eds. (2019). *Inside Countries: Subnational Research in Comparative Politics*. Cambridge University Press.

Kapiszewski, D. (2012). *High Courts and Economic Governance in Argentina and Brazil*. Cambridge University Press.

Karamaneff, L. (2022). *¿Desarrollo económico sin capacidades estatales? El caso de la promoción industrial en Argentina (1982–1992)*. Doctoral thesis, School of Politics and Government, Universidad Nacional de San Martín. Available at: https://ri.unsam.edu.ar/handle/123456789/2160

Kenawas, Y. (2015). *The Rise of Political Dynasties in a Democratic Society*. EDGS Working Paper, Northwestern University.

Kurtz, II, D. M. (1989). The Political Family: A Contemporary View. *Sociological Perspectives* 32(3), 331–352. https://doi.org/10.2307/1389121

Kurtz, II, D. M. (2001). First Families in Japan, Mexico, and the United States: 1946-2001. *International Journal of Comparative Sociology* 42(5), 461–478. https://doi.org/10.1163/156913201753397675

Mendoza, R. U. Beja Jr E. L., Venida, V. S. & Yap, D. B. (2012). An Empirical Analysis of Political Dynasties in the 15th Philippine Congress. *Philippine Political Science Journal* 33(2), 132–145. https://doi.org/10.2139/ssrn.1969605

Querubin, P. (2011). *Political Reform and Elite Persistence: Term Limits and Political Dynasties in the Philippines*. Harvard Academy for International and Area Studies.

Rossi, M. A. (2014). Family Business: Causes and Consequences of Political Dynasties. Documento de Trabajo No. 114, Universidad de San Andrés. Available at: chrome-extension://efaidnbmnnnibpcajpcglclefindmkaj/https://webacademicos.udesa.edu.ar/pub/econ/doc114.pdf

Secretaría de Minería (2022). Empleo por provincia de la minería argentina. Available at: chrome-extension://efaidnbmnnnibpcajpcglclefindmkaj/https://www.argentina.gob.ar/sites/default/files/2022.10_empleo_provincial.pdf. Accessed on May 30th, 2024.

Sidel, J. T. (2014). Economic Foundations of Subnational Authoritarianism: Insights and Evidence from Qualitative and Quantitative Research. *Democratization* 21(1), 161–184. https://doi.org/10.1080/13510347.2012.725725

Smith, D. M. (2018). *Dynasties and Democracy: The Inherited Incumbency Advantage in Japan*. Stanford University Press.

Snyder, R. (2001). Scaling Down: The Subnational Comparative Method. *Studies in Comparative International Development* 36, 93–110. https://doi.org/10.1007/BF02687586

Van Coppenolle, B. (2017). Political Dynasties in the UK House of Commons: The Null Effect of Narrow Electoral Selection. *Legislative Studies Quarterly* 42(3), 449–475. https://doi.org/0.1111/lsq.12164

Vilas, C. (1992). Family Affairs: Class, Lineage and Politics in Contemporary Nicaragua. *Journal of Latin American Studies* 24(2), 309–341. https://doi.org/10.1017/S0022216X00023403

Whitehead, L &. Behrend, J. (2016). Uneven Processes and Multiple Pathways. In Behrend, J & Whitehead, L., eds. *Illiberal Practices: Territorial Variance within Large Federal Democracies*. Johns Hopkins University Press.

7 The effects of warring and civil oligarchs on Colombia's subnational democracy

Jan Boesten and Daniel Llanos

The Colombian puzzle – relatively robust democratic institutions with high levels of (political/criminal) violence – relates to an apparent core/periphery divide: violence is most often concentrated in the latter, while the former may even enjoy boom cycles at the very same time. Behind this divide lie subnational institutions that have very little in common with the democratic promises of the country's constitution. These institutions, elsewhere identified as subnational oligarchic citizenship defects (Boesten 2022b), cannot be solely reduced to the effects of armed actors nor nefarious political actors. Rather, these two factors work in tandem in a functional alliance, and the argument of this chapter is that oligarchic modes of rule can conceptually bridge these apparent contradictions.

Jeffrey Winters defines oligarchy[1] as "the politics of wealth defence by materially endowed actors"; variation emerges via the degree to which oligarchs are involved in the provision of coercion to defend that material wealth (2011: 7). Two types of oligarchic rule matter for this chapter: warring and civil oligarchs. Warring oligarchies are marked by *warlordism*, while civil oligarchs are entirely disarmed (2011: 35–36). In legal theoretical terminology, between them runs the line of legality, and it is precisely in this context – the margin of legality[2] – that the Colombian case can provide new insights into the traits of oligarchic rule. The longevity of Colombia's experience with armed non-state actors (hereafter: ANSAs) financing their coercive capabilities through the drug trade, combined with political clans[3] that divide public offices amongst themselves, has produced an oligarchic system that is internally differentiated and provides functional benefits to each side.

The novelty of the argument here is that behind the internal differentiation sits an oligarchic system that exhibits the presence of both types of oligarchs, warring and civil, who operate autonomously from each other, yet are informally linked. Their inter-relations are often contractual rather than organic, and accordingly unstable (Duncan 2006), but nevertheless sufficiently advantageous to both sides to produce a durable sub-optimal outcome: ineffective state institutions. What is more, since civil oligarchs and their clans are competing on the legal playing field, and warring oligarchs, functionally dissociated, compete on the extra-legal playing field, this configuration also explains why competitive elections are held, but the rule of law is weak. The

DOI: 10.4324/9781003519195-7

contribution to theories of oligarchy lies in the importance of the uncertainty of legality that creates that divide. After all, Winters argues that oligarchies operate at an optimum "during 'the politics of the ordinary'" (2011: 18), when oligarchs can best bring their versatile material and power resources to subordinate the "atomized common citizens across society" (19). The Colombian case displays oligarchic structures that are seemingly stable and persistent in a political playing field *and* where linkages with the politics of the extra-ordinary play a crucial role.

In order to make the case for Colombia's peculiarity in the theatre of different oligarchies, we will explore the rise and transformation of the paramilitary phenomenon in the Caribbean region from the mid-1990s (after the fall of the large cartels), through their demobilization in the 2000s, until their restructuring in the course of peace processes with the AUC (Spanish abbreviation for United Self-Defence Forces of Colombia) and FARC-EP (Spanish acronym for Revolutionary Armed Forces of Colombia-People's Army; hereafter simply FARC).[4] It highlights the *contractual* relations between political clans and paramilitaries that (informally) connect the coercive capacities of the latter with the political hegemony of the former.

Between warring and civil oligarchy: The characteristics of oligarchic modes of rule

In Colombia, oligarchic rule occurs at *the margin of legality*. This phrase, encountered in research interviews with judges of the Constitutional Court (Boesten 2022a), formulates a key contention of the Colombian puzzle in legal theoretical terms: its inability to guarantee the inalienable right to physical integrity. This propensity for violent conflict places the question of legality itself, and not regime contentions, as central to understanding Colombia's democratic deficits. Scholars have identified Colombia's democratic defects outside the polyarchic regime that nevertheless affect the republican dimension of weak public institutions (Bejarano & Pizarro 2005: 237; Boesten 2022b). Sociologically, the margin of legality inevitably involves exploring the source of law's positivity: the monopoly of violence (Weber 1968). Therefore, if Colombia's primary democratic deficits are subnational oligarchic structures outside the institutional playing field (Boesten 2022b), we must understand how the ineffective monopoly of violence breeds those armed non-state actors that undermine key republican rights – the right to vote and freedom of assembly – through locally enforced territorial control.

If we disaggregate the state of democracy in Colombia according to the template proposed by Cameron and Jaramillo (2022; see Table 7.1 below), we see that one element of the electoral component is at odds with the others: electoral processes at times are very fraudulent, while virtually all other elements are exemplary.

Table 7.1 The disaggregation of democracy in Colombia

Democratic component		*Score*	*Evidence*
Electoral component	Officials acquiring the right through periodic election	2	Elections are held without restrictions, and results are respected.
	Electoral processes are not fraudulent	−1	Coercion and vote buying prior to casting votes fundamentally damage the accuracy of the process.
	Active right to vote	2	Active right to vote is not restricted.
	Passive right to vote	2	Passive right to vote is not restricted.
Concomitant conditions	Freedom of expression	−1	Ownership concentration of outlets and violence against journalists.
	Freedom of association/ assembly	−1	The systematic assassination of social leaders.
	Alternative sources of information	1	Colombia's rich journalistic tradition produces a wide variety of journalistic outputs.
	Access to justice and other rights	2/1	The tutela has broadened access to justice fundamentally and extensively. Corruption in the Supreme Court is tainting the judiciary's reputation.
Democratic State	Rule of law and horizontal accountability	1	The Constitutional Court's horizontal accountability is exemplary.
	Civilian oversight of armed forces	0	Colombia's army is apolitical but susceptible to cooperation with illegal armed actors.
	Nonelected officials do not arbitrarily terminate terms	2	No evidence of the termination of terms of elected officials
Citizenship Capacities	Citizens are agents and participate in choices that affect their lives	0	Inequality provides opportunity structures for the illicit economy, armed actors, and clientele relations.
	Citizens are free from violence, intimidation, and discrimination	−2	Endemic violence undercuts collective action at the local level.

Source: Authors (The scores run from +2 through 0 to −2).

Behind this defect lie the effects of armed non-state actors' locally enforced territorial control, the same flaw that undermines "citizenship capacities." Colombia's democracy combines highly authoritarian elements (armed non-state actors exercising local coercive control with few constraints) with democratic elements (fair elections and a functioning liberal constitution). Between these two poles sits a third element: the presence of family clans dominating regional political offices, whose exercise of power blurs not only private and public interests, but also legality and illegality. More precisely still: paramilitary structures' competitive advantage over other non-state armed actors was their ability to delegate votes (Acemoglu et al. 2013) to preferred candidates.[5] It opened opportunity structures for those groups to link up with the lawful side of the margins of legality. The recipients of those votes evidently also received tangible benefits with the added advantage that they did not have to fully embrace the illegality of the organizations that procured the votes – agreements between these actors were informal, and plausible deniability was an important caveat of this arrangement. This bargain at the nexus between legality and illegality, which co-opts but does not destroy the electoral component of Colombia's democracy, produces an equilibrium between legal politics and illegal armed actors, which is violent and fragile at times, but nevertheless robust in that it reproduces, rather than consumes, itself over time. The result is a locked-in suboptimal outcome with relative stability that sets detrimental incentives for the monopolization of violence (Acemoglu et al. 2013); this link also creates the space for oligarchic modes of rule in Colombia.

The functional equilibrium between actors populating the legal and extra-legal spectrum of the margin of legality poses some challenges to the definition of oligarchy. To foreshadow my argument, and also limit the discussion to key models, we can list the central elements of how oligarchy functions on Colombia's Caribbean Coast: (1) the presence of families that dominate politics with little regard to the difference between private and public; (2) civil and warring oligarchs coexist, have acted in concert at the margin of legality in certain regions, but are not identical, and their interests also have clashed; (3) oligarchy is said to best function in the politics of the ordinary (Winters 2011), but the fact that this occurs at the margin of legality means that the politics of the extraordinary are never far away. This section will lay out the definitional foundation of oligarchy, its effects on politics, and the variation in the monopolization of violence it produces.

It is conventionally argued, with Aristotle, that oligarchy is a deviant form of rule, in which the few govern the many myopically in their own interest. Yet, as Winters observes, "[i]t comes as a surprise to many social scientists that the number of people ruling is not the primary foundation of Aristotle's theory of oligarchy or democracy" (2011: 2). Aristotle agrees, arguing that "the real thing in which democracy and oligarchy differ from each other is poverty and wealth, and wherever some rule on account of wealth, whether a minority or a majority, this is necessarily an oligarchy" (1984: 96). Winters is therefore correct to observe that oligarchs are "actors who command and control massive concentrations of material resources that can be deployed to defend or enhance their personal wealth and exclusive social position" (2011: 6) and that generically "[o]ligarchy refers to the politics of wealth defence by materially endowed actors" (7). The crucial point of this theorization is that it can neither neglect the political aspects of oligarchy – power and control – nor the economic basis of rule – concentration of material wealth. "It is a perspective influenced as much by Marx's historical materialism as by Weber's emphasis on the locus of the means of coercion in his classic definition of the modern state," Winters implores (10).

Power, coercion, and the modern state add important caveats to the conceptual analysis of oligarchy, because the role of coercive power "as a component of individual power profiles has changed so radically over the course of civilization" (Winters 2011: 15). The monopoly of violence in the hands of *one* legitimate actor is the defining difference from pre-modern forms of rule, and, since the modern state effectively disarmed individuals, "the most significant historical line of demarcation among oligarchies divides those before and after the rise of the modern nation-state" (32). Incidentally, this line of demarcation, when translated into legal positivistic terms, is the same line that runs between legality and illegality – and the margins of legality extend from that line.

Given it is precisely the ineffectiveness of Colombia's state institutions that has allowed space for ANSAs to compromise the monopoly of violence (Boesten 2022b), it matters greatly how Winters translates that line of demarcation into types of oligarchy. His differentiation is contingent on four dimensions: involvement in the provision of coercion, involvement in governance, factionalism between oligarchs, and (internal or external) constraints on them. Two models that derive from Winters' categorization are important for this essay: *warring* and *civil oligarchy*.[6] When fragmentation and lateral conflicts between oligarchs preying on territorial and social control are prevalent, Winters identifies a *warring oligarchy* (essentially warlordism). It is marked by the coterminous importance of coercive and material power resources. Sultanistic and civil oligarchs have surrendered their coercive capacities; in the case of the former to an individual oligarch (hence the non-application to the Colombian case), and in the latter to an institutionalized body of laws that provide external coercive guarantees (for their property claims).

It is, of course, peculiar that we can identify the persistent coexistence of warring and civil oligarchies in Colombia – ostensibly, the polar opposite on Winters' spectrum of modes of rule. Yet, the Colombian case and its eponymous puzzle are known to traverse categorizations that, at least intuitively, do not make good pairs: democratic but violent, deep constitutional traditions with equally profound traditions of illegality. This also applies to oligarchic modes of rule in Colombia: civil and warring oligarchs operate autonomously from each other and fulfil particular functions of local coercive control and national political brokerage – functions that have benefits to the respective other side. Interestingly, scholars have increasingly argued that it is not the absence of the state *per sé* that presents the biggest challenge to local governance and the rule of law, but how other (non-state) actors fill those spaces in concert with state and legal institutions (Ballvé 2020). Even after peace processes with the FARC-EP and the AUC targeting those extra-legal actors, patterns of violence have reappeared, accompanied by political structures that replicate previous political networks (Boesten 2022b). The politics of the ordinary and extraordinary remain intrinsically bound up with one another at the margin of legality, producing highly corrupted patterns of democratic competition paired with a context of ANSAs obfuscating the certainty of legality. Both phenomena conjoined together – a corrupted version of the politics of the ordinary combined with the uncertainty of legality – best explain the coexistence of the ineffective monopolization of the legitimate means of violence and relatively democratic institutions in Colombia's Caribbean.

The trajectory of paramilitarism in Colombia's counter/insurgency war

Scholars (Duncan 2006) distinguish between three generations of paramilitaries between 1968 and 2005 when the Uribe government passed the Justice and Peace Process for the demobilization of the AUC (Table 7.2). With the implementation of the peace processes with the AUC (2006) and the FARC (2017) under way, we are now in a new, post-counterinsurgency phase of Colombia's conflict, in which ANSAs combine various traits of their predecessors but are much more

Table 7.2 Periodization of paramilitary structures in Colombia

Period	*Characterization of paramilitary structures*	*Socio-political traits*
1968–1975	Legalization of vigilante groups against guerrilla	Counterinsurgency strategy of Cold War/National Security Strategy
1975–1995	Private armies of assassins (*sicarios*) by cartels	Contract enforcement in the narcotics trade
1995–2006/2017	Armed non-state actor/warlordism	Territorial control and political networks
2006/2017–present	Criminal bands (BACRIMs) in post-counterinsurgency conflict/warlordism	Combination of some territorial control, contract enforcement, and governance

Source: Authors.

criminally inclined.[7] In its entire history, paramilitary groups displayed two key characteristics that remain prevalent with their successor groups today: linkages with landed interests and alliances with the state. The first generation of paramilitaries were private vigilante groups, which the state legalized through Law 48 in 1968 as part of the National Security Strategy of the Cold War. The second generation refers to the cartels' armies of sicarios. The third generation of paramilitaries is the culmination of the paramilitary project into a political project under the umbrella of the AUC (López 2010). The latest incarnation consists of those post-AUC groups (and post-FARC groups) that ultimately did not disarm, have become much more criminal than their predecessor groups, but combine criminal motivations with their governance know-how.

From the very beginning, paramilitarism was part of the state's counterinsurgency strategy advised by the United States.[8] When Congress passed Law 48 in 1968, several armed groups (the FARC and ELN in 1964) had officially declared themselves Marxist/Castroist guerrillas. Landowners' legalized vigilante groups, although part of the state's strategy to thwart communist insurgencies, were never included in the army's ranks (Duncan, 2006). This autonomy as an ANSA would only grow over the decades with the influx of illicit capital and is an important caveat for our understanding of the modes of oligarchic rule in the Colombian Caribbean.

The modern paramilitary project grew out of the riches of the drug economy, but somewhat counterintuitively as the offspring of the cartels that would ultimately devour their flamboyant capos. In fact, it is Escobar's downfall that suggests the importance of the functional separation of oligarchic roles at the margins of legality. The potential oligarch cannot be both civil and warring simultaneously. Importantly, his empire lacked the core attribute of paramilitaries, who became the main actors in the cocaine economy: territorial control.[9] Already in the 1980s, something called *traquetización* opened the margins of legality for actors to move beyond contract enforcement in the illicit economy.[10] Rank and file members of the cartels laundered their money by buying land in the countryside. The FARC's extortion strategy provided the fuel that fused them with the traditional landowning class. This new social class, rich in illicit resources and with little interest in sharing either wealth or access to power (Gutiérrez-Sanín & Vargas 2017), reaped mutual benefits: landowners could finance their security, while *narcos* gained status in the social fabric of rural society (Gutiérrez Sanín & Barón 2006: 44; Duncan 2006). The intrinsic competitive advantage of territorial control in the cocaine economy became evident when state prosecution closed in on cartel leaders. Running from state prosecution, the former capos were trapped in deals of protection with those *narcos* exercising territorial control. These deals were made in a disequilibrium and the new *señores de la Guerra* had no obligations to comply. The result was that former capos became dependents of warlords, effectively reversing the hierarchy in the illegal economy (Duncan 2006: 234; Ávila Martínez 2010: 109). Through the lens of oligarchic theory, this process did not merely fuse together a heterogeneous group of landowners and drug traffickers; it created actors for whom material wealth and coercive capacities were coterminous with their political power.

Escobar's death made the guerrilla the prime public security target, and the symbiosis between sectors of the armed forces and paramilitaries further deepened through vigilante policy programmes and, subsequently, through the formation of an umbrella organization, AUC. The CONVIVIR programme (Spanish acronym for Vigilante Cooperatives and Private Security, 1994–1997), essentially a rendition of the 1968 law to legalize self-defence groups, supported the formation of "neighbourhood watch groups," thereby setting incentives for the privatization of security in the periphery. The political initiative came from governors who were closer to FARC activity in Colombia's periphery – above all, Álvaro Uribe from Antioquia.[11] Its effects were twofold. First, it was a crucial *legal* vehicle for expansion, cementing informal alliances of regional politicians to counter the strengthening guerrilla. Second, it enabled paramilitaries to expand precisely into those key areas of the *illegal* economy that had come under FARC control or presence, without facing consequences from the state, as its counternarcotics policies were often corrupted by counterinsurgency strategies.[12] After the illegalization of the CONVIVIRs, the various vigilante groups pulled together into a confederation under the leadership of the Castaños, the AUC. Defending the status quo – ostensibly, a capitalist, constitutional democracy as opposed to a classless utopia – served as the bonding mechanism for relatively autonomous coercive bodies.[13]

The third generation of paramilitaries came to full fruition when their coercive structures concocted parasitic relationships that functioned along state structures. Beyond police and army, this also had a political side and implied what Boesten (2022a) elsewhere termed the *parainstitutionalization* of Colombia's political regime: the co-optation of Colombia's representative institutions by armed non-state actors. This is the sphere where civil oligarchs reign and occupy various public offices in the regional state and Congress. The benefits of paramilitary expansion for civil oligarchs in Colombia's political institutions are manifold and interdependent. It shielded political elites from the electoral changes of the 1991 Constitution (Ávila Martínez 2010: 117). Colombia's presidentialism has always been checked by strong regional clusters of power (Archer and Shugart 1997), but national circumscription for Senate elections threatened those power bases. The same rule, however, also made regional power brokers independent from traditional party labels. It turns out that paramilitaries could mobilize voters, either through coercion or material persuasion, and thereby shield regional elites from constitutional changes. Electoral entrepreneurs, the atomization of the two-party system, and the wide-ranging criminalization of Colombia's legislature were the result (Gutiérrez Sanín 2007). Together, by functionally demarcating a legal and an extra-legal playing field, this informal set-up had clear advantages for all sides: regional elites could successfully compete in relatively democratic elections, and in exchange provided legislative support to legalize paramilitaries' land grabs, reduce their exposure to criminal prosecution, and assert favourable conditions in the peace process (López Hernández 2010; Acemoglu et al. 2013). In short, it created a system of wealth defence, in which civil and warring oligarchs operated side-by-side.

The picture that emerges from this short history of paramilitary structures is an entangled one, assembling multiple actors interacting or clashing with each other. The outcome is hardly contested: paramilitarism "united a good sector of Colombian society: *ganaderos* (agro industrialists), industrialists, narco-traffickers, militaries, some national politicians, and the entire regional elite" (Ávila Martínez 2010: 120). It is a functional whole that is internally separated into a legal and extra-legal playing field. Drug traffickers could not be politicians at the same time without facing serious consequences, as the fate of Pablo Escobar tells us.[14] Three factors stand out to explain the contingency of this process of differentiation: international obligations, constitutional politics, and the politics of monopolizing the means of violence. Modern vigilantism was born in the context of the counter/insurgency war that ended with the demobilization of the FARC-EP. Policies facilitating the privatization of security in Colombia's periphery emerged during the Cold War and were deepened in the war on drugs, thus always involving US interests – even if policies in either arena were often muddled and contradictory. As the far weaker "partner" in the US–Colombia relationship, the United States always had leverage over Colombia to strong-arm counterinsurgency and antinarcotics policies; becoming a narco-state, in which drug barons occupied public offices, was not a viable option, and the differentiation into a legal and extra-legal playing field was therefore also a function of international politics (Gutiérrez Sanín 2019).

Oligarchic modes of rule associated with paramilitarism emerged at the nexus between legality and illegality, not only in the criminal/legal sense but, more importantly, in the Weberian sense; in spaces where territorial control is at stake. The state, as the source of legality itself, demarcates the politics of the ordinary, in which political and economic elites operate, from the politics of the extraordinary, where the *Señores de la Guerra* operate in a contest over territorial control. The former terrain, while potentially very corrupt, must operate on the legal side of the medal, whereas the latter operates outside the factual legality of the Colombian state. The circumstance that Colombia boasts a constitutional democracy with a free public sphere reinforces this contingency, constraining political actors in how far they can venture into the extra-legal sphere. The next section will detail the trajectory of paramilitarism in the Caribbean, from the 90s to the early 2000s, to explore the emergence of two distinct types of oligarchic modes of rule: warring and civil oligarchies.

Warring oligarchs: Paramilitarism in the Caribbean

Colombia is a country with five macro-regions,[15] with distinct dynamics of violence resulting from the presence of a multitude of armed actors. Colombia's Caribbean consists of seven departments.[16] While it is true that the Colombian conflict, for the duration of the counter/insurgency war, was essentially a tripartite conflict between the state, various guerrilla groups, and paramilitary groups, this is not entirely the case here. Since the early '90s, "paramilitaries have taken root…and guerrilla groups have basically disappeared from the Caribbean coast."[17] This outcome is telling for our analysis of oligarchic modes of rule because it largely reflects and illustrates the above-cited process of *traquetización*. From the beginning of the narcotics trade in the late 1960s, when the marijuana boom produced the first trafficking routes to the United States, through Escobar's conversion of the same routes into cocaine highways to the hidden beaches of Florida, to the modern traffickers of the *Clan del Golfo*, the region has been of high strategic importance to various armed non-state actors. The trajectory described in this section shows the evolution of actors on either side of margins of legality (political clans and armed structures), their mutually beneficial but nevertheless fractious linkages, to argue that both operate with unique interests and constraints. Transgressing those boundaries carries existential risks to either side.

The International Federation for Human Rights (FIDH) writes that several guerrilla groups populated the region in the 1970s, "with differing levels of social, military, and territorial control" (2021: 9). The first to arrive was the ELN, but the FARC followed in the early to mid-1980s. Three fronts (9th, 59th, and 41st) formed the Caribbean bloc, "were spread across La Guajira, Magdalena and Cesar", and cooperated with the ELN. They used the area as a "refuge to mobilise their troops [as well as] exercise control over economically and militarily strategic areas" (FIDH 2021: 9). During the same period, drug lords were "purchasing their way into the landed gentry" (Dudley 2004: 62), not only transforming landowner class compositions but also initiating counter land reform by accruing around 15% of all arable land in rural Colombia – not least in the Caribbean Magdalena Medio Valley (Stone: 12). The FARC had taxed growers already in the 1970s, but after the 7th Guerrilla Conference in 1982, they "decided to impose taxes on traffickers themselves"; a strategic decision that helped them grow from 17 to 28 *frentes in* 1984. Traditional landowners themselves were either pressured into political agreements to redistribute land to *campesinos* or were directly extorted to pay the *vacuna* (Berman-Arévola 2021: 354). *Traqueticazión* in the Caribbean was driven by *narco* profits, social class transformations, and aggressive FARC strategies serving as the veneer that tied interests together. As elsewhere, vigilantism offered opportunities to escape those caveats of guerrilla presence.

The political clans that have been dominating the eastern part of the Caribbean Coast are well-known, and "have relied on the illicit economy to help them boost their standing, particularly contraband gasoline from Venezuela" (Stone 2016: 70). The most prominent are the Bautes, Rojas, Araújos, Nogueras, Pupos, Cote, and Gneccos, who comprise the civil oligarchy in the region, as they have limited coercive means.[18] They often have had overlapping interests (particularly, vis-à-vis the guerrilla), but also compete with each other for political offices and a larger share of the economic pie (including illicit profits). Yet, even if they are deeply entrenched in the illegal narcotics trade, they are not identical with warring oligarchs, for whom coercive capacities are coterminous with wealth protection. Rather, the different warring oligarchs offer a menu from which civil oligarchs can construct their web of allies to protect their wealth against guerrilla threats and increase leverage in the competition with other civil oligarchs. The other side of that medal is, however, that warring oligarchs also have a choice from various political clans to construct their web of allies that serves their interests.[19] This concoction is at the root of the uncertainty that has been befalling the Caribbean Coast since at least the late 1960s.

Jorge Gnecco and his clan serve as the example to illustrate civil oligarchs in Colombia's Caribbean because he ventured far to the illegal side of the margin of legality only to get burnt in his Icarian quest to play in both worlds. He was also the most important political person at the turn of the century in the region when AUC expansion was at its climax. The Gneccos were of contraband fame, originally arriving in the nineteenth century, and by the 1990s had built an important transportation hub in Santa Marta. The crown jewel in that trucking enterprise was contracts with coal producer Drummond Inc. and palm oil producers to move their products to the port in Santa Marta, effectively traversing contested territory of high importance to the illicit economy. The Gneccos – in particular Jorge – had also amassed substantial landholdings themselves, which not only made them *ganaderos* (ranchers) but also enabled him to tap into the illicit economy itself. Jorge was elected only to one sole term in public office (Assembly of Cesar 1982–1984), but new riches produced more successful political campaigns in the 1990s. His older brother Lucas was twice elected governor (1992–1995 and 1998–2000), his brother "Peppe" Senator in 1998, and Luis Alberto Monsalvo Gnecco became a Representative in the Chamber. In those elections, the Gneccos consolidated their grip on Cesar's political apparatus, defeating rival clans in several elections – above all the Araújos – and amassing control over numerous public offices throughout the region.[20]

The cases of Rodrigo Tovar Pupo (hereafter by his nom de guerre "Jorge 40") and Hernán Giraldo are emblematic of warring oligarchs on the Colombian Caribbean Coast. Giraldo came to Santa Marta in 1969 and probably settled in the early 1970s in the Sierra Nevada, moving from coffee to timber extraction. That brought him into contact with traffickers' illicit crops that were permeating the mountainous slopes. By the late 1970s, drug-infused violence was at critical levels in Santa Marta, so, with other settlers from the *Sierra,* he founded his first group, the *Chamizos,* which offered "'protection' to the Santa Marta market traders and marijuana growers in the Sierra Nevada [involving] selective assassinations and extortion of the city's merchants."[21] By the mid-80s, he controlled the transfer of shipments from and through the Sierra Nevada de Santa Marta and, as a consequence, was in open conflict with the FARC. From these clashes resulted his first proper paramilitary group – the Peasant Self-Defence Forces of Magdalena and La Guajira – that used "land transactions for narco-paramilitary money laundering" and employed a "combination of coercive and juridical strategies" to accrue land (Berman-Arévalo: 359). In this context of the early 90s, Giraldo must have done business with Jorge Gnecco and his trucking network (Stone 2016: 91); and crossed paths with Jorge 40.

Jorge 40's rise to the summit of the paramilitary project in the Caribbean was different. His family name was one of traditional fame. He was the grandson of a cattle rancher, Oscar Pupo, and at one time "tended to the Pupo family's cattle ranches" (Stone: 86–87), which made him a target of the FARC's aggressive military tactics. In the late 1980s, his family's political connections opened a career path with stints in the army and municipal bureaucracy, where he experienced the establishment of what scholars have termed "armed clientelism": the embezzlement of mayoral funds by the guerrilla that ran their own candidates in newly institutionalized local elections (Peñate 1999).[22] By 1995, the paramilitaries had started to organize their project in Colombia's regions. Jorge 40 joined first as a foot soldier, but his elite connections with various political clans quickly opened the doors to the leadership of the AUC. He became the protégé of Carlos Castaño himself and, more importantly, Salvatore Mancuso, who wanted to consolidate the political nature of their project and connect with "potential funders and political operators" (Stone: 89). When Jorge 40 was released from prison, proving the versatility of his own connections in the local state apparatus, they made him the commander of the Northern Bloc of the AUC.

Hannah Stone reports that for Jorge 40 "Mancuso was his military [and] Jorge Gnecco his political boss" (2016: 91). This constellation is important because the subsequent conflict between Jorge 40 and Giraldo not only disjointed that arrangement but also showed that paramilitaries themselves were hardly monolithic – in fact, that has been a key difference to the FARC guerrilla (Gutiérrez Sanín 2008) – and their political allies even less so organic co-conspirators. As Jorge 40 spearheaded the expansion of the AUC's Northern Bloc, a strategic alliance emerged between him and Jorge Gnecco to monopolize trafficking routes in the Caribbean region, since drug trafficking constituted a substantial portion of the paramilitary's finances. Key cocaine export ports were located in Magdalena under Giraldo's control, with whom Gnecco also had alliances because they had recognized the financial potential to increase transit levies on paramilitary operations in that area.[23]

The emerging (complex) picture allows for two plausible interpretations: (1) Gnecco at the top of a pyramid as the political oligarch and patron of several armed clients and (2) a horizontal arrangement of different (types of) oligarchs. Subsequent events clarified the structure:

> problems between the paramilitary groups became particularly tense when Hernán Giraldo got into a dispute with the Rojas family, an ally of the House of Castaño that moved illegal drugs and other illicit products along the coast. Over time, the rift grew and drew in Jorge Gnecco. Gnecco's power was at its apex throughout the region, and he took sides with Giraldo. It was a pivotal moment in the battle for the Grand Magdalena. At stake was more than just the illicit trafficking routes that motored the paramilitary war against the guerrillas and its expansion. Political power in the north-eastern corner of Colombia, and possibly that of the entire country, was now in play.
>
> (Stone, 2016: 91)

It is ironic that some of the most violent clashes in Colombia's counterinsurgency war occurred between vigilante groups professing common enemies in the guerrilla, but "in 1999 until 2002, there was a very tough war between the paramilitaries of Carlos Castaño and the paramilitaries of Hernán Giraldo."[24] During this clash, and despite his political power, Jorge Gnecco did not return alive from a meeting with Jorge 40 in 2001. Militarily, Jorge 40 did indeed bring Giraldo's army to the brink of collapse, so much so that in 2002 Giraldo surrendered, renegotiated with the *Casa Castaño*, and joined the AUC as the *Bloque Resistencia Tayrona* under Jorge 40's leadership. Importantly, Giraldo retained leadership of his military capacities, which remained largely intact to be rebuilt.

Politically, the intra-paramilitary war that cost Gnecco's life also weakened his family's political fortunes without entirely eliminating the clan as a political force. Jorge 40 moved his support to the Araujo Family, who reaped the rewards with several important offices during the Uribe years from 2002 to 2010: Hernando Molina Araujo (Governor in 2004), Álvaro Araújo Castro (Senate: 2002 and 2006), María Consuelo Araújo (two-time minister in the Uribe administration). The Gneccos lost substantially in relative power to the other clans but did not perish, and after 2010, they recuperated some important offices (e.g., Luis Alberto Monsalvo Gnecco became governor in 2012).

The narrative of events unfolding in the Caribbean at the turn of the century illustrates some of the key elements of oligarchic rule that were theorized in the first section of this chapter: the autonomy of the armed actor from the political actor, the fragmentation of the armed actor itself (characteristic of warring oligarchies), and the political competition within a democratic playing field amongst civil oligarchs. Different types of oligarchies can be aligned by mutual interests, but the synergies also leave plenty of autonomous space on either side of the legal-to-extra-legal spectrum, creating fragile equilibria that often erupt into violent confrontations. In the realm of civilian oligarchs, numerous established clans compete for economic dominance and political positions. Conversely, within the domain of warring oligarchs, conflicts arise between warlords vying for territorial control and resources.

Peace processes and the persistence of warring oligarchs

Boesten and Idler (2021) argue that in the context of internal armed conflict, peace processes with ANSAs are liminal spaces, in which existing systems of order are disrupted and new patterns of order have not yet emerged. In Colombia, there have been two major peace processes in the last two decades with the two most powerful armed non-state actors, the AUC and the FARC. The process with the counterinsurgents of the AUC also included Jorge 40 and Hernán Giraldo, who were eventually extradited by the Uribe administration. In the post-FARC era, beginning in 2017, the situation in the Caribbean looks very similar to the early 2000s. Curiously enough, the armed actors now confronting each other have lineages that run directly to Jorge 40 and Giraldo. As evidence of the *persistence* of the previously described phenomena, it is only prudent to map the subsequent evolutions in the security panorama in the region. Testimonies and reports give clues about the attributes of warring oligarchs in the system of violence in Colombia's Caribbean, including institutional caveats of their domination.

The added implication of peace processes as liminal spaces is that the trajectory ought not to be understood as moving along binaries, that is, from conflict to peace. The empirical evidence suggests that the disappearance of one hegemon in a violence system compels competitors to fill that vacuum unless the state dispels them with decisive action. It is therefore unsurprising that after peace processes with the AUC (2006) and the FARC (2017), the number of ANSAs did not tend toward zero but rather increased, and the security landscape became accordingly complex. In the Caribbean, *BACRIMs* (Spanish acronym for Criminal Bands; post-AUC groups that did not demobilize and continued in illicit activities) are of more significance than the post-FARC groups, since the FARC had not much presence from the early 90s onwards. The number included under this government categorization of armed groups has fluctuated between 16 in 2008[25] and 5 in 2022.[26]

The two dominant actors in the Caribbean, the AGC and the Conquering Self-Defence Forces of the Sierra – or *Clan del Golfo* and *Pachencas*, respectively – are currently embroiled in a confrontation that eerily resembles the one from the early 2000s. The AGC grew out of the AUC units from the area of the Gulf of Urabá (hence the name *Clan del Golfo*), and took over Vicente Castaños' trafficking routes after his death in 2007 (Ballvé 2020). They extended their influence over the entire Caribbean Coast after 2008, usurping various smaller groups along the way (essentially the remnants of Jorge 40's group). Giraldo formed the first incarnation of the *Pachencas* as the *Oficina del Caribe* to regulate contracts in the local narcotics trade around 2006. It survived his extradition in 2008 and continued under the banner of *Giraldos* and then *Pachencas*. Since 2012, relations between the *Pachencas* and the AGC have been alternating between conflict over control of drug trafficking territory and unstable alliances to move drugs conjointly through local corridors. By the end of the decade, the *Pachencas* were weakened by a high leadership turnover, as several were either killed or arrested, and the AGC moved in to take advantage of that void.[27] The conflict broke out openly in 2020 and continues until today.

In such times of relative upheaval, the political side of oligarchic modes of rule has also been rife with competition between the clans that operate on that side of the margin of legality. A jurist for an indigenous organization in Santa Marta explained that today (2023) "we have the Vives family, we have the Cote family, we have the Diazgranados family, we have the Dávila family."[28] At times, the lines of distinction between clans become blurred because of alliances that have the goal "to circulate [their respective leaders] among the most important posts and positions in the region."[29] These same lines of distinction become more apparent, though, when clans clash with each other over gains in the electoral arena, which remains competitive as they *contest* for political offices: "the Dávila and the Cotes don't want anything to do with each other, are at war," because the current governor, Carlos Eduardo Caicedo, has been supported by the Dávilas against the other families. The Dávilas "control almost all the housing of Santa Marta, the port, and they have Davón, a company that exports bananas and foodstuffs in general from the banana-growing area, where all their farms are."[30] Competitiveness in this contest for public power remains contingent on the ability to ally with actors on the extra-institutional playing field: "they have military, paramilitary and even ex-guerrilla alliances, with traditional politicians, with new politicians, they also have alliances with Petro; it's crazy, they play in every game."[31] Political operations are not ideological or programmatic, but rather a form of melodramatic *alliancism* between political networks vying for hegemony. The ability to compete relies on material wealth (that can literally buy votes) and informal linkages with ANSAs present in the region (who help to "mobilize" voters). Thus, local elections may be competitive, but usually they are not free or fair.

Evidence shows that actors on the extra-institutional playing field still rely on their ability to enforce a local monopoly of violence and are constrained by the competition for territorial control. An officer of the *Defensoría* in the region explains, Giraldo used to control everything, "had military power, economic power, the whole drug business" under his control, and after his extradition, "families related to Hernán" control everything.[32] That control has gone beyond the illegal economy and its trading routes. Everyone, from tour organizers for tourists to "the sellers of water or beer [on the streets], has to pay a tax [to the

Pachencas] for each of the things they sell."[33] This paints a picture in which territorial control, enforced through violence against competitors (and selectively against social leaders), combined with efforts of taxation of the licit and illicit economy, enables warring oligarchs to maintain their position on the extra-legal playing field.

In essence, this section shows that most recent developments have reproduced structures similar to the revelations of *parapolítica*: civil and warring oligarchs operate on different sides of the margin of legality, are functionally autonomous from each other, but at the same time are connected through informal linkages. The struggle between the AGC and the *Pachencas* has not seen a definite winner, and it seems unlikely that the former can eject the latter because the *Pachencas* exercise extensive territorial and social control in those rural areas so important for the narcotics trade. Politically, some commentators have lamented that the left in Colombia has been in government since Petro's election in 2022, but not in power.[34] The reason for that frustration is local systems of wealth defence that are internally differentiated into civil and warring modes of oligarchic rule that leave little space for transformative capacities to bloom.

Conclusion: The functional differentiation of civil and warring oligarchy in Colombia's Caribbean Coast

"The number of people ruling is not the primary foundation of Aristotle's theory of oligarchy or democracy," Winters (2011: 2) observes. It is material wealth. Consequently, oligarchs are "actors who command and control massive concentrations of material resources that can be deployed to defend or enhance their personal wealth and exclusive social position," and "[o]ligarchy refers to the politics of wealth defence by materially endowed actors" (Winters 2011: 6–7). This essay also borrows the key variable of variation of oligarchies: the degree to which oligarchs are involved in the provision of coercion to defend their wealth. In warring oligarchies, coercive capacities are coterminous in importance for securing their wealth, while civil oligarchs are fully disarmed.

Empirically, this chapter showed that there are curious consistencies. The conflict between Jorge 40 and Hernan Giraldo's armies of the early 2000s remanifested itself in the conflict between AGC and the *Pachencas;* the aims also appear ominously similar (control over a section of the illicit economy), and the means through which that control is exercised are also relatively identical (territorial and social control). This remains true, even though the superstructure of an umbrella organization that connects such groups under one collective political project, namely, the AUC, is lacking (that political project never entailed pooling all coercive capacities into one structured organization to begin with).

The consistencies extend to the political, that is, civil, side of oligarchic modes of rule in Colombia's Caribbean Coast. We have identified a list of political families dominating the eastern part of the Caribbean Coast. This portfolio of important families has not substantially changed, and most public posts are rotated amongst members from within their respective political networks. Important features of their privileged social position are the control of most legal businesses (e.g., transportation, agrarian industries, banking, ports, and contracts with multinationals), aforementioned control of public offices, and tight-knit networks reinforced by family bonds. Crucially, they generally do not operate with coercive capacities, even when venturing into criminal enterprises – certainly not on par with those warring oligarchs.

The argument here is that there exists a functional differentiation between the legal and extra-legal sides of the margin of legality that is populated by civil and warring oligarchs, respectively. And it is this functional differentiation that explains some caveats of Colombia's democratic deficit, namely, that you have competitive, but by no means free and fair, (local) elections. Actors on each side of the playing field have different goals and face different constraints. Civil oligarchic modes of rule take place in public and therefore must remain relatively legal. The basis of their wealth is also largely legal, and it is important that it remains thusly. Their political position is greatly helped by the availability of warring oligarchs, whose services they contract to protect their landed wealth and generate votes in elections.

It has also become clear that actors from one side cannot operate on the respective other side of the playing field without incurring serious consequences. If they attempt to bridge that functional separation from legal to illegal (and vice versa), they end up losing: Jorge Gnecco could not compete with the AUC commanders, and AUC commanders were extradited once they had to engage politically during the peace process. Viewing these developments through the lens of the "margins of legality" shows us why that is: the games that each side engages in have different objectives, and actors face different constraints. There is a "political level that determines the distribution of public posts,"[35] which is decided through alliances or ruptures amongst political clans. This game is public and therefore must remain relatively legal. The other side of that game takes place "in rural areas, [where] we continue to see how they are confronting each other militarily."[36] Hence, we argue that civil and warring oligarchs operate on different sides of the margins of legality, are functionally autonomous from each other, and reinforce their respective positions through informal linkages. The costs for the distribution of public goods are enormous: this

> generates insecurity, not only in terms of violence in the city and in the countryside, but also political insecurity, because there is no clarity about who is with whom, who does what, and in the long run nobody does anything.[37]

The result: "the department and the city are completely abandoned to their fate: [...] insecurity is skyrocketing, hunger, poverty, everything is skyrocketing, [while] they are fighting amongst themselves over land. Well, and power."[38]

Notes

1 The importance of oligarchy as a concept has recently been rediscovered by Latin Americanists (for an overview, see Cameron 2021).
2 The *margins of legality* are those grey areas within an internationally recognized state territory, where the monopoly of violence is razor-thin and armed non-state actors not only control territory but also regulate public (in particular: political) life through codes of conduct and levies for resource extraction. Consequently, it is also the geographical space in which the positivity of law is uncertain.
3 In this chapter, we use the terms political clans or political families interchangeably. Behrend (2021) differentiates between political families and dynasties in Mexico's federal states, arguing that the former encompass multiple members who are involved in politics at various levels without clear patterns of succession, while the latter are characterized by a lineage of family members holding high-level elected positions over several generations, often in succession. Notwithstanding that in FN 19 we identify emerging patterns, this chapter focuses on the differentiation between warring and civil oligarchs and not on the succession within the ranks of (civil) oligarchic families. That is a task for the next step in this research project.
4 In this essay, FARC always denotes the armed non-state actor, not the political party founded after its demobilization.
5 Guerrillas were politically and ideologically diminished in their capacity to build political networks equal in depth to those of paramilitaries. The systematic differences between paramilitaries and guerrillas (above all the FARC-EP) are well documented and explained. They have engaged with the narcotics trade in contrasting capacities, because of different know-how in the illicit economy (Taylor & Saab 2009), displayed opposite social compositions reflective of ideological predispositions (Gutiérrez Sanín & Wood 2014), and engaged different remuneration systems that served their distinct organizational structures (Gutiérrez Sanin 2008).
6 Sultanistic and ruling oligarchies are outside the scope of this essay.
7 See our Interdisciplinary Group for the Study of Peace and Conflict (IGSCP): Mesa, William. "Policy Brief. Hacia una comprensión de la Paz Total: Trayectorias, enfrentamientos y acercamientos entre grupos armados ilegales y el Estado colombiano." March 2023. Online at: https://www.lai.fu-berlin.de/termine_lai_archiv/veranstaltungen_2023/ressourcen/Policy-Brief_hacia-un-paz-total.pdf. Last consulted: 16 February 2024.
8 Headquarters, U.S. Army Special Warfare School, Subject: Visit to Colombia, South America, by a Team from Special Warfare Center, Fort Bragg, North Carolina, 26 February 1962. Kennedy Library, Box 319, National Security Files, Special Group; Fort Bragg Team; Visit to Colombia; 3/62. "Secret Supplement, Colombian Survey Report."
9 It is true that Escobar had a massive army of *sicarios* and, through the formation of the MAS (Spanish acronym for "Death to Kidnappers"), founded something akin to a vigilante group, ventured into local governance by providing public goods (housing), and ran for Congress. However, his *sicarios* were for the most part contracted and did not replace state structures in Medellín (those were mostly corrupted). In addition, after the source of his wealth became known, politics turned on him.
10 The term comes from *traquetos,* which Colombians used to describe all those associated with the drug trade, because their guns had a distinct rippling sound – onomatopoetically: "*trr trr trr*" (Boesten 2022a). It is the process when the utilization of coercion *and* accompanying territorial control became the key competitive advantage in the narcotics trade (see Duncan 2006)

11 Congress was dominated by regional interests, and they procured the votes for any political initiative (Boesten 2022a; for the influence of regional power brokers on the presidency, see: Gutiérrez Sanín 2007).

12 See also commentary by Whitehead, Laurence & Jan Boesten. "Petro en Colombia, una elección sin precedentes." 27 July 2023. Online at: https://agendapublica.elpais.com/noticia/18163/petro-colombia-eleccion-sin-precedentes. Last consulted: 16 February 2024.

13 Their terror strategy was clearly anything but democratic, but that should not dissuade from the fact that the paramilitary project was a *political* project, consisting of a coordinated national expansion plan, internal organizational structures and statutes, public relations initiatives, and codes of conduct imposed to exert long-lasting territorial control – very draconian codes accompanied by selective killing campaigns that make any form of independent political action an impossibility.

14 Below we will see that the reverse, a politician operating on the extra-legal playing field, also carries existential risks.

15 Pacific, Andes, Amazon, Caribbean and the Islands Region.

16 La Guajira, Magdalena, Cesar, Atlántico, Bolívar, Sucre, and Córdoba. The Caribbean islands – San Andrés, Providencia, and Santa Catalina – are another category within the broader region itself.

17 Interview, 17 July 2023, Santa Marta, Colombia.

18 This list is by no means exhaustive. In fact, there is some interesting variation amongst these families, some being able to trace their origin to the circle of hegemonic clans to the immediate aftermath of independence, while others – such as the Chars in *Atlantico*, who started their business in the 1950s – are a more recent addendum to the circle of oligarchic families. The continuation of this research project involves mapping the various families and tracing their corresponding linkages with the illicit world more comprehensively. A clear pattern emerges that seemingly applies to most, if not all, of them: the core of their economic activity is in the legal economy, even if all of them entertain proven relations with the illicit economy. Most also have a stake in "grey area" business activities such as real estate in urban and rural areas, mining, and banking. And virtually all of them have entertained some form of alliance with paramilitary groups.

19 Stone affirmingly writes:

> these families had their own political and economic interests, and regardless of the payoff of ridding themselves of the guerrillas, they were not willing to hand these interests to the AUC. What's more, they had their own armed groups, which did not operate under the purview of the AUC.
>
> (77)

20 For example, Gnecco's influence extended well into La Guajira, where his principal allies included Juan Francisco "Kiko" Gómez, his cousin and former mayor of Barrancas, and Samuel Lopessierra, a former senator involved in smuggling. See Semana. "Mafia y política: una tenaza peligrosa." 26 October 2013. Online at: https://www.semana.com/nacion/articulo/relaciones-gobernadores-con-la-mafia/362629-3/. Last consulted: 9 February 2024.

21 Fundación Paz y Reconcilliación (Pares). "El legado de Hernán Giraldo en las Autodefensas Conquistadoras de La Sierra (Los Pachencas)." 4 November 2022. Online at: https://www.pares.com.co/post/el-legado-de-hern%C3%A1n-giraldo-en-las-autodefensas-conquistadoras-de-la-sierra-los-pachencas. Last consulted: 14 February 2024.

22 This was a strategy that paramilitaries later perfected and extended to congressional offices to build their political networks.
23 Semana. "Un genio del mal." 25 November 2006. Online at: https://www.semana.com/nacion/articulo/un-genio-del-mal/82272-3/. Last consulted: 10 February 2024.
24 Interview, 17 July 2023, Santa Marta, Colombia.
25 Center for International Security and Cooperation. Freeman Spogli Institute. Stanford University. "Mapping militants. Bandas Criminales." August 2019. Online at: https://cisac.fsi.stanford.edu/mappingmilitants/profiles/bandas-criminales. Last consulted: 15 February 2024.
26 France 24. "Colombia agrees ceasefire with five largest armed groups." 1 January 2023. Online at: https://www.france24.com/en/americas/20230101-colombia-agrees-ceasefire-with-five-largest-armed-groups. Last consulted: 15 February 2024.
27 Even the return of Hernan Giraldo from US prison in 2022 could not ascertain the leadership question, as he is facing further charges for sexual violence in Colombian courts.
28 Interview, 17 July 2023, Santa Marta, Colombia.
29 Interview, 17 July 2023, Santa Marta, Colombia.
30 Interview, 17 July 2023, Santa Marta, Colombia.
31 Interview, 17 July 2023, Santa Marta, Colombia.
32 When at the apex of his power, many campesino families in territory controlled by Giraldo were forced to offer their (often underage) daughters to him. He is currently awaiting trial for those crimes in a Colombian prison. It is one of the bitter ironies of the Colombian conflict that Giraldo's armed group survived his extradition, precisely because he was a sexual predator of minors and now has "more than 30 sons" that run the group.
33 Interview, 17 July 2023, Santa Marta, Colombia.
34 Zelik, Raul. "Kolumbien: An der Regierung, aber nicht an der Macht." 23 August 2023. Online at: https://www.rosalux.de/news/id/50936. Last consulted: 15 February 2024.
35 Interview, 17 July 2023, Santa Marta, Colombia.
36 Interview, 17 July 2023, Santa Marta, Colombia.
37 Interview, 17 July 2023, Santa Marta, Colombia.
38 Interview, 17 July 2023, Santa Marta, Colombia.

References

Acemoglu, Daron, James A. Robinson, and Rafael J. Santos. 2013. "The Monopoly of Violence: Evidence from Colombia." *Journal of the European Economic Association* 11 (1): 5–44. https://doi.org/10.1111/j.1542-4774.2012.01099.x.

Archer, Ronald. P., and Shugart, Matthew. S. (1997). "The Unrealized Potential of Presidential Dominance in Colombia." In *Presidentialism and Democracy in Latin America*, edited by S. Mainwaring & M. S. Shugart, 110–159. Cambridge University Press. https://doi.org/10.1017/CBO9781139174800

Aristotle. 1984. *The Politics*. Chicago: University of Chicago Press.

Ávila Martínez, Ariel Fernando. 2010. "Injerencia Política de Los Grupos Armados Ilegales." In *Y Refundaron La Patria. De Cómo Mafiosos y Politicos Reconfiguraron El Estado Colombiano*, edited by Claudia. López Hernández, 79–215. Bogotá: Corporación Nuevo Arco Iris.

Ballvé, T. 2020. *The Frontier Effect: State Formation and Violence in Colombia*. Cornell Series on Land: New Perspectives on Territory, Development, and Environment. Ithaca, NY: Cornell University Press.

Behrend, Jacqueline. 2021. "Political Dynasties and Democracy in Contemporary Mexico." *Latin American Policy* 12 (2): 385–404.

Bejarano, Ana Maria, and Pizarro, Eduardo. (2005). From "Restricted" to "Besieged": The Changing Nature of the Limits to Democracy in Colombia. In *The Third Wave of Democratization in Latin America*, F. Hagopian and S. P. Mainwaring, 235–260. Cambridge University Press. https://doi.org/10.1017/CBO9780511791116.009

Berman-Arévalo, Eloisa. 2021. "Mapping Violent Land Orders: Armed Conflict, Moral Economies, and the Trajectories of Land Occupation and Dispossession in the Colombian Caribbean." *The Journal of Peasant Studies* 48 (2): 349–67. https://doi.org/10.1080/03066150.2019.1655640.

Boesten, Jan. 2022a. *Constitutional Origin and Norm Creation in Colombia. Discursive Institutionalism and the Empowerment of the Constitutional Court.* Abingdon: Routledge.

Boesten, Jan. 2022b. "Colombia: A Liberal Democracy Besieged." In *Challenges to Democracy in the Andes: Strongmen, Broken Constitutions, and Regimes in Crisis*, edited by Maxwell A. Cameron and Grace M. Jaramillo, 143–66. Boulder, CO: Lynne Rienner Publishers.

Boesten, Jan, and Annette Idler. 2021. "Mutual Recognition in the Context of Contested Statehood." In *Armed Non-State Actors and the Politics of Recognition*, edited by Anna Geis, Maéva Clémen, and Hanna Pfeifer. Manchester University Press. https://doi.org/10.7765/9781526152763.00022.

Cameron, Maxwell A. 2021. "The Return of Oligarchy? Threats to Representative Democracy in Latin America." *Third World Quarterly* 42 (4): 775–92. https://doi.org/10.1080/01436597.2020.1865794.

Cameron, Maxwell A., and Grace M. Jaramillo. 2022. *Challenges to Democracy in the Andes: Strongmen, Broken Constitutions, and Regimes in Crisis*. Edited by Maxwell A. Cameron and Grace M. Jaramillo. Boulder, CO: Lynne Rienner Publishers. https://doi.org/10.1515/9781955055598.

Dudley, Steven. 2004. *Walking Ghosts*. Routledge. https://doi.org/10.4324/9780203499566.

Duncan, Gustavo. 2006. *Los Señores de La Guerra. De Paramilitares, Mafiosos y Autodefensas En Colombia*. Bogota: Editorial Planeta Colombiana.

FIDH - International Federation for Human Rights. 2021. "The Wound in the Heart of the World: Crimes against Humanity Committed against Indigenous Peoples of the Sierra Nevada de Santa Marta, Colombia." Paris. https://www.fidh.org/en/region/americas/colombia/colombia-crimes-against-humanity-against-indigenous-people-of-sierra.

Gutierrez Sanin, Francisco. 2019. *Clientelistic Warfare. Clientelistic Warfare*. London: Peter Lang UK. https://doi.org/10.3726/b11179.

Gutiérrez Sanín, Francisco. 2007. *Lo Que El Viento Se Llevo: Democracia y Partidos Politicos En Colombia 1958–2006*. Bogota: Grupo Editorial Norma.

Gutiérrez Sanín, Francisco. 2008. "Telling the Difference: Guerrillas and Paramilitaries in the Colombian War." *Politics & Society* 36 (1): 3–34. https://doi.org/10.1177/0032329207312181.

Gutiérrez Sanín, Francisco, and Mauricio Barón. 2006. "Re-Stating the State: Paramilitary Territorial Control and Political Order in Colombia (1978–2004)." *Crisis States Research Centre, DESTIN, LSE.*

Gutiérrez-Sanín, Francisco, and Jenniffer Vargas. 2017. "Agrarian Elite Participation in Colombia's Civil War." In *Journal of Agrarian Change*, 17: 739–48. https://doi.org/10.1111/joac.12235.

López Hernández, Claudia. 2010. *Y Refundaron La Patria. De Cómo Mafiosos y Politicos Reconfiguraron El Estado Colombiano.* Bogotá: Corporación Nuevo Arco Iris.

Peñate, Andres. 1999. "El Sendero Estratégico Del ELN: Del Idealismo Guevarista Al Clientelismo Armado." In *Reconocer La Guerra Para Construir La Paz*, edited by María Victoria Llorente and Malcolm D. Deas, 53–98. Bogota.

Saab, Bilal Y., and Alexandra W. Taylor. 2009. "Criminality and Armed Groups: A Comparative Study of FARC and Paramilitary Groups in Colombia." *Studies in Conflict & Terrorism* 32 (6): 455–75. https://doi.org/10.1080/10576100902892570.

Gutiérrez Sanín, Francisco, and Elisabeth Jean Wood. 2014. "Ideology in Civil War." *Journal of Peace Research* 51 (2): 213–26. https://doi.org/10.1177/0022343313514073.

Stone, Hannah. 2016. "Colombia Elites and Organized Crime." Washington, DC. https://insightcrime.org/investigations/colombia-elites-and-organized-crime-introduction/.

Weber, Max. 1968. *Economy and Society. An Outline of Interpretive Sociology.* Edited by Guenther Roth and Claus Wittich. New York: Bedminster Press Incorporated.

Winters, Jeffrey A. 2011. *Oligarchy*. Cambridge: Cambridge University Press. https://doi.org/10.1017/CBO9780511793806.

8 After the stealth intervention

Civil–military relations and rule of law in post-Bolsonaro Brazil

Karabekir Akkoyunlu and José Antonio Lima

Introduction

More than a year after the election of Lula as president for a third term in November 2022, Brazil's institutions were still recovering from the crisis and instability triggered during four tumultuous years under President Jair Bolsonaro and its dramatic finale. No other institution was as invested in the Bolsonaro presidency – and arguably none experienced as profound a schism and reputational damage – as the Armed Forces of Brazil (FA), whose carefully crafted image as a "moderating power" and guarantor of the constitution suffered a major setback when Bolsonaro supporters, rejecting the outcome of the presidential election and calling for a military intervention, ransacked the Planalto Palace, Congress, and the Federal Supreme Court (STF) in the Brazilian capital on 8 January 2023, with the quiet acquiescence – and apparent complicity – of a sizeable number of military officers.

We previously described the kind of military activism and militarization of politics that started around the impeachment process of Dilma Rousseff, accelerated during the Temer presidency, and reached its height under Bolsonaro as a "stealth military intervention"; a gradual yet systematic attempt to interfere in and redesign national politics without formally stepping outside the law, suspending the democratic process, or overthrowing elected leaders (Akkoyunlu and Lima, 2022). In this chapter, we discuss what the turbulent end of the Bolsonaro presidency has meant for the military's stealth intervention and set out to assess the state of civil-military relations and rule of law in Brazil after a year under President Lula.

We argue that the stealth intervention ended in failure because the Bolsonaro campaign undermined its core logic – that it should remain stealthy and within the formal boundaries of the law. Bolsonaro's explicit confrontation of Brazil's post-1988 constitutional framework, of which the Armed Forces is one of the architects and on which a delicate balance of institutional powers rests, created a rift inside the FA and generated social, political, and judicial pushback. This pushback, however, has been mostly limited to containing Bolsonaro and Bolsonarismo, rather than reckoning with the underlying condition that enabled the stealth intervention in the first place: unreformed military praetorianism and

DOI: 10.4324/9781003519195-8

tutelary privileges. Unpacking the complex relationship between the military, the presidency, and the judiciary during the first year of the Lula administration, we demonstrate that Brazil's key political actors have been preoccupied with damage control and re-establishing a new institutional equilibrium after Bolsonaro, with the military on the backfoot and the judiciary on the offensive, while avoiding any substantial reform agenda necessary to strengthen democracy and the rule of law in the country.[1]

A house divided: Stealth military intervention and its failure

A stealth military intervention involves the combination of three factors. The first, a background condition, is the existence of a permissive legal-institutional framework (or tutelary structure) that enables activist officers to play an enhanced political role without formally breaking the law or suspending the constitution as in an open coup. Officers with a praetorian mindset can activate their "dormant" prerogatives and gradually intervene in national politics when, (1) there is a sustained socio-political crisis that erodes public trust in democratic actors and processes and boosts support for the military, and (2) there are civilian politicians in key positions seeking a pact with the soldiers, drawing them into politics.

All three conditions were present in Brazil in the mid-2010s. Having overseen the transition from dictatorship to democracy in the 1980s, the Armed Forces still maintained important prerogatives and privileges. The Amnesty Law of 1979 prohibited the prosecution of dictatorship-era crimes. Military courts enjoyed an extensive remit. The Armed Forces held sway over the defence budget, education and indoctrination, promotions and retirements, salaries and pensions, while active-duty officers could be appointed to civilian positions in government. For many in the FA, these prerogatives and privileges did not constitute a contradiction to the rule of law in a democracy. On the contrary, they continued to view the Armed Forces as the guarantor of law and order, a role that was enshrined in four of the five Brazilian constitutions prior to 1988. In the process of drafting the 1988 Constitution, the Army senior command successfully inserted – through negotiations, pressures, and threats – this clause into the new text (Zaverucha, 1998; Bachtöld, 2020; Marsiglia, 2022). Article 142, which confers upon the FA the duty to "guarantee the constitutional branches, and, on the initiative of any of them, law and order," thus came to symbolize "the very identity of the Armed Forces," and the constitutional recognition of its institutional autonomy and political role (De Oliveira and Soares, 2000: 105).

It is important to note that the FA managed to retain these powers and privileges partly due to its continued popularity and reputation among considerable segments of the Brazilian population as a relatively moderate and competent institution. State violence and repression under the dictatorship had affected fewer people than in countries like Argentina and Chile. The military had not lost any wars, akin to the Argentinian defeat in the Malvinas/Falklands, or major political battles, such as the Chilean plebiscite in 1988. The generals could take credit for the "economic miracle" of the 1970s, leaving it to civilian governments to deal with its long-term consequences, from increased inequality to massive foreign debt and rising inflation. Finally, having steered the transition, it was able to avoid the type of public reckoning with the abuses of the dictatorship that took place with the Trial of the Juntas in Argentina or the Truth Commission in Chile, thereby preserving its status as well as those of its civilian allies in politics, the business community, and the media.

From 2015 onwards, amidst right-wing mass demonstrations against the Workers' Party (PT) government fuelled by economic crisis, the *Lava Jato* investigation, and the impeachment process against President Rousseff, the military top brass led by then Army chief Eduardo Villas Boas found a favourable socio-political environment to become increasingly outspoken about and engaged in government affairs. Under Rousseff's replacement Michel Temer, and even more so under Bolsonaro, a former Army captain whose election the activist generals enthusiastically supported, Brazil witnessed a dramatic expansion of the military's presence in and influence over the federal government, with the appointment of hundreds of active-duty and reserve officers to key positions in state agencies and ministries (Akkoyunlu and Lima, 2022: 44–46). Crucially, while executing their stealth intervention, the generals routinely emphasized their commitment to democracy and the law, for instance distancing themselves from the small but vocal and persistent pro-coup demonstrations between 2015 and 2018 (Brooks and Boadle, 2018; Ramalhoso, 2018). Theirs was a subtle and gradual way of influencing national politics without blatantly overstepping their already expansive legal-institutional boundaries, all the while maintaining an image of rationalism and moderation.

Not known for his subtlety, it was Bolsonaro who undermined and ultimately sabotaged this strategy. First, the president's reckless handling of the Covid-19 pandemic, coupled with mounting evidence of corruption and criminal links implicating his family and entourage, created ground for a popular anti-Bolsonaro rainbow coalition that would serve as Lula's electoral base in 2022. The involvement of active-duty officers in these public failures and scandals, most notably at the Health Ministry under General Eduardo Pazuello, led to growing unease within the FA about the reputational costs of the military's political activism and close association with Bolsonaro (Godoy, 2020). This concern was not unfounded: a nationwide poll in July 2021 suggested that 62% of Brazilians were against the participation of military officers in political events, while 58% opposed officers serving in civilian posts (Gielow, 2021) – a dramatic swing in the national mood from January 2019, when 62% had expressed support for military involvement in government.

Secondly, the Bolsonaro camp's open clashes with and repeated threats against Congress and the Supreme Court helped unite Brazil's fractured political establishment against Bolsonarismo. They also turned the unease within the Armed Forces into an institutional rift between Bolsonaro loyalists and their "legalist" counterparts. This rift came to the surface in March 2021, when commanders of all three forces resigned after Bolsonaro sacked his defence minister, General Fernando Azevedo e Silva, for resisting his demands for personal loyalty. It continued to widen in the run-up to presidential elections in October 2022, as well as afterwards, reaching a climax with the 8 January 2023 events in Brasília.

Lula's narrow election victory, which was immediately congratulated by a long list of world leaders as if in a coordinated effort to pre-empt any anti-democratic interference, spelled the end of the stealth intervention (Casarões, Monte, and Hernandez, 2024). While Bolsonaro, after having claimed voting fraud for months, refused to concede defeat, the Armed Forces published a report shortly after the second round confirming the integrity of the electoral system (Downie, 2022). Feeling betrayed, many Bolsonaro loyalists and supporters apparently concluded that the only way to annul "the stolen election" was to force an open intervention by patriotic officers, which led to the storming of the capital on 8 January.[2] Although the attempt ended in failure, shocking scenes of violent mobs vandalizing the Congress, the Presidential Palace, and the Supreme Court as military officers and the police looked on deepened the sense of insecurity and distrust among Brazil's civilian institutions and the military. Overcoming this distrust to establish a working relationship with the Armed Forces, while containing Bolsonarismo and dealing with those who oversaw the 8 January insurrection, became a key challenge for Lula in his first year in office.

The limits of executive pushback: Civil–military relations after the stealth intervention

The first year of the new Lula government was marked by attempts by the executive branch, the judiciary, and the military to strike a fragile balance. This was a period when, according to Lula's Defence Minister José Múcio Monteiro, "everyone was suspicious of everyone" (Gularte, 2024). The Armed Forces were divided and on the back foot. Besides the reputational damage the institution had suffered, a growing number of officers were facing legal charges as a result of the allegations surrounding the Bolsonaro presidency and its chaotic final act. Although the legalist officers seeking some kind of damage control and normalization had gained the upper hand following Lula's victory and the 8 January events, their position was hardly enviable. While being heckled by Bolsonaro allies and supporters as cowards and traitors, they were not particularly thrilled about Lula's return to the Planalto Palace either. A candid expression of this faction's sentiments came in a private speech that General Tomás Paiva, then commander of the Southeast, delivered to his subordinates three days before stepping up as the head of the Army in January 2023. In the leaked address, the general lamented the election outcome as "unfortunate" and "undesired" by the Armed Forces, but also defended the integrity of the vote and the election system against fraud allegations (Feitoza, 2023a).[3] The fact that, despite these setbacks and divisions, the generals were able to protect the FA's core prerogatives and privileges demonstrated their political strength even in times of crisis.

For their part, Brazil's civilian leaders showed little interest in seizing the moment to review civil-military relations in a substantial manner. Throughout 2023, relations between civilians and the military were marked by mutual "gestures" and "signs" in search of a *modus vivendi*, reminiscent of the political climate at the end of the dictatorship (Pedretti, 2023). After early signs to the contrary, Lula also appeared satisfied with a return to the *status quo ante*. This was not out of line with his political character, as he displayed a penchant for striking pragmatic bargains with Brazil's conservative forces. During his first two terms in office, he had carefully avoided "rocking the boat" and kept the Army content through generous budget increases. While in prison in 2018, he had even reached out to those generals who had openly worked to push him out of the presidential race, signalling his willingness to cooperate with the military (Monteiro, 2018). Although visibly shaken by the attempted coup on 8 January, having been elected on a rainbow coalition and facing a legislature dominated by conservatives (including Bolsonaro allies), Lula also knew he had little time and political capital to wage a drawn-out war to reform civil–military relations. Consequently, his administration prioritized ensuring the president's security and clearing the way to focus on issues seen as more pressing, such as the economy.

Before taking office, Lula isolated military and defence matters from public deliberation, setting up transition commissions in all areas of government with the participation of civil society groups, except for defence. The transition was overseen by an Army general and a brigadier, both personally trusted by Lula, and Múcio, the future Minister of Defence (Viana, 2023). Immediately after taking office, the government moved to reduce the number of military officers working in the executive branch. As many as 1,400 commissioned personnel were dismissed in the first week alone, including all military officers who occupied high-ranking civilian positions (Weteman and Frazão, 2023). These efforts intensified after 8 January, as evidence of military involvement in the coup demonstrations mounted. Declaring that the Armed Forces were not the "moderating power" that they perceived themselves to be (Spechoto and Fagundes, 2023), the president started putting in place measures to distance the soldiers from his administration. Between January and April, he removed military personnel from his personal security, temporarily entrusting it to the Federal Police (Soares and Hekally, 2023), transferred the Brazilian Intelligence Agency (ABIN) from the military-controlled Institutional Security Office (GSI), which under Bolsonaro had turned into a veritable barracks inside the federal executive, to his own Chief of Staff (Machado, 2023), fired the Army chief (Landim and Arbex, 2023) as well as the military commander of Planalto (Alves, 2023), and withdrew from Congress a Bolsonaro-era bill exempting military personnel from punishment during GLOs (law and order operations) (Holanda, 2023).

However, the government avoided direct confrontations with the military. In March, Lula took the seat of his vice president, Geraldo Alckmin, in weekly meetings with the chiefs of the Army, the Navy, and the Air Force. These were mediated by the Minister of Defence, José Múcio, who played the role of interlocutor between the Armed Forces and the government.[4] Among other things, Múcio made sure that sensitive proposals underwent a conciliatory "filter." In January, the Justice Ministry proposed creating a National Guard to assume several functions, including the security of federal buildings in Brasília, traditionally a military prerogative (Vilela, 2023). But the proposal never went forward to Congress. In February, a deputy from Lula's Workers' Party proposed amending Article 142 of the Constitution and ending the military-led GLO operations (Borges, 2023), but this did not receive support from Planalto. Instead, the government proposed another measure requiring active-duty officers seeking elected positions to go to the reserve. First announced in March after receiving the Army leadership's nod of approval (Fernandes, 2023), the proposal to "depoliticize" the military was negotiated for a further six months and watered down to allow active-duty officers to hold Minister of State positions, before being approved in the Senate in November (Vinícius, 2023; Agência Brasil, 2023).

Lula and his allies also did not seek to discipline the military in budgetary terms. The president encouraged investments in the arms industry, as he had done in his first terms in office. As part of a major public investment initiative that was announced in August, the government earmarked R$52 billion for defence projects, surpassing the funding allocated to the health sector (Holanda and Machado, 2023). In November, Planalto supported a Bolsonaro-aligned senator's proposal mandating the government to invest 2% of GDP in the defence sector (Pitta, 2023). Defence spending was spared from the budget cuts announced in early 2024, maintaining a privilege jealously guarded by the Armed Forces (Holanda et al., 2024).

Finally, the government did little to support the largely symbolic efforts to condemn and hold the dictatorship to account. The National Truth Commission continued to operate with a very low budget. The promise to re-establish the Special Commission on Political Deaths and Disappearances, abolished by Bolsonaro on his last day in office, was not fulfilled. Citing discomfort in the barracks, the Ministry of Defence kept postponing the publication of its legal opinion on the matter, a necessary formality, thereby undermining Ministers Sílvio Almeida (Human Rights and Citizenship) and Flávio Dino (Justice and Public Security) who had publicly committed to recreating the commission by 25 October, the anniversary of the assassination of journalist Vladimir Herzog in 1975, known as Democracy Day. In a meeting at the end of September, Múcio advised Almeida to pursue the matter at a "more opportune" moment (Hupsel

Filho, 2023). The episode sparked outrage among the families of the victims, who felt that the country was being led by "two governments, one civilian and the other military" (Otávio, 2023).

The president's "gestures" were reciprocated by the Armed Forces. After assuming the leadership of the Army, General Paiva stated that the soldiers who were involved in the 8 January events would be punished and prohibited his officers from maintaining profiles on social media platforms where they could be identified by their names and ranks (Braga, 2023; Feitoza, 2023b). In March, amid debates about depoliticizing the military, the Army, Navy, and the Air Force gave their officers 90 days to disaffiliate from political parties (Feitoza, 2023c; Roxo and Gularte, 2023).[5] The Armed Forces and the Defence Ministry stopped commemorating the 1964 coup, which under Bolsonaro was celebrated as a "milestone for democracy" (Mazui, 2023).[6] The generals did not raise an objection when Lula decided to maintain the Federal Police (PF) in charge of his and the first lady's personal security, instead of returning the task to the military-controlled GSI when the PF's temporary mandate expired.

With the Federal Police investigations into the 8 January events advancing, and with fresh allegations of corruption implicating Bolsonaro-era military personnel, the Armed Forces leaned on the Minister of Defence to protect their interests. Múcio personally invited Vice President Alckmin, the head of the PF Andrei Rodriguez, and Supreme Court Justice Alexandre de Moraes to the Soldier's Day ceremony on 25 August. In private, the generals suggested the purpose of these invitations was to "guarantee a good institutional relationship." According to the Defence Minister, the appearance of key figures from the government, the judiciary, and the federal police at a military event was "very important to show society that we are all on one side" (Chaib and Feitoza, 2023).

The rulers of law: The judiciary and the military before and after Bolsonaro

In the story of civil–military relations and rule of law in Brazil, both past and present, the judiciary plays at least as central a role as the military and the executive branch – and arguably a more complex one than both. Sectors of the judiciary have enabled the military's stealth intervention and also later contained it. From the *Lava Jato* investigation to the Supreme Court, activist judges and prosecutors have made critical decisions precipitating the fall (and return) of Lula, as well as the rise (and fall) of Bolsonaro, in the process themselves turning into political celebrities. Given this importance and complexity, it is surprising that the relationship between the judiciary and the military has received little scholarly attention since re-democratization. In light of this gap, it is worth briefly touching upon the background of this relationship before turning to how it has helped shape the post-Bolsonaro political field in Brazil.

The Brazilian Judiciary and the Armed Forces have intertwined stories. In a highly stratified society built upon colonial foundations that only established universal suffrage in the mid-1980s, traditional careers in law and the armed forces have been signifiers of social status and gateways to political power.[7] To this day, both institutions display hereditary characteristics, with many in the leadership strata pursuing careers in line with their family's professional legacy (Silva, 2013; Oliveira, 2018). Not surprisingly, the two institutions share a common goal in preserving their extensive privileges and prerogatives within the country's political framework, although how they pursue this goal necessarily differs. While the 1988 Constitution compels the Armed Forces to exert influence indirectly, such as by applying pressure on the executive branch, it bestows upon the judiciary a direct role as the arbiter of disputes among political actors (Sadek, 2004).

The two courts in Brasilia in particular, the Supreme Federal Court (STF) and the Superior Court of Justice (STJ), are entrenched in a political culture that evolved during the 1980s and aimed to insulate the political system from transformative social forces that emerged during the final years of the dictatorship. Within this framework, key actors strive to maintain their veto powers in order to safeguard other interests, such as their generous salaries and pensions (Nobre, 2013: 45; 2022). Members in the higher echelons of the judiciary tend to prefer "the discreet enjoyment of their material and status privileges" over the burden of governance and accountability, notes legal scholar Conrado Hubner Mendes (2018). This preference appeared evident in the way the STF and the STJ helped preserve the political system by dismantling two major anti-corruption investigations (*Satiagraha* and *Castelo de Areia*) prior to *Lava Jato*. The STF has also been instrumental in shielding the Armed Forces from legal accountability by upholding the Amnesty Law of 1979. In 2010, the Supreme Court voted against revoking the law, calling it "the foundation of Brazilian democracy" (Schneider, 2011).

The military's stealth intervention was executed by activist officers who were dissatisfied with the political direction of the country under the PT governments, especially the Rousseff administration, and wanted to return to the decision-making circles from which they were marginalized during re-democratization. In reasserting themselves into politics without appearing to overstep the law, they sought and received support from members of the judiciary who were sympathetic to their cause or found it expedient to work with the military. This was a reunion of sorts, reminiscent of the collaboration between jurists and officers in creating an "authoritarian legality" that was used to legitimize both the Estado Novo dictatorship (1937–1945) and the military dictatorship (1964–1985) (Teixeira, 2011: 165; Bechara and Rodrigues, 2015: 592).

In September 2018, for instance, the new president of the STF, José Antonio Dias Toffoli, in an attempt to entrench his position, sought to establish a bridge with the Armed Forces and appointed a military man as his advisor; an unprecedented move at the time (Recondo and Weber, 2023). Recommended by then Army Commander General Villas Boas, the appointee was Fernando Azevedo e Silva, who went on to become Bolsonaro's Defence Minister. This was after Villas Boas had issued a thinly veiled ultimatum on the eve of a critical decision by the STF on Lula's *habeas corpus* request, which was rejected by six votes to five, landing the former president in prison and out of the presidential race of 2018. Throughout that year, there were frequent exchanges between active-duty officers and the judges overseeing Lula's trial as part of the *Lava Jato* case; a relationship that led General Villas Boas to praise the "synergy between the two institutions."[8] In August, when a regional court suspended Lula's release order, Bolsonaro's vice-presidential candidate General Hamilton Mourão invited the court's president to the Military Club in Rio, where he thanked him for "asserting, with firmness and determination, the rule of law" (Rezende, 2018). Important magistrates openly supported Bolsonaro's candidacy (Lima, 2018). Most notable of these was Sergio Moro, the celebrity judge of *Lava Jato,* who became Bolsonaro's Minister of Justice and Public Security.

What disrupted this "synergy" was, as we noted earlier, the autocratic impulses and anti-establishment discourse of President Bolsonaro, which after a brief honeymoon period brought the executive branch to loggerheads with the judiciary, in particular the Supreme Court. Bolsonaro's attempts to dismantle constitutionally established participatory bodies, weaken accountability mechanisms, exert personal control over autonomous agencies, cover up criminal investigations into his allies and family, and rule by decree were met with growing resistance from the STF, uniting its members and turning it into the first line of defence against the president's anti-democratic agenda (Vieira et al., 2023). The Court became particularly interventionist during the Covid-19 pandemic, responding promptly to requests to act upon the president's denialist and anti-vaccine stance and attempts to derail public health measures adopted by state governments.

Frustrated by such roadblocks, Bolsonaro took to openly insulting and threatening individual members of the STF, mobilizing and provoking his supporters against the constitutional branches of power, and spreading conspiracy theories about electoral fraud in the 2022 election, which implicated another judicial body, the Supreme Electoral Court (TSE), whose president and vice-president are also STF members (Human Rights Watch, 2021). In turn, the STF judges turned even more activist, launching ex officio investigations and pushing their own legal boundaries in the process. A case in point is the STF inquiry headed by Justice Alexandre de Moraes into the spread of fake news, as part of which the "crusading judge" ordered raids, censorship of social media accounts and arrests of pro-Bolsonaro figures, in the process turning into Bolsonaro's public enemy number one (Savarese and Goodman, 2023).

Ultimately, what was Brazil's gravest constitutional crisis since re-democratization fractured the military and alienated Bolsonaro's allies; Sergio Moro, for instance, stepped down as justice minister in April 2020, citing the president's attempts to cover up the PF investigation against his family. It also made strange bedfellows out of Bolsonaro's diverse opponents. It was in this context that Lula, the politician most likely to defeat Bolsonaro in an election, was released from prison when the STF reversed its earlier decision on defendants' right to remain free until all appeals options were exhausted, and eventually threw out his case on grounds of unlawful collusion between Sergio Moro and the prosecutors of the *Lava Jato* investigation.

Following Lula's victory and the 8 January events, the Armed Forces sought to affirm good relations with the STF, in particular with Moraes, who presided over the Supreme Electoral Court and led both the 8 January inquiry and the ongoing investigations launched during the Bolsonaro government into crimes committed by the former president's associates, including military figures. Moraes was also due to cast the decisive vote in an impending ruling at the STF on whether military courts should maintain the right to try civilians who commit crimes against members of the military or the institution of the Armed Forces. In fact, behind the scenes, Moraes and other members of the STF had been in close contact with active-duty officers during the final stretch of the Bolsonaro presidency, and the jurists reportedly felt emboldened to confront Bolsonaro upon reaching the conclusion that the troop commanders would not support a coup attempt (Recondo and Weber, 2023).

Under the new government, dialogue between the Armed Forces and the STF was spearheaded by General Tomás Paiva and Air Force Brigadier Joseli Parente Camelo, who in March 2023 became the president of the Superior Military Court (STM). Paiva was one of the officers who had reassured Moraes after the election that "only crazy people supported a coup" and that such an act would generate a backlash "from the rest of the world" (Recondo and Weber, 2023: 193). Upon taking over as Army chief, Paiva initiated a series of meetings with the STF members, which were well received by the judges. More importantly, the general expressed his support for Moraes' decision to try the military personnel involved in the 8 January insurrection (Araújo and Netto, 2023).[9] Camelo also endorsed the decision to judge these soldiers in a civilian court and implemented a more assertive communication policy in the STM, emphasizing intolerance for partisan behaviour and threats to the rule of law.

Throughout 2023, Moraes took a series of decisions impacting the Armed Forces. In May, he ordered the arrest of Lieutenant Colonel Mauro Cid, Bolsonaro's former aide, as part of a PF investigation into the illicit sale of jewellery gifted to Bolsonaro by foreign dignitaries during his presidency. The Army discharged the officer in September upon the judge's request (Araújo and Borges, 2023). In August, Mauro's father, General Lourena Cid, was also arrested, as was Second Lieutenant Osmar Crivelatti. Lourena was a prestigious four-star general and part of the military high command while on active duty, and his arrest shocked the FA. Mauro Cid's right-hand man, Crivelatti, was also known to be close to General Villas Boas. It was at this moment that the Defence Minister decided to draw the Armed Forces closer to the leadership of the Federal Police and invited its chief to the Soldiers' Day Parade, along with Moraes.

In October 2023, the Electoral Court, under Alexandre de Moraes' presidency, found Bolsonaro and General Walter Braga Netto, Bolsonaro's former Minister of Defence and running mate in the 2022 election, guilty of turning the bicentenary celebrations of Brazil's Independence in Rio de Janeiro into a campaign event, and banned them from running for office for eight years. The expectation before the ruling was that Moraes would spare Braga Netto from conviction so as not to disturb the delicate relationship between the judiciary and the military (Brígido, 2023). By condemning the general and criticizing the Army in his ruling for cancelling the official parade in 2022 to increase attendance in the pro-Bolsonaro demonstration in Rio de Janeiro, the judge asserted the judiciary's – and his own – authoritative position in the institutional balance of powers. The generals did not contest the ruling or defend Braga Netto but voiced concern over the damage that the series of unfavourable rulings and investigations had inflicted on the corporate spirit of the Armed Forces (Folha de S.Paulo, 2023).

At the same time, Moraes was careful not to overplay his hand, making gestures and decisions that also pleased the generals. In September, when condemning the first group of civilian defendants in the 8 January inquiry, the judge emphasized that "the Brazilian military did not subscribe to this coup fantasy," distinguishing between the perpetrators of the insurrection and the Armed Forces as an institution; a distinction that was well received by the defence minister and the military top brass (Arbex, 2023). Finally, in November, Moraes cast the decisive vote in the STF judgement over the military court's prerogative to try civilians, in favour of its continuation.

In short, the judiciary, and in particular the Supreme Court, came out strengthened from its confrontation with Bolsonaro. Lula's decision to appoint Robert Lewandowski, the former president of the STF who was critical of *Lava Jato* and cast several votes in favour of both Lula and Dilma over the years, as justice minister in January 2024, suggests the president also recognizes the Court's increased weight and wants to have an interlocutor in his relationship with the judges. In turn, while the Armed Forces suffered a setback, it was still able to maintain its privileges and prerogatives. This is evidenced by the generals' compliance with those rulings perceived as unfavourable to the military, but also by the decisions that pleased the generals.

At the time of writing in early 2024, the cases against Mauro and Lourena Cid and Crivelatti were ongoing. No military personnel had been convicted by the STM or the STF in connection with the 8 January inquiry, although a major escalation in February 2024 saw the Federal Police seize Bolsonaro's passport, issue search warrants for Generals Braga Netto and Heleno, and arrest three officers close to the former president for plotting to overturn the election results in 2022.[10] While these were unprecedented developments in a country where the military is not typically held to account for its actions, it remained doubtful whether the investigations would have an impact beyond Bolsonarist coupism and help tackle the underlying issue of military tutelage (Prazeres, 2024).

Conclusion

Our overview of the political dynamics and relationship between the military, the government, and the judiciary during the first year of the new Lula administration leads us to three observations about the state of civil–military relations, the rule of law and democracy in post-Bolsonaro Brazil. The first is that while the activist generals exerted an influence over national politics during the Bolsonaro presidency that was reminiscent of the dictatorship, an era that they never ceased to glorify, it was also their close association with Bolsonaro that spelt the end of the military's stealth intervention. In carrying the military to the centre of executive power, Bolsonaro made the generals accomplices in his crimes and anti-constitutional outbursts. This undermined the stealth nature of the military's intervention and the carefully constructed image of a rational and patriotic army that is the protector of the constitution, acts within the law, and exerts itself soberly and reluctantly on national affairs due to popular demand and political invitation. While there was a clear craving within the officer corps for a more central role for the Armed Forces in steering the country's affairs, only the most committed Bolsonaro loyalists displayed an appetite to upend the constitutional order or pick a damaging fight with the judiciary, which not only had a firmer legal basis for intervening in politics, but also had been key to protecting some of the military's core privileges and prerogatives.

The military's misadventure with Bolsonaro echoes an increasingly familiar story that we encounter, with some variation, across a wide geography. This is a story in which rivalries within a fractured political establishment propel one group of elites (often the conservatives, such as the Republican Party in the United States, the military in Turkey, or the hardliner clerics in Iran) to seek a pact with an anti-establishment outsider (such as Trump, Erdogan, or Ahmadinejad) with whom they share a certain worldview and a common foe (often the left or liberal wing of the establishment). These Faustian bargains, however, rarely succeed as the anti-establishment outsiders turn out to be more ambitious and unruly than previously assumed, slowly taking over the political base of their establishment allies and threatening the very edifice that these elites stand on, ultimately forcing them to put aside their differences and unite against their popular (and populist) tormentors. In Brazil, it took a rainbow coalition spanning from the far-left to the centre-right, Lula's exceptional political skills, and unprecedented activism by the Supreme Court to defeat Bolsonaro

– although Bolsonarismo is very much alive in society and politics, and will bide its time for a comeback.

The second observation is that such clashes with anti-establishment disrupters often feature the judiciary playing an unusually activist and interventionist role, and Brazil has been no exception. In resisting and containing Bolsonaro and Bolsonarismo, the Supreme Court successfully executed its post-dictatorship mission of safeguarding the political system from transformative social forces, this time emanating not from the left but from the far-right. The fact is that facing a direct challenge from a populist outsider with autocratic instincts, the STF stepped in to safeguard Brazil's elitist democracy. The ordeal has left the Supreme Court even more powerful than before, with individual judges testing and stretching their own legal boundaries. It is too early to tell whether the executive and the legislative branches (or for that matter the military) will accept the judiciary's elevated status as the new normal, rendering Brazil's democracy more juristocratic, or push back against it to reach a different equilibrium.[11] What seems clear is that the figure of a politically-inclined celebrity judge acting as a caped crusader to the delight of some groups and the horror of others will remain a feature of Brazil's polarized socio-political landscape for the foreseeable future.

The third and final observation is that even though the Brazilian military has suffered legal and reputational setbacks, and has been fractured and demoralized, it has managed to preserve its core tutelary privileges and prerogatives. The Amnesty Law remains in place, the generals control the education and indoctrination of the soldiers, the military courts continue to have an extensive remit, and there is still no ban on active-duty officers taking up civilian posts – all of which undermine the democratic control of the Armed Forces. Lula, in his pragmatic prudence and contending with a conservative-dominated Congress, has shied away from confronting these prerogatives, while the judiciary never appeared bothered by them in the first place. It is important to remember, however, that it was these tutelary prerogatives that enabled the activist generals to initiate their stealth intervention, as part of which they provided Bolsonaro with the organizational mechanism that carried him to the Planalto Palace. Indeed, many of the legalist officers, who have been engaged in a charm offensive and damage control, were onboard with the stealth intervention until it got derailed by Bolsonaro.

In 2016, when asked to reflect on how the Armed Forces had changed since 1964, General Eduardo Villas Boas said, "the Army is still the same as that period, with the same values, the same principles, and the same objectives. But the circumstances have changed" (Odilla, 2017). In early 2024, there was little to suggest that the Armed Forces as an institution had categorically moved away from this self-image, which underpins their tutelary prerogatives and extensive privileges. Without a comprehensive socio-political and institutional reckoning with unreformed praetorianism and tutelage, one cannot rule out another stealth intervention when circumstances change again in the future.

Notes

1 A comprehensive evaluation of the relationship between these institutions and Congress, as well as between different actors inside Congress, while important, remains outside the scope of this chapter, although we bring the legislative branch into the discussion when relevant.
2 When asked whether Lula had won the election by receiving more votes than Bolsonaro, 40% of the respondents to a poll conducted on 9 and 10 January 2023 answered "no," while 37% said they were in favour of a military intervention to annul the election (Ribero, 2023).
3 In a later statement, this time made in public, the general condemned the disinformation campaign during the vote and said that the military should fulfil its duties regardless of who the president was (Tavares, 2023).
4 A member of ARENA, the official party of the Brazilian dictatorship, from 1966 to 1979, Múcio maintained strong ties with the generals. But, having served as a minister during the first Lula administration, he also enjoyed a close relationship with Lula and was trusted by the president.
5 Although active-duty officers were already banned from joining political parties, this ban was not being enforced.
6 We should note that the FA had stopped commemorating the anniversary of the coup only under Dilma Rousseff, who was imprisoned and tortured during the dictatorship. It was also Rousseff who launched the Truth Commission in 2011, which published extensive findings of human rights abuses during the dictatorship in 2014. Although the commission was largely toothless due to the Amnesty Law of 1979, its creation and findings nonetheless caused much displeasure within the Armed Forces (D'Araújo, 2012).
7 It is not by chance that of Brazil's 38 presidents since the formation of the Republic, 19 had a background in law, while 10 were military men.
8 Tweets by Eduardo Villas Boas (@Gen_VillasBoas) on 3 April and 6 June 2018.
9 The Commission of Inquiry into the 8 January events indicted 60 individuals, half of whom were military personnel, including key figures in the stealth intervention such as Walter Braga Netto and former ministers Augusto Heleno and Luiz Eduardo Ramos, as well as several generals, including a former Minister of Defence and former commanders of the Army and the Navy.
10 These are Colonel Marcelo Câmara (former advisor to President Bolsonaro), Colonel Bernardo Romão Corrêa Neto, and Lieutenant Colonel Rafael Martins de Oliveira.
11 At the time of writing, there were emerging signs, particularly in conservative public opinion, of impatience with the normalization of the activist conduct of Supreme Court judges, especially Alexandre de Moraes. See, for example, the editorial of the centre-right *Estadão* newspaper on 1 January 2024 (O Estado de S.Paulo, 2024).

References

Agência Brasil. (2023). CCJ do Senado aprova PEC que proíbe militares da ativa se candidatarem. 29 November. https://agenciabrasil.ebc.com.br/politica/noticia/2023-11/ccj-do-senado-aprova-pec-que-proibe-militares-da-ativa-se-candidatarem

Akkoyunlu, K., & Lima, J. A. (2022). Brazil's Stealth Military Intervention. *Journal of Politics in Latin America*, 14(1), 31–54. https://doi.org/10.1177/1866802X211039860

Alves, F. (2023). Governo Lula exonera general Dutra do Comando Militar do Planalto na véspera de depoimento à PF. *O Globo*. 12 April. https://oglobo.globo.com/politica/

noticia/2023/04/governo-lula-exonera-general-dutra-do-comando-militar-do-planalto-na-vespera-de-depoimento-a-pf.ghtml

Araújo, C., & Netto, P. R. (2023). Exército concorda com decisão de Moraes sobre julgamento de militares. *UOL*. 27 February. https://noticias.uol.com.br/colunas/carla-araujo/2023/02/27/exercito-concorda-com-decisao-de-moraes-sobre-julgamento-de-militares.htm

Araújo, C., & Borges, S. (2023). Após ordem de Moraes, Exército afasta Cid de suas funções. *UOL*. 10 September. https://noticias.uol.com.br/politica/ultimas-noticias/2023/09/10/exercito-mauro-cid-afastamento.htm

Arbex, T. (2023). Voto de Moraes agrada à Defesa e ao Exército por separar atuação de militares golpistas de Forças Armadas, dizem fontes. *CNN Brasil*. 14 September. https://www.cnnbrasil.com.br/politica/voto-de-moraes-agrada-defesa-e-exercito-por-separar-atuacao-de-militares-golpistas-de-forcas-armadas-dizem-fontes/

Bachtöld, F. (2020). Pressão militar gestou artigo vago da Constituição usado hoje em atos pró-intervenção. *Folha de S.Paulo*. 23 May. https://www1.folha.uol.com.br/poder/2020/05/pressao-militar-gestou-artigo-vago-da-constituicao-usado-em-atos-pro-golpe.shtml

Bechara, G. N., & Rodrigues, H. W. (2015). Ditadura Militar, Atos Institucionais e Poder Judiciário. *Revista Justiça do Direito*, 29(3), 587–605. https://seer.upf.br/index.php/rjd/article/view/5611

Borges, B. (2023). Deputado tenta viabilizar PEC que altera artigo 142 da Constituição e delimita poderes de militares. *G1*. 17 February. https://g1.globo.com/politica/noticia/2023/02/17/deputado-tenta-viabilizar-pec-que-altera-artigo-142-da-constituicao-e-delimita-poderes-de-militares.ghtml

Brígido, C. (2023). TSE tenta evitar que julgamento de Bolsonaro provoque atrito com militares. *UOL*. 31 October. https://noticias.uol.com.br/colunas/carolina-brigido/2023/10/31/tse-tenta-evitar-que-julgamento-de-bolsonaro-provoque-atrito-com-militares.htm

Brooks, B., & Boadle, A. (2018). The squadron of ex-military men behind Bolsonaro's rise in Brazil. *Reuters*. 23 October. https://www.reuters.com/article/us-brazil-election-generals-insight/thesquadron-of-ex-military-men-behind-bolsonaros-rise-in-brazil-idUSKCN1MX1QX

Braga, J. (2023). Comandante do Exército diz que militares envolvidos no 8 de janeiro serão punidos. *Folha de S.Paulo*. 13 February. https://www1.folha.uol.com.br/colunas/painel/2023/02/comandante-do-exercito-diz-que-militares-envolvidos-no-8-de-janeiro-serao-punidos.shtml

Casarões, G., Monte, D., & Hernandez, M. (2024). Safeguarding Brazilian democracy from the outside-in: transnational democratic networks and the illiberal threat in contemporary Brazil. *Third World Quarterly*. Forthcoming.

Chaib, J., & Feitoza, C. (2023). Militares vivem clima de desconfiança com PF, e ministro da Defesa tenta contornar rusgas. *Folha de S.Paulo*. 3 September. https://www1.folha.uol.com.br/poder/2023/09/militares-vivem-clima-de-desconfianca-com-pf-e-ministro-da-defesa-tenta-contornar-rusgas.shtml

D'Araújo, M. C. (2012). O estável poder de veto das Forças Armadas sobre o tema da anistia política no Brasil. *Varia Historia*, 28(48), 573–597. https://doi.org/10.1590/S0104-87752012000200006

De Oliveira, E. R., & Soares, S. A. (2000). Forças Armadas, direção política e formato institucional. In M. C. D'Araujo & C. Castro (Eds.), *Democracia e Forças Armadas no Cone Sul*. Rio de Janeiro: Ed. Fundação Getulio Vargas.

Downie, A. (2022). Brazil military finds no evidence of election fraud, dashing hopes of Bolsonaro supporters. *The Guardian*. 10 November https://www.theguardian.com/world/2022/nov/10/brazil-military-finds-no-evidence-of-election-dashing-hopes-of-bolsonaro-supporters

Feitoza, C. (2023a). Comandante disse que vitória de Lula foi indesejada no Exército e infelizmente ocorreu. *Folha de S.Paulo*. 28 February. https://www1.folha.uol.com.br/poder/2023/02/comandante-disse-que-vitoria-de-lula-foi-indesejada-pelo-exercito-mas-que-infelizmente-ocorreu.shtml

Feitoza, C. (2023b). Comandante do Exército cobra tropa para não ter perfil nas redes com função militar e patente. *Folha de S.Paulo*. 2 March. https://www1.folha.uol.com.br/poder/2023/03/comandante-do-exercito-reforca-a-militares-sobre-veto-a-redes-sociais-atreladas-a-forca.shtml

Feitoza, C. (2023c). Lula se encontra com almirantes, e Marinha dá 90 dias para oficiais se desfiliarem de partidos. *Folha de S.Paulo*. 15 March. https://www1.folha.uol.com.br/poder/2023/03/lula-se-encontra-com-almirantes-e-marinha-da-90-dias-para-oficiais-se-desfiliarem-de-partidos.shtml

Fernandes, M. C. (2023). O comandante que silenciou o Exército. *Valor Econômico*. 31 May. https://valor.globo.com/publicacoes/especiais/rumos-da-economia/noticia/2023/05/31/o-comandante-que-silenciou-o-exercito.ghtml

Folha de S.Paulo. (2023). Militares tentam se descolar de Braga Netto e dizem que TSE não afeta Forças Armadas. 1 November. https://www1.folha.uol.com.br/poder/2023/11/militares-tentam-se-descolar-de-braga-netto-e-dizem-que-tse-nao-afeta-forcas-armadas.shtml

Gielow, I. (2021). Datafolha: Maioria diz que militar da ativa não deve ir a manifestação política nem ter cargo no governo. *Folha de S.Paulo*. 11 July. https://www1.folha.uol.com.br/poder/2021/07/datafolha-maioria-diz-que-militar-da-ativa-nao-deve-ir-a-manifestacao-politica-nem-ter-cargo-no-governo.shtml

Godoy, M. (2020). 'Bolsonaro gera crises e tenta envolver as Forças Armadas em ruptura', diz brigadeiro. *O Estado de S.Paulo*. 8 June. https://www.estadao.com.br/brasil/bolsonaro-e-os-militares/bolsonaro-gera-crises-e-tenta-envolver-as-forcas-armadas-em-ruptura-diz-brigadeiro/

Gularte, J. (2024). Do golpe ao PAC entenda a strategia para pacificar militares sob Lula um ano após o 8/1. *O Globo*. 5 January. https://oglobo.globo.com/politica/noticia/2024/01/05/do-golpe-ao-pac-entenda-a-estrategia-para-pacificar-militares-sob-lula-um-ano-apos-o-81.ghtml

Holanda, M. (2023). Lula pede retirada de projeto de Bolsonaro que poderia isentar militares de punição em GLO. *Folha de S.Paulo*. 6 April. https://www1.folha.uol.com.br/poder/2023/04/lula-pede-retirada-de-projeto-de-bolsonaro-que-poderia-isentar-militares-de-punicao-em-glo.shtml

Holanda, M., & Machado, R. (2023). Novo PAC investirá R$ 52,8 bi em projetos da Defesa em gesto aos militares. *Folha de S.Paulo*. 11 August. https://www1.folha.uol.com.br/mercado/2023/08/novo-pac-investira-r-528-bi-em-projetos-da-defesa-em-gesto-aos-militares.shtml

Holanda, M., Resende, T., Feitoza, C. (2024). Lula poupa militares de cortes nas emendas parlamentares. *Folha de S. Paulo*. 26 January. https://www1.folha.uol.com.br/poder/2024/01/lula-poupa-forcas-armadas-de-cortes-nas-emendas-em-meio-a-gestos-a-caserna.shtml

Hübner Mendes, C. (2018). Magistocracia, a 'gran famiglia' judicial brasileira. *Época*. 2 April. https://epoca.globo.com/politica/Conrado-Hubner/noticia/2018/04/magistocracia-gran-famiglia-judicial-brasileira.html

Human Rights Watch. (2021). Brazil: Bolsonaro Threatens Democratic Rule. 15 September. https://www.hrw.org/news/2021/09/15/brazil-bolsonaro-threatens-democratic-rule

Hupsel Filho, V. (2023). Comissão sobre ditadura militar trava, e governo Lula não cumpre promessa. *Veja*. 25 October. https://veja.abril.com.br/coluna/maquiavel/comissao-sobre-ditadura-militar-trava-e-governo-lula-nao-cumpre-promessa

Landim, R., & Arbex, T. (2023). Lula demite comandante do Exército. *CNN Brasil*. 21 January. https://www.cnnbrasil.com.br/politica/lula-demite-comandante-do-exercito/

Lima, J. A. (2018). O Judiciário poderá conter um presidente Bolsonaro? *Yahoo Notícias*. 16 October. https://web.archive.org/web/20181103163712/https://br.noticias.yahoo.com/o-judiciario-podera-conter-um-presidente-bolsonaro-142510685.html

Machado, R. (2023). Governo Lula retira Abin das mãos de militares e a transfere para a Casa Civil. *Folha de S.Paulo*. 2 March. https://www1.folha.uol.com.br/poder/2023/03/governo-lula-transfere-abin-para-a-casa-civil.shtml

Marsiglia, I. (2022). 'Perdemos': a crise militar que impôs o Artigo 142 à Constituição de 88. *UOL*. 15 November. https://tab.uol.com.br/noticias/redacao/2022/11/15/a-crise-entre-ulysses-e-os-militares-sobre-o-artigo-142-da-constituicao.htm

Mazui, G. (2023). Forças Armadas não comemoram golpe militar no 31 de março pela 1ª vez em cinco anos. *G1*. 31 March. https://g1.globo.com/politica/noticia/2023/03/31/forcas-armadas-nao-comemoram-golpe-militar-no-31-de-marco-pela-1a-vez-em-cinco-anos.ghtml

Monteiro, T. (2018). PT escala emissários para sondar militares. *O Estado de S.Paulo*. 10 October. https://politica.estadao.com.br/noticias/eleicoes,pt-escala-emissarios-para-sondar-militares,70002541446

Nobre, M. (2013). *Imobilismo em Movimento – Da Abertura Democrática ao Governo Dilma*. São Paulo: Companhia das Letras.

Nobre, M. (2022), *Limites da Democracia – De Junho de 2013 ao Governo Bolsonaro*. São Paulo: Todavia.

Odilla, F. (2017) 'Exército é o mesmo de 1964, mas circunstâncias mudaram', diz comandante sobre pedidos de intervenção militar. *BBC*, 13 November. https://www.bbc.com/portuguese/brasil-41929572

Oliveira, R. C. (2018). Genealogias Políticas do Judiciário. *Revista NEP – Núcleo de estudos paranaenses da UFPR*, 4, 317–330. http://dx.doi.org/10.5380/nep.v4i1.60229

Otávio, C. (2023). "O país é conduzido por dois governos, um civil e outro militar', diz parente de desaparecido sobre demora na recriação de comissão para vítimas da ditadura." *O Globo*. 6 October. https://oglobo.globo.com/brasil/noticia/2023/10/06/o-pais-e-conduzido-por-dois-governos-um-civil-e-outro-militar-diz-parente-de-desaparecido-sobre-demora-na-recriacao-de-comissao-para-vitimas-da-ditadura.ghtml

O Estado de S.Paulo. (2024). É hora de encerrar os inquéritos contra golpistas. *O Estado de S.Paulo*. 1 January. https://www.estadao.com.br/opiniao/e-hora-de-encerrar-os-inqueritos-contra-golpistas

Pedretti, L. (2023). A mão amiga de Lula. *Piauí*. 15 December. https://piaui.folha.uol.com.br/mao-amiga-de-lula/

Pitta, I. (2023). Governo sinaliza apoio a PEC da oposição que eleva orçamento da Defesa a 2% do PIB. *CNN Brasil*. 22 November. https://www.cnnbrasil.com.br/politica/governo-sinaliza-apoio-a-pec-da-oposicao-que-eleva-orcamento-da-defesa-a-2-do-pib/

Prazeres, L. (2024). Cúpula militar na mira da PF: o impacto da inédita investigação de envolvimento em plano de golpe. *BBC*. 19 February 2022. https://www.bbc.com/portuguese/articles/cz9e4xyd1kwo

Ramalhoso, W. (2018). Intervenção militar, como foi pedida nos protestos em rodovias, seria golpe e inconstitucional. *UOL*. 30 May. https://noticias.uol.com.br/politica/ultimas-noticias/2018/05/30/o-que-manifestantes-pediram-foi-golpe-militar-nao-intervencao.htm

Recondo, F., & Weber, L. (2023). *O Tribunal - Como o Supremo se uniu ante a ameaça autoritária*. São Paulo: Companhia das Letras.

Rezende, C. (2018). Mourão recebe no clube militar desembargador que manteve Lula preso. *O Estado de S.Paulo*. 20 August. https://www.estadao.com.br/politica/eleicoes/mourao-recebe-no-clube-militar-desembargador-que-manteve-lula-preso/

Ribero, G. (2023). Continued terrorist threat. *The Brazilian Report*. 11 January. https://brazilian.report/newsletters/brazil-daily/2023/01/11/brasilia-riots-china-trade

Roxo, S., & Gularte, J. (2023). A exemplo da Marinha, Exército e Aeronáutica pedem que militares se desfiliem de partidos políticos. *O Globo*. 24 March. https://oglobo.globo.com/politica/noticia/2023/03/a-exemplo-da-marinha-exercito-e-aeronautica-pedem-que-militares-se-desfiliem-de-partidos-politicos.ghtml

Sadek, M. T. (2004). Judiciário: mudanças e reformas. *Estudos Avançados*, 18(51), 79–101. https://www.scielo.br/j/ea/a/rmr7WmNQZLyrPJ7VfWLFPyc/

Savarese, M., & Goodman, J. (2023). Crusading judge tests boundaries of free speech in Brazil. *Associated Press*. 25 January. https://apnews.com/article/jair-bolsonaro-brazil-government-af5987e833a681e6f056fe63789ca375

Schneider, N. (2011). Impunity in Post-authoritarian Brazil: The Supreme Court's Recent Verdict on the Amnesty Law. *European Journal of Latin American and Caribbean Studies*, 90, 39–54. https://www.jstor.org/stable/23047819

Silva, C. R. (2013). Famílias de militares: explorando a casa e a caserna no Exército brasileiro. *Revista Estudos Feministas*, 21(3), 861–882. https://doi.org/10.1590/S0104-026X2013000300006

Soares, I., & Hekally, K. (2023). PF ganha protagonismo na segurança pessoal de Lula após atos golpistas. *Correio Braziliense*. 16 January. https://www.correiobraziliense.com.br/politica/2023/01/5066381-pf-ganha-protagonismo-na-seguranca-pessoal-de-lula-apos-atos-golpistas.html

Spechoto, C., & Fagundes, M. (2023). 'Forças Armadas não são poder moderador como pensam', diz Lula. *Poder360*. 12 January. https://www.poder360.com.br/governo/forcas-armadas-nao-sao-poder-moderador-como-pensam-diz-lula/

Tavares, G. (2023). Tem que respeitar o resultado da urna', diz comandante militar do Sudeste. *UOL*. 20 January. https://noticias.uol.com.br/politica/ultimas-noticias/2023

/01/20/tem-que-respeitar-o-resultado-da-urna-diz-comandante-militar-do-sudeste.htm
Teixeira, M. (2011). O Poder Judiciário brasileiro durante a ditadura militar e os desafios para a construção de uma justiça de transição. *Diké* , v. 3, 153–187.
Viana, N. (2023). 'Militares atuaram em 8 de janeiro por omissão e também por ação', diz historiador. *Agência Pública*. https://apublica.org/2024/01/militares-atuaram-em-8-de-janeiro-por-omissao-e-tambem-por-acao-diz-historiador/
Vieira, O. V., Glezer, R., & Barbosa, A. L. (2022). Supremocracia e infralegalismo autoritário: o comportamento do supremo tribunal federal durante o governo Bolsonaro. *Novos Estudos Cebrap*, 41(3), 591–605. https://doi.org/10.25091/501013300202200030008
Vilela, P. R. (2023). Proposta de criação da Guarda Nacional está pronta, diz ministro. *Agência Brasil*. 26 January. https://agenciabrasil.ebc.com.br/politica/noticia/2023-01/proposta-de-criacao-da-guarda-nacional-esta-pronta-diz-ministro
Vinícius, C. (2023). Governo recua e PEC não vetará militar de ser ministro. *Poder360*. 30 August. https://www.poder360.com.br/governo/governo-recua-e-pec-nao-vetara-militar-de-ser-ministro
Weteman, D., & Frazão, F. (2023). 'Desbolsonarização' no governo Lula atinge militares em cargos políticos. *O Estado de S.Paulo*. 7 January. https://www.estadao.com.br/politica/desbolsonarizacao-no-governo-lula-atinge-militares-em-cargos-politicos/
Zaverucha, J. (1998), "Sarney, Collor, Itamar, FHC e as Prerrogativas Militares (1985–1998)". *Prepared for delivery at the 1998 meeting of the Latin American Studies Association*, The Palmer Hilton House Hotel, Chicago, Illinois, September 24–26, 1998.

9 National referendums on natural resources

Are they effective for conflict resolution?

Yanina Welp

Introduction

Direct democracy mechanisms (DDMs) have proliferated throughout Latin America, thanks to a wave of constitutional reforms that has swept the region, including in Colombia (1991), Peru (1993), Ecuador (1998 and 2008) and Venezuela (1999). In fact, some kind of mechanism for popular consultation now exists in every Latin American nation (Ruth-Lovell and Welp 2024). The triggering or attempted triggering of such mechanisms has also become more common. While these mechanisms have been analyzed in terms of their relationship with the quality of democracy and with populist leaderships (Altman 2010, Lissidini 2015, Tuesta and Welp 2020), this paper shines a light on their effectiveness in resolving conflicts pertaining to an especially hot topic in contemporary debates on development: natural resources.

Public interest in environmental protection and natural resource management has been identified with post-materialist concerns attributed to the world's richest and most industrialized countries. But empirical evidence refutes this idea. According to the EJAtlas, the largest number of protests about these issues are actually concentrated in the global south, where their origins are profoundly material and linked to local living conditions, especially those of Indigenous and peasant populations (Martinez Allier 2004, Temper et al. 2018).

In Latin America, debates over development, the state, and democracy are often centred around natural resources (Acosta 2012, Campello and Zucco 2020). This is not new. Since they gained their independence, Latin American states have been concerned with natural resources due to their potential to generate economic growth, and because this growth has a non-linear relationship with social welfare. While the former occurs through the insertion of countries into global markets, the latter is part of the political dispute over whether or not to impose taxes and retentions on exports of primary goods which can, in turn, be invested in the development of industrial or social policies. It is no coincidence, then, that an extensive literature has grown up around the economic, social, and political consequences of production models that revolve predominantly around the primary sector (whether through agricultural and livestock production or the

DOI: 10.4324/9781003519195-9

extraction of gold, silver, and fossil fuels such as gas and oil, to which rare minerals such as lithium have more recently been added) (Svampa 2015).

With the arrival of the twenty-first century, these disputes have not diminished but rather expanded. Practices such as open-pit mining, oil extraction, and the use of transgenics and pesticides often pit the interests of large corporations against the opposition of environmental movements and Indigenous and peasant communities (Martínez Allier 2015, Spalding 2023). Disputes over production models are materialized in specific conflicts rooted in particular territories and entail a struggle over the exercise of political rights to define who can and should decide (with some of the possible options including the affected communities, the whole nation, or elected representatives), as well as *how* to decide (from the various possible mechanisms and procedures).

In recent years, scholars have tried to map environmental protests (Temper et al. 2018) in order to understand both patterns of dispute and the multidimensional consequences of extractive activities (Svampa 2015, Glazebrook and Opok 2018). An emerging literature additionally focuses on the outcomes of international mechanisms such as "prior consultations" (Zaremberg and Torres Wong 2018, Perreault, 2015). The picture is a complex one. There are numerous case-studies,[1] as well as analyses of specific mechanisms such as prior consultation,[2] that set out to identify their possibilities and limitations. But there is no research that comparatively analyzes the triggering processes for national-level direct democracy mechanisms aimed at deciding on the use of natural resources. It is worth asking whether this absence is due to the simple disinterest of the citizenry in initiating mechanisms that are costly to implement in terms of time and resources, or because of other factors, including the fact that initiation attempts may not be successful (see Raventós 2020, Pozo 2020, Tuesta and Welp 2020).

In order to contribute to the production of knowledge on the subject, this paper examines the conditionalities and outcomes of the activation of national-level DDMs to decide on the ownership and use of natural resources in Latin American countries between 1980 and 2023. First, it offers a state-of-the-field summary of citizen participation in decision-making on natural resources, before presenting a similar overview of direct democracy mechanisms. Then, based on original research, it systematically analyzes those referendums and popular initiatives that have been successfully initiated (whether or not they have reached the voting stage), considering the nature of each procedure as well as its consequences. Finally, the results of this analysis are discussed, and the overall conclusions of the paper are presented.

Legitimacy and the inclusion of the citizenry

The rivalry between different models of development has shaped the relations between economic and political power throughout Latin America. In Argentina, this is illustrated by the concept of "hegemonic standoff" (Portantiero 1977), which accounts for the tensions between a powerful agricultural sector and an incipient, state-dependent industrial bourgeoisie over the course of the twentieth century. This case is not an isolated one, although each has its own particularities as well, as suggested by the emergence of peasant guerrillas in Nicaragua, or the disputes between Central American countries such as Guatemala and large, foreign-owned companies such as United Fruit. The Panamanian case is perhaps the most emblematic, in that the US controlled part of the country's territory from a few days after it won its independence from Colombia, all the way through the twentieth century to 1977, when the Torrijos-Carter Treaties became effective (Brown Araúz and Nevache 2023).

In recent decades, as Indigenous communities have been recognized and an ever greater concern is felt for the environment, the interests at stake in such conflicts have diversified and the field of struggle has broadened. This can be seen clearly in environmental protests, which often involve a variety of actors, including local communities, government agencies, the private sector, and international organizations. Because of their consequences – which for some actors may include the suspension of extractive industrial activity – supranational institutions such as the World Bank and the ILO have supported demands for the adoption of mechanisms for citizen participation. These processes vary greatly due to a range of different factors, including who they involve (communities, local units, or more extensive territorial units) and their consequences (such as whether they are consultative or binding). That said, it is still possible to distinguish three basic varieties of mechanism: social licence, prior consultation, and popular consultations – the latter designed to facilitate a decision-making process via the ballot box (whether convened from above by governments, or from below by the citizenry).

"Social licence" is a term introduced in the late 1990s at a World Bank conference (Geert and Björn 2016). The idea addresses the need to obtain society's endorsement of a given economic activity because otherwise its rejection by the population could lead to the stalling or limiting of projects (in the original discussion, it was mining projects that communities were rejecting). A social licence differs from a legal licence in that it appeals to the citizenry, rather than the judiciary, for acceptance. It is usually linked to projects that have a significant territorial impact, such as mining, tourism, or particularly polluting industries. An instrumental notion of legitimization can be observed in this origin. The idea of the social licence emerged from within the milieu of economic development and investment, and it has been promoted as a way of avoiding protests that could jeopardize the sustainability of investments. The procedures established for it are neither particularly rigorous nor systematic.

The case of Prior Consultation, established by ILO Convention 169, is distinct. Prior Consultation is aimed at Indigenous and other ethnic communities and concerns projects that directly affect their territories. It applies in countries that have ratified the Convention and requires informed consultation to be carried out with the affected populations. However, extensive research on the subject shows that such consultations are rarely successful, especially when communities are organized and manage to establish support networks (Falleti and Riofrancos 2018). In general, in the best of cases, prior consultations seem to favour the renegotiation of benefits, rather than the questioning of projects (Acuña 2022, Torres Wong 2018, Walter and Urkidi 2016). In some countries, such as Colombia, prior consultation is usually carried out under the tutelage of the central government and functions as a deliberative mechanism without any electoral component (Acuña 2022). Studies such as that of Zaremberg, Torres Wong, and Guarneros-Meza (2018) attest to the presence of these and other local institutions of citizen participation in Mexico, too, where their initiation is authorized by federal law in relation to neo-extractive mega-projects (such as mining and hydrocarbons) and alternative energy industries (such as wind and hydroelectric power).

Another issue worthy of consideration is the expansion of the ideology of "good living" and the recovery of Indigenous rights under the auspices of what is often called the "new Latin American constitutionalism" (Acosta 2012), which initially supported political projects such as those promoted in Ecuador and Bolivia in the mid-2000s. However, even here, the tension between rival models of development quickly reared its head. In Bolivia, one prominent example was the 2009 road construction project in the Isiboro Secure Indigenous Territory and National Park (TIPNIS). Its rejection by local communities generated protests that were repressed by the government in what was identified as a conflict between "communitarians" (Indigenous communities) and "developmentalists" (represented by then-Vice President Alvaro García Linera). This conflict was a watershed moment.[3] Similar tensions arose during the Ecuadorian Constituent Assembly in 2007, in which the "developmentalists" also triumphed, although not without cost to the legitimacy of these political projects (Welp 2022).

The case of the TIPNIS, for which no public consultation was ever held, reveals the contradiction between the participatory discourses surrounding these projects and practices of keeping decision-making controlled. Despite this, popular consultations have become an ever more prominent mechanism of resistance for communities or population groups at the local level (Flemmer and Schilling-Vacaflor 2016). These consultations usually take place in municipalities and communities and are strongly conditioned by the relevant legal frameworks, the organizational capacity of local actors, and multilevel political contestation (for a detailed investigation of these factors, see Acuña 2022). Depending on the legal framework, popular consultations can be self-convened or convened by the authorities. Sometimes, the dispute can end up in the Constitutional Courts, as happened in Colombia (Hincapié 2017, Muñoz and Peña Niño 2019).

Referendums and initiatives in Latin America

Unlike participatory processes that aim to grant "social licence" to a project or achieve its approval through "prior consultation" – neither of which appear to be effective ways of resolving conflicts – the scenarios analyzed in this section suggest that national-level DDMs can be powerful mechanisms for channelling conflicts institutionally. But when and under what conditions do they function in this manner?

National-level DDMs enable the incorporation of citizens into the decision-making process by electoral means that go beyond the election of representatives. Research into the consequences of such mechanisms warns of risks linked to their strategic use by leaders who might initiate them in order to circumvent institutional obstacles. Indeed, in Latin America, there have been numerous cases of leaders who lack a legislative majority promoting their agendas by appealing to the will of the citizenry, which can lead to conflicts between legality and legitimacy (Ruth-Lovell and Welp 2024). On the other hand, mandatory mechanisms to ratify decisions such as constitutional changes, and mechanisms activated by signature collection that could allow the repeal of laws passed by congress or the proposal of legislation that is not on the institutional agenda, stand out as DDMs that have the potential to strengthen democracy (Lissidini 2015, Altman 2010, Ruth et al 2017, Welp 2022).

In contrast to the limitations of prior consultations and social licence – whose scope is confined to directly affected communities and groups, whose results are non-binding, and whose procedures are largely adaptable to the criteria of their promoters – it may be that referendums and popular initiatives, and above all those that can be initiated by the citizenry, can allow for broader and more effective debates to be held over models of development and help to legitimize decisions made at the level of the nation-state by providing a framework of clear and fair rules. But can they operate in this way? And what legal and other requirements would need to be contemplated to this end? To answer the question, we must first explore the nature of the regulations that allow for DDMs to be initiated.

In recent decades, every country in the region has embarked on constitutional reforms that incorporate DDMs, although there are marked differences in terms of the specific regulations. Essentially, there are three types of procedures: those initiated by the authorities (the executive and/or the legislature); those initiated due to constitutional obligations; and those initiated through the collection of signatures. While presidentially initiated mechanisms have in practice been rather flexible,[4] the mandatory and signature-driven procedures require regulation. Eleven countries allow their citizens to activate a popular initiative or referendum: Bolivia, Colombia, Costa Rica, the Dominican Republic, Ecuador, Honduras, Mexico, Nicaragua, Peru, Venezuela, and Uruguay (each one with regulations that vary considerably – for details see Linares and Welp

2020), while seven also mandate that referendums be held to ratify constitutional reforms.[5]

In general (taking into account every possible thematic area), Uruguay and Ecuador are the countries in which these mechanisms have been activated most frequently, although according to different patterns: in Uruguay via the collection of signatures, and in Ecuador by presidential initiative (Ruth et al. 2017). In mid-twentieth century Uruguay, the "popular initiative" (an instrument that could be activated by signature collection but had to first be initiated by parties with a parliamentary presence) played an important role in transferring to the citizenry the ability to decide party-political disputes. A 1967 reform expanded the mechanism so that it could be initiated by any person or civil society association. With the transition to democracy, popular initiatives became important once again in terms of human rights issues (for example, in debates over the repeal of the "Law of Expiry" that prevents the investigation of crimes committed during the dictatorship, rejected twice in 1989 and 2009), and against the privatization process in the 1990s (in which the Broad Front, an opposition grouping made up of trade unions, civil society organizations and political parties, played a key role; see Monestier 2011). More recently, such mechanisms have also played into the hands of conservative parties, which tried to use them to block the extension of new rights to groups such as transgender people (regarding which a pre-referendum was activated and rejected, see Lissidini 2021). The last plebiscite to be initiated was in opposition to the Urgent Consideration Law (a broad package of reforms that the government of President Lacalle Pou passed via an emergency procedure during the pandemic), which failed to force the Law's repeal in 2022.

In Ecuador, the democratic transition of 1978 included a vote on the constitution, and since the 1990s, practically every one of the country's presidents has held a popular consultation. Rafael Correa successfully used them on several occasions to alter the distribution of political power, and consultations were also later organized by both Lenín Moreno and Guillermo Lasso. In the rest of the Latin American nations, popular consultations have been less frequent, although displaying notable differences in goals, procedures, and results (see Lissidini 2015, Ruth et al. 2017).

In the studies that have been conducted into the functioning of these mechanisms in Latin America, two central findings stand out. The first is that deficits in institutional design tend to inhibit the citizens' ability to initiate them, thanks to regulatory contradictions, high thresholds, and/or broad thematic exclusions. Thus in Ecuador, at least half a dozen citizen initiatives failed during the 2010s because the law lacked clarity as to whether the National Electoral Council should authorize the collection of signatures before, or after, the constitutionality of the initiatives had been verified, causing the initiatives to be sent from one institution to another until they were shelved (Tuesta and Welp 2020). In Costa Rica, an exhaustive list of excluded topics and the Constitutional Court's high level of discretionary power prevented the authorization of at least ten initiatives (Raventós 2020). And the same can be said of Mexico until the passing of legal reforms in 2018. A lack of safeguards has also affected processes in other countries, such as Colombia, where a participation threshold of 33% was required for an anti-corruption consultation to be officially valid, while a more questionable level of only 13% was imposed on the peace plebiscite. In summary, comparative and case analyses show that in general, and with the exception of Uruguay, referendums have mainly been activated by the executive in order to circumvent institutional obstacles, which has entailed subtle or flagrant violations of legal frameworks in a significant number of cases (see Lissidini 2015, Altman 2010, Tuesta and Welp 2020 and Linares and Welp 2020, Ruth et al. 2017).

However, despite this tentative conclusion, a second important finding is that plebiscites have been frequently used to try to channel conflicts. A good example is that of Peru in 2018, where then-President Martín Vizcarra held a consultation to ratify a raft of reforms in order to try and circumvent an ongoing political crisis (Tuesta 2020). Also worthy of note is the Chilean experience, where in response to the popular uprising of 2019, the best-represented political parties at the time agreed to organize a plebiscite on constitutional reform. But now we must move onward to our analysis of nationwide consultations over natural resources.

Analysis

In this section, we map the initiation of popular consultations (whether via the collection of signatures, or by the authorities, or as a result of constitutional mandates) in Latin America in the period 1980–2023, identifying: (1) the countries in which DDMs have been formally initiated to make decisions on natural resources, (2) the dynamics of these processes, and (3) their consequences. The criteria for selecting the cases were as follows:

1. The type of mechanism initiated. For the launching of popular consultations by the executive and/or the legislative branch, the existence of an enabling legal framework is not essential since these authorities can, and in many cases have, called for these consultations on an *ad hoc* basis. Sometimes this has prompted the intervention of other organs of state either to endorse or reject the call. Both of these types of cases were included in the study (an example being Panama 2023). In contrast, popular initiatives triggered by the collection of signatures require a legal framework through which to become institutional processes. For this reason, only those signature-based initiatives formally initiated in countries with laws that regulate these processes (as listed in the previous section) were considered for analysis.
2. The topic. Only those consultations referring to the management, use, and ownership of natural resources – including issues such as water, extractive

industries, infrastructure with high environmental impact, and packages of measures including any or all of these (as in Costa Rica 2007) – were considered relevant for this study.

3. Formal initiation (or attempted initiation). The criterion for recognition in this sense was, ideally, that a formalized proposal (often a decree or legislative decision) had been presented and was subsequently processed through the corresponding legal channels. It was not always this clear-cut, however, especially in the case of citizen initiatives in Ecuador and Costa Rica, where a considerable number of petitions were registered and then presented either to the electoral body or to the legislative body, only to be dismissed during the initial phases of the process and prior to the collection of any signatures.[6]

All in all, initiations or attempted initiations of national-level referendums or popular initiatives aimed at deciding questions of natural resources have been identified in seven different countries: Bolivia, Colombia, Costa Rica, Ecuador, Mexico, Panama, and Uruguay.[7] These cases are presented below.

Bolivia: The resolution of two specific conflicts

In October 2003, in what became known as the "Bolivian gas conflict," a mass mobilization by citizens against the export of natural gas through Chilean territory led to the resignation of President Sánchez de Lozada. Vice President Carlos Mesa took office and promised to call a binding referendum in order to resolve the conflict. To carry it out, the country's constitution was reformed. The referendum was held on 18 July 2004. The consultation included five questions regarding the repeal of the law that Lozada had approved, state ownership of hydrocarbons at the wellhead, the recovery of shares in private hands, and the use of resources obtained from gas extraction for investments in development and social policies.[8] In the end, the "yes" vote triumphed, provisionally stabilizing the government and setting a political precedent as well as popular expectations for the use of DDMs in the resolution of conflicts between political actors (Salazar Elena 2009). Salazar Elena's study focuses on a central issue for our current analysis: the kind of normative framework that determines, or aims to determine, how to practically implement the resolutions made via the consultation. For example, question two – "Do you agree with the recovery of the ownership of all hydrocarbons at the wellhead for the Bolivian State?" – opens the door to a whole series of resolutions that are not defined. Does this "recovery" imply expropriation, and if so, with or without indemnification? Different actors took different positions in relation to these questions. But the interesting thing is that the president launched an intense campaign throughout the nation's territory to put forward his point of view and to announce subsequent resolutions to be taken in case the consultation was approved.

Bolivia's second popular consultation linked to the management and ownership of natural resources took place in 2009, in combination with a consultation over the ratification of the new constitution, and was called the "settlement referendum." This vote sought to resolve an issue on which the constituent assembly had been unable to reach an agreement, and which it therefore decided to transfer to the citizenry. The issue at stake was the extension that an unproductive large estate had to have – whether 5,000 or 10,000 hectares – in order for the state to be able to expropriate it. The option to set the expropriation threshold at 5,000 hectares triumphed with 80% of the vote. Since then, there have been no further initiations of national-level DDMs on questions of natural resources (although Bolivia has nevertheless seen intense conflicts over these issues, as mentioned above in relation to the TIPNIS).

*Colombia: A*nother popular consultation process frustrated

Colombia's 1991 constitution was the first in Latin America to incorporate a wide range of civic participation institutions, including DDMs. But in practice, their use has been rare, as well as marked by the frustration of the 2016 Plebiscite for Peace and the subsequent failure of the 2018 Anti-Corruption Consultation to gain sufficient signatures to validate its results. Regarding issues of natural resources, numerous consultations took place at the subnational level (Acuña 2022), but only one at the national level, for which 60 civil society organizations gathered two million signatures but nonetheless failed to reach the voting stage. The initiative was a reaction against previous legislation commercializing water distribution and sought the enshrinement of access to drinking water as a fundamental right, as well as the free provision of the minimum quantity needed for subsistence, the special protection and priority use of ecosystems essential to the water cycle, and public, state, and community management of water and sewage services. The process was frustrated in its passage through parliament due to conflicts between the benches (see Gómez Bustos 2014), and also because the consultation would have coincided with another promoted by President Alvaro Uribe to approve the possibility of his re-election, which was suspended as unconstitutional (see Londono 2020). The high thresholds required to activate these mechanisms and validate them in a country with high abstention rates, and the lack of definition suffered by the DDMs under citizen control (see Linares and Welp 2020), suggest that the regulatory framework surrounding them is in need of review.

Costa Rica: The citizenry cannot act as veto player

In Costa Rica, constitutional reforms in 2002 introduced changes intended to halt the democratic system's increasing loss of legitimacy, which included the possibility of triggering DDMs. However, it was not until 2007, after a judicial appeal was filed by civil society organizations and endorsed by the Constitutional

Court, that these mechanisms were finally regulated (See Raventós 2020). The civil society lawsuit was initiated with the intention of collecting signatures to reject a free trade agreement recently signed by the government. Raventós' work provides an account of the inequalities and undue pressures exerted on social movements during the signature-gathering stage. President Oscar Arias finally decided to take the initiative, suspending the citizen-led process and instead calling the consultation "from above." During the subsequent campaign, pressures on public officials were denounced, as were problems of severe inequality in terms of access to material resources and media space. The vote resulted in a close victory for supporters of the free trade treaty, in a process perceived by its opponents as unfair (Raventós 2018). The country's second consultation process is an initiative in favour of oil exploitation and was registered with the Supreme Electoral Tribunal (TSE) in 2020, but there is no record as to whether progress has been made in collecting signatures.[9] As in other cases analyzed here, the amending of standards is common. In Costa Rica, a legislative reform was approved in 2021 that charged the TSE with consulting the Constitutional Chamber regarding *a priori* constitutionality. This is positive because it avoids the initiation of signature-collection without knowing if an initiative is constitutional, but it also boosts the power of the Constitutional Chamber, which acquires greater say and influence in this area.

Ecuador: A common practice that rarely meets its objectives

In 2007, President Rafael Correa promoted the Yasuní ITT initiative in defence of the environment, which proposed to leave the area's oil in the ground in exchange for economic compensation from the richest and most polluting countries. After a few years and in the absence of any such compensation, he proposed instead to exploit the oil. In response, in 2013, the Yasunidos association, which brought together environmentalists, peasants, and Indigenous communities, tried to organize a popular vote on the issue, with the intention of prohibiting exploitation. The National Electoral Council argued that sufficient signatures had not been obtained and did not allow a vote to take place, in a highly-contested process that would be reactivated in the following years.

On 2 April 2017, Lenín Moreno (Alianza País) was elected president with a narrow majority (51.16%) in a runoff poll. He faced his first political crisis only a few days after taking office due to serious corruption allegations involving Vice President Jorge Glas. The governing party split into two factions: that of President Moreno and that of the former president, Rafael Correa. In the previous decade, tensions had grown between Correa's government and a range of other groups, including social movements, media outlets, and opposition parties. It was in this context that Moreno decided to open a process of "National Social Dialogue" (Decree 49 of 20 June 2017), which gave rise to the idea of calling a popular consultation. This initiative was in line with the perception, widespread in the Ecuadorian political arena, that directly consulting the population serves as an instrument of legitimization. Moreno invited the citizenry to send in proposals on what to include in the vote. On October 2, the president announced that he had sent to the Constitutional Court a list of seven questions that would together constitute the "Popular Consultation and Referendum."[10] Five of these were classified as referendums, and two as popular consultations. Two concerned natural resources: one regarding the prohibition of metallic mining, and another on limiting oil extraction in the Yasuní area.[11] Both were approved, but their implementation has since been questioned.

When Guillermo Lasso subsequently took office in 2021, he did just as his predecessor Moreno had done and promoted a popular consultation with the aim of legitimizing his rule and strengthening his control of the country (necessary because his party was a minority in the legislative assembly). Thus, on 29 August 2023, he initiated a popular consultation that once again concerned Yasuní: "Do you agree that the Ecuadorian government should keep the crude oil of the ITT [Ishpingo-Tambococha-Tiputini oil field], known as Block 43, indefinitely in the subsoil?" The proposal passed with 59% of the vote, and a period of one year was settled on for the region's oil exploitation infrastructure to be dismantled. The conclusion that would seem to emerge from the Ecuadorian case, then, is that while consultations are used often, the implementation of their results tends to remain in limbo.

Mexico: Tools in the hands of parties and the government

Mexico was the last country in the region to incorporate DDMs into its constitution. It did so in 2012 and subsequently expanded and modified them in 2018 (Sandoval 2020). In December 2013, a group of citizens affiliated with the Party of the Democratic Revolution (PRD) were among the first to present a popular initiative to the Senate, which aimed to modify a law passed by the Peña Nieto administration opening up the management of national oil revenue to the private sector. More than two million signatures were gathered, and the initiative was admitted and referred to the National Supreme Court of Justice (SCJN) to be checked for constitutionality. There it was rejected on the grounds of formal defects. Another group of people from the same party subsequently presented a similar initiative in the House of Representatives. A resolution was made to combine both consultations, and it was again passed to the SCJN, which this time declared it unconstitutional due to its subject matter. A group of citizens linked to the National Regeneration Party (MORENA) put forward a third initiative that falls within our thematic field in 2014, with similar content to the initiatives presented by the PRD. The proposed question was: "Do you agree or disagree with the granting of contracts or concessions to private parties, national or foreign, for the exploitation of oil, gas, refining, petrochemicals, and the electricity industry?" This was also declared unconstitutional on the grounds that the consultation impinged upon the country's revenues (suggesting the existence of regulatory deficits that inhibit the successful activation of consultations; see the analysis of Sandoval 2020).

Finally, two other consultations relevant to our analysis were held during the period between Andrés Manuel López Obrador's presidential election victory in June 2018, and his actual installation as president in December: one in opposition to the construction of the new Mexico City airport at Texcoco, and another in support of the "Mayan Train" project. Both took place outside the usual legal framework of Mexican DDMs, since the National Electoral Institute refused to implement them because the president had not yet assumed office. López Obrador's position triumphed in both consultations, but in conditions that did not comply with the minimum requirements of a fair and competitive vote and with low levels of participation. Ultimately, López Obrador did not intend them to be effective decision-making processes, but rather used them as tools to give electoral legitimacy to decisions that he could otherwise have implemented with legislative support.

Panama: From the canal to the mine

In 1977, the Torrijos-Carter Treaties, which stipulated that the United States would return control of the Panama Canal to Panama, were put to a referendum and won the approval of two-thirds of voters. Giannareas (2020: 100) defines it as "a vote in favour of decolonization and a second and deeper independence."[12] The country's 1972 Constitution, which provided the framework for that referendum, established in its Article 274 that the construction of a new canal or a third set of locks would need to be submitted to a national plebiscite. A 2004 constitutional reform re-emphasized the necessity of referendums for validating decisions related to the Canal. One such vote took place in 2006 regarding the Canal's expansion, with three out of four voters approving the proposal in a referendum with a very low turnout of 43% (for details, see Giannareas 2020).

The next (failed) attempt at initiating a referendum occurred in 2023. That October, the legislature fast-tracked the approval of a contract with Minera Panama (a subsidiary of Canada's First Quantum Minerals), sparking public outcry over environmental issues as well as allegations of corruption. The government initially declared it would uphold the decision already taken by the legislature, but as protests continued to escalate, President Laurentino Cortizo announced his willingness to hold a popular consultation on December 17 so that the citizenry could decide. This process was rejected by the Electoral Tribunal; however, while the Constitutional Court concurrently declared the contract itself unconstitutional.

Uruguay: Water as a human right

As we have already mentioned, Uruguay is the most prolific country in the region in terms of initiating popular consultations, of which we have identified three linked to natural resources. The first took place on 31 October 2004 and saw 65% of the voters approve a measure giving the state exclusive responsibility for sanitation and the distribution of drinking water. The plebiscite was promoted by the National Commission for the Defence of Water and Life, an alliance between the trade union of the state water and sanitation company (OSE) and several civil society groups. The next initiative, in 2017, sought to repeal a law (Law n.°19553, "Irrigation Destined for Agriculture," passed by the Ministry of Livestock, Agriculture and Fisheries (MGAP)), which increased the amount of water available for agricultural production. A third, in 2018, attempted to halt the implementation of the Aratirí Project (a huge open-cast iron ore mine spanning parts of the Florida, Durazno, and Treinta y Tres departments). Neither of these latter initiatives managed to progress beyond the signature collection phase, and both generated internal conflicts within the ruling Frente Amplio party between "developmentalists" and defenders of the environmental agenda (see Lissidini 2021).

Discussion

Our review shows that popular consultations have been formally initiated on at least 20 occasions in seven different Latin American countries. Civil society groups initiated seven of these consultations, of which only one was actually voted on (Uruguay 2004). The remaining initiatives either failed to meet signature collection thresholds or were suspended due to instrumental issues (Costa Rica 2007, Colombia 2009, Ecuador 2013). Opposition political parties used signature collection processes to push forward three other initiatives, all of which similarly failed to reach the voting stage because they were declared unconstitutional (Mexico).

Of the nine promoted either by constitutional mandate (Panama 2006), by institutional agreement (Bolivia 2009), or by the executive, all of them, with the exception of Panama 2023, resulted in referendums in which the president's proposal won the day. However, if we judge them on the basis of their political objectives – institutionally channel conflicts, introduce or veto legislation, or legitimize a decision already taken (see "political function" in Table 9.1) – it appears that only a few of these consultations were truly successful. Among these would be the Bolivian consultation on energy policy of 2004, which managed to defuse a serious conflict, and to a lesser extent the Costa Rican consultation of 2007, which also resolved a conflict but at the cost of its own legitimacy, given that social organizations and civil society movements subsequently denounced numerous irregularities that had affected the vote. Along the same lines, President López Obrador's informal consultations in Mexico failed both to mobilize the grassroots and to generate processes considered as politically and legally valid.

Conclusions

In Latin America, debates over development, the state, and democracy often centre on natural resources, which have long occupied a key role due both to

Table 9.1 Initiation or attempted initiation of DDMs on natural resources (1980–2023)

Country	*Year*	*Issue*	*Promoted by*	*Political function*	*Result*
Bolivia	2004	Energy Policy, five questions	Interim president (Carlos Mesa)	Channel pre-existing conflict	Approved by vote
	2009	Agrarian Reform, two options	Constitutional mandate	Channel pre-existing conflict	Approved by vote
Colombia	2009	Water as a fundamental right	Civil society	Introduce legislation	Archived
Costa Rica	2007	Free-trade agreement with US (ALCA)	President	Channel pre-existing conflict/ legitimize	Approved by vote
Ecuador	2007	Oppose the ALCA	Civil society	Veto a decision	Archived
	2020	Authorize exploitation of natural resources	Civil society	Introduce legislation	No data
	2013	Against petroleum exploitation in Yasuní	Civil society	Veto a decision	Archived
	2018	Prohibition of mining of metals	President (Lenín Moreno)	Legitimize	Approved by vote
	2018	Reduce area of petroleum exploitation in Yasuní	President (Lenín Moreno)	Legitimize	Approved by vote
	2023	Prohibit petroleum exploitation in "Block 43" (Yasuní)	President (Guillermo Lasso)	Legitimize	Approved by vote
Mexico	2014	Energy reform (presented to Chamber of Deputies)	Political party (PRD)	Channel pre-existing conflict	Cancelled
	2014	Energy reform (presented to Senate)	Political party (PRD)	Channel pre-existing conflict	Cancelled
	2014	Energy Reform	Political party (Morena)	Channel pre-existing conflict	Cancelled
	2020	Regarding the new airport	President-elect (not yet in post)	Legitimize	Informal vote
	2020	Regarding the Mayan Train project	President-elect (not yet in post)	Legitimize	Informal vote
Panama	2006	Expansion of the Canal	Obligatory	Legitimize	Approved by vote
	2023	Regarding the mining contract	President	Channel pre-existing conflict	Cancelled
Uruguay	2004	Water as a fundamental right	Civil society	Introduce legislation	Approved by vote
	2017	Against the agrarian law	Civil society	Veto legislation	Signatures not collected
	2018	Against mining	Civil society	Veto legislation	

Source: Author's own elaboration.

their potential to generate economic growth, and because this growth has a non-linear relationship with social welfare. Disputes about the "best" or most "correct" use of natural resources thus entail a struggle over the exercise of political rights to define who can and should decide. Reviewing the research that has been conducted on these issues reveals that it is supranational bodies that have promoted the need to apply "prior consultation" processes (ILO Convention) or to obtain a "social licence" (World Bank) for certain kinds of cases. These initiatives are not binding and concern only the territories directly affected by a project – normally relatively small areas with Indigenous and/or peasant populations. It, therefore, appears that direct democracy mechanisms – namely, referendums and popular initiatives – have greater potential as decision-making processes. On these grounds, we set out to investigate their relevance. We began by noting that governments are reluctant to initiate such mechanisms unless they can be used to resolve high-level political conflicts or disputes with civil society (especially when these involve powerful civic protest movements). Meanwhile, popular initiatives may enable the citizenry to widen debates with the aim of trying to veto laws (such as those enabling oil exploitation in Ecuador) or to introduce them (one example being Uruguay's "right to water" legislation).

In most of the 20 or so initiatives analyzed here, the use of DDMs has not served as an effective way of resolving conflicts. In some cases, this is because they have been declared unconstitutional or inappropriate, while in other cases, even when they have reached the voting stage, they have not managed to legitimize decisions already made by governments (except in the cases of Bolivia in 2004 and 2009, and to a lesser extent Costa Rica in 2007, in which the process was heavily critiqued), or resulted in the implementation of new determinations made by voters. Are these limitations related to the rule of law? The answer is yes, although the nature of regulatory frameworks cannot make for an exhaustive explanation, and/or their role is compounded by the ways in which different actors instrumentalize these mechanisms for their own benefit (although they do not always manage to benefit in the end).

We observe, in the first place, that elected representatives often lack political responsibility. This is evident in cases such as that of Mexico, where President López Obrador activated popular consultations – such as those concerning the Mayan Train and the construction of the new airport – in defiance of official procedure.

Second, institutional designs are flawed (which is evident from the Costa Rican, Ecuadorean, and Colombian cases cited here, although even these do not attest to the total number of design elements that should be reconsidered to facilitate the legitimate initiation of DDMs). There are multiple ways of designing institutions and there is no one correct path, but certain criteria exist that should guide the formulation of questions for popular consultation (as covered in the OAS white paper on referendums, for example). Thresholds for signatures are central to drawing the line between initiatives that can be efficiently used to channel the demands of the citizenry, and those that are no more than useless paper, but there is much more that can also be done. Poorly-designed "rules of the game" hinder the functioning of DDMs, which happens all too often, especially in those cases where civil society organizations or social movements try to initiate them. It is evident that the inclusion of these mechanisms in the region's new or updated constitutions has not, in general, been accompanied by their effective regulation, resulting in gaps in the legislation that allow citizens' initiatives to be all too easily blocked.

Third, there are also problems with the weaknesses (if not outright co-optation) of procedural control and oversight bodies, which particularly affect electoral institutions and constitutional courts but are not limited to these bodies either. The experience of Costa Rica, where President Arias blocked a popular initiative and improperly activated state resources for political campaigning, is one clear illustration of this issue. The same could be said of the manipulation and blocking of popular initiatives in Ecuador in 2013 (Yasuní), and in Bolivia in 2009 (TIPNIS).

Finally, there is a last issue that not only concerns the rule of law but is also linked to regulatory frameworks: namely, that the instances of public opinion formation must be regulated, and that there must be guarantees that the information available for decision-making will be complete and sufficient. The mechanisms of direct democracy operate in a particular kind of system that conditions their own development. If the rules are not clear, or the actors are not willing to respect them, then it is difficult for DDMs to offer a real solution to a country's conflicts.

Notes

1 Among others, see Dietz, 2019; Garcés Villamil and Rapalino Bautista 2015; Walter and Martinez-Alier 2010; and Hincapié 2017.
2 See Falleti and Riofrancos, 2018; McGee, 2009; Perreault, 2015; and Zaremberg and Wong, 2018.
3 In 2011, a group of NGOs and representatives of social movements published a critique titled "For the Recuperation of the Process of Change By and For the People," denouncing the continuity of the extractive model. A few days later, Linera published "'NGOism': Infantile Illness of the Right (Or, How the 'Taking Back' of the Process of Change is the Neoliberal Restoration)," in which they identified the signatories of the former as "bitter politicians," many of whom had been part of previous governments.
4 Having pushed forward numerous such exercises despite this not being their prerogative, as occurred in Argentina in 1984 with the "Consultation of the Argentinian People Regarding the Southern Margins of the Beagle Canal Zone," for the ratification of the treaty with Chile.
5 Obligatory referendums apply in Bolivia, Panama, Paraguay, the Dominican Republic, Venezuela, Uruguay, and Peru (although in the latter, constitutional reforms are also possible if two consecutive legislatures approve them). Neither obligatory nor signature-initiated referendums apply in Argentina, Brazil, Chile, El Salvador, and Guatemala.

6 For example, Raventós (2020) identifies 45 popular consultation initiatives presented in Costa Rica between 2006 and 2018, of which only two fit within the thematic classification that we are considering in this study (Raventós, 2020).
7 The cases were identified via the revision of the C2D database, my personal archive, electoral institutions, and conversations with other researchers. I owe many thanks here to Fabián Acuña, Alicia Lissidini, and Carolina Ovares y Ciska Raventós.
8 "1. Do you agree with the abrogation of Hydrocarbons Law Nº 1689 passed by Gonzalo Sánchez de Lozada? 2. Do you agree with the recovery of the ownership of all hydrocarbons at the wellhead for the Bolivian State? 3. Do you agree with restoring YPFB and taking back state control of the shares held by Bolivians in the capitalized oil companies, so the state can participate in every stage of the hydrocarbon production chain? 4. Do you agree with the policy of President Carlos Mesa of using gas as a strategic resource for attaining a functional and sovereign outlet onto the Pacific Ocean? And 5. Do you agree that Bolivia should export gas in line with a national policy that: covers the gas consumption of the Bolivian women and men, foments the industrialization of gas within the national territory, charges taxes and royalties on the oil companies at a level of 50% of the value of gas and petroleum on behalf of the nation, and channels the returns on the exploitation and industrialization of gas principally towards education, health, roads and employment?"
9 N.° 5870-E9-2020. "Autorización del formulario para la recolección de firmas necesarias para convocar a referéndum, por iniciativa ciudadana, el proyecto de ley denominado 'Aprovechamiento de los Recursos Energéticos Nacionales'." See https://www.tse.go.cr/juris/
10 I took part in the Electoral Observation Mission organized by the OAS, which gave me the opportunity to interview numerous social, political, and academic figures as well as carry out a detailed study into the prior participative process and the popular consultation. The mission's report can be consulted here: http://www.oas.org/eomdatabase/GetFileA.aspx?id=398-1126-28-0
11 "Do you agree with amending the Constitution of the Republic of Ecuador to prohibit the mining of metals in all of its stages, in protected areas, intangible zones and urban centers, according to Annex 5?" And, for popular consultation, "Do you agree with increasing the intangible zone to at least 50,000 hectares and reducing the area of petroleum exploitation authorized by the National Assembly in the Yasuní National Park from 1,030 hectares to 300 hectares?"
12 The same author argues that the third that opposed the Treaties voted against them because, above all, they considered the period marked out for devolution to be excessive (1999) and doubted their effectiveness.

References

Acosta, A. (2012). Extractivismo y neoextractivismo: dos caras de la misma maldición. In M. Lang and D. Mokrani (Eds.), *Más Allá del Desarrollo: Grupo Permanente de Trabajo sobre Alternativas al Desarrollo*. Quito: Ediciones Abya Yala, Fundación Rosa Luxemburg.

Acuña, F. (2022). Doctoral thesis. ¿Y después de la consulta…? factores que inciden para la implementación de las decisiones producto de la democracia directa: el caso de las consultas comunitarias y populares contra proyectos extractivos en América Latina (1996–2021) http://flacso.repositorioinstitucional.mx/jspui/handle/1026/403

Altman, D. (2010). Plebiscitos, referendos e iniciativas populares en América Latina: Mecanismos de control político o políticamente controlados? *Perfiles Latinoamericanos* 35: 9–34.

Arce, M. (2015). *La extracción de recursos naturales y la protesta social en el Perú.* Lima: Fondo Editorial PUCP.

Brown Araúz, H. and Nevache, C. (2023). Durmiendo con el enemigo ; la larga importan del populismo en Panamá, en Casullo, Maria Esperanza y Brown Araúz, Harry, *El Populismo en América Central*, Buenos Aires: Siglo XXI.

Campello, D. and Zucco, C. (2020). *The Volatility Curse: Exogenous Shocks and Representation in Resource-Rich Democracies.* Cambridge: Cambridge University Press.

Dietz, K. (2019). Direct Democracy in Mining Conflicts in Latin America: Mobilising against the La Colosa Project in Colombia. *Canadian Journal of Development Studies*, 40(2), 145–162.

Falleti, T. and Riofrancos, T. (2018). Endogenous Participation. Strengthening Prior Consultation in Extractive Economies, *World Politics*, 70(1), 86–121.

Flemmer, R. and Schilling-Vacaflor, A. (2016). Unfulfilled Promises of the Consultation Approach: The Limits to Effective Indigenous Participation in Bolivia's and Peru's Extractive Industries. *Third World Quarterly*, 37(1), 172–188.

Garcés Villamil, M. Á. and Rapalino Bautista, W. G. (2015). La Consulta Popular como mecanismo de participación ciudadana para evitar actividades mineras. *Justicia Juris*, 11(1), 52–62.

Geert, D. and Björn, F. (2016). The Social License to Operate. *Journal of Business Ethics,* 136(4), 675–685.

Giannareas, J. (2020). Los demonios de la democracia panameña. In F. Tuesta Soldevilla and Y. Welp (Eds.), *El diablo está en los detalles*. Lima: Fondo editorial PUCP.

Glazebrook, T. and Opoku, E. (2018). Defending the Defenders: Environmental Protectors, Climate Change and Human Rights. *Ethics and the Environment*, 23(2), 83–109.

Gómez Bustos, I. (2014). La acción colectiva del agua en colombia y el referendo como acercamiento de democracia directa. *Análisis Político*, 27(80), 79–103.

Hincapié, S. (2017). Entre el extractivismo y la defensa de la democracia. Mecanismos de democracia directa en conflictos socioambientales de América Latina. *RECERCA, Revista De Pensament I Anàlisi,* 21, 37–61.

Linares, S. and Welp, Y. (2020). Las iniciativas ciudadanas de referéndum en su laberinto. *Revista Latinoamericana de Política Comparada*, 15, 55–77.

Lissidini, A. (2015). Democracia directa en América Latina: avances, contradicciones y desafíos. *Nueva sociedad* website. Available at http://nuso.org/

Lissidini, A. (2021). Democracia directa contra déficit democrático: el caso uruguayo. *RECERCA. Revista De Pensament I Anàlisi*, 28(1). https://doi.org/10.6035/recerca.5600

Londono, J. F. (2020). ‘El referéndum en Colombia: un amor no correspondido.’ In F. Tuesta Soldevilla and Y. Welp (Eds.), *El diablo está en los detalles*. Lima: Fondo editorial PUCP.

Martínez Allier, J. (2004). *El ecologismo de los pobres. Conflictos ambientales y lenguajes de valoración,* Barcelona: Barcelona.

Martínez-Alier, J. (2015). Ecología política del extractivismo y justicia socio-ambiental. *Inter-Disciplina*, 3(7), 57–73. http://dx.doi.org/10.22201/ceiich.24485705e.2015.7.52384

McGee, B. (2009). The Community Referendum: Participatory Democracy and the Right to Free, Prior and Informed Consent to Development, *Berkeley Journal of International Law*. http://dx.doi.org/doi:10.15779/Z38T94C

Monestier, F. (2011). Movimientos sociales, partidos políticos y democracia directa desde abajo en Uruguay: 1985–2004. Consejo Latinoamericano de Ciencias Sociales-CLACSO.

Muñoz, M. T. and Peña Niño, J. (2019). Estudio de caso: Auge y decadencia de las consultas populares como mecanismo de participación y refrendación de la voz ciudadana en el sector extractivo en colombia. Bogotá: Fundación Foro Nacional Por Colombia. Available at https://foro.org.co/wp-content/uploads/2020/07/Casos-Consultas-Populares.pdf

Perreault, T. (2015). Performing Participation: Mining, Power, and the Limits of Public Consultation in Bolivia. *The Journal of Latin American and Caribbean Anthropology*, 20(3), 433–451.

Portantiero, J. C. (1977). Economía y política en la crisis argentina: 1958–1973. *Revista Mexicana de Sociología*, 531–565.

Pozo, J. P. (2020). Ecuador: la consulta popular, entre lo ciudadano y lo político. In F. Tuesta Soldevilla and Y. Welp (Eds.), El diablo está en los detalles. Lima: Fondo editorial PUCP.

Raventós, C. (2020). Democracia directa en Costa Rica: el diablo está donde se definen y aplican las reglas. In F. Tuesta Soldevilla and Y. Welp (Eds.), *El diablo está en los detalles*. Lima: Fondo editorial PUCP.

Raventós, C. (2018). *Mi corazón dice No. El movimiento de oposición al TLC en Costa Rica*: Editorial UCR.

Ruth, S., Welp, Y. and Whitehead, L. (Eds.). (2017). *Let the people rule? Direct democracy in the twenty-first century*. Colchester: ECPR Press.

Ruth-Lovell, S. and Welp, Y. (2024). Are Latin American Populists More Likely to Introduce Direct Democracy? *Contemporary Politics.*

Salazar Elena, R. (2009). *El referéndum en Bolivia, in Welp, Yanina and Serdült, Uwe, Armas de doble filo.* Buenos Aires: Prometeo.

Spalding, R. J. (2023). *Breaking Ground: From Extraction Booms to Mining Bans in Latin America*. Oxford: Oxford University Press.

Sandoval, M. (2020). In F. Tuesta Soldevilla and Y. Welp (Eds.), *El diablo está en los detalles*. Lima: Fondo editorial PUCP.

Svampa, M. (2015). Commodities consensus: Neoextractivism and enclosure of the commons in Latin America, *South Atlantic Quarterly*, 114(1), 65–82.

Temper, L., Demaria, F., Scheidel, A., del Bene, D. and Martínez-Alier, J. (2018). The Global Environmental Justice Atlas (EJAtlas): Ecological Distribution Conflicts as Forces for Sustainability. *Sustainability Science,* 13(3), 573–584.

Torres Wong, M. (2018). *Natural Resources, Extraction and Indigenous Rights in Latin America. Exploring the Boundaries of Environmental and State-Corporate Crime in Bolivia, Peru, and Mexico*. London: Routledge. https://doi.org/10.4324/9781351210249

Tuesta, F. and Welp, Y. (Eds.). (2020). *El diablo está en los detalles. Referéndum y poder político en América Latina*. Lima: Ediciones PUCP.

Walter, M. and Martinez-Alier, J. (2010). How to Be Heard When Nobody Wants to Listen: Community Action against Mining in Argentina. *Canadian Journal of Development Studies,* 30(1–2), 281–301.

Walter, M. and Urkidi, L. (2016). Community Consultations: Local Responses to Large-Scale Mining in Latin America. In F. De Castro, B. Hogenboom, and M. Baud (Eds.), *Environmental Governance in Latin America* (pp. 287–325). London, UK: Palgrave Macmillan.

Welp, Y. (2022). *The Will of the People. Populism and Citizens Participation in Latin America.* Berlín: De Gruyter.

Zaremberg, G. and Wong, M. T. (2018). Participation on the Edge: Prior Consultation and Extractivism in Latin America. *Journal of Politics in Latin America*, 10(3), 29–58.

Zaremberg, G., Torres Wong, M. and Guarneros-Meza, V. (2018). Descifrando el desorden: Instituciones participativas y conflictos en torno a megaproyectos en méxico. *América Latina Hoy,* 79, 81–102.

10 Prosecutors as rule of law gatekeepers in contemporary Latin America

A survey

Laurence Whitehead and Susana Berruecos

Prosecutors as gatekeepers

This paper is an overview of the critical role occupied by state prosecutors (*fiscales*) in regulating law enforcement in contemporary Latin America. It presents them as a crucial – but understudied – component of the subcontinent's longstanding overall republican rule of law system, a pivotal element that has become more central as judicial institutions have reformed and gained salience in the first two decades of this millennium. Prosecutors serve as gatekeepers to the whole criminal law enforcement process.[1] Moreover, they also play a strategic role in elite political game-playing, functioning as the discretionary filter determining which allegations of high crimes and political misdemeanours are prioritized, which are processed in a routine manner, and which are relegated to the Greek calends.

Therefore, from a legal predictability standpoint, and also in terms of democratic governance, they are the fulcrum of a republican justice system which derives its legitimacy from its track record of reliability and impartiality. That is the theoretical ideal, but in practice, the gatekeeping literature also alerts us to how omissions and misapplications of due process can undermine societal trust in the reliability and impartiality of the rule of law (Manzi, 2022). All too often, substantial sectors of public opinion find through observation and experience that their prosecutors cannot always be relied upon to perform their duties consistently, and without fear or favour. Given their substantial budgets, extensive formal powers, and their capacity to create (or suppress) "legal facts," these gatekeepers can either generate or dissipate public confidence in the entire justice system. Public trust in courts and prosecutors needs to be rebuilt, or citizens may be tempted to defect from compliance with legal norms to "un-rule of law" strategies and practices.

In all legal systems, the rule of law envisages a hierarchy of rights and duties backed up by specific enforcement procedures, whether through arbitration, punishment, or protection. In principle, rule of law architecture is supposed to be comprehensive, coherent, and in some sense equitable. It prescribes sanctions for unacceptable conduct and should provide predictability to those subjects who seek its benefits or attempt to avoid violating its prohibitions. This

DOI: 10.4324/9781003519195-10

is, however, an idealized construct likely to mesh imperfectly with underlying social norms and practices – not least so in unequal and poorly integrated societies such as those prevalent in most of Latin America. In practice, therefore, hemispheric lawmakers must reckon with the existence of substantial groups (beneficiaries as well as losers) for whom compliance with the law is a second best to evasion or extra-legal recourse to informal alternatives. In addition, some important sectors of society may correctly understand that officially promised avenues of redress may not actually be available to them, and that supposedly impartial enforcement procedures can be subject to capture and misuse. When, for such reasons, ostensibly beneficial legislation produces unsatisfactory results, a common legislative response is to enact still more unrealistically positive laws, rather than to examine how to improve the take-up of existing provisions.

Across Latin America, the outcome has frequently been that formally ambitious and inclusive legal guarantees cannot be taken at face value. They are "aspirational" rather than enforceable laws that promise far more than they can deliver to most citizens. In such a setting, prosecutors' offices become far more powerful, discretionary, and potentially arbitrary than would be the case in a harmonious and effective rule of law system, because the many who will receive poor legal service – or indeed may be entirely disserved by the justice system – can see themselves as the victims of negative selection by a narrowly ocused, overloaded, and perhaps even elite-captured gate-keeping filter.

To address these complex and understudied issues, the paper takes a synoptic view. It surveys the current institutional landscape, reflecting on the main endogenous and exogenous factors involved. To focus the analysis, given the limited empirical evidence at our disposal, we draw mostly on data from contemporary Bolivia, Colombia, Ecuador, Guatemala, and Perú, and pay particular attention to the issues of political bias and possible elite capture that have attracted the most media attention and that may have had much impact in eroding public trust in the democratic rule of law. At the same time, we also tentatively open a discussion on options for institutional strengthening and reform.

The many variants on prosecutorial gatekeeping in contemporary Latin America

Gatekeeping is a feature of all rules-based systems of distribution where individual cases are complex/non-homogeneous. It is through the acquisition and transmission of relevant information that the gatekeeper exercises control. Such gatekeeping operates in information systems, and in neuroscience (the thalamus can be studied from this perspective), as well as in political and legal arenas. In penal case law, a decision-maker is needed to determine the eligibility/priority/processing channel applicable to each dossier. This assignment function requires the preliminary assessment, classification, and allocation of all relevant cases.

Such legal gatekeepers may be neutral, technical, and highly professional, but even so, such operations inherently involve a degree of discretionary power, leaving open the possibility of some mistake, partiality, or discrimination in the treatment of a particular dossier. In a high-quality democratic rule of law system, such shortcomings are isolated and easily remedied, and public confidence in the overall reliability of the process is secure. In "un-rule of law" contexts, on the other hand, even the most conscientious of legal gatekeepers may be suspected of manipulation and unjust treatment. As we shall see, quite a few of the region's prosecutors have attracted such suspicions, sometimes for good reason.

Much of the scholarly literature on legal gatekeeping refers to common law and English-language regimes that reflect a different tradition from the fiscalías of concern here. Still, there are several points of interest that apply more widely. It is generally agreed that legislatures, courts, and police agencies have received more attention in rule of law studies than has been accorded to public prosecutors.[2] Traditionally these were viewed as minor actors rather than as pivotal elements in the overall justice system. For example, the House of Commons examination of England's Crown Prosecution Service (2009: 3) says:

> Historically, it has been seen as the minor partner, the handmaiden, to other organizations such as the police. In reality, the decisions made by the prosecutors are pivotal…the role has only developed incrementally over time, in response to specific challenges, rather than with clear expectations or direction…The CPS has, amongst other things, taken on responsibilities about charging, a power formerly belonging to the police, and gained powers to recommend conditional cautions, arguably giving it the function of a sentencer.

By contrast, Ireland's Attorney-General has delegated the function of prosecution to the DPP and concentrated instead on serving as an independent "guardian of the Constitution" and enforcer of public rights (including a key role in extradition). However, Kenny and Casey (2019: 2) consider that it operates in secrecy and "there is a mismatch between the importance of the AG to the Irish legal system and the level of critical analysis it has received."[3] Casey and Kenny (2022: 664) continue with this theme of gatekeepers of the constitutional order, by comparing four English-language systems (the UK, Canada, the United States, and Ireland) and concluded:

> that the practice of constitutional review by executive lawyers is highly variable, changing between places and over time along four axes that can either constrain or empower the executive to varying degrees. It can restrain executive action by holding it within constitutional boundaries; it can bolster the executive power by giving legalistic credibility to its actions while providing little restraint in practice; or it can create policy distortion by overly tightly binding executive and legislative action.

More directly concerning the political constraints on the decisions taken by federal prosecutors in the United States, a major recent study notes that:

> vast prosecutorial discretion exists for nearly all decisions, from before criminal cases are filed through the sentencing of offenders...Federal and state courts in the United states have repeatedly ratified this "unfettered discretion" for prosecutors in 'crucial areas of decision making' that are "beyond review" and "free of accountability."
>
> (Boyd, 2021: 103–104)

They track indicators of how both political leaders and public opinion may influence each stage of the exercise of this considerable gatekeeping power, concluding that:

> Federal prosecutors sit in an incredibly important position as the true agenda setters for much of the federal criminal justice system. This means that everything that comes after the prosecutor – from sentencing, to incarceration, to community corrections – depends on (politically tinged) prosecutorial behaviour. While federal law has grown in scope in recent years, the federal prosecutor's decision-making has remained largely free from judicial oversight or legislative guidelines.
>
> (Boyd, 2021: 194).

Turning to Latin America's prosecutors, we again encounter a pivotal but understudied component of the constitutional rule of law system, one that has risen to prominence recently with major implications both for the penal system and for the exercise of executive power. As with English-language counterparts, these agencies display considerable variability over time and national context. To understand their present powers and how they might contribute to or detract from a trustworthy rule of law system, it is necessary to study not just their internal characteristics, but in particular how they interact with (and potentially marginalize) other components of the overall justice system. Public understanding of their roles, and approval of their performance, is increasingly important for the legitimacy of the whole legal edifice. By comparing the diverse variants in operation across the subcontinent, it should also be possible to identify some practices to avoid and some pathways toward democratic reform and improved public confidence.

Across Latin America, as episodes of constitutional government alternated with periods of emergency or authoritarian rule, the emergence of an autonomous public prosecution service was more delayed and contested than in North America, and these less secure institutions were more readily cowed or even captured by incumbent rulers. The developmental trajectory of professionalized prosecutions is specific to each republic and requires historical reconstruction beyond what is possible here. The next chapter (on Mexico) illustrates what this involves. In general, contemporary prosecution services across the subcontinent have gained much of their current authority from relatively recent constitutional dispensations (1988 in Brazil, 1991 in Colombia, 1994 in Argentina, etc.) and from the associated democratization processes. But previous history and current controversies make each case distinctive, so all that can be provided here is an overview of the major common features together with a mapping of the most salient patterns of variation. The task of filling out these contours to provide in-depth nationally specific prosecutorial profiles remains to be undertaken later.

Shared characteristics

Twenty-first century prosecutors' offices are large specialized bureaucratic institutions that absorb substantial fiscal resources and require high levels of technical expertise. Not only are legal draughtsmanship, advocacy skills, good record keeping, and knowledge of case history required. Forensic techniques, digital recovery capacities, financial auditing expertise, public relations management, and political intelligence are also vital. Among other sub-fields of enquiry, modern prosecutors need considerable scientific and technical competence to deal effectively with money laundering, cyber-crime, human trafficking, refugee flows, gender violence, environmental crimes, and of course, narcotics smuggling. They also require accurate and timely intelligence on domestic legislative and regulatory changes, and on international standards and external monitoring initiatives that could affect their activities. All these demands must be balanced "in-house" and under conditions of secrecy, given the sensitivity of information about internal decision-making and the risk that affected parties could benefit from leakages. So, the recruitment, supervision, coordination, and disciplining of a large personnel base adds a further level of complexity to the operation of these prosecutorial services. All these demands would exert great pressure on any agency even when its sole purpose is to deliver professional outputs.[4] In addition to that core objective, prosecutors also exercise a high degree of discretion that may serve other interests as well. Consequently, they often become the subject of partisan criticism and factional contestation. Keeping up good standards of performance while under fire from often ill-informed campaigns and pressures is a further strain on these agencies. Moreover, they cannot operate in a vacuum. To deliver on their purposes, they need to interact with other parts of the justice system (courts, police, jails) that are also subject to public pressures. They all need to maintain functional working relationships that require some degree of mutual trust, and yet when something goes wrong, each agency will seek to shift the blame for failings to their various counterparties. Prosecutors necessarily become past masters at blame-shifting. For them, public trust is at a premium. They have the benefit of controlling critical information, but they therefore also face high risks if caught misusing their privileges.

Range of variation

Although contemporary prosecution services across the 20 republics of Latin America[5] share important common features, they also vary substantially on a variety of dimensions. A comprehensive grid of variations would require more space and fuller background detail than we can provide in this short overview. Naturally, the textual provisions of each constitutional charter provide the essential starting point for a comparative analysis of prosecutorial systems (e.g., Brazil's 1988 Constitution contrasts markedly with Bolivia's 2009 counterpart on the critical issue of delivering justice for indigenous peoples). Most Latin American prosecutorial systems have long followed the continental European inquisitorial model, but latterly the US-led adversarial and accusatory alternative has gained traction (e.g., recently adopted in Mexico), although not in Argentina or Brazil, at least so far. Whereas in most countries with accusatory systems, prosecutors are part of the executive branch, Colombia combines that procedure with direction from the Supreme Court.[6] The rise of multi-party democracy has also provided institutional scope for more independent legislatures to exercise influence concerning prosecutorial appointments, in partnership with the executive and judicial branches of government.

Beyond this essential framework of formal rules, in practice the legal communities of each nation have evolved specific routines and expectations concerning the prosecutorial function. Two complementary perspectives require consideration here: variations in how prosecutorial officials may understand their professional responsibilities, and the range of factors perceived by external analysts as the main structural constraints on Fiscalía performance in different republics.

Under the first rubric, while any modern prosecution service is bound to be a highly specialized operation needing considerable autonomy of action and control over information, it will also understand its scope as strictly limited. It is not a separate branch of government, but just one component of a larger justice system which exercises delegated authority in a specific functional domain. As such, even the most autonomous and prestigious Fiscalías remain ultimately subject to oversight by a higher constitutional authority. Where variation of self-understanding can arise is over whether this last resort monitoring and supervision power is located in the executive or the judicial branch. Both options have a long historical track record in the annals of Latin American constitutionalism. Hence, some modern prosecutors are likely to view themselves as essentially accountable to the judiciary, while in addition owing a duty of respect for executive power. The alternative view would be that in a presidential system, the prosecutors are substantively aligned with executive authority, tempered by judicial obligations on the procedural front. In a well-ordered republican system, these two standpoints can typically be harmonized, although they are evidently in tension. But much of Latin America – both historically and at present – displays a pattern of seesawing between executive and judicial assertions of authority that often proves both persistent and disruptive (Llanos and Marsteintredet, 2023). Moreover, transitions to multi-party electoral competition render the legislature an additional regulator of prosecutorial activities, especially when a divided assembly becomes critical to the appointment and renewal of top Fiscales. The professional autonomy and policy orientations of prosecutorial officialdom can be expected to vary between countries and over time in response to these larger rivalries between republican branches of government.

In addition to such considerations shaping the self-understanding of Fiscalía responsibilities within the epistemic community of legal professionals, there is also a complementary second perspective. External analysts, comparativists, and opinion leaders may direct attention to various structural factors affecting the relative standing and performance of such agencies across the twenty republics under consideration here. The presence or absence of the following five dimensions merits consideration – (1) federalism, (2) sovereignty, (3) institutional dominance, (4) security, (5) reform. Each can be accompanied by illustrative examples.

(1) Federalism

Argentina, Brazil, and Mexico are federations (like the United States), whereas Chile, Colombia, Guatemala, Perú, and Uruguay are among those that are constitutionally unitary. Prosecutors in such federal systems may have considerable leeway to shape outcomes in many subnational judicial hearings, but state-level laws are not uniform, and local legislation requires a separate prosecution agency in each jurisdiction. The national prosecutor's office is therefore confined to acting on a restricted range of cases and must either defer to, or share with, local prosecutors' offices on a substantial subset of offences. Defining the boundaries between cases can become a major source of litigation in its own right. In unitary systems, this problem does not arise, and yet in countries such as Colombia and Perú, local diversity and uneven coverage of the rule of law can in any case generate considerable territorial subsidiarity and diversity of enforcement patterns. The federal/unitary divide on prosecution issues is therefore important, but should be understood as a continuum (federal Argentina is relatively centralized), with national/local powers subject to renegotiation, rather than as an absolute binary split.

(2) Sovereignty

At one extreme, Puerto Rico lacks national sovereignty, and its system of prosecution depends directly on the US Department of Justice, with ultimate recourse to the US Supreme Court (although the Commonwealth also has its own legal authority, and an insular Supreme Court and Attorney General). At the opposite extreme, Brazil has a very authoritative Supreme Court and a constitutionally guaranteed prosecution service. Like the United States, Brazil has tended to resist the transfer of international law into domestic jurisdiction (although this stress on national sovereignty has recently softened a bit, at least as regards human rights law). In between these two poles, there is again a continuum, with some unstable shifting positions, for example concerning extradition practices and international migratory laws. The most spectacular recent example of instability on sovereignty issues concerns the establishment and termination of the International Commission against Impunity in Guatemala (CICIG) in 2019.[7] External (mostly US) intervention has profoundly reshaped Guatemalan public life ever since the 1950s, but without the steadying effect transmitted to colonial Puerto Rico. On paper, the 1985 Constitution established the pre-eminence of international law and created an autonomous public prosecutor's office as well as an Attorney General and an ombudsman. In practice, however, the seesaw between domestic and international pressures had more to do with Cold War, civil-military, and refugee dynamics. External pressure for rule of law enforcement peaked between 2009 and 2016, but has waned thereafter. A huge international effort to purge Guatemala of political corruption was resisted internally by vested interests that could also shelter behind the sovereignty claims of the *Tribunal Constitucional*. Successive public prosecutors have alternated between reformist virtue and corrupt lawfare with drastic but as yet still unresolved legacies of political confrontation. Other republics such as Perú and Colombia have also displayed similar tensions, but none have yet proved quite so extreme as in Guatemala (notably so in 2024).

(3) Institutional dominance

As just noted in the case of Guatemala, the creation of an autonomous prosecution service can be accompanied by the establishment of other rights-enabling agencies that could serve both as supports and as rival institutions. For example, Ombudsman offices (*Defensorías del Pueblo*) may assist public prosecutors by sifting citizen grievances and reinforcing public support for legal enforcement of neglected citizen rights. But their powers and modus operandi are very different, and the two agencies can also compete in the same arena, possibly even clashing. Similarly, with Information transparency agencies and specialized courts on matters such as labour rights, electoral law, military justice, and environmental regulation. Brazil's 1988 Constitution "set up the prosecutors as a fourth branch of government, with guarantees of autonomy similar to those that protect the courts, and with a broad mandate to protect the constitutional order from private or public, individual or collective actors" (Botero, et. al., 2022: 17). Such institutional dominance is, however, by no means the regional norm. In Mexico before President Andrés Manuel López Obrador, the exponential growth of more than ten "autonomous constitutional bodies" acquired functions related to the administration of justice, etc. "Given the amount of law-making, supervision, management and adjudication powers these bodies accumulate, portraying the separation of powers without them would be grossly misleading" (Giménez, 2022: 211). In November 2024, the Mexican Congress finally approved constitutional reforms proposed by López Obrador back in February which eliminated these autonomous bodies. Here is another dimension affecting the mapping of prosecutors' offices across Latin America – again along an unstable continuum.

(4) Security

The worst risk facing a US District Attorney for Puerto Rico is probably an early reposting by the Department of Justice, whereas in May 2022, Paraguay's Prosecutor General suffered assassination while on his honeymoon in the Caribbean without the protection of his regular bodyguards (US Department of State, 2022). In between these two extremes, most senior prosecutors in Latin America are forced to live highly constrained personal lives, and many worry not only about their own security — as Ecuadorean prosecutor Diana Salazar has claimed — but also the risks of kidnap and extortion directed against their families. Beyond this danger, they also face severe pressures from the business, political, and media sources that could be hurt by their decisions.[8] Previous and prospective holders of the same office may also pose a challenge to their tenure of office, and rival factions within the law enforcement bureaucracy can also bring them down. The counterpart of high discretionality and strong secrecy is that these offices are also highly vulnerable and attract strong enmities. Formal rules concerning term limits and security of tenure may provide some protection, but comparative career trajectories suggest that it is often the shelter of informal ties that provides the best assurance of a successful life path. Such subjective factors impede international comparisons of prosecutorial security, but the general picture indicates high levels of unpredictability with large upswings and downswings.

(5) Reform surges and backlashes

The Botero, Brinks, and González-Ocantos (2022) volume draws attention to a considerable variety of cyclical episodes affecting prosecutorial zeal across the subcontinent. The *Lava Jato* scandals that spread from Brazil to almost a dozen other countries provide the obvious focus for such studies, not least now that even in Brazil the impulse to persist with an anti-corruption agenda has evaporated. The CICIG offers a further case study, and other episodes follow a similar script (CICIG, *Caso Odebrecht*). Overall, the contest between forces favouring more resolute and effective crime prevention and offsetting warnings of overreach remains unresolved either way. In some countries, lasting progress may be attainable; in others the scope for near-term rule of law breakthroughs may seem remote. But in almost all, the two alternatives both possess a depth of support. Among the factors determining each outcome, international pressures and constraints sometimes require as much attention as the domestic correlation of forces.

International influences

In general terms, Latin America's engagement with liberal rule of law institutions of European origin has a very long historical pedigree. Montesquieu theorized the standard separation of powers doctrine that prioritized judicial independence, and most of the region's constitutions drew heavily on United States, French, and Spanish precursor models. As noted above, its current reaffirmation of such traditions owes much to externally encouraged democratizations and post-Cold War liberal internationalism. Par Engstrom and Courtney Hillebrecht (2019) has documented the importance of region-wide judicial co-ordination (notably from the Costa Rica-based Inter-American Court of Human Rights) as a reinforcement of various national undertakings. The same reasoning applies at the more specific level of modern prosecutorial institution-building. Just as central bankers and electoral integrity specialists have built epistemic communities and collaborative support networks across the region, so public prosecutors have also constructed their own associations.

In 1954, Brazil hosted the foundation of the Ibero-American Association of Public Prosecution Officers (*Asociación Ibero-Americana de Ministerios Públicos* – AIAMP).[9] Moreover, the Netherlands hosts an International Association of Prosecutors which now organizes a biennial regional conference in Latin America, and in addition to the specialized areas mentioned above, promotes collaboration on counter-terrorism and e-crime. The World Justice Project also provides guidance and monitoring services, and includes public trust in prosecutors as one of its concerns. Beyond these mutual support initiatives, external actors such as the DEA and the US State Department, and agencies such as the European Parliament, the German Party internationals, and Spain's Co-operation ministry also exert some influence. Besides sharing evidence-based knowledge concerning challenges of crime and violence in Latin America by scaling up pilot programmes, the Inter-American Development Bank (IDB) is also enhancing the analytical capabilities of financial intelligence units to strengthen their ability to detect money laundering.[10] What remains to be determined is how deeply any of these external influences affect the development paths of the various Latin American prosecution services, and whether or not their activities generate positive results. Whereas the operations of external economic and financial advisers have clearly delivered powerful cumulative effects in Latin America, early research on legal training programmes indicated a poor match between foreign models and local receptivity.[11] This mismatch contributes to the troubled conditions facing many Latin American prosecutors even today.

High politics and prosecutorial scandals

In recent years, Latin America has produced a remarkable array of political scandals and legal processes involving top prosecutors and leading national politicians. This pattern of interactions is so prominent and recurrent that it demands comparative study. The purpose of this paragraph is not to sideline the more institutional and structural issues of prosecutorial gatekeeping, or to reduce the topic to its most fleeting and sensational manifestations. Such scandals do grip public opinion and can distract attention from the deeper problems of law and order that should be our primary concern. Sometimes they may prove insubstantial, but enough of them prove consequential to add an extra layer of tension and instability to what is, in any case, a troubled policy domain. Debates about the widespread impact of so-called "lawfare" may often become imprecise and over-excited, but they are too impactful to be disregarded. What follows is an illustrative sample of prominent controversies, each of which deserves fuller exposition than is possible here.

In Ecuador, the General Prosecutor became more prominent after President Rafael Correa changed the constitution to abolish the Ministry of Justice and replaced it with a new Transparency Branch (Viti, 2023). The Prosecutor's Office currently employs a staff of over 3,700, with an annual budget of almost $150 million (FGE, 2023). When the Odebrecht scandal reached Quito, a rising Afro-Ecuadorean prosecutor, Diana Salazar, led the case against Correa's Vice President, Jorge Glas, who was convicted and jailed for six years. She also exposed the nexus between judges and police with crime as part of investigations known as "Metástasis." In 2019 (under Lenin Moreno, an anti-Correa administration), Salazar won a merit contest to be elected the new Attorney General for a six-year term (Art. 196), ending in 2025 (Asamblea Nacional de Ecuador, 2017; FGE, 2019). That term has coincided with an intense succession of high political dramas involving the prosecutors in multiple legal controversies. Salazar faces a political trial and has recently announced being pregnant. The Asamblea has suspended the hearing after she argued that women's rights should protect her from extreme stress at the trial. In such a polarized climate, the future course of the prosecution service will be a major source of contention in a violently divided contest.

In Guatemala, the political upheavals associated with the CICIG have already been outlined. In 2019, the mandate of CICIG was allowed to expire. In May 2022, Consuelo Porras and the new head of FECI, Rafael Curruchiche, were both sanctioned as "anti-democratic and corrupt" actors on the US State Department's (2022) Engel List,[12] notwithstanding which Porras was re-elected for a second four-year term (ending in 2026) (Ministerio Público Guatemala, 26 May 2023). While under the current Constitution, Porras can only be removed from office before the end of her term (May 2026) if convicted of a major crime, in May 2024, President Bernardo Arévalo presented to the Congress (Congreso de la República de Guatemala, 6 May 2024) an initiative to reform the internal law of the Public Prosecutor's Office that would allow the Executive to remove the Prosecutor earlier for additional reasons. These highly political struggles seem likely to run on, as Porras has responded that President Arévalo's actions violate the Constitution and threaten the independence of the Prosecutor's Office.

Colombia has also become entangled in the Guatemala imbroglio. Two leading Colombian lawyers played a critical role in guiding CICIG at the peak of its activism. Ivan Velásquez is now Minister of Defence in Gustavo Petro's administration, and in March 2024 his close colleague Luz Adriana Camargo was selected by the Supreme Court (with 18 votes out of 23) as Colombia's new General Prosecutor (Corte Suprema de Justicia, Oficina de Comunicaciones, 12 March 2024). Under the 1991 constitution, the Prosecutor's office is part of the judiciary but has administrative and budgetary autonomy (Constitución República de Colombia, 2012). It currently employs almost 6,000 staff and operates with a budget of over US $1 billion (FGN, 2024). Between 2005 and 2014, Camargo and Velásquez had led investigations of ties between Colombian paramilitary groups and politicians that resulted in the incarceration of more than 80 congressmen and governors. They then moved to CICIG. In January 2023, President Alejandro Giammattei accused Minister Velásquez of crimes related to his work as a special prosecutor in Guatemala. Among the sensitive domestic dossiers now bequeathed to Camargo, she will have to handle fraud and bribery charges directed both against former President Álvaro Uribe and the current President's eldest son, Nicolás. Camargo may have the credentials to restore a reputation for institutional integrity, but the polarized state of Colombian party politics makes it hard for her to manage such top-level corruption cases without eliciting partisan backlash.

In principle, Peru's Nation Prosecutor is appointed by the *Junta de Fiscales Supremos* (JNJ) for a three-year term, with provision for a two-year extension, to head an agency comparable in size and budget to that of Colombia (Diario Oficial El Peruano, 2023). But in practice, over the past decade, no fewer than nine officials have occupied the post – at a time when seven presidents and ten ministers of the interior also succeeded each other. Since the return of democracy in 2000, successive presidents of Perú have been imprisoned for a variety of serious crimes, many traceable to the Odebrecht corruption scandal. The Congress has taken the lead in many of these cases, but the national prosecutor is usually also involved. In such a turbulent political setting, it is hardly surprising that top prosecutors have been appointed and dismissed mainly in accordance with their expected performance as allies or enemies of these incumbent executives. There have also been intense and recurrent confrontations between specialized units within the Fiscalía, often involving the two competing top courts, the JNJ, and dominant coalitions in the legislative assembly. The track record of Peruvian democracy over the past decade contains an apparently unbroken sequence of "lawfare" operations and presidential scandals that seem unlikely to end in any legitimate "rule of law" settlement any time soon.

Ecuador, Guatemala, Colombia, and Perú may currently present the most spectacular cases of prosecutorial entanglement in elite political scandals, but they are by no means exceptional. The next chapter on Mexico covers some similar ground. Overall, as the previous volume in this series demonstrated (Llanos and Marsteintredet, 2023), the political questioning of executive and legislative discretionality and impunity is a fundamental source of tension and instability throughout the subcontinent. Even if the judiciary tries to avoid capture and delegitimization by contending political actors, a professional justice system is inescapably stretched and battered by the associated excesses. In such settings, large and expensive prosecution agencies cannot confine their work to limited "horizontal" aspects of law enforcement. They are magnets for political controversy, and even what at first seemed like a simple case of business bribery (Petrobras contracts in Curitiba) can easily escalate into major tests of "vertical" political accountability.[13] In short, as justice gatekeepers, prosecutors' offices are required to contend simultaneously with routine law and order prosecutions, low-level criminal abuse and social violence, deep-rooted human rights and structural injustice challenges, and also large-scale elite political shenanigans. To add to their burdens, the police, courts, and prisons may not be fit for service, the media may misinform, and career incentives within the service can be misaligned. Remedies for such a list of maladies can only at best be partial and incremental.

Balance sheet

An effective and legitimate prosecution service is not just an abstract normative ideal; it also involves a sequence of rule-bound procedural practices that provide a horizon of possibility, generating collective confidence in the impartiality of justice. The rule of law can be considered a "necessary fiction," necessary in the sense that an ordered society rests on shared assumptions about correct conduct, and fictional in the sense that the lived realities of individual experience can only incompletely match these collective expectations. Modern prosecutorial agencies are assigned a demanding responsibility for aligning such general principles as closely as possible with the complexities of individual cases. Dominant elites derive benefit from public trust in these specialized agencies, but they may also seek to control an apparatus that could encroach on their inherited privileges or that might be used against them by their enemies. This helps explain why public prosecutors in Latin America can become a magnet for political contestation.

As the gatekeepers of the subcontinent's rule of law systems, public prosecutors exercise great discretionary power. They have both the capacity and the duty to classify individuals according to a binary schema — "separating the sheep from the goats" – after which it is up to the courts and the rest of the justice system to follow through on matters of judgement and law enforcement. This should be a strictly focused and institutionally contained filtering process. In principle, it should only serve to draw a clear line between two categories of citizens: those liable to further investigation and potential prosecution, and those free from any such liability. A good prosecution service is one that maximizes the proportion of individuals correctly classified, minimizing both omissions and "false positives," and that then processes these individuals fairly and objectively up to the point of judgement. In practice, however, both the binary classification and the ensuing sorting of cases can be highly flawed. The subcontinent's public ministries are required to adjudicate a cumbersome range of disparate offences, working in conditions of secrecy and poor co-ordination, with inadequate information and resources, and often with unreliable information and under severe resource limitations. Moreover, on sensitive cases, they can come under strong informal pressures to act strategically rather than professionally, especially when dealing with powerful elites and contested laws. These agencies are also expected to deliver value for money to the taxpayer. If they seem to fall short in these duties, they can easily become the target of public reproach, not just for their own failings but also for deficiencies in policing, sentencing, and the application of sanctions. Even so, the evidence shows that through patient and well-informed incremental reforms, it is still possible to make potentially faltering prosecutorial systems more fit for purpose.

The World Justice Project is prominent among the international monitoring services that track the strengths and weaknesses of justice systems on an annual basis, including subnational variations and citizen trust in the various rule of law component entities. Across Latin America, it registers a huge variation in 2023 outcomes, with Uruguay rating 25th out of 142 countries while Venezuela rates last. In between, Argentina is 63rd, Brazil 83rd, Colombia 94th, and Mexico 116th. Within Mexico, there is also huge subnational variation, with Querétaro and Yucatán far ahead and the drug trafficking Pacific coast states much worse than average. There is also considerable diversity between different components of the WJP 8-factor rule of law index – in Mexico, the "effectiveness of criminal investigations" indicator is particularly poor, for example. While this very mixed picture is in some ways highly disconcerting, this vast diversity of results also has a positive side. Even in the worst settings, there may be "islands of integrity" with the potential to spread best practices where they are lacking. Understandably, citizen trust fluctuates greatly across jurisdictions, component agencies, and over time – but the record shows that it can be recovered when credible reforms acquire traction.

On value for money, for example, these complex and expensive bureaucratic agencies require accurate monitoring and well-informed accountability. This can be built up over time through peer group evaluation – for example, from academia, the *Colegio de Abogados*, or from properly informed congressional oversight hearings, as well as an independent media and human rights NGOs reinforced by international advice and comparative assessments.

As regards proposals for institutional reform, it is easier to proclaim the need for radical improvements than to provide the steady and consistent pressure and guidance needed to upgrade prosecutorial performance. In general, the risks of disruptive upheaval can easily outweigh the benefits of imposing yet another blueprint for reform. The safer presumption is usually to promote better implementation of the existing institutional provisions rather than to scrap them and start again. By contrast, across much of Latin America, the most frequent elite response to failures of service delivery or the eruption of popular protests over scandals and injustices is to upend the agency, dismissing many of those most experienced in its operations, and once more restructuring its organizing principles. A radical approach to reform may enable the incoming authorities to blame their predecessors for past failings and to create new patronage opportunities under the pretext of designing a new best practice regime. But during the process of negotiating the new package, demoralization and planning blight can afflict the existing structures of provision. So the disruption and costs of adjustment associated with the transition can prove a heavy deadweight loss. Parts of the existing structure that worked well are liable to be dismantled together with the flawed legacies. Institutional memory and professional expertise can be squandered, while the fundamental underlying sources of poor performance often remain unaddressed.

In extreme cases, it could become unavoidable to sweep aside parts of the established justice system and, in effect, to start again. No doubt there are some policy areas (e.g., prison services) where root and branch restructuring may be the only option. But prosecution services rarely fit this template. The burden of this chapter is that effective and legitimate justice gatekeeping must rest on social trust. Such practices take hold not because they are relentlessly imposed upon a passive population, but rather because they come to embody shared understandings of fairness and appropriateness. They, therefore, require community interpretation, understanding, and acceptance. Such routinization is built up gradually through experience and adaptive learning. In order to reinforce such social foundations of a law-abiding collective disposition, innovations in prosecution practices need to be infrequent and patiently justified. Draconian new systems tend to carry with them many unforeseen costs and unintended consequences. The following chapter looks more closely at Mexico and tracks an example of ambitious prosecutorial reforms that seem to be going astray.

Notes

1 On prosecutorial gatekeeping, see House of Commons Justice Committee (2009); Casey and Kenny (2022); Elderbroom and Eisen (2015) .

2 A notable recent exception is González-Ocantos, Munoz, Pavao, and Baraybar (2023).
3 Kenny and Casey (2019) . Compare also Casey and Larkin (2022).
4 For example, Gallagher and Contesse (2022) hypothesize that even the most professional of prosecutorial staff may have "strong personal and systemic incentives against filing in ways that implicate other state agents, and an aversion to creating more work" (Botero, et al., 52).
5 Beyond Latin America's diverse presidential systems, comparable issues also arise in various other constitutional democracies, notably over recent years in the parliamentary monarchy of Spain. Jose Maria Maravall (2001) provided an early but still highly pertinent analysis. For a contemporary update, see the message from premier Pedro Sánchez to the nation on 2 May 2024 ("La Fiscalía- de qué depende?") in which, following an accusation against his wife, he urged reform of the Ley de Enjuiciamiento Criminal.
6 A distinctive feature stressed by the incoming Fiscal General in her inaugural interview in Semana, 23 March 2024.
7 On 12 December 2006, the United Nations and the Government of Guatemala signed the agreement to establish the International Commission against Impunity in Guatemala – Comisión Internacional contra la Impunidad en Guatemala (CICIG) – which was ratified by the Congress on 1 August 2007. CICIG's mandate is unprecedented among United Nations (UN) or other international efforts to promote accountability and strengthen the rule of law as it was established as an independent and international body designed to support the Public Prosecutor's Office, the National Civil Police, and other state institutions. See CICIG
8 In 2015, the Argentinean prosecutor, Alberto Nisman, died hours before he was due to testify against former president Cristina Fernández de Kirchner. Two years later, a federal judge found he died from a gunshot wound before testifying that the government covered up alleged Iranian involvement in a deadly bombing at a Jewish centre in Buenos Aires in 1994.
9 AIAMP was founded in 1954 in Brazil. It currently brings together public prosecutors from 22 nations – including Spain, Portugal, and Andorra, hosting an annual conference and promoting seven specialized networks of cooperation, covering organized crime, people trafficking, cybercrime, counter-narcotics, corruption control, gender violence, and environmental protection.
10 According to the IADB (2024), its portfolio of citizen security and justice projects for 2024 will be its largest annual investment in technical and financial support through lending operations for this issue.
11 Gardner (1980) which dealt with Brazil, Chile, and Colombia in the 1970s.
12 According to De Luca, et al. (2021),

> the United States-Northern Triangle Enhanced Engagement Act, passed by Congress in December 2020, provides for "targeted sanctions to fight corruption in El Salvador, Guatemala, and Honduras," and requires a report identifying individuals in the Northern Triangle who, according to the State Department, engaged in corruption or undermined democracy. Then, in July 2021, the State Department published what has come to be called the "Engel List," which named 55 purportedly "corrupt and undemocratic actors for Guatemala, Honduras, and El Salvador."

13 In fact, the uncertainty about where a given scandal may lead suggests that an additional "diagonal" dimension of responsibility deserves consideration.

References

Arévalo, Bernardo (2024) *Presidente Arévalo insta a diputados a aprobar reforma a ley del MP*, 6 May 2024 https://bernardoarevalo.presidencia.gob.gt/presidente-arevalo-insta-a-diputados-a-aprobar-reforma-a-ley-del-mp/

Asociación Ibero Americana de Ministerios Públicos (AIAMP) https://www.aiamp.info/index.php/la-asociacion/quienes-somos.

Botero, Sandra, Daniel M. Brinks, and Ezequiel A. González-Ocantos (2022) *The Limits of Judicialization: From Progress to Backlash in Latin America*, Cambridge, Cambridge University Press.

Boyd, Christina L., Michael J. Nelson, Ian Ostrander, and Ethan D. Boldt (2021) *The Politics of Federal Prosecution*, Oxford, Oxford University Press.

Casey, Conor Casey and David Kenny (2022) "The Gatekeepers: Executive lawyers and the executive power in comparative constitutional law" in *International Journal of Constitutional Law* 20, 2.

Center for Economic and Policy Research, 14 December 2023, *Facing Possible Impeachment, Ecuador's Prosecutor General Cracks Down on Judicial Oversight Authority* https://cepr.net/press-release/facing-possible-impeachment-ecuadors-prosecutor-general-cracks-down-on-judicial-oversight-authority/

CICIG, *Informe final de Labores* https://www.cicig.org/cicig/informes_cicig/informe-de- labores/informe-final-de-labores/#informe

CICIG, *Caso Odebrecht* https://www.cicig.org/casos/caso-odebrecht/

Congreso de la República de Guatemala, *Propuesta de Ley presentada por el Presidente de la república que reforma la Ley del Ministerio Público*, 6 May 2024 https://www.congreso.gob.gt/noticias_congreso/10413/2023/1

Constitución República de Colombia, 2012. https://www.fiscalia.gov.co/colombia/wp-content/uploads/2012/01/Constitucion_Politica.pdf

Corte Suprema de Justicia, Oficina de Comunicaciones, 12 March 2024 https://cortesuprema.gov.co/luz-adriana-camargo-garzon-nueva-fiscal-general-de-la-nacion/

De Luca, Martin, Wade Weems and Scott Nielson *Anti-corruption report. The Engel List Foreshadows U.S. Enforcement in Central America*, 1 December 2021. https://www.anti-corruption.com/18589031/the-engel-list-foreshadows-u-s-enforcement-in-central-america.thtml

Driscoll A., Nelson MJ. (2015) "Judicial Selection and the Democratization of Justice: Lessons from the Bolivian Judicial Elections", *Journal of Law and Courts*, 3(1), 115–148.

Diario Oficial El Peruano (2023) *Resolución No. D000661-2023-JUS/PGE-PG*, 30 December 2023 https://busquedas.elperuano.pe/dispositivo/NL/2249286-1 (Procuraduría General del Estado, S/ 64,073,281.00 Soles https://busquedas.elperuano.pe/dispositivo/NL/2249286-1)

Engstrom, Par, and Courtney Hillebrecht (2019) *Progress and Resilience in the Inter-American Human Rights System: The Law and Politics of Institutional Change*, Cambridge University Press.

Elderbroom, Brian and Lauren-Brooke Eisen (2015) "*The Gatekeepers: Four Ways Prosecutors can Improve their Decision-Making*" *The Marshall Project*, (16 March 2015 commentary).

Fiscalía General de la Nación de Colombia (2024) *Presupuesto General de la Nación 2024.* https://www.fiscalia.gov.co/colombia/la-entidad/presupuesto-general-asignado/

Fiscalía General del Estado (2023) Ecuador, *Informe de Labores* Enero-Diciembre 2023 https://www.fiscalia.gob.ec/transparencia/2024/rendicion-de-cuentas/6-Redaccion-Informe.pdf

Fiscalía General del Estado (2019) Ecuador, *Press Release*, 8 April 2019 https://www.fiscalia.gob.ec/diana-salazar-mendez-fue-posesionada-como-fiscal-general-del-estado/

Gallagher JK and Contesse J. (2022) Critical Disconnects: Progressive Jurisprudence and Tenacious Impunity in Mexico in Botero S, Brinks DM, Gonzalez-Ocantos EA, eds. *The Limits of Judicialization: From Progress to Backlash in Latin America*, Cambridge University Press, pp.: 39–65.

Gardner, James A (1980) *Legal Imperialism: American Lawyers and Foreign Aid in Latin America*, Madison: Wisconsin UP.

Giménez, Francisca Pou (2022) "The Constitution of Mexico" in Conrado Hubner Mendes, Roberto Gargarella, and Sebastian Guidi, (eds) *The Oxford Handbook of Constitutional Law in Latin America,* Oxford: OUP.

González-Ocantos, Ezequiel, Paula Munoz, Nara Pavao, and Viviana Baraybar Hidalgo (2023) *Prosecutors, Voters, and the Criminalisation of Corruption in Latin America: The Case of Lava Jato,* Cambridge: Cambridge University Press.

House of Commons Justice Committee (2009) *The Crown Prosecution Service: Gatekeeper of the Criminal Justice System* (Ninth Report of 2008/9 session), London: HMSO.

Inter-American Development Bank (IDB), *Citizen Security in Latin America and the Caribbean*, 7 March 2024https://www.iadb.org/en/news/citizen-security-latin-america-and-caribbean

Kenny, David and Conor Casey (2019) A One-Person Supreme Court? The Attorney General, Constitutional Advice to Government, and the Case for Transparency *Dublin University Law Journal* 42,1.

Llanos, Mariana and Leiv Marsteintredet (eds) (2023) *"Latin America in Times of Turbulence: Presidentialism under Stress"* Routledge.

Manzi, Lucia (2022) "Prosecutorial Gatekeeping and its Effects on Criminal Accountability: The Roman Prosecutor's Office and Corruption Investigations in Italy, 1975-1994" *Justice System Journal* 3, 43.

Ministerio Público Guatemala, 26 May 2023 https://www.mp.gob.gt/noticia/doctora-maria-consuelo-porras-argueta-primera-mujer-en-la-historia-de-latinoamerica-y-del-pais-en-ser-reelecta-como-fiscal-general/

Maravall, Jose Maria (2001) "The Rule of Law as a Political Weapon", Working Paper 160, *The Juan March Institute*, Madrid, Spain

Romero, Franco (2017) *Estado de Indecisión en la Asamblea por Glas*, Asamblea Nacional Ecuador, 1 September 2017 https://www.asambleanacional.gob.ec/es/blogs/franco-romero/51241-estado-de-indecision-en-la-asamblea-por-glas

Sánchez, Pedro, Message to the nation, 2 May 2024 ("La Fiscalía- de qué depende?").

Semana, "Por Primera vez habla Fiscal Luz Adriana Camargo, Luz Adriana Camargo, en diálogo con SEMANA, se refirió por primera vez a sus retos en la Fiscalía, su relación con la Casa de Nariño, la oposición y las investigaciones más relevantes",

23 March 2024 https://www.semana.com/politica/articulo/por-primera-vez-habla-la-fiscal-luz-adriana-camargo-en-entrevista-con-semana-se-refiere-a-su-relacion-con-petro-e-ivan-velasquez-la-oposicion-y-las-investigaciones-relevantes/202414/

República de Colombia. Corte Suprema de Justicia, Oficina de Comunicaciones, 12 March 2024 https://cortesuprema.gov.co/luz-adriana-camargo-garzon-nueva-fiscal-general-de-la-nacion/

US Department of State (2022) Press Release, *Designation of Attorney General María Consuelo Porras Argueta de Porres for Involvement in Significant Corruption and Consideration of Additional Designations*, 16 May, 2022.

US Department of State (2022) *Reward Offer for Unknown Co-conspirators Responsible for Murder of Paraguayan Prosecutor Marcelo Daniel Pecci Albertini*, 17 November 2022 https://www.state.gov/reward-offer-for-unknown-co-conspirators-responsible-for-murder-of-paraguayan-prosecutor-marcelo-daniel-pecci-albertini/

Viti Katherine (2023) *Country Report Ecuador*, Global Trends in Judicial Reform, https://law.stanford.edu/publications/country-report-ecuador-general-judicial-reforms/

WOLA joint statement (2021) *"El Salvador's Constitutional Court Paves Way for President Bukele to Seek Reelection Following Purge of Country's Judiciary"* 9 September 2021

11 Mexico's new *Fiscalía General de la República*

Still misfiring

Susana Berruecos and Laurence Whitehead

Mexico's rule of law is faltering in the face of mounting pressures from drug cartels, other organized crime groups, surging homicides, femicides, and disappearances, accelerating international migratory flows, arms and organ trafficking, and lingering traditions of elite impunity. Such challenges threaten to overwhelm the entire justice system (courts, police, prisons, and prosecutors) since it is under-resourced, slow to adapt, and vulnerable to politicization. Resort to external forms of backup, such as extraditions and trials in US courts, tends to demoralize and undermine the effectiveness of national justice institutions. Among these, the *Fiscalíá General de la República* (FGR) (General Prosecutor's Office) and the associated 32 state prosecutor's offices occupy a pivotal role, and efforts have recently been made to enhance their prosecutorial capacities. Despite initial promises, this chapter finds that the new system has so far failed to redress accumulated deficiencies or to restore public trust. If anything, a downward spiral of impunity and criminal complicity has accelerated, bequeathing dire rule of law prospects to the next administration. Nevertheless, since some state-level and sectoral centres of excellence still survive within a generally dysfunctional prosecutorial system, there is still some potential for a renewal of zeal and effectiveness. Overall, however, this chapter finds the early results of the latest reforms a major disappointment, and gravely lagging behind still worsening pressures of lawlessness.

From Procuraduría General de la República (PGR) to an autonomous Fiscalía

For decades, Mexico's Attorney General's Office (Procuraduría General de la República, PGR) remained part of the executive branch, and the Attorney General (Procurador General) was appointed by and reported directly to the president. During this time, executive control of the *PGR* led to the politicization of many criminal investigations and prosecutions. The 1824 and 1857 Constitutions placed the Attorney General (and a Prosecutor, or *Fiscal* after 1857) under the Supreme Court. It was only in 1900 that a constitutional reform transferred these two offices to the executive branch, meaning direct appointment by President Porfirio Díaz. Following the Revolution, the 1917 Constitution gave the Senate

DOI: 10.4324/9781003519195-11

the last word on such presidential nominations and dismissals.[1] But once the PRI established one-party hegemony, the upper chamber hardly challenged such executive decisions or seriously questioned the professionalism/independence of its nominees. No specific term limits were prescribed, but the convention became that each new president would make new appointments.

Subordination to the executive continued until the judicial constitutional reform of 1994, which at last began responding to longstanding opposition and civil society demands for more autonomy concerning the rule of law. The assassination of PRI presidential candidate Luis Donaldo Colosio and related shocks enhanced perceptions of weak legality, especially given that outgoing President Carlos Salinas had appointed five successive Attorney Generals during his six-year term. After 1994, Attorney Generals were assigned oversight over *amparos* and constitutional controversies, and the role of the Senate in vetting and ratifying presidential nominees was reinforced.[2] President Ernesto Zedillo sought to enhance the stability and impartiality of the position by the appointment of an opposition congressman, subsequently replaced by a human rights lawyer.

PRI dominance of Congress ended in 1997, and it lost the Presidency in 2000, opening the way to a transitional justice process. President Vicente Fox then created a Special Prosecutor's Office charged with investigating federal crimes of repression over the previous 30 years (FEMOSPP).[3] But after five years, this operation ended in 2006 with his presidency, having produced no convictions. All indictments were rejected on procedural grounds invoking statutes of limitations, or remitted to military courts which buried them.[4] Although President Fox contemplated a constitutional reform to create an autonomous Prosecutor's Office, this project had to be dropped after adverse mid-term elections, and was not resurrected until 2018.

By the mid-2000s, the Mexican criminal justice system faced a serious crisis. Less than 4% of reported crimes resulted in anyone being brought to justice, and less than 1% in someone being sentenced (Shirk, 2010). President Calderon's war on drugs included the adoption, in 2008, of a far-reaching constitutional reform.[5] This redefined "organised crime" and assigned it exclusively to federal jurisdiction. It expanded the powers of public prosecutors and established such novel features as asset forfeiture. It also introduced public monitoring of court proceedings, mandated three independent judges to serve on all trials, and established an adversarial model with oral testimony.

The Peña Nieto presidency and the new *Fiscalía General de la República*

The main concerns in the context of the 2012 presidential election were public security and corruption (Parametría, 2012). Since over 90% of murders in Mexico remained unresolved, one of the 266 commitments in Enrique Peña Nieto's electoral campaign was to create a "National Anti-Corruption Commission" (NAC) and an autonomous Prosecutor General's Office. Mexico's National Institute of Statistics and Geography's Annual Victimisation Survey (ENVIPE, 2014)[6] found an uptick in crime rates over the previous year, as well as an increase in the so-called "black number" (*cifra negra*), a higher percentage of crimes going unreported with respect to 2012.

In spite of various reforms to improve public security, an independent Prosecutor's Office was one of the most difficult challenges for the transformation of Mexico's criminal justice system. It took almost five years for the Senate to approve a secondary law. The 2014 reform created a new National Prosecutor's Office (*FGR*) as an independent body, separate from the executive, with its own legal character and assets. It eliminated the presidential practice of nominating a single candidate as Attorney General and granted the Senate the power to assess a list of candidates and shortlist ten. From that list, the president proposes a list of three final candidates, from which the Senate selects the national prosecutor. The president maintained the power to remove the national prosecutor or high-ranking PGR/FGR officials from the post for "serious causes" (though the Senate can object to this decision).[7]

The 2014 reform established a nine-year term for the General Prosecutor, guaranteeing that whoever held the post would continue beyond the six-year term of the Presidency. The hope was that a General Prosecutor would have the freedom to investigate sensitive cases. However, the reform introduced the so-called "automatic pass," allowing the incumbent Attorney General to automatically become the first Prosecutor General for a nine-year term. Thus, the immediate effect was to replace Attorney Generals who had served little more than a year or two in office with a secure long-term prosecutor who turned out to be Alejandro Gertz Manero.[8]

The political context helps to explain these two legal reforms. President Peña Nieto needed to differentiate his administration from the excesses of the preceding "war on drugs." The PRI had returned to office but governed in a "tacit" pact with the outgoing PAN. On rule of law issues, the pact included anti-corruption and prosecutorial autonomy provisions. Historical transitional justice issues gave way to more immediate human rights, criminal violence, and political corruption crises. In particular, the disappearance of 43 students from Ayotzinapa's Rural Normal School in the state of Guerrero since 26 September 2014; multiple gubernatorial corruption cases (some subject to US court hearings); the Brazilian construction company Odebrecht corruption scandal; and widespread atrocities attributable to proliferating drug cartels all put pressure on the government to produce a reinforced security posture.

The 2008 justice reforms only came fully into effect in 2016, and by then it was apparent that they fell short of addressing all these rule of law failings. For example, the PGR may have been assigned sole responsibility for prosecuting organized crime, but the Ayotzinapa case might also involve state crimes in Guerrero, human rights violations of international significance, and perhaps even military justice issues. Similarly, although Odebrecht was an anti-corruption case, it might also involve illicit electoral financing.

Regarding the FGR, civil society, human rights, and anti-corruption groups demanded an end to the practice of appointing the Attorney General without first assessing the candidate's qualifications and suitability for the post. A Washington Office on Latin America (WOLA) report entitled "Mexico needs an autonomous and effective Prosecutor General to fight impunity" listed more than 300 organizations insisting that the new Prosecutor should be elected through an open, transparent, and public process. However, in October 2016, President Peña nominated Raúl Cervantes, a former PRI Senator, as the third Attorney General of his presidency. He was ratified by the Senate with 85 votes and 3 against.[9]

Critics argued that Cervantes could not become the first impartial nine-year prosecutor given his PRI-based career. The media widely covered the *#VamosPorUnaFiscaliaQueSirva* movement, which on 29 August 2017 presented a report to create an independent and autonomous General Prosecutor Office.[10] The lack of scrutiny by the Senate was seen "as a worrying sign for the consolidation of the Anti-Corruption National System and the future of an autonomous Prosecutor General's Office."[11]

Cervantes resigned in October 2017 with the homicide rate at its highest level. His resignation was considered a victory for civil society and the result of social pressure to have an autonomous prosecutor. According to Miguel Carbonell, "society is expecting a more neutral, balanced, prestigious figure that enjoys autonomy and credibility" (New York Times, 17 October 2017). High-profile cases such as Ayotzinapa remained unresolved, and only three out of seventeen investigations against former state governors had gone to trial.

In his short tenure as interim prosecutor, Alberto Beltrán found it difficult to bring charges against officials connected to the Odebrecht case. After admitting to paying nearly 800 million dollars in bribes to secure government contracts in various Latin American countries and in Mexico for more than ten million dollars, no high-profile PRI government official faced any consequences. Cervantes had travelled to Brazil, but Mexico only banned Odebrecht from doing business in the country for two and a half years and did not bring criminal charges against the company.[12] Nor did Beltrán make any progress on other bribery cases. He oversaw the dismissal of former electoral chief prosecutor, Santiago Nieto, after he led an investigation involving Peña Nieto's campaign funding.[13] Beltrán was later investigated for an alleged unjustified increase in his assets of two million dollars between 2014 and 2018.

This cursory survey of Mexico's prosecutorial history should suffice to demonstrate the close and enduring entanglement between the republican law enforcement system and its turbulent high politics. Given this entrenched reality, it would be remarkable if the 2018 creation of the FGR had delivered a quick and clear-cut break with traditional practices. The rest of this chapter concerns the early years of the new system. Whereas Salinas appointed five Attorneys General, Zedillo and Fox two each, Calderón three, and Peña Nieto four, President López Obrador has only appointed one General Prosecutor, with a term that extends into the first half of the next administration.

The Lopez Obrador presidency and the new FGR (2018–2027)

In the context of the 2018 election, fighting corruption and strengthening the rule of law remained primary concerns for Mexicans. After the 2014 reform, the Attorney General's Office continued to be in charge of investigating federal crimes, but the Prosecutor's office remained vacant.

After President López Obrador took office in December 2018, Alejandro Gertz Manero, who served as a security advisor in his presidential campaign, was appointed as acting Attorney General. As soon as the Senate approved the secondary law, Gertz was elected as the first national Prosecutor with 91 out of 128 votes to serve until 2028. While he declared himself non-partisan (*El Economista*, 1 January 2019), various groups criticized Gertz for being too close to President López Obrador. Mexico Evalúa,[14] an independent think tank, highlighted that "priority was given to closeness and the use of practices that don't contribute to the transformation of the country." WOLA and Transparencia Mexicana also considered that it had been an accelerated process without civil society participation or a true assessment of the candidates.[15]

An amended organic law for the Prosecutor General was enacted in May 2021. It defined the structure of the office with its own civil service and five autonomous Specialized Prosecutors.[16] The Prosecutor General was also granted power to submit to the Supreme Court of Justice constitutional controversies or unconstitutional actions. More importantly, Chapter III established budgetary autonomy for the Prosecutor General in its Article 87.

The Inter-American Commission on Human Rights (IAHCR) requested that any additional changes made to the Office of the Attorney General be debated with significant citizen participation and a human rights perspective to reflect Mexico's international commitments. The IAHCR urged Mexico to ensure open and transparent legislative discussions, as well as to enable an assessment of the impact of potential changes on the country's compliance with its international obligations concerning human rights.[17]

Prosecutor General's structure and budget

The Prosecutor General's structure in 2024 was composed of 12 major units, including 8 Specialized prosecutors.[18] According to the FGR's Structure and Remuneration 2024 Manual, there were 24,760 positions available in 2022, of which 5,935 were vacant.[19]

To build a strong infrastructure of specialized public officials might seem to require a rising budget, but in fact in 2019 the FGR was assigned fewer resources than any the PGR had received in the preceding decade. Even with a 14.5% increase the following year to almost $800 million USD, this was still the lowest amount since 2011. An analysis of 2020's federal budget by México Evalúa (Sánchez, 2019) found that most funds had been allocated towards maintaining the structure under which PGR operated, while little was invested in improvements to the institution's structure or investigative practices. In 2020, FGR's budget decreased 20% in real terms compared to 2013 and 8% compared to 2018. At $1,135 million USD, the 2023 allocation was still a decrease of 2.6% in real terms as compared to the 2022[20]. FGR's 2024 allocation was identical to 2025's budget proposal, although in real terms the latter was 0.20% lower (SHCP, 2024: 71). Whereas López Obrador has pressed "republican austerity" on the civilian public sectors, his administration has also allocated generous funding without much budgetary transparency to the military, who have taken up increased law enforcement responsibilities, as well as to major infrastructure projects.

Rule of law and corruption in Mexico

During the AMLO presidency, Mexico fell from 99th in 2019 to 116th in 2023 and 118th in 2024 on the overall World Justice Project Rule of Law Index. According to Americas Quarterly's "2023 Capacity to Combat Corruption" Index, Guatemala and Mexico are the only two countries whose overall scores have decreased every year since 2019 (when the index began). Likewise, in 2023 Transparency International ranked Mexico 126th in its more comprehensive list of 180 countries.[21]

Although specialized corruption Prosecutors' Offices were created at the state level in 2017, while 28 states reported having opened 58,822 cases in the last five years, recent data from 16 state Prosecutors' Offices suggest that under 1% of these have reached closure.

Prosecutors' overview

A report by the DPLF and WOLA (2020) analyzed the FGR's performance under Alejandro Gertz during his first eighteen months in office. While some progress is noted in a small number of emblematic cases, "there is a need for further action and progress in order to become an independent, autonomous and efficient institution, capable of operating free from political influence and ensuring justice for all Mexicans."[22]

According to the report, indicators about the effectiveness of the investigations by the police and the Prosecutor's Office continue to be the greatest challenge in criminal justice. INEGI estimates that nine out of ten crimes that occurred in Mexico were not investigated by law enforcement institutions. Nearly 90% of victimization events go missing from official crime statistics. In 2023, the percentage of unreported crimes with the highest *cifra negras* were kidnapping (98.6%), extortion (97.9%), fraud (96.7%), car robbery (94.4%), and house robbery (90.6%) (INEGI, ENVIPE 2021). Mexico Evalúa's (2022) report indicated that only 4.3% of the cases opened in 2022 (96,500 out of 2.2 million) resulted in a formal investigation.

After four years of Alejandro Gertz's appointment, his first report as prosecutor general recognized that there is "an unjustified delay in more than 300,000 cases that have not been solved," confirming that more than 30,000 new claims received in only 100 days still needed to be processed (Comunicado FGR 216/19). INEGI's (Censo Nacional de Procuración de Justicia Federal, 2024) latest figures show that from more than two million cases opened in Mexico in 2023, the FGR started 80,169 files but more than half (53,604) have not been solved.

According to Amnesty International, by the end of 2022, more than 109,000 people were registered as missing and disappeared, most of them after 2006. In December 2023, the *Comisión Nacional de Búsqueda* confirmed 92,000 disappearances after identifying 16,681 from 110,964 registered in August 2023.[23] President López Obrador criticized that this report is being used politically against his government, guaranteeing there is no manipulation of data and that accurate information will be presented monthly.[24]

Killing of journalists and human rights defenders also remained at record levels. Since 2000, Article 19 – an independent organization that defends freedom of expression – has documented assassinations of 163 journalists, 47 during Peña Nieto's government and 43 since 2018.[25] The NGO *Causa en Común (2023)* lists 2,482 policemen assassinated in the 5 years beginning June 2019, of whom three-fifths were poorly paid municipal officers,[26] one third were state police, and the rest were at the national level. Over the same period, the assassination of candidates in election contests has also reached epidemic levels.

The FGR and high-profile corruption cases

The Specialized Prosecutor Office to Fight Against Corruption (FEMCC in Spanish) was created in March 2019 and is responsible for investigating corruption cases since December 2019. In 2020, the *Instituto de Investigación en Rendición de Cuentas y Combate a la Corrupción (IIRCCC)* found that only nine of over 30,000 probes into presumed acts of corruption advanced to the next stage of investigation. By June 2022, 2,749 claims had been presented, but only 24 (0.87%) had led to a judicial process.

Over the past years, the Prosecutor General has made some progress in a few high-profile cases of corruption. Most of these prosecutions have been highly politicized and mediatized. While the FGR reported 1,150 favourable rulings in 2023, the Prosecutor General has faced ozens of legal setbacks in high-profile processes – seven between 2019 and 2022 and 27 ruled in 2023, as will be discussed below.

Not that Gertz has always taken a soft line on prosecutions. As Freeman (2023) has commented concerning various Latin American prosecutors, "they may be less focussed on prosecuting complex crimes than on pursuing cases of personal interest." This might include the decision by Gertz Manero, as soon as he became General Prosecutor, to reopen a case concerning the Jenkins Foundation and the funding of a private university in Puebla, where he had previously served as the director.

Gertz also activated a long-running case concerning the death of his ailing 82-year-old brother. While the forensic study identified "visceral congestion" as the cause, Gertz argued that his brother's death was the result of mistreatment and "negligent homicide" by his partner (Laura Morán) and daughters (Laura and Alejandra Cuevas). His 94-year-old former sister-in-law and her daughter were convicted, in an action that was belatedly nullified by a unanimous Supreme Court ruling, with a former president of the Court referring to a risk to judicial impartiality, and a former legal adviser to the presidency complaining that the Prosecutor's Office was being used to litigate personal matters.

After months of negotiations and an intense public campaign by the Cuevas family, the Court accepted the case in November 2022. Former President of the Court, Arturo Zaldívar, argued that "there was danger of influences that did not give room to impartiality of justice." On 28 March 2023, the Supreme Court made a historic unanimous verdict ordering the immediate release of 69-year-old Alejandra Cuevas. One month after the Court's ruling, former legal adviser to President López Obrador, Julio Scherer, filed a legal claim against Gertz for influence peddling and abuse of power. Scherer specifically criticized Gertz for using the Prosecutor's Office to "litigate personal matters and obtain benefits" (El Universal, 22 April 2023)[27].

The Odebrecht case in Mexico

The most visible case related to Odebrecht is the one against Emilio Lozoya, the former Chief Executive Officer of Petróleos Mexicanos, who was accused of accepting US$10.5 million in bribes from the Brazilian construction conglomerate between 2012 and 2014. In 2020, Lozoya was arrested in Spain and extradited to Mexico. Lozoya faced two corruption cases as he was linked to the process of criminal association for money laundering (Odebrecht) and by allegedly receiving bribes from the steel company Altos Hornos de México (AHMSA) – owned by Alonso Ancira – in exchange for Pemex's irregular purchase of an inoperative fertilizer plant abandoned in 2014. Lozoya and former PAN senator, Jorge Luis Lavalle, have been the two main public officials in prison as a result of the Odebrecht scandal.[28] While in March 2022 the Prosecutor seemed willing to let Lozoya walk free if he could reach a so-called "restitution agreement" with Pemex and the Financial Intelligence Unit to repair the damage caused by the Odebrecht and Agronitrogenados affairs, he was acquitted in the latter case based on the restitution agreement with Alonso Ancira in 2021.

Amid wider tensions between López Obrador's government and the judiciary,[29] the FGR alleged that the Supreme Court as well as district and federal judges were showing bias in Lozoya's favour. In September 2023, an appeals court judge ruled that details of Lozoya's bank accounts in Switzerland and Brazil could not be admitted as evidence as these were not obtained by a court order. The Court's ruling in favour of Pemex former CEO's property was appealed by the FGR in November. President López Obrador criticized the judge's decision, which released assets "letting alleged criminals go free by excuses," and reinforced his plans to reform a "rotten" judiciary (24 November 2023). Moreover, Lozoya was released from prison on 20 February 2024 after a local court granted him house arrest, considering he is no longer a flight risk. While the FGR will pursue the Agronitrogenados case, Lozoya's legal team has denied his own claim, arguing that the FGR altered his file.

González Ocantos contrasts (2022: 146–7) legal inaction in Mexico with active anti-corruption leadership in Brazil and Perú.

> In sum, the Mexican story is one in which the institutional environment conspired against the emergence of skilled and committed prosecutors required to observe anti-corruption crusades...The space is therefore left wide open for obstructionist shenanigans. Corruption investigations are left at the mercy of extra-legal political dynamics and fail to gain any degree of autonomy.

Genaro García Luna and the role of US courts

Another high-profile case is related to former Secretary of Public Security (2006–12), Genaro García Luna, who was arrested in Texas in December 2019 for drug-trafficking conspiracy and making false statements. According to the indictment and other court filings by the government, from 2001 to 2012, García Luna received millions of dollars in bribes from the Sinaloa Cartel in exchange for providing protection for its drug trafficking activities. It is worth noting that former Mexican Secretary of National Defense, General Salvador Cienfuegos, was also arrested in the United States on charges of money laundering and conspiracy to manufacture, import, and distribute narcotics into the United States. After this arrest, the Mexican FGR opened its own investigation and requested evidence from the Department of Justice.[30]

Even though Mexico confirmed in early 2020 that it had asked the United States to extradite García Luna, he was finally sentenced in February 2023 to 20 years imprisonment for drug-related violations, international cocaine distribution, and making false statements, among others. Following the New York court ruling, García Luna is now facing a civil lawsuit in a Florida court brought by President López Obrador's administration. Three months later, the Mexican

General Prosecutor Office informed that it received apprehension orders against García Luna and 60 others, including members of his family.[31] After Luis Cárdenas Palomino, one of García Luna's closest former aides, was exonerated in Sonora from an arms trafficking claim (Fast & Furious), the US Courts have rescheduled García Luna's ruling to October 2024.

Other recent ongoing high-level political cases handled by the FGR include the three-year (2020–2023) preventive detention of former Mexico City Mayor, Rosario Robles[32]; the arrest in 2022 of a former Attorney General (2012–2015), Jesús Murillo Karam;[33] and a court case currently ongoing that concerns the alleged 2019 purchase by the Mexican military of Pegasus spyware used against critical journalists and opposition figures.

US (and international) courts are playing an active role in duplicating or displacing the work of Mexican prosecutors concerning important high-profile cases. Various major arrests have been initiated abroad (Emilio Lozoya, Genaro García Luna, General Salvador Cienfuegos, etc.) and only followed up by the FGR. Setbacks include cases against Lozoya, García Luna, Jorge Sánchez Ortega (Colosio case), Rosario Robles, Juan Collado, Juan Carlos García (Pegasus), police and military involved in the Ayotzinapa students' massacre, among others.

The currently pending US trials of key Mexican drug lords, including "Mayo Zambada," are notable here. The FGR was incapable of capturing him despite his notoriety and his many decades as the country's pivotal crime lord. But, in July 2024, he was detained by the Drug Enforcement Administration (DEA) in El Paso under circumstances that the FGR has labelled "treasonable"[34], and if he plea bargains to the judge in New York, he can severely damage the reputations of many Mexican office holders of all political persuasions.

The autonomy and politicization of state prosecutors

Following up on the federal government's reforms that aimed to strengthen the role of the national prosecutor's office in combating corruption and violence, Mexico's 32 states have also initiated a transition to an autonomous prosecutor's office, independent from the executive/governor's office. Some local constitutions have been reformed to ban individuals who have held an elected office or a political position within the past 1–3 years from being selected as prosecutors. However, prosecutor's offices at the state level are facing various challenges beyond autonomy and politicization. These offices are mostly understaffed, under-resourced, and poorly trained.

It is also worth highlighting the threat that organized crime poses to prosecutors' security. Prosecutors in Latin America are increasingly becoming victims of targeted assassinations. While in the previous chapter we discussed the murders of Ecuador's prosecutors - Federico Estrella and César Suárez – who were killed while leading criminal investigations, in Mexico the highest alert so far has been at the subnational level.

On 10 September 2023, a regional prosecutor was assassinated two days after his appointment in Tierra Caliente, Guerrero. On 24 January 2024, Mexico's most populous state, the State of Mexico's prosecutor, José Luis Cervantes, was the victim of an armed attack. Although the attack was downplayed as an isolated event, the incident is indicative of the high levels of violent crime registered in the second deadliest state. According to the federal security ministry (SSPC), the State of Mexico recorded 2,597 murders in 2023, second to Guanajuato with 3,104. In December 2023, citizens of Texcaltitlán killed ten alleged members of the criminal organization *Familia Michoacana* who were extorting members of the municipality.

MEXICO City'S attorney general

After a series of reforms to Mexico City's Constitution, Ernestina Godoy was elected as local Attorney General on 10 December 2019.[35] Godoy had a political background and requested a leave as local legislator. Among other controversies, an article published by the *New York Times* on 9 November 2023 revealed Godoy's office had ordered Mexico's largest telecommunications company, Telcel, to hand over phone and text records of prominent Mexican officials and politicians from the ruling Morena party and its allies. According to the publication, Telcel "acknowledged in a court filing reviewed by The Times that it had received the orders and handed over the records, which spanned from 2021 until earlier this year."[36]

While the Mexico City Attorney's office argued that the information was being sought in connection with investigations into disappearances and kidnappings, the federal Prosecutor General's office "categorically denied" requesting phone records and said that no such criminal investigations were on file. On 13 November, the *New York Times* highlighted that the information provided by Godoy's office did not contradict their report.

In spite of criticism from opposition parties and civil society "*No más fiscal carnal*" ("no more partial prosecutor"), the Citizen Judicial Council voted in favour of Godoy continuing as Mexico City's prosecutor in November 2023 for another four-year term. President López Obrador and other government officials also backed Godoy publicly. Nevertheless, after hours of discussions on 13 December 2023, the local Congress postponed Godoy's ratification process to January 2024 and finally rejected her in an extraordinary session.[37] President López Obrador asserted that this decision was a political revenge as Godoy had openly confronted the opposition's real-estate corruption in the mayoralty of Benito Juárez.[38]

While presenting her last annual report as local prosecutor, Godoy highlighted that her team achieved a reduction of 42% in homicides and 18% in femicides between 2019 and 2023, deactivated 83 criminal groups, and captured 102 leaders from various drug trafficking cartels. Godoy made several political statements against opposition representatives and used the "real estate cartel" as an explanation for Congress' rejection, especially against the capital's 2024 mayoral candidate, Santiago Taboada, "for his failures as mayor of Benito Juárez." Godoy also mentioned "there can be no doubt that Mexico City is better than in 2018 under Mexico City's previous mayor, Miguel Angel Mancera" (FGJ CdMx, 9 January 2024).

Ernestina Godoy had to be temporarily replaced by Ulises Lara with an interim appointment (who coincidentally obtained his degree in law on the same day). In turn, Godoy was included as Morena's candidate for the Senate and has recently been appointed by president-elect Claudia Sheinbaum as her government's legal adviser. The fact is that the selection process of one of the most important state prosecutors in Mexico has been criticized for being highly politicized.

Most recently, it is worth highlighting that Lara intervened in favour of former Chihuahua's governor, Javier Corral, who was going to be detained in a restaurant in Mexico City by Chihuahua's corruption prosecutor office for various charges including misuse of public funds. While President López Obrador considered the actions against Corral to be a "political revenge," Chihuahua's prosecutor strongly criticized Lara's response as a "severe obstruction of justice" (Rojas, El Economista, 15 August 2024).

Guanajuato

The north-central state of Guanajuato has become one of the country's most violent places. Despite being only the sixth largest in terms of population, Guanajuato has seen the highest number of homicides in the country. According to the National Executive Secretariat of Public Security 2022 figures, Guanajuato has been the most violent state for three consecutive years. A war between the Santa Rosa de Lima and Jalisco Nueva Generación cartels has been reported since 2019.[39]

President López Obrador has continuously criticized Guanajuato's security policy and insisted on replacing the local prosecutor. In 2020, the President suggested "there was corruption or collusion with some of the drug cartels fighting bloody battles in Guanajuato." Responding to another massacre in Salvatierra, Guanajuato on 20 December 2023, López Obrador called for the removal of state prosecutor Carlos Zamarripa, alleging he had been in office for 13 years and had "amassed excessive power and acts as if **he** were the governor supported by powerful groups."[40] Thus far, Zamarripa has remained in his position although the newly elected PAN governor, Libia García, has said he will not be part of her government.

Guerrero

After the local Congress did not approve Governor Evelyn Salgado's proposals for state prosecutor in 2021, she appointed Army Lieutenant Sandra Valdovinos for a six-year term until 2027. This decision was strongly criticized for militarizing public security responsibilities, as well as for Valdovinos' lack of experience and partiality (El País, 29 December 2021).[41] Two years later, in the midst of a wave of increasing violence associated with organized criminal activity in Guerrero, Valdovinos requested the local Congress a temporary leave from office for six months due to personal matters (14 February 2024), which was postponed. Instead, the governor decreed the dismissal of the prosecutor, who objected that this was contrary to the state Constitution. After President López Obrador supported the Governor's decision (Escobar, 2024), in April the local Congress elected a replacement state prosecutor, putting an end to this dispute, but at the same time demonstrating the lack of autonomy.

Morelos

A case that transcended the state's jurisdiction is related to Morelos Prosecutor Uriel Carmona. The death of a 27-year-old single mother became a source of conflict between Carmona and the Mexico City prosecutor. Mexico City's then-mayor (and subsequently the next president) Claudia Sheinbaum declared that "Morelos state prosecutor is trying to cover up a femicide."[42] Carmona was a vocal critic of President López Obrador. In 2023, the Mexico City prosecutor arrested him for obstructing the femicide investigation. President López Obrador argued that this was "lawful as his immunity protected him only from federal crimes." In a partisan vote, the federal lower chamber then impeached Carmona (by 230 votes to 22 with 170 abstentions), as the Morelos state assembly blocked the federal prosecutor from acting against the state prosecutor. This is the second time in the last five years that a local legislature has voted against the federal Congress and invalidated this decision. After the victory of Morena's candidate, Margarita González Saravia, in the 2024 gubernatorial election, Uriel Carmona reiterated that he has not considered resigning in spite of criticisms and threats to replace him.

Nayarit

According to Mexicanos contra la Corrupción, during Roberto Sandoval's PRI Government, police coordinated by the state prosecutor Edgar Veytia extorted hundreds of people while facilitating that Cartel Jalisco Nueva Generación stored drugs in Manzanillo. When Sandoval's government ended, protests against both emerged, and the first claims were presented to the new prosecutor, Petronilo Díaz, who later confirmed formal investigations were opened.

In 2019, former Nayarit Prosecutor Edgar Veytia was sentenced to 20 years in prison in the United States for drug trafficking conspiracy on behalf of the Beltrán Leyva cartel, to which he confessed. He later became a state witness against Genaro García Luna and testified that in 2011 the Governor of Nayarit had told him that President Felipe Calderón and García Luna were backing

Leyva's rival, Chapo Guzmán. In April 2024, Veytia's sentence length was reduced to ten years after declaring as a protected witness in García Luna's case.

Nuevo León

Since the beginning of his term, Nuevo León Governor Samuel García has openly confronted the acting head of the State's Prosecutor's Office, Pedro Arce. On 7 June 2023, García denounced an armed break-in by the Prosecutor´s Office in the government's building and travelled to Mexico City calling for Arce´s dismissal due to his lack of independence and links with the PRI. President López Obrador publicly backed García, acknowledging the governor would request the Senate the state prosecutor. Nevertheless, the Supreme Court resolved that Arce could not be removed until the constitutional controversy (238/2022) was resolved.

The confrontation between García and Arce, as well as with the local congress, continued throughout 2023–2024. After García requested a six-month leave to contend as Movimiento Ciudadano's presidential candidate in 2024, the deputy prosecutor, Luis Enrique Orozco, was appointed interim governor. As Garcia confirmed he would finally not be running as a candidate on 2 December, Congress determined he could resume his activities and govern the state.

On 14 February 2024, the Supreme Court ruled in favour of García, ordering the renewal of the prosecutor's selection process. After 21 months of attempting to replace the state prosecutor, on 12 August 2024, the local congress elected four finalists, including Pedro Arce. It is expected that Governor Garcia will oppose the selection process again, especially considering PRI victories in Nuevo León and the capital, Monterrey.

Balance sheet and prospects

Reliable and impartial prosecution is both indispensable to Mexico's rule of law ambitions and also an inevitable focus of anxiety and contention. Over the past two centuries, although the republican system has been periodically interrupted by external invasions and internal upheavals, the society's core commitment to constitutional principles has taken deep root. Compared to other adjoining republics, Mexico's legal order is remarkably durable and relatively authoritative. There is a hunger for impartial justice, and since multi-party democracy arrived over the past quarter century, important reforms have been adopted to reinforce the rule of law and potentially also to boost the reach and credibility of the prosecutorial system. Over the same period, however, the weight of prior history and the uncertain commitment of successive governments to the full realization of these upgrades have tended to redirect or even obstruct such reformist impetus. The project of converting aspirations for a trustworthy justice system and an impartial prosecution service into practical improvements that deliver real benefits to the citizenry at large has at best so far proved no more than a work in progress.

Meanwhile, the pressures on law enforcement in Mexico have grown ever more severe. As in various other Latin American republics, political democratization does not necessarily work to the benefit of citizen security or effective law enforcement.[43] Among the various general impediments, the security forces often reduced their vigilance as they found their prestige downgraded; decentralization and market liberalization opened up new spaces for the growth of crime; and the expense of competitive elections led some candidates to seek funding from dubious sources. These generic problems took a more drastic turn in those countries located along major narcotics corridors serving the vast US market for illegal drugs. Mexico's Pacific coast and frontier states were, of course, fundamental to this trade, which was further aggravated by the reverse flow of illicit weaponry and associated people trafficking and white-collar crimes. For a mixture of generic and nationally specific reasons, twenty-first-century Mexico's rule of law regime has displayed cumulative and metastasizing failures as severe as almost any in the subcontinent. Pressures from the US Drug Enforcement Agency and the US courts have underscored the extent of these deficiencies, which are now being compounded by vast refugee and undocumented migratory flows. In sum, whatever the partial advances in law enforcement attributable to the justice reforms of the past two decades, they have been dwarfed by this explosion of violent criminality.

This negative balance of forces was already fully on display before the electoral watershed of 2018. The new federal General Prosecutor's Office began its work as the "*abrazos no balazos*" ("hugs not bullets") approach was proclaimed. In practice, however, the Lopez Obrador administration has prioritized the assignment of public order tasks to the military, rather than empowering civilian law enforcement agencies. If an effective public prosecution service requires open communications and the marshalling of public trust, reliance on a National Guard (*Guardia Nacional)* to fill gaps in a broken policing system points in the opposite direction, especially when the authorities seem tempted to suppress evidence of poor outcomes, rather than conduct truthful audits of criminal justice outcomes. In this context, the appointment of an irremovable federal prosecutor with a guaranteed nine-year term may prove little advancement over the previous parade of 16 attorney generals over 30 years. (It should be noted that Alejandro Gertz Manero was almost 79 when he started a term scheduled to end near his 88th birthday.) In every previous administration, the incoming president has selected a like-minded top prosecutor, but this precedent is due to be broken in 2024. It remains to be seen whether such *continuismo* can serve to strengthen the delivery of justice, or whether it slows the stock-taking and renewal that the results of 2018–2024 surely demand.

A final paragraph on the prospects for law enforcement under the next administration is inevitably speculative. The conflict between lagging reform and intensified challenges could prove explosive. However, sexennial renewal also offers the hope that long-delayed necessities might be tackled with fresh energy by a new team. Much depends upon the clarity of the incoming authorities concerning the problems they have inherited and their margins of freedom to break with evident errors of the past. At the time of writing, there are huge speculations concerning a possible radical overhaul of the entire court system, perhaps including the direct election of all judges. But no attention has been given to the misfiring of the FGR, and there seems little prospect that the present incumbent will soon be replaced by a more effective successor, whether elected or nominated. It seems no quick or simple remedies are available. In any case, the incipient capacities of the existing prosecutorial system need to be nurtured and reinforced, rather than disrupted.

Gaps in coverage between federal and state prosecutorial services can only be bridged gradually, and as a result of careful audit and skilled bargaining. This chapter has provided multiple examples of prosecutorial weakness at both at the federal and state levels. There are some "islands of excellence" within the overall system, but there is no easy way to transmit success in, say, Yucatán, to the broken structures of Michoacán or Guerrero.[44] Within the FGR, some special prosecutor's offices display more reformist zeal than others, but the transmission of good practice can all too easily reverse rather than diffuse. More generally, successive Mexican administrations faced with intractable rule of law challenges are mostly inclined to pursue "bait and switch" tactics. That is to say, they seek to gain political capital by launching appealing innovations. But then to shield themselves from criticism when results are slow to appear, they covertly switch course and resort to protective expedients intended to defer true rule of law disciplines to the next *sexenio*. If this is the tactic pursued by the next administration, longer run reforms of the FGR will continue to misfire.

Notes

1 Article 102 of the 1917 Constitution, which took effect when terms of appointment were specified in August 1919 and responsibilities were defined in 1934.
2 Secretaría de Gobernación (1994).
3 Diario Oficial de la Federación (2001); Valencia, Salvador (2009).
4 Silvia Dutrenit (2011); Chapter 5 of González-Ocantos (C.U.P. 2016). and Treviño-Rangel (October 2022).
5 See Gobierno Federal, 2008.
6 As official crime statistics in Mexico do not provide an accurate picture of major crime types that occur, INEGI runs a yearly victimization survey. This survey aims to identify the share of crime missing from official statistics – excluding homicide – by sampling over 100,000 households across more than 1,700 municipalities in Mexico.
7 While the concentration of power by the national prosecutor was not concerning in itself, the 2019 Due Process of Law Foundation (DPLF) & Washington Office on Latin America (WOLA) report highlighted: (1) a lack of transparency in the Prosecutor's appointing process and (2) Mexico's Constitution states that the president is the only public official who can remove the prosecutor. Neither the Senate nor the Prosecutor's

Office's Citizens' Council can initiate a motion for removal, even when evidence suggests the prosecutor committed a grave offense.

8 For a polemical but informative biography see Lemus J. Jesús, 2023.

9 Fundación para el Debido Proceso, 2016. See also: Presidencia de la República 2016; Redes de Organizaciones Civiles 2016; .RedTDT (2016).

10 IMCO, 2017.

11 The group #FiscaliaQueSirva brought together more than 100 human rights organizations, victims' associations, academics, journalists, and business leaders united to guarantee a truly autonomous and robust Fiscalía General. Fundación para el Debido Proceso, 2017.

12 Ezequiel González-Ocantos et al., 2023, pp. 141–7.

13 In an interview held in October 2017, Santiago Nieto claimed that Emilio Lozoya, former Pemex CEO, had pressured him to clear his name in a bribery case tied to the 2012 presidential election. Nieto was fired on the grounds that he broke a code of conduct and violated laws governing criminal proceedings, but later joined López Obrador's campaign team and became the head of the Financial Intelligence Unit (UIF). The UIF also announced in 2019 that it would examine accounts belonging to former acting prosecutor Alberto E. Beltrán.

14 México Evalúa (2019).

15 See WOLA (2018); WOLA (2020); TM (2019).

16 https://fgr.org.mx/. The Fiscalía Especial para los Delitos de Violencia contra las Mujeres (FEVIM), created in 2006, was replaced on 20 May 2021 by the Fiscalía Especializada para los Delitos de Violencia contra las Mujeres y Trata de Personas (FEVIMTRA). See also: Senado de la República (2020); Monreal (2020).

17 Inter-American Commission on Human Rights, 2021.

18 See https://fgr.org.mx/.

19 FGR, 2024, p. 10–13. See also: Cámara de Diputados (2024).

20 Secretaría de Hacienda, 2023; Cuenta Pública 2008-2022.

21 Transparency International, 2022.

22 Due Process of Law Foundation, 2020. See also Justice in Mexico (2021); Fundación por la Justicia y el Estado Democrático de Derecho (2020); Indacochea (2019).

23 In 2022, the CNB had a structure of 243 personnel and is part of the federal government (Ministry of the Interior). The CNB reported that 48% of actions to identify disappeared people have been implemented collaboratively with local Fiscalías, 24% with FGR, 9% with FGE and FGR, and 19% independently. https://comisionacional debusqueda.gob.mx/busqueda/ Disappearances of girls and women have also become a serious concern. While 20,292 women have been murdered between 2018 and May 2023, Amnesty International has pointed out that only 5,065 were classified as femicides. A report published in 2022 noted that over the last six years, the number of disappeared girls and women has tripled (Instituto Mexicano de Derechos Humanos y Democracia A.C, 2022).

24 Andrés Manuel López Obrador, Morning press conference, 27 December 2023.

25 Artículo 19, https://articulo19.org/periodistasasesinados/.

26 Dávila, Proceso, 1 August 2023.

27 Since May 2022, the FGR has been investigating the real assets of Julio Scherer in addition to other accusations for alleged acts of corruption. See Gomez Bruera, Hernán (2023); Ferri (2021); Garcia Angeles; Contra la Corrupción.

28 While in the case of Emilio Lozoya the FGR is seeking a 46-year sentence, Lavalle reached an agreement for provisional release after being prosecuted for investigations stemming from the complaint filed by Lozoya. In spite of being under provisional release, Lavalle was appointed Campeche's Economic Development Secretary on 4 December 2024.

29 In August 2023, Minister President Norma Piña submitted the 2024 budget proposal for the judicial power of US $4.93bn. President López Obrador considered it "excessive" and for months he embarked on an open confrontation with the judiciary on the use of trust funds (*fideicomisos*) for judges' health and pensions. An unconstitutional action was filed with the Court and the use of these trust funds by the federal government has been provisionally suspended.
30 US Department of Justice, 2020.
31 Gobierno de México, 2023
32 Rosario Robles was imprisoned in 2020 for improper exercise of public service. After three years of imprisonment and an open media debate about the politicization of her case led by her daughter, a federal judge ordered her release. See Robles (2024).
33 In August 2022, Murillo Karam was arrested on charges that under his administration abuses had been committed in the investigation of the Ayotzinapa disappearances. It was not only the first arrest of a former Attorney General in recent history, but also the biggest mass arrest of Mexican army soldiers ever by civilian prosecutors. More recently, the FGR identified misuse of public funds by Murillo involving more than 176 million US dollars.
34 FGR 415/24, 11 August 2024. Amid accusations of manipulation of the case, the Sinaloa prosecutor resigned on 16 August 2024. See Ibarra, Proceso, 18 August 2024.
35 Local congressmen, mainly from Morena, modified Article 44 to change from three to one year the time required for Attorney candidates of not holding elected positions by popular vote (Ordaz, Forbes, 11 December 2019).
36 Abi-Habib, et al. New York Times, 2023.
37 With 41 votes in favour and 25 against, the local Congress did not reach the qualified majority to ratify Godoy as Prosecutor (8 January 2024).
38 For years, PAN officials have been accused of allegedly setting up construction companies with family members and handing out illegal permits in exchange for flats.
39 See: Gobierno de México, 3 January 2023; 17 January 2023.
40 According to Guanajuato's prosecutor, members of a local cartel opened fire on a group of friends during a holiday celebration, where 11 people died and more than 15 were injured. (Camhaji, El País, 20 December 2023).
41 Barragán, El País, 29 December 2021.
42 McDonnell, Los Angeles Times, 2023.
43 For an early warning, see e.g. Bergman and Whitehead (2009).
44 World Justice Project (2024).

References

Abi-Habib, M., Kitroeff, N. and Rodríguez Mega, E. (2023) In Mexico, Surveillance Orders That Read Like a Political Power List. *New York Times*, 9 November 2023. https://www.nytimes.com/2023/11/09/world/americas/mexico-surveillance-attorney-general.html

Anderson, L.E. and González-Ocantos, E.A. (2016) *Shifting Legal Visions: Judicial Change and Human Trials in Latin America*, Cambridge University Press.

Artículo 19, *Periodistas asesinados en México* https://articulo19.org/periodistasasesinados/

Barragán, Al. (2021). Evelyn Salgado nombra a una militar en activo como fiscal general de Guerrero. *El País,* 29 December 2021. https://elpais.com/mexico/2021-12-29/evelyn-salgado-nombra-a-una-militar-en-activo-como-fiscal-general-de-guerrero.html

Botero, Sandra, Daniel M. Brinks and Ezequiel González Ocantos (2022) *The Limits of Judicialization*, Cambridge University Press.

Cámara de Diputados. *Ley de la Fiscalía General de la República* (2024, 1 de abril). Diario Oficial de la Federación. https://www.diputados.gob.mx/LeyesBiblio/ref/lfgr.htm

Camhaji, E. (20 December 2023). López Obrador eleva la presión sobre el fiscal de Guanajato y cuestiona su versión sobre la masacre de Salvatierra: "No es suficiente". *El País*. https://elpais.com/mexico/2023-12-20/lopez-obrador-eleva-la-presion-sobre-el-fiscal-de-guanajuato-y-cuestiona-su-version-sobre-la-masacre-de-salvatierra-no-es-suficiente.html

Causa en Común (2023) Bajando el switch… un país sin denuncia y con probable manipulación de cifras sobre inseguridad. https://www.wilsoncenter.org/sites/default/files/media/documents/publication/wp236_national_security_and_armed_forces_in_mexico.pdf

Congreso de la Unión (2021) https://www.canaldelcongreso.gob.mx/noticias/14214/Remiten_al_Ejecutivo_decreto_que_expide_la_Ley_de_la_Fiscala_General_de_la_Repblica

Contra la Corrupción https://contralacorrupcion.mx/tablero-de-la-impunidad/gertz-manero-y-caso-udlap/

Cuenta Pública (2008–2022) https://www.cuentapublica.hacienda.gob.mx/ Annex Análisis del Ejercicio del Presupuesto de Egresos FGR.

Dávila, Patricia (2023) Lanzan alerta por homicidios de policías en México in *Proceso*, 1 August 2023 https://www.proceso.com.mx/nacional/2023/8/1/lanzan-alerta-por-homicidios-de-policias-en-mexico-311851.html

Diario Oficial de la Federación, Estatuto Orgánico de la Fiscalía General de la República, 19 June 2023, https://www.dof.gob.mx/nota_detalle.php?codigo=5692571&fecha=19/06/2023#gsc.tab=0 Artículo 102 de la Constitución https://www.dof.gob.mx/nota_detalle.php?codigo=5332025&fecha=10/02/2014#gsc.tab=0 Ley de la Fiscalía General de la República, 20 May 2021 https://www.diputados.gob.mx/LeyesBiblio/ref/lfgr.htm Ley Orgánica de la Fiscalía General de la República, 14 December 2018 (https://dof.gob.mx/nota_detalle.php?codigo=5546647&fecha=14/12/2018#gsc.tab=0) Decreto por el que se Reforma, Adiciona y Derogan Diversas Disposiciones de la Constitución Política de los Estados Unidos Mexicanos, en Materia Política-Electoral, 10 February 2014. Acuerdo por el que se disponen diversas medidas para la procuración de justicia por delitos cometidos contra personas vinculadas con movimientos sociales y políticos del pasado, 27 November 2001, https://www.dof.gob.mx/nota_detalle.php?codigo=758894&fecha=27/11/2001#gsc.tab=0

Due Process of Law Foundation (2020) *How Mexico is Lagging in Transforming its National Prosecutor's Office: New Report Examines the Institution's Performance and Identifies Challenges Ahead to Address Impunity*, 19 August 2020. https://www.dplf.org/en/news/how-mexico-lagging-transforming-its-national-prosecutors-office-new-report-examines

Dutrenit Bielous, Silvia (2011) "Una gestión atrapada: el caso de la FEMOSPP" in *La crisis de las instituciones políticas en México* (pp. 111–144) UNAM-FCPyS.

Escobar, Dalia (2024) AMLO da espaldarazo a Evelyn Salgado tras ceses de secretarios de Guerrero. *Proceso,* 15 March 2024. https://www.proceso.com.mx/nacional/2024

/3/15/amlo-da-espaldarazo-evelyn-salgado-tras-ceses-de-secretarios-de-guerrero-325674.html

Ferri, P. (2021) El fiscal Gertz encara la peor ola de reproches desde su nombramiento. *El País*. 28 September 2021. https://elpais.com/mexico/2021-09-28/el-fiscal-gertz-encara-la-peor-ola-de-reproches-desde-su-nombramiento.html

Fiscalía General de la República (FGR), ACUERDO Estructura ocupacional de la FGR y expide el Manual que regula las remuneraciones de los servidores pública de la FGR para ejercicio fiscal 2024, 22 February 2024, https://www.dof.gob.mx/nota_detalle.php?codigo=5717655&fecha=22/02/2024#gsc.tab=0

ACUERDO Estructura ocupacional de la FGR y expide el Manual que regula las remuneraciones de los servidores pública de la FGR para ejercicio fiscal 2022 (http://aplicaciones.pgr.gob.mx/normatecasustantiva/Normateca%20Sustantiva/ACUERDO%20A-OM-001-2022.pdf) (pp. 10–13)

municado FGR 415/24, 11 August 2024. https://www.fgr.org.mx/es/FGR/Prensa?suri=http%3A%2F%2Fwww.FGR.swb%23fgr_Boletin%3A14798 Comunicado FGR 216/19. Conferencia de prensa del Fiscal General de la República, sobre los primeros 100 días de la institución. https://www.gob.mx/fgr/prensa/comunicado-fgr-216-19-conferencia-de-prensa-del-fiscal-general-de-la-republica-sobre-los-primeros-100-dias-de-la-institucion Comunicado FGR 530/2022 https://www.gob.mx/fgr/prensa/comunicado-fgr-530-22-fgr-obtiene-vinculacion-a-proceso-por-el-caso-segalmex Informe Anual Actividades de la Fiscalía General de la República (2019–2022) https://stastdgv2portfgr032.blob.core.windows.net/transparencia/InformesActividades Informes de Seguridad, https://seguridad.sspc.gob.mx/documentos/

Freeman, Will (2023) Do Latin America's Top Prosecutors Have Too Much Power? In *Americas Quarterly*, 30 November 2023. https://www.americasquarterly.org/article/do-latin-americas-top-prosecutors-have-too-much-power/

Fundación por la Justicia y el Estado Democrático de Derecho (2020, 19 de enero) *¿1 año de justicia y autonomía de la FGR? Balance ciudadano de la gestión del fiscal general de la República, Dr. Alejandro Gertz Manero*. https://www.fundacionjusticia.org/1-ano-de-justicia-y-autonomia-de-la-fgr-balance-ciudadano-de-la-gestion-del-fiscal-general-de-la-republica-dr-alejandro-gertz-manero/

Fundación para el Debido Proceso, Anexo, 25 October 2016 https://www.dplf.org/sites/default/files/anexo_ii_posicionamiento_pgr_y_sfp.pdf #Fiscalía que Sirva, 2017, https://www.dplf.org/es/programa/fiscaliaquesirva

undación para la Justicia https://www.fundacionjusticia.org/wp-content/uploads/2020/01/FINAL_DIGITAL_A-UN-A%C3%91O-DE-JUSTICIA-Y-AUTONOMIA.pdf

García Ángeles, D. (s.f.) *Contra la Corrupción. Gertz Manero y caso UDLAP*. https://contralacorrupcion.mx/tablero-de-la-impunidad/gertz-manero-y-caso-udlap/

García Ángeles, D. (2022) *La Fiscalía General de la República ¿una oficina particular del fiscal?* https://contralacorrupcion.mx/encuesta-mcci-reforma-2022/como-vivimos-mexicanas-y-mexicanos-la-corrupcion/la-fiscalia-general-de-la-republica-una-oficina-particular-del-fiscal/

Gobierno de México, La red de corrupción de Genaro García Luna, 1 March 2023 https://www.justice.gov/opa/pr/joint-statement-attorney-general-united-states-william-p-barr-and-fiscal-general-mexico Informe de Seguridad, 17 January 2023 https://seguridad.sspc.gob.mx/documento/304/informe-de-seguridad Resultados de la

Estrategia Nacional de Seguridad Pública 2022, 3 January 2023 https://seguridad.sspc.gob.mx/documento/302/resultados-de-la-estrategia-nacional-de-seguridad-publica-2022; https://seguridad.sspc.gob.mx/documento/304/informe-de-seguridad Establecimiento de la Procuraduría General de la República. La PGR nació con la reforma judicial de 1900. https://www.gob.mx/cms/uploads/attachment/file/341895/IV._ESTABLECIMIENTO_DE_LA_PROCURADUR_A_GENERAL_DE_LA_REP_BLICA.pdf Federal government registry of missing persons at www.gob.mx/sesnsp/acciones-y-programas/registro-nacional-de-datos-de-personas-extraviadas-o-desaparecidas-rnped Reforma Constitucional de Seguridad y Justicia. Guía de consulta. ¿En qué consiste la reforma? Texto constitucional comparado antes y después de la reforma (2008) http://biblioteca.diputados.gob.mx/janium/bv/hcd/lx/refcons_segjus_gc.pdf

Gómez Bruera, Hernán (2023) *Traición en Palacio: El negocio de la justicia en la 4T*, Editorial Grijalbo.

González-Ocantos Ezequiel, Chirinos, P.M., Pavao, N., & Hidalgo, V.B. (2023) Prosecutors, Voters and the Criminalisation of Corruption in Latin America: The Case of Lava Jato in *Cambridge Studies in Law and Society*, Cambridge University Press.

Ibarra, Adrián (2024) La de Sinaloa, una Fiscalía "autónoma" atada al "consejo" del gobernador in *Proceso*, 18 August 2024. https://www.proceso.com.mx/nacional/2024/8/18/la-de-sinaloa-una-fiscalia-autonoma-atada-al-consejo-del-gobernador-335070.html

IMCO, Centro de Investigación en Política Pública (2017) 28 August 2017 https://imco.org.mx/vamosporunafiscaliaquesirva/

INEGI, Censo Nacional de Procuración de Justicia Federal (cnpjf), 2024 y Censo Nacional de Procuración de Justicia Estatal (cnpje), Comunicado de Prensa 583/24, 3 October 2024. https://www.inegi.org.mx/app/saladeprensa/noticia.html?id=9330

INEGI, Encuesta Nacional de Victimización y Percepción sobre Seguridad Pública. Principales Resultados, September 2021. https://www.inegi.org.mx/contenidos/programas/envipe/2021/doc/envipe2021_presentacion_nacional.pdf.

Instituto Mexicano de Derechos Humanos y Democracia A.C. (2022) *Diagnóstico de mujeres desaparecidas*, September 2022. https://www.imdhd.org/wp-content/uploads/2022/11/IMDHD-Diagnostico_Nov2022.pdf

Instituto de Investigación en Rendición de Cuentas y Combate a la Corrupción (IIRCCC) (2020) SOBRE EL COMBATE A LA CORRUPCIÓN EN MÉXICO, Informe País, Universidad de Guadalajara. https://combatealacorrupcion.mx/wp-content/uploads/Sobre-el-combate-a-la-corrupcion-en-Mexico-2020_Reporte-completo-1.pdf

Inter-American Commission on Human Rights (2021) IACHR Calls on Mexico to Ensure that Any Changes to its Constitutional Law on the Office of the Attorney General Are Debated with Significant Citizen Participation and Reflect the Country's International Human Rights Commitments, 22 February 2021, https://www.oas.org/en/iachr/jsForm/?File=/en/iachr/media_center/preleases/2021/037.asp

IMCO, Reforma Constitucional respecto del diseño de la Fiscalía General de la República, 29 August 2017 https://imco.org.mx/wp-content/uploads/2017/08/Resumen-reforma-a-FGR-VXUFQS-28agosto2017-1.pdf

Indacochea, Úrsula, DPLF and Maureen Meyer, *"The Implementing Law of Mexico's National Prosecutor's Office. Progress and Pending Issues,* WOLA, March 2019 (https://www.wola.org/wp-content/uploads/2019/03/FiscaliaENG.pdf) https://

justiceinmexico.org/envipe-study-shows-uptick-in-victimization-increase-in-cifra-negra-of-unreported-crimes/

Justice in Mexico, 16 March 2021 https://justiceinmexico.org/prosecutorial-reform-in-mexico-assessing-the-progress-of-the-national-prosecutors-office/

Justice in Mexico. (2014). *ENVIPE Study shows uptick in victimization, increase in "cifra negra" of unreported crimes.* https://justiceinmexico.org/envipe-study-shows-uptick-in-victimization-increase-in-cifra-negra-of-unreported-crimes/

Lemus, J. Jesús (2023) *El Fiscal Imperial: El eslabón más oscuro de la 4T.* Harper Collins Mexico.

López Obrador, Andrés Manuel, morning conference, 27 December 2023 https://lopezobrador.org.mx/2023/12/27/informe-de-avances-en-busqueda-de-personas-desaparecidas-se-presentara-cada-mes-presidente/

Mexico Evalúa, Hallazgos (2022) Seguimiento y evaluación de la justicia penal en México (2022) https://www.mexicoevalua.org/hallazgos-2022-evaluacion-de-la-justicia-penal/ Hallazgos (2021) Seguimiento y evaluación del sistema de justicia penal en México, https://www.mexicoevalua.org/wp-content/uploads/2022/10/hallazgos2021vf-4oct.pdf De PGR a FGR: lineamientos hacia la transición (2019) 21 March 2019 http://www.proyectojusticia.org/wp-content/uploads/2019/03/PGRaFGR.pdf Proceso de Designación del Primer Fiscal General de México ha sido una Simulación (2019) 18 January 2019, https://www.mexicoevalua.org/proceso-designacion-del-primer-fiscal-general-mexico-ha-sido-una-simulacion/

McDonnell, P.J. (2023) Amid femicide epidemic, Mexico prosecutor charged with cover-up in a single mom's death. *Los Angeles Times.* 5 August 2023 https://www.latimes.com/world-nation/story/2023-08-05/mexico-city-arrests-neighboring-states-attorney-general-alleging-femicide-coverup

Mendoza, V. (2024) FGJEM investiga como robo de vehículo muerte de quien aparentemente era chef del fiscal. *Proceso.* 16 March 2024 https://www.proceso.com.mx/nacional/estados/2023/12/6/fgjem-investiga-como-robo-de-vehiculo-muerte-de-quien-aparentemente-era-chef-del-fiscal-319913.html

Monreal, Ricardo (2020) *Iniciativa con Proyecto de Decreto por el que se expide la Ley de la Fiscalía General de la República, se abroga la Ley Orgánica de la Fiscalía General de la República y se reforman, adicionan y derogan diversas disposiciones de distintos ordenamientos legales*, 9 October 2020. https://ricardomonrealavila.com/ley-de-la-fiscalia-general-de-la-republica/

New York Times, 9 November 2023 https://www.nytimes.com/2023/11/09/world/americas/mexico-surveillance-attorney-general.html

Ordaz Díaz, A. (2019) No fue adecuado el proceso de elección de Ernestina Godoy como fiscal. *Forbes.* 11 December 2019 https://www.forbes.com.mx/no-fue-adecuado-el-proceso-de-eleccion-de-ernestina-godoy-como-fiscal-de-cdmx-experto/)

Parametría, El reto de la seguridad pública en México, 30 Noviembre 2012. https://www.parametria.com.mx/estudios/el-reto-de-la-seguridad-publica-en-mexico/

Presidencia de la República, Press Release (29 November 2016) https://www.gob.mx/epn/prensa/epn-proposes-constitutional-amendment-to-senate-to-prevent-attorney-general-from-automatically-becoming-new-public-prosecutor?idiom=en

Proyecto de Presupuesto de Egresos de la Federación 2023. Estrategia Programática. https://www.ppef.hacienda.gob.mx/work/models/8uLX2rB7/PPEF2023/mo2h2PK/docs/49/r49_ep.pdf

Redes de Organizaciones Civiles (2016) Presidencia y Senado atentan contra una Fiscalía autónoma y la consolidación del SNA Ciudad de México, 26 September 2016 https://www.dplf.org/es/programa/fiscaliaquesirva https://www.dplf.org/sites/default/files/anexo_ii_posicionamiento_pgr_y_sfp.pdf

RedTDT (2016) Presidencia y Senado atentan contra una Fiscalía autónoma y la consolidación del SNA, 26 September 2016. https://redtdt.org.mx/archivos/7417

Robles, Rosario (2024) *Rosario de México, Testimonio de una infamia.* Editorial Grijalbo.

Rojas Arturo (2024) Intento frustrado de detención de Javier Corral: AMLO dice que se trata de una venganza política in *El Economista*, 15 August 2024, https://www.eleconomista.com.mx/politica/Detencion-de-Javier-Corral-AMLO-dice-que-se-trata-de-una-venganza-politica-20240815-0050.html

Sánchez, Andrea (2019) *El rumbo de la Fiscalía General está escrito en el Presupuesto*, México Evalúa, 30 December 2019, https://www.mexicoevalua.org/rumbo-la-fiscalia-general-esta-escrito-en-presupuesto/

Secretaría de Hacienda (2023) Proyecto de Presupuesto de Egresos de la Federación 2023. Estrategia Programática (resumen) https://www.ppef.hacienda.gob.mx/work/models/8uLX2rB7/PPEF2023/mo2h2PK/docs/49/r49_epr.pdf (last consultation 26 April 2024)

Secretaría de Gobernación (1994) Iniciativa de Decreto por el que se reforman y adicionan diversos artículos de la Constitución Política de los Estados Unidos Mexicanos, 5 December 1994, http://sil.gobernacion.gob.mx/Archivos/Documentos/1994/12/asun_1087_19941206_742675.pdf

Secretaría de Hacienda, Proyecto de Presupuesto de Egresos de la Federación para el Ejercicio Fiscal 2025, November 2024, pp 1-183. https://www.ppef.hacienda.gob.mx/work/models/GYPPF25Q/PPEF2025/lurbgnma/paquete/egresos/Proyecto_Decreto.pdf

Senado de la República (2020) Iniciativa de Decreto por el que se expide la Ley de la Fiscalía General de la República, 9 October 2020 https://lfgr.senado.gob.mx/docs/lfgr/IMLFGRLOFGR.pdf

Shirk, David A. (2010) Drug Violence in Mexico: Data and Analysis from 2001–2009. *Trends Organ Crim* 13, 167–174. https://doi.org/10.1007/s12117-010-9096-7

Transparency International (2022) Corruption Perceptions Index https://www.transparency.org/en/cpi/2022/index/mex

Transparencia Mexicana (2019) Proceso de Designación del Primer Fiscal General de la Nación ha sido una simulación, 18 January 2019 https://www.tm.org.mx/proceso-de-designacion-del-primer-fiscal-general-de-mexico-ha-sido-una-simulacion/

Treviño-Rangel, Javier (2022) "El pasado autoritario de la justicia transicional mexicana" Latin American Research Review 58, 3 October 2022.

US DEPARTMENT OF JUSTICE, Office of Public Affairs, Press Release, November 2020 https://www.justice.gov/opa/pr/joint-statement-attorney-general-united-states-william-p-barr-and-fiscal-general-mexico

Valencia Carmona, Salvador (2009) "Constitución y Nuevo Proceso Penal", in *Reforma Judicial, Revista Mexicana de Justicia*, Num. 13 http://historico.juridicas.unam.mx/publica/rev/refjud/cont/13/pjn/pjn4.htm

Winter Brian and Geert Aalbers "*2023 Capacity to Combat Corruption (CCC) Index, Assessing Latin America's ability to detect, punish and prevent corruption*",

Anti-Corruption Working Group, Americas Quarterly and Control Risks https://www.americasquarterly.org/wp-content/uploads/2023/06/CCC_2023_Report.pdf

WOLA (2020) *Where does Mexico stand in its fight against impunity, New Autonomous National Prosecutor's Office has Yet to Realize its Potential*, August 2020 https://www.wola.org/wp-content/uploads/2020/08/ENG-FGR-Gertz-FINAL.pdf

WOLA, 2018 https://www.wola.org/wp-content/uploads/2018/04/Fiscalia-Report-SPN.pdf

World Justice Project, Indice de Estado de Derecho en México 2022–2023 https://worldjusticeproject.mx/wp-content/uploads/2023/06/IEDMX-2022-2023_Digital.pdf World Justice Project Rule of Law Index. MEXICO https://worldjusticeproject.org/rule-of-law-index/country/Mexico Indice Global de Estado de Derecho, 2023 https://worldjusticeproject.mx/wp-content/uploads/2023/10/ROLI23_MX.pdf Indice de Estado de Derecho en México, 10 junio 2024 https://worldjusticeproject.mx/indice-de-estado-de-derecho-en-mexico/

12 Confronting extractivism

The Inter-American Human Rights System and indigenous rights in Latin America

Par Engstrom and Edward Pérez

Introduction

Across Latin America, where extractivism remains the dominant model of development, the surge in socio-environmental conflicts in recent decades constitutes a distinct challenge to the rule of law and basic governability. From lithium extraction in Chile, hydro-electrical projects in Brazil, oil exploitation in Ecuador, to gold mining in Colombia and Guatemala, the typically private-driven, export-oriented extraction, and exploitation of land and natural resources has generated widespread opposition by local communities, with governments regularly responding to popular resistance with repression and violence. The region's indigenous and Afro-descendent communities are particularly affected, given the significance of land and natural resources for their livelihoods, and in many contexts, their collective survival.

In this context, the Inter-American Human Rights System (IAHRS), consisting of the Inter-American Commission on Human Rights (IACHR) and the Inter-American Court of Human Rights (IACtHR), has become increasingly involved in conflicts over land and natural resource extraction. While the IAHRS has explicitly recognized the importance of the extractive industry for economic development, it has developed human rights standards that seek to regulate projects, as well as obligations of both states in the region and external actors to respect and guarantee human rights. The Commission has emphasized the state's duty to adopt "appropriate and positive steps with due diligence to prevent, investigate, punish and redress human rights violations that result from the execution of these projects," including adopting an appropriate regulatory framework (IACHR, 2015b, 2016). The IACtHR, for its part, has been in the vanguard of the international development of indigenous rights as they pertain to land and natural resources. In a series of landmark cases, the Court has recognized the notion of collective rights of indigenous communities to ancestral lands and natural resources based on their importance for the distinct cultural identities of these communities. Moreover, the Court has recognized the right of indigenous communities to consultation and participation in all matters that could directly affect them.

DOI: 10.4324/9781003519195-12

These jurisprudential developments notwithstanding, tensions remain between, on the one hand, the preservation of cultural identity and traditional values of indigenous peoples through the protection of their right to lands and natural resources, and, on the other hand, economic development projects and extractive industries. Despite cyclical shifts in electoral politics during recent decades, characterized by alternating right- and left-wing governments, the extractive mode of development endures in Latin America. This phenomenon, termed the "extractivism consensus" by Svampa (2015), transcends ideological and political divides and reveals a deeply ingrained commitment to resource extraction as a primary driver of economic growth. However, resistance to extractivism persists in Latin America. This resistance is often manifested in disorderly and occasionally violent public protests, fuelled in part by the perceived inadequacy of formal protections. Repressive state responses to protests have made Latin America stand out as the deadliest region for environmental defenders.

In parallel, a trend of increasing recognition for international rights of prior consultation and indigenous land and territorial rights has emerged amongst regional states. Notably, the IAHRS has played a vanguard role in developing these international human rights standards and policy guidelines. For groups able to leverage the IAHRS's norms and standards, the System presents a unique transnational opportunity structure for communities to contest domestic public policies and development projects. These developments highlight the complex tensions between formal legal advancements, on the one hand, and the lived experiences, on the other hand, of communities on the ground, where the extractive frontier continues to expand (Picq, 2020).

This chapter examines how the IAHRS has navigated the tensions between the protection of local communities, particularly indigenous people, and large-scale extractivism promoted and supported by governments. It explores the transnational dimensions affecting the governability for development by examining the IAHRS's engagement with conflicts arising from tensions and trade-offs generated by development projects affecting indigenous and local interests and rights. It is divided into three main parts. The first part provides a contextual overview of extractivist trends in Latin America with the aim to identify the main drivers of extractivism in the region and how they affect local communities, including indigenous people. The second part discusses how the IAHRS has engaged with the human rights implications of extractivism in Latin America, with specific focus on the development of what we term a tripartite regulatory framework emphasizing the obligations of states to ensure the *effective participation* of affected communities, to elaborate a prior and independent *environmental and social impact assessment*, and to ensure the *sharing of reasonable benefits* with affected communities. The third part develops a tentative assessment of the effectiveness of the IAHRS in its engagement with the human rights implications of extractivism.

Extractivism in Latin America: The (un)rule of law and the allure of development

The extractive imperative

In Latin America, recent decades have witnessed an intensification of extractivism as the dominant development model, taking a contemporary form as a private-sector-driven, export-orientated strategy for exploiting and extracting natural resources (Farthing & Fabricant, 2018). Extractivism expanded during the political shift to the left in the first decade of the 2000s, further deepening the extraction-based development model in the region (Burchardt & Dietz, 2014). Extractivism generated substantial revenues for governments to fund social spending and public infrastructure investments, consolidating political support among traditionally disadvantaged sectors of Latin American societies. However, while seeking to fulfil promises of poverty reduction and inequality mitigation without resorting to forceful fiscal redistribution, Latin American governments have not only left the core dynamic of resource extraction unchanged but also further entrenched the perception of nature as a collection of exploitable resources for modernization (Arsel et al., 2016).

The persistent appeal of extractivism notwithstanding, its actual development record in Latin America has been highly uneven, at best. The allure of resource wealth for national development often prioritizes centralized benefits, potentially overlooking or neglecting the concerns and hardships faced by rural communities directly impacted by extraction activities. Most notably, the surge of extractivism, such as large-scale mining, in recent decades has led to significant encroachment on protected lands and indigenous territories (Kröger & Lalander, 2016). Extractivist activities often fuel tensions and conflicts in regions and communities where they take place (Avilés, 2019). These impacts have been exacerbated in recent years with the expansion of extractivism in Latin America encompassing not only traditional sectors such as oil, gas, and mining, but also extending to novel extractive frontiers related to renewable energy, often under the guise of "green extractivism" (Hernandez & Newell, 2022).

Popular resistance to extractivism

The expansion of extractivism has been accompanied by widespread resistance and a surge in socio-environmental conflicts in Latin America (McNeish, 2018). On some estimates, over half of the world's conflicts over extractivist activities are taking place in the region (Özkaynak et al., 2015). Much of the resistance tends to be articulated locally, by communities directly affected and people whose livelihoods, health, and cultures are threatened by large-scale extractivist projects (Tetreault, 2015). Communities affected by extractivism often deploy a combination of strategies and diverse legal and institutional avenues (Bebbington et al., 2018; Kingsbury, 2021). Domestically, rule-of-law strategies encompass domestic litigation within national courts (Auz, 2022), leveraging legal advancements pioneered by Latin American environmental constitutionalism (Gómez-Betancur et al., 2022). Internationally, efforts range from lobbying foreign governments and multinational companies, to shareholder activism, transnational NGO mobilization, and engagement with development banks, the United Nations system, and the IAHRS. Resistance to extractivism is not contained in formally institutionalized spaces, however. Communities across the region have regularly engaged in transgressive forms of contention, including street blockades and occupation of extractive companies' facilities. Some communities, such as the Mapuche in Chile, have developed "indigenous forms of 'collective bargaining by riot' by attacking the local extractivist network" (Schmalz et al., 2023).

Communities resisting extractivism encounter inherent difficulties in generating effective resistance at a scale that might affect government policy. However, with increasing intensification of conflicts over extractivism, resistance has nationalized in some contexts, and new political spaces for human rights-based resistance have emerged (Picq, 2020). There have even been tentative attempts to move away from extractivism in parts of Latin America, following resistance and collective mobilization against extractivist projects by communities (Spalding, 2023). For example, highly contentious anti-mining social movements in El Salvador led to the adoption of a law banning all metal mining in the country (Edenhofer, 2022).

Individual examples of successful resistance to extractivism do not change the fact, however, that the effectiveness of social mobilization is often highly limited. For example, Orihuela et al. (2022) have found that "successful resistance represents only 2–5% of the total universe of Peru[vian] mining conflicts." Moreover, there is no regional mass movement against extractivism, as was the case with the regional coordination of social movements mobilizing against neoliberalism in the 1990s (Almeida, 2014). The effectiveness of collective mobilization against extractivism in Latin America is also increasingly constrained by a shrinking political space, due to the escalation of repressive measures adopted by governments (Raftopoulos, 2017). The criminalization of social protest and violence against environmental defenders has made Latin America a high-risk region for collective mobilization against extractivism (Lakhani, 2020).

Violence is, however, not necessarily the principal obstacle to anti-extractivism mobilization. Any assessment of the impact of contentious collective action against extractivism needs to recognize the inherent limits of any policy change "without durable shifts in the structures that keep development models that prioritize the large-scale extraction of natural resources in place" (Silva et al., 2018). Moreover, the development needs facing communities and individual members thereof, combined with the economic benefits promised by extractivist companies, can undermine collective resistance. Contentious collective action often prioritizes conventional economic concerns and resolutions over environmental justice goals, leading to conflicts being settled through compensation schemes and financial agreements (Orihuela et al., 2022). As a result, community resistance may co-exist, however uneasily, with social acceptance in many contexts (Carrasco, 2016). Compensation programmes often face significant limitations, however. Though purporting to directly compensate affected individuals and communities and secure their support, these initiatives frequently disregard the fundamental demands of many community-based resistance movements to exercise their "right to effectively exercise autonomy over the decision to accept or reject extractive projects" (Tetreault, 2020). The common disconnect between extractivist projects and affected communities highlights the often-irreconcilable objectives and demands of extractivism as a development model on the one hand, and local community needs and aspirations on the other hand.

That said, extractivism encompasses a diverse array of practices, some of which engender significantly greater local resistance compared to others. The level of resistance is often contingent upon the scale of the environmental degradation associated with the extractive activity relative to the potential socio-economic benefits that may accrue to the affected community. In contexts characterized by robust and impartial rule of law, it may be possible to construct broad-based coalitions of support and minimize environmental harms, thereby achieving a mutually beneficial outcome. Conversely, in situations where the regulatory system is weak or susceptible to capture, resistance is likely to be significantly amplified, resulting in unacceptable societal costs.[1]

The Inter-American Human Rights System, indigenous rights, and extractivism

In a regional context of local mobilization against extractivism combined with limited opportunities for communities to challenge extractivism at home, the IAHRS has developed a set of human rights standards and principles with a view of strengthening the scope of obligations states have to respect and guarantee human rights at stake in extractivist activities. This part of the chapter examines how the IAHRS has navigated the tensions between the protection of local communities, particularly indigenous people, on the one hand, and large-scale extractivism promoted and supported by governments, on the other hand. While the IAHRS recognizes the importance of extractivist activities for regional economies, the IAHRS has sought to address the negative impacts of extractivism on human rights through the development of a set of primarily procedural obligations of states to respect and guarantee human rights.

The Inter-American Human Rights System: Origins, development, and mandate

The IAHRS has its origins in the creation of the Organization of American States (OAS) and the adoption of the American Declaration on the Rights and Duties of Man in 1948. While the IACHR was created in 1959 with a general mandate to promote human rights in the region, it took OAS member states until 1978 to agree on a legally binding American Convention on Human Rights. With the entry into force of the Convention, the IAHRS adopted the institutional structure that has remained to this day, composed of a Commission and a Court.

The IAHRS was created and experienced its initial development in a region marked by the Cold War and long periods of repressive and authoritarian rule, from the 1950s to the mid-1980s. During this period, the IAHRS primarily sought to identify general patterns of human rights violations rather than focusing on individual cases. However, with the general return to democracy in Latin America, the System turned its attention to the challenge of improving the quality of democratic rule and efforts to address human rights challenges in a regional context where electoral democracy has made significant advances but also where there continue to be widespread human rights abuses. Since the introduction of the right of individual petition, the system has become more responsive to regional human rights challenges; although the capacity of domestic litigants to turn to the regime varies considerably between countries in the region (Engstrom & Low, 2019). The institutional limitations and political constraints facing the IAHRS notwithstanding, the System has developed ambitious human rights norms that, to a significant degree, draw from regional legal traditions of expansive formal constitutional rights protections.

The IAHRS and extractivism

Over the course of several decades, the IAHRS has gradually developed its engagement with the human rights impacts of extractive activities. In 1997, the Commission published a report on Ecuador that addressed the situation of extractive industries and their impact on human rights in the country (IACHR, 1997). The Commission stressed its concerns about the potential human rights violations that could result from the planned oil exploitation activities in the traditional lands of the Huaorani people and threats to their very existence (IACHR, 1997). Following this initial report, the IACHR's concern with respect to extractivism has intensified as it has sought to develop legal standards through a series of thematic reports, including a 2015 report on indigenous peoples, Afro-descendent communities, and natural resources (IACHR, 2015a) and a 2019 report on indigenous and tribal peoples of the Pan-Amazon region (IACHR, 2019).

The IAHRS has also responded to extractivism in the region through the adoption of so-called interim measures, with the aim to prevent the occurrence of irreparable human rights violations or to put an end to ongoing human rights violations (Saldarriaga González, 2019). The IACHR has issued such measures with respect to extractivist activities on several occasions. One particularly noteworthy example was the Commission's adoption of interim measures in *Belo*

Monte in 2011, related to the construction of a hydroelectric dam in the Xingu River Basin, in Pará, Brazil. The Brazilian government under then-President Dilma Rousseff responded strongly by suspending its annual contribution to the Commission and by withdrawing its former Human Rights minister Paulo Vannuchi's candidacy to become a member of the Commission. In response to the backlash, the IACHR toned down its approach and requested broader measures, including that Brazil "adopt measures to protect the lives, health, and physical integrity of the members of the Xingu Basin indigenous communities in voluntary isolation and to protect the cultural integrity of those communities," as well as measures to protect the health and property rights of the communities (OAS, 2009). It is also relevant to note that when the IACtHR faced a similar request in *Ngöbe*, also related to the construction of a hydroelectric dam (in this case in Panama) within the affected community's ancestral lands, it declined to order interim measures, citing a lack of evidence.

It is in its standard-setting role, however, that the IAHRS has left its distinctive imprint in its response to the multiple negative impacts of extractive activities on human rights. Through its primary focus on the development of procedural obligations of states, the IAHRS has sought to balance the need of many (nearly all) Latin American societies for development through extractive activities against the obligation of states to uphold their commitments under international human rights law (IACHR, 2015a, 2019). The IAHRS's engagement with extractivism has been particularly noteworthy in relation to its development of indigenous rights.

The IAHRS and indigenous rights

The IAHRS has developed an internationally prominent approach to the rights of indigenous people. Most notably, the IAHRS has recognized the right of indigenous peoples to own and control their land as a fundamental aspect of their self-determination. The System has established guidelines to safeguard these lands, including the demarcation of territories, granting of land titles, prevention of illegal use by third parties, and preservation of natural resources (IACHR, 2019). Furthermore, the IAHRS has acknowledged the integral connection between indigenous peoples' land and natural resources and their means of subsistence and livelihood (e.g., *Lhaka Honhat* and *Yakye Axa)*. The IACtHR's jurisprudence has been particularly influential in the System's development of indigenous rights. The Court has advanced notions of the rights of indigenous people to demand free, prior, and informed consent to any major development and economic projects affecting their livelihoods. The Court has recognized indigenous peoples' right to consultation and participation in all matters that could directly affect them, particularly regarding the recognition of their communal property rights over their ancestral lands and natural resources that they have traditionally used. Additionally, the Court has interpreted the scope of these rights in a broad manner, including the protection of the right of members of indigenous communities to enjoy their own culture and traditional practices, as different peoples (Fuentes, 2017).

The first landmark case in this respect was the Court's 2001 ruling in *Awas Tingni*. This was the first case by an international tribunal that recognized the rights of indigenous people to communal property of their traditional lands. The Court argued that this right was protected under Article 21 (right to property) of the American Convention. Since the adoption of the landmark ruling in *Awas Tingni*, the IACtHR has developed extensive indigenous rights jurisprudence. In *Saramaka* concerning mining and logging activities on the lands of the Saramaka people, a tribal community in Suriname, the IACtHR issued its first ruling where it expressly analyzed the tensions that arose from extractive projects. Since that initial ruling, the IACtHR has adjudicated another case from Suriname (*Kaliña*), as well as cases from Ecuador (*Sarayaku)*, Honduras (*Triunfo de la Cruz, San Juan)*, Guatemala (*Maya Q'eqchi'),* and Argentina (*Lhaka Honhat)*, finding States responsible for failing to ensure human rights protections in the context of extractive projects. The IACtHR's jurisprudence on the topic is likely to develop further as it currently (at the time of writing this chapter, March 2024) has several high-profile cases on its docket concerning Colombia (*U'wa)*, Ecuador (*Tagaeri y Taromenane)*, and Peru (*La Oroya)* still pending final decisions. The IACtHR has also developed legal standards regarding extractivism through an advisory opinion on the right to a healthy environment, in which the Court explicitly recognized the autonomous status of the right (Mardikian, 2023). Moreover, a final decision on an advisory opinion on human rights and climate change, which is likely to address extractivism, is still pending before the Court.

The IACtHR has progressively expanded its interpretation of the scope of protection of the right to property to include the protection of the "close ties of indigenous peoples with their traditional lands and the native natural resources thereof, associated with their culture, as well as any incorporeal element deriving therefrom" (*Sawhoyamaxa)*. The basic rationale of the IACtHR's jurisprudence regarding indigenous land rights is that special positive measures are required on behalf of the members of indigenous communities "to guarantee that they may continue living their traditional way of life, and that their distinct cultural identity, social structure, economic system, customs, beliefs and traditions are respected, guaranteed and protected by States" (*Saramaka)*. This is to ensure the protection and preservation of the physical and cultural survival of indigenous people. The Court has acknowledged the communitarian character of collective land tenure among indigenous communities; in the process, departing quite dramatically from the classic concept of the (individual) right to property. The Court's notion of communal property rights does not merely include a right to traditional lands, but also a right to natural resources that indigenous communities have traditionally used within their territories (*Kaliña*).

The application of communal property rights in practice has occasionally been contentious. The IACtHR, for instance, recently faced a challenge in which different representatives of the same indigenous community presented conflicting demands concerning the scope of their communal land rights claims. Although the IACtHR acknowledged the existence of multiple leadership claims within the community, the Court ultimately favoured the representation of the leadership that had been involved in the proceedings since the initial submission of the petition to the IACHR (*Maya Q'eqchi',* para.44). Recognizing its limitations in resolving the internal leadership dispute, the IACtHR emphasized dialogue within the community and with the state concerned and prioritized finding an effective remedy with full participation of the community, rather than getting involved in competing claims within the community (*Maya Q'eqchi',* para.343).

It is important to note that for the IAHRS, the right to property is not absolute, including for indigenous peoples. For example, in its efforts to balance potential conflicts between human rights law and the benefits associated with extractive activities, the IAHRS has developed a proportionality test (*Saramaka)* that seeks to balance the risks and benefits of extractive activities with human rights concerns. Moreover, the IACtHR has also sought to strike a balance between indigenous property rights and those of third parties. For example, in *Yakye Axa, Sawhoyamaxa, and Xákmok Kásek,* the traditional land rights claims of indigenous communities conflicted with existing land holdings of Mennonite groups (Correia, 2021). In all three cases, while the IACtHR ordered Paraguay to return ancestral lands to the indigenous communities, the Court added that if the lands were in private hands and "objective and reasoned" motives existed to be unable to return the lands to the community, Paraguay would be obliged to give the affected indigenous community alternative lands selected with community approval. This was the case with the Yakye Axa community, who agreed to alternative lands on the condition that the state built an adequate road to those new lands (*Yakye Axa*, 2022).

Tripartite regulatory framework: Consultation, impact assessment, and allocation of *benefits*

Overall, the IAHRS has emphasized a set of primarily procedural approaches to address the human rights implications of extractive activities. First, the IAHRS's most extensively developed procedural obligation concerns the right to an adequate consultation process. Most extractivism conflicts addressed by the IAHRS focus on whether indigenous peoples' consultation rights were adequately protected. The IAHRS understands consultation rights as protecting both indigenous communities' lands and their right to participate in public affairs (*Kaliña, Maya Q'eqchi')*. In *Saramaka*, the Court established, for the first time, a state duty of consultation. For the Court, the state duty to ensure adequate consultation means that the Saramaka People must be included in discussions concerning any development, investment, exploration, or extraction plans within their territory. The Court ruled, in addition, that given the large-scale character of the extractivist activities on Saramaka lands, no extractive activities should have been allowed without consent from the Saramaka people. This ruling further contributed to addressing the application of indigenous rights standards to Afro-descendent communities, such as the Maroons in Suriname, even though these communities may have distinct relationships with land compared to indigenous peoples (*Saramaka,* para.79; Dulitzky, 2010).

Since the 2007 *Saramaka* ruling, the IACtHR has developed an extensive case law on the issue of consultation. In 2012, the Court found that indigenous communities had to be consulted "from the first stages of the planning or preparation of the proposed measure, so that the indigenous peoples can truly participate in and influence the decision-making process" (*Sarayaku*). In 2015, it further specified that consultations must be continuous and ongoing throughout each stage of a development project's implementation (*Kaliña*). In a 2023 ruling, the IACtHR emphasized that consultation processes must be culturally appropriate and linguistically accessible to the affected indigenous community. Additionally, indigenous communities must be provided with sufficient information to enable meaningful participation (*Maya Q'eqchi'*). The IAHRS's approach to consultation rights has progressively evolved towards ensuring that the participation of the indigenous peoples is effective (IACHR, 2015a) and not mere formalities (IACHR, 2019, p. 10).

A second procedural state obligation developed by the IAHRS concerns prior environmental and social impact assessment. The IACtHR recognizes that conducting thorough impact assessments is crucial to ensure that restrictions on indigenous communities' property rights do not jeopardize their very survival as distinct peoples. For the Court, impact assessments have become a cornerstone of consultation processes, ensuring participating indigenous communities have the information necessary for meaningful engagement (*Triunfo de la Cruz,* paras 179–180). The Court, however, has not defined the specific standards for these assessments. The Court has only indicated in *Triunfo de la Cruz* that impact assessments should comply with relevant international standards, respect cultural traditions, and be completed before granting concessions or licenses. This requirement aims to ensure communities are informed about projects and can effectively participate in decision-making processes.

In the Court's jurisprudence, the assessment of environmental and social impact is closely tied to the responsibility of states to protect the right to a healthy environment (Tigre & Urzola, 2021). In its advisory opinion on the matter, the Court held that states must regulate and supervise activities that have the potential to cause harm, conduct environmental impact assessments, and take steps to mitigate any damage caused by extractive industries. For the Court, an environmental impact assessment is essential in determining whether an action would result in "significant harm" to human rights, including the right to life, personal integrity, and a healthy environment. Based on this advisory opinion, if an environmental impact assessment shows that significant harm would occur due to an extractive activity, then it should not be carried out. This link between environmental and human rights illustrates how the Court has contributed to the "greening" of human rights in indigenous cases (Sena, 2020; Tigre et al., 2021). The Court may further develop its position on the scope of state obligations with respect to the adoption of environmental protections, building on its indigenous rights jurisprudence. For example, *La Oroya* was decided by the Court at the end of 2023, though at the time of drafting this chapter, its ruling had not yet been published (IACtHR, 2023). The case concerns the negative consequences of contamination to the environment, health, and life produced by a mining and metallurgical industry in Peru. The Commission argued before the IACtHR that Peru had failed to adopt adequate regulations, permitted the emission of highly harmful substances, and had failed to supervise and monitor the industry's activities. It further argued that Peru failed to ensure a progressive development duty insofar as it favoured drastic flexibilities on its standards of air quality without reason. This case presents the IACtHR with an opportunity to develop legal guidelines related to environmental restrictions on extractive activities, extending beyond those affecting indigenous communities.

A third duty identified by the IAHRS concerns the allocation of reasonable benefits derived from extractive activities for affected communities. In *Saramaka*, the IACtHR ruled that this protection arose from the legal principle prohibiting the deprivation of property without just compensation. The IACtHR affirmed that "benefit sharing may be understood as a form of reasonable equitable compensation resulting from the exploitation of traditionally owned lands and of those natural resources necessary for the survival of the Saramaka people" (*Saramaka,* para.140). Both in *Saramaka* and *Kaliña*, Suriname was found liable for failing to guarantee that the communities impacted by extractive activities had access to reasonable benefits. While the IACtHR has consistently upheld the right to reasonable benefits, it has refrained from offering a clear definition of the term.

In summary, the IAHRS has prioritized procedural obligations to uphold the rights of indigenous peoples during the development and implementation of extractive activities in the region. The IACtHR's stance on consultation rights as part of the right to participation suggests a potential expansion of these standards and regulatory frameworks to non-indigenous groups. The IACtHR has increasingly established that consultation rights are independently protected under the American Convention as part of the right to participation. This would broaden the scope of the right beyond its traditional association with the 1989 International Labour Organization (ILO) Convention 169 on Indigenous and Tribal Peoples (IACHR, 2015a). Developing the notion of an independent right to consultation that is not contingent on the victim's membership in an indigenous community could broaden the applicability of these regulations beyond indigenous cases.

The IACtHR has been particularly explicit in its extension of procedural protections for non-indigenous communities with respect to environmental impact assessments, which are mandatory in any instance of extractive activities that may pose a threat to the life, livelihood, and right to a healthy environment of people (IACtHR, Advisory Opinion on the Environment).

Towards an assessment of the effectiveness of the IAHRS

The IAHRS has become increasingly engaged with the human rights implications of extractivism in Latin America. However, how effective is the IAHRS in addressing extractivism? Clearly, extractivism poses a complex test of the institutional effectiveness of the IAHRS, given the substantial political and socio-economic stakes involved. Extractive industries often wield significant influence, making it difficult for the IAHRS to enforce protections for vulnerable communities and environments.

In this part of the chapter, we explore three areas that highlight the IAHRS's potential and limitations in effectively addressing extractivism in Latin America. First, we address the formal and informal constraints on access to the IAHRS for affected communities, which constitute formidable barriers to the IAHRS's ability to fundamentally challenge extractivism. Second, the nature of the IAHRS's response to communities affected by extractivism is far from transformational. Particularly, the IAHRS's primarily procedural approach to state obligations to regulate extractivism raises persistent concerns regarding the efficacy of participation and consultation mechanisms, as well as the processes for calculating and distributing "shared benefits" from extractivist projects. This highlights not only the issue of weak enforcement of existing state obligations but also the normative limitations of the IAHRS's framework in terms of offered protections. Third, the IAHRS's effectiveness is undeniably challenged by problematic state responses embedded within the enduring political economy of extractivism in the region.

Mobilizing the IAHRS

The IAHRS constitutes a distinct international opportunity structure for groups and communities that seek to challenge extractivism in Latin America (Engstrom & Low, 2019). The System can be used to expose human rights violations caused by extractivist activities. Communities can leverage the institutional mechanisms of the IAHRS, such as friendly settlement procedures, to negotiate with states over specific extractivist projects. The IAHRS provides standards and norms to frame social and political debates on the desirability of extractivism. The System can promote the interests of politically and economically marginalized groups that would otherwise have few opportunities to be heard in their domestic political systems. The jurisprudence of the IACtHR can strengthen litigation efforts before domestic courts by providing litigants and judges with judicial standards to articulate demands and legitimize judicial decisions. The IAHRS also offers groups and communities opportunities to pursue regional and international networking and build alliances with groups facing similar circumstances in other parts of the region.

Accessing the IAHRS can be challenging, however. The use of the IAHRS requires legal know-how and the ability to navigate complicated institutional avenues. Proceedings before the IAHRS are also lengthy and costly. It should also be noted that in many countries in Latin America, the risks associated with human rights work remain considerable. Human rights activists seeking to challenge extractivist projects in many parts of the region face regular and widespread low-level police harassment, political vilification, paramilitary violence, and threats of assassination. As a result, the capacity of actors to access and to mobilize the IAHRS is highly unequal.

Using the IAHRS is particularly challenging for traditionally marginalized groups, such as indigenous communities. Beyond the resource constraints facing indigenous groups and their representatives before the IAHRS, there is also the need to be able to formulate claims and struggles in the human rights language and terms recognized and accepted by the System (Loperena, 2020). In addition, only a minuscule number of cases reach a final judgement by the IACtHR in a timely manner. While the increasing number of petitions to the Commission has translated into a significantly increased caseload for the IACtHR, the Court deals with a handful of cases on an annual basis.

Considering these multiple constraints and the obstacles to mobilizing the IAHRS, how useful is the System for struggles against extractivism, and particularly those of indigenous communities? In the first instance, it is crucial to acknowledge the extensive expertise indigenous communities have acquired in international law through continuous mobilization, often through transnational networks and alliances. Indigenous people regularly leverage their rights, particularly those related to consultation and self-determination. Through legal victories at the IACtHR, indigenous communities have established significant legal precedents, securing judgements that compel states to formally recognize indigenous territorial authority. The landmark case of *Sarayaku* exemplifies the Court's role in upholding the right to free, prior, and informed consent. The Court issued a binding decision against Ecuador for its failure to consult the Sarayaku people before allowing a foreign oil company to operate on their ancestral lands. Even in highly inhospitable conditions and against the odds, indigenous groups seek to leverage the IAHRS in their struggles against often existential threats, as demonstrated in the Wayúu's pursuit of water rights "lawfare" in Colombia (Vidal Parra, 2019). In this particular case, the IACHR issued precautionary measures in favour of the elderly, women, and children that suffer the consequences of the water rights claims, which have led to a Constitutional Court decision aimed at protecting their rights (*Wayúu)*. The IACHR recently monitored this situation through an on-site visit (IACHR, 2022).

In other words, human rights strategies, including those seeking to deploy the IAHRS, have become critical tools in the political contestation surrounding indigenous and environmental issues, particularly as natural resource extraction emerges as an increasingly controversial development model (Raftopoulos, 2017). This highlights that, though far from guaranteeing rights, international human rights institutions, such as the IAHRS, have the potential to legitimate claims, raise public awareness, and increase the costs of non-compliance for governments (Anagnostou & Mungiu-Pippidi, 2014). This also demonstrates how human rights advancements depend on the capacity of social movements and human rights advocates to mobilize international human rights law and institutions to effectively pressure domestic authorities for the implementation of change. While the IAHRS by itself is not sufficient, it can be strategically utilized as part of a broader campaign for change, potentially serving as a catalyst for tangible improvements at the local level, even in cases where state authorities demonstrate resistance to the IAHRS.

The IAHRS' (mildly) reformist critique of extractivism

Another area highlighting the potential and limitations of the IAHRS's approach to extractivism concerns the character and scope of the obligations that it seeks to impose on states. The IAHRS has privileged the development of mainly procedural types of state obligations. The growing recognition of extractivism's detrimental impacts has prompted policy concerns urging improved natural resource governance. Such policies typically seek to enhance the regulatory frameworks through the adoption of transparency and accountability measures for extractive projects, increase "stakeholder engagement" via strengthened civil society participation in oversight, and combine with targeted social investments in extractive regions to mitigate social unrest.

There are, however, significant problems with procedural approaches to extractivism, as demonstrated with respect to the IAHRS's emphasis on the rights of consultation of affected communities. Consultation processes, promoted by international actors in both the public and private sectors, have become an integral part of the global governance of extractivism and are at the centre of conflicts over extractivism in Latin America (Schilling-Vacaflor, 2017), particularly involving indigenous communities. Yet, the privileging of procedural guarantees in the form of consultation processes is problematic for several interlocking reasons. First, the general absence of indigenous ownership in consultation processes presents a significant challenge. These processes can potentially function as a "counter-insurrectionary device" that reinforces the existing power imbalances between state, corporate, and elite interests on one hand, and indigenous communities on the other hand. As such, consultation processes may simply serve as a marketing tool for development projects, creating an illusion of genuine dialogue, negotiation, and democratic decision-making (Dunlap, 2018).

A second challenge lies in the difficulty indigenous groups often face in articulating and defending their distinct visions for development and specific demands regarding extractivism. Third, a significant challenge arises from the often-limited outcomes generated by consultation processes. Even when consultation legislation is adhered to, the weakness of state institutions significantly undermines their effectiveness.

In short, there is a substantial implementation gap with respect to the consultation of indigenous people (Wright & Tomaselli, 2019). The frequent failures, whether deliberate or through neglect, of the prior consultation regime leave communities with limited options, often giving rise to disruptive and disorderly protests (Gamu & Soendergaard, 2023). However, some argue that agreements between governments, corporations, and indigenous groups hold the potential for the latter to gain greater control and benefit from extractivism. This would suggest that such agreements may transcend simple categorization as a "neoliberal technology" (O'Faircheallaigh & Babidge, 2023). Indeed, the meaning and application of consultation and participation rights are continuously subject to negotiation in practice.

These potential opportunities for affected communities notwithstanding, the circumscribed nature of consultation rights exposes weaknesses in enforcement capabilities and potential shortcomings in the normative framework of the IAHRS pertaining to the scope of protections offered. The scope of remedies available through the IAHRS remains restricted, preventing it from addressing the deeply entrenched marginalization and exclusion indigenous peoples face in Latin American societies. These limitations are reflected in the Court's tendency to frame indigenous rights within the narrow normative confines of property rights, sidelining the broader cultural and societal dimensions of such rights for indigenous communities (Antkowiak, 2013). The IAHRS also encounters the inherent tensions between, on the one hand, its efforts to safeguard cultural identity and traditional values through the protection of ancestral lands and resources and, on the other hand, government development priorities that often involve extractive industries.

Despite its many limitations, however, there are opportunities for the IAHRS to develop responses conducive to a more sustainable future. One such emerging response lies in the recognition of the rights of nature and their connection to human rights, exemplified by initiatives such as granting legal personhood to rivers in Colombia (Álvez-Marín et al., 2021) or forests in Ecuador (Prieto, 2021). The IACtHR has argued that

> as an autonomous right, the right to a healthy environment, unlike other rights, protects the components of the environment, such as forests, rivers and seas, as legal interests in themselves, even in the absence of the certainty or evidence of a risk to individuals.

endorsing the tendency "to recognize legal personality and, consequently, rights to nature" (IACtHR Advisory Opinion on the Environment, para.62). Such interpretive frames challenge the anthropocentric paradigm that views nature solely as a resource for human exploitation, potentially offering novel legal frameworks for environmental protection. However, while it is possible that the forthcoming advisory opinion by the IACtHR on climate change will lead to the development of specific obligations of non-state actors on the need to mitigate the impact of extractive activities, it is likely that the Court will refrain from acknowledging nature as rights bearers. This more restrained interpretative framework would partly reflect the Court's reading of the American Convention's Article 1.2 that restricts rights bearers to human beings, and partly its moderate position limiting its own competence while potentially deferring to the development of rights of nature by domestic courts in the region. Moreover, practical considerations remain regarding the implementation and enforcement of these rights, particularly in balancing them with legitimate human development needs.

A second area concerns the IAHRS's approach to business and human rights. In 2019, the IACHR published a report that digested its normative framework in response to human rights affected by corporations in the region. In 2021, the IACtHR issued a judgement in *Miskitos*, concerning the lack of supervision and auditing of the extractive fishing industry's labour conditions of indigenous people. The case established landmark standards concerning business and human rights that address the lack of accountability for the impact of extractive industries (do Amaral & Palacio Revello, 2018). While the IAHRS continues to prioritize state obligations over direct corporate accountability, the System has sought to advance notions of state responsibility to prevent, investigate, sanction, and provide remedies for human rights violations committed by non-state actors, including corporations (Cantú Rivera, 2023). Pressures on the IAHRS are increasing, however, to develop "more robust standards directly addressing corporations and to integrate the United Nations Guiding Principles on Business and Human Rights […] into its framework" (Gonza, 2016).

The (hard) realities of the political economy of extractivism

The IAHRS also confronts effectiveness challenges given the centrality of the political economy of extractivism for development in Latin America. There are several dimensions to these challenges. First and foremost, the allure of extractivism for governments in Latin America poses a formidable challenge to the IAHRS. Governments in the region are confronted with extensive social and economic demands from their electorates. Extractive projects constitute well-trodden pathways towards the generation of resources needed to meet these expectations.

Furthermore, the IAHRS's institutional responses to extractivism confront entrenched state interests embedded within the enduring political economy of resource extraction in the region. As noted by Raftopoulos, while human rights discourses empower social movements and activists to challenge extractivism and critique prevailing development models, their application has yielded limited tangible outcomes (Raftopoulos, 2017). To a significant extent, this limited effectiveness stems not only from state fragility and weaknesses of regulatory frameworks, but also from the willingness of governments to prioritize development objectives and override their commitments to human and environmental rights.

It is also important to recognize that in the IAHRS, as elsewhere, human rights implementation varies with "overall legal infrastructure capacity and government effectiveness of a state" (Anagnostou & Mungiu-Pippidi, 2014). Weak state capacity and dysfunctional domestic judiciaries partly explain the unevenness in state compliance with the IAHRS. The IAHRS's impact on public policy formulation and implementation depends heavily on its institutionalization within state structures. Effective remedies for human rights violations hinge on whether states have organized their institutions in ways that facilitate such remedies. As Huneeus explains, the more coordination required from national authorities, the lower the levels of compliance with the IAHRS (Huneeus, 2011).

Confronted with these pressures, a persistent challenge for the IAHRS lies in calibrating its response to extractivism. The IAHRS's engagement with the human rights implications of extractivism underscores the centrality of concerns regarding the rule of law (access to justice, due process) and the rights of historically marginalized groups, particularly indigenous peoples, within the regional human rights agenda. This shift signifies a broader trend in human rights politics in Latin America, characterized by a move away from a focus on traditional human rights abuses perpetrated by state actors as part of deliberate state policies towards increasing concerns regarding the responsibilities of non-state actors, including multinational corporations (*Miskito*).

These trends present significant challenges to the established normative frameworks and institutional mechanisms developed by the IAHRS, designed towards the protection of individuals from state actions. Its basic foundations rest on legal concepts of state responsibility and the assumption that pressure can be applied to states, as they possess the primary levers for improvement. The challenge of extractivism for the IAHRS lies precisely in the extent to which state regulation of extractive activities remains — by a combination of commission and omission — underdeveloped, underlining the limited capacities of states to effectively assume their responsibilities to prevent negative human rights impacts.

Another related challenge for the IAHRS concerns the fact that it is no longer primarily concerned with "naming and shaming" repressive military and authoritarian regimes. It seeks, rather, to engage democratic regimes through a (quasi) judicial process that assumes at least partially responsive state institutions. This raises the question of the appropriate level of deference accorded to (democratic) states and their prioritized development agendas by the IAHRS. While some critics argue that the IAHRS does not show sufficient deference to local political preferences and solutions (Contesse, 2016), proponents of a more active and intrusive regional human rights system point to the deficiencies of Latin American democracies, both in terms of the degree to which the interests of many groups remain woefully under-represented and in terms of what political systems in the region actually deliver to the people they are supposed to serve.

Conclusion

This chapter has examined the role of the IAHRS in shaping the governance of extractivism in Latin America. It has highlighted the human rights implications associated with the region's dependence on extractive industries. We have noted the key challenge in balancing the potentially contradictory policy objectives of poverty alleviation, reduced consumption, environmental protection, and the demands of politically and economically marginalized groups, particularly in a region with a historical reliance on resource extraction. Crucially, the impacts of extractivism and the promise of local development opportunities vary depending on the specific interests at stake. While negative impacts are multifaceted and experienced heterogeneously across and within local communities over time and space, the commodification of natural resources can also bring the promise of local development.

Specifically, the chapter has examined the IAHRS's engagement with conflicts arising from tensions and trade-offs generated by development projects affecting local interests and rights. The focus has been on how these conflicts affect indigenous communities specifically, given the significant impact of extractivism on their way of life. In its approach, the IAHRS has developed a primarily procedural set of state obligations, which we refer to as a tripartite regularly framework. This framework emphasizes the right to effective participation of affected communities, the requirement for a prior and independent environmental and social impact assessment, and the need to share reasonable benefits with these communities. Furthermore, the System has recognized the concept of collective rights held by indigenous communities over ancestral lands and natural resources, acknowledging their vital importance in preserving the distinct cultural identities of these groups.

The chapter has attempted to be sober about the multiple challenges facing the IAHRS in its engagement with extractivism and indigenous rights. These are, indeed, formidable, both in terms of the realities of the political economy of extractivism and in terms of what the IAHRS can realistically offer communities affected by extractivism. And yet, against the odds, it is quite remarkable the extent to which groups, both indigenous and non-indigenous, have developed strategies and specific tactics that draw on the resources and opportunities provided by the IAHRS in their ongoing struggles against extractivism in Latin

America. The IAHRS can provide prominent political spaces for policy debates and negotiation between the key actors involved in efforts to address the human rights implications of extractivism. The System provides an authoritative set of norms and standards to regulate extractivism, and it adds an additional layer of political pressure, momentum, and urgency to the issue.

Note

1 The authors are indebted to Laurence Whitehead for the formulation of this point.

References

Almeida, P. (2014). Mobilizing Democracy: Globalization and Citizen Protest. JHU Press.

Álvez-Marín, A., Bañales-Seguel, C., Castillo, R., Acuña-Molina, C., & Torres, P. (2021). Legal personhood of Latin American rivers: Time to Shift Constitutional Paradigms? *Journal of Human Rights and the Environment*, 12(2), 147–176. https://doi.org/10.4337/jhre.2021.02.01

Anagnostou, D., & Mungiu-Pippidi, A. (2014). Domestic Implementation of Human Rights Judgments in Europe: Legal Infrastructure and Government Effectiveness Matter. European Journal of International Law, 25(1), 205–227. https://doi.org/10.1093/ejil/chu001

Antkowiak, Thomas M. (2013). Rights, Resources, and Rhetoric: Indigenous Peoples and the Inter-American Court. *University of Pennsylvania Journal of International Law*, *35*(1), 113–188.

Arsel, M., Hogenboom, B., & Pellegrini, L. (2016). The Extractive Imperative in Latin America. The Extractive Industries and Society, 3(4), 880–887. https://doi.org/10.1016/j.exis.2016.10.014

Auz, J. (2022). Human Rights-Based Climate Litigation: A Latin American Cartography. Journal of Human Rights and the Environment, 13(1), 114–136. https://doi.org/10.4337/jhre.2022.01.05

Avilés, W. (2019). The Wayúu Tragedy: Death, Water and the Imperatives of Global Capitalism. Third World Quarterly, 40(9), 1750–1766. https://doi.org/10.1080/01436597.2019.1613638

Bebbington, A. J., Sauls, L. A., Rosa, H., Fash, B., & Bebbington, D. H. (2018). Conflicts over Extractivist Policy and the Forest Frontier in Central America. European Review of Latin American and Caribbean Studies / Revista Europea de Estudios Latinoamericanos y Del Caribe, 106, 103–132.

Burchardt, H.-J., & Dietz, K. (2014). (Neo-)extractivism – A New Challenge for Development Theory from Latin America. Third World Quarterly, 35(3), 468–486. https://doi.org/10.1080/01436597.2014.893488

Cantú Rivera, H. (2023). Business and Human Rights in the Inter-American System. In A. Ewing (Ed.), Teaching Business and Human Rights (Vol. 1). Edward Elgar Publishing Ltd. https://www.e-elgar.com/shop/gbp/teaching-business-and-human-rights-9781802201123.html

Carrasco, A. (2016). A Biography of Water in Atacama, Chile: Two Indigenous Community Responses to the Extractive Encroachments of Mining: A Biography of Water in Atacama, Chile. The Journal of Latin American and Caribbean Anthropology, 21(1), 130–150. https://doi.org/10.1111/jlca.12175

Contesse, J. (2016). Contestation and Deference in the Inter-American Human Rights System Subsidiarity in Global Governance. Law and Contemporary Problems, 79, 123–146.

Correia, J. E. (2021). Infrastructures of Settler Colonialism: Geographies of Violence, Indigenous Labor, and Marginal Resistance in Paraguay's Chaco. In S. Hirsch, P. Canova, & M. Biocca (Eds.), Reimagining the Gran Chaco: Identities, Politics, and the Environment in South America (p. 0). University Press of Florida. https://doi.org/10.5744/florida/9781683402114.003.0008

do Amaral, A. Jr., & Palacio Revello, V. (2018). Human Rights and Extractive Industries in Latin America: What Responsibility of Corporation and Their States of Origin for Human Rights Violations in the Inter-American Human Rights System? Section II: Dossie Especial: Business and Human Rights. Brazilian Journal of International Law, 15(2), 243–254.

Dulitzky, A. E. (2010). When Afro-Descendants Became 'Tribal Peoples': The Inter-American Human Rights System and Rural Black Communities. UCLA Journal of International Law and Foreign Affairs, 15(1), 29–81.

Dunlap, A. (2018). "A Bureaucratic Trap:" Free, Prior and Informed Consent (FPIC) and Wind Energy Development in Juchitán, Mexico. *Capitalism Nature Socialism*, 29(4), 88–108. https://doi.org/10.1080/10455752.2017.1334219

Edenhofer, N. (2022). Mining Boom and Contentious Politics across Central America: Elites, Movements and Party Systems. Journal of Latin American Studies, 54(2), 253–281. https://doi.org/10.1017/S0022216X22000207

Engstrom, P., & Low, P. (2019). Mobilising the Inter-American Human Rights System: Regional Litigation and Domestic Human Rights Impact in Latin America. In P. Engstrom (Ed.), The Inter-American Human Rights System: Impact Beyond Compliance (pp. 23–58). Palgrave Macmillan. https://doi.org/10.1007/978-3-319-89459-1_2

Farthing, L., & Fabricant, N. (2018). Open Veins Revisited: Charting the Social, Economic, and Political Contours of the New Extractivism in Latin America. Latin American Perspectives, 45(5), 4–17. https://doi.org/10.1177/0094582X18785882

Fuentes, A. (2017). Protection of Indigenous Peoples' Traditional Lands and Exploitation of Natural Resources: The Inter-American Court of Human Rights' Safeguards. International Journal on Minority and Group Rights, 24(3), 229–253. https://doi.org/10.1163/15718115-02403006

Gamu, J. K., & Soendergaard, N. (2023). Governance Capture and Socio-Environmental Conflict: A Critical Political Economy of the Global Mining Industry's Prior Consultation Regime. Review of International Political Economy, 0(0), 1–25. https://doi.org/10.1080/09692290.2023.2265976

Gómez-Betancur, L., Vilardy Q., S. P., & Torres R., D. (2022). Ecosystem Services as a Promising Paradigm to Protect Environmental Rights of Indigenous Peoples in Latin America: The Constitutional Court Landmark Decision to Protect Arroyo Bruno in Colombia. Environmental Management, 69(4), 768–780. https://doi.org/10.1007/s00267-021-01483-w

Gonza, A. (2016). Integrating Business and Human Rights in the Inter-American Human Rights System. Business and Human Rights Journal, 1(2), 357–365. https://doi.org/10.1017/bhj.2016.18

Hernandez, D. S., & Newell, P. (2022). Oro Blanco: Assembling Extractivism in the Lithium Triangle. The Journal of Peasant Studies, 49(5), 945–968. https://doi.org/10.1080/03066150.2022.2080061

Huneeus, A. (2011). Courts Resisting Courts: Lessons from the Inter-American Court's Struggle to Enforce Human Rights. Cornell International Law Journal, 44, 493–534.

IACHR. (1997). Report on the Situation of Human Rights in Ecuador (OEA/Ser.L/V/II.96 Doc. 10 rev. 1). https://www.cidh.org/countryrep/ecuador-eng/Chaper-9.htm

IACHR. (2015a). Indigenous Peoples, *Afro-Descendent Communities, and Natural Resources: Human Rights Protection in the Context of Extraction, Exploitation, and Development Activities* (OEA/Ser.L/V/II.OEA/Ser.L/V/II.). https://www.oas.org/en/iachr/reports/pdfs/ExtractiveIndustries2016.pdf

IACHR. (2015b). *Indigenous Peoples, Communities of African Descend, Extractive Industries* (OEA/Ser.L/V/II. Doc. 47/15).

IACHR. (2016, April 6). IACHR Presents Report on Extractive Industries and Human Rights. https://www.oas.org/en/iachr/media_center/preleases/2016/048.asp

IACHR. (2019). *Situation of Human Rights of the Indigenous and Tribal Peoples of the Pan-Amazon Region* (OAS/Ser.L/V/II. Doc. 176). https://www.oas.org/en/iachr/reports/pdfs/Panamazonia2019-en.pdf

IACHR. (2022, November 30). Visita a Colombia: REDESCA observa serios desafíos para la garantía de los DESCA en La Guajira. https://www.oas.org/es/CIDH/jsForm/Default.asp?File=/es/cidh/prensa/comunicados/2022/265.asp

IACtHR. (2023, December 8). Corte Interamericana de Derechos Humanos celebró el 163 período ordinario de sesiones. https://corteidh.or.cr/docs/comunicados/cp_91_2023.pdf

Kingsbury, D. V. (2021). Latin American Extractivism and (or after) the Left. Latin American Research Review, 56(4), 977–987. https://doi.org/10.25222/larr.1668

Kröger, M., & Lalander, R. (2016). Ethno-Territorial Rights and the Resource Extraction Boom in Latin America: Do Constitutions Matter? *Third World Quarterly*, 37(4), 682–702. https://doi.org/10.1080/01436597.2015.1127154

Lakhani, N. (2020). Who Killed Berta Caceres?: Dams, Death Squads, and an Indigenous Defender's Battle for the Planet. Verso Books.

Loperena, C. A. (2020). Adjudicating Indigeneity: Anthropological Testimony in the Inter-American Court of Human Rights. American Anthropologist, 122(3), 595–605. https://doi.org/10.1111/aman.13415

Mardikian, L. (2023). The Right to a Healthy Environment before the Inter-American Court of Human Rights. International & Comparative Law Quarterly, 72(4), 945–975. https://doi.org/10.1017/S0020589323000416

McNeish, J. A. (2018). Resource Extraction and Conflict in Latin America. Colombia Internacional, 93, Article 93.

OAS. (2009, August 1). *Precautionary Measures—Indigenous Peoples* [Text]. https://www.oas.org/en/iachr/indigenous/protection/precautionary.asp

O'Faircheallaigh, C., & Babidge, S. (2023). Negotiated Agreements, Indigenous Peoples and Extractive Industry in the Salar de Atacama, Chile: When Is an Agreement More than a Contract? *Development and Change*, 54(3), 641–670. https://doi.org/10.1111/dech.12767

Orihuela, J. C., Pérez Cavero, C., & Contreras, C. (2022). Extractivism of the Poor: Natural Resource Commodification and Its Discontents. The Extractive Industries and Society, 9, 100986. https://doi.org/10.1016/j.exis.2021.100986

Özkaynak, B., Rodriguez-Labajos, B., Aydın, C. İ., Yanez, I., & Garibay, C. (2015). *Towards Environmental Justice Success in Mining Conflicts: An Empirical Investigation* (EJOLT Report 14). EJOLT.

Picq, M. L. (2020). Resistance to Extractivism and Megaprojects in Latin America. In Oxford Research Encyclopedia of Politics. https://doi.org/10.1093/acrefore/9780190228637.013.1742

Prieto, G. (2021). The Los Cedros Forest has Rights: The Ecuadorian Constitutional Court Affirms the Rights of Nature. Verfassungsblog. https://verfassungsblog.de/the-los-cedros-forest-has-rights/

Raftopoulos, M. (2017). Contemporary Debates on Social-Environmental Conflicts, Extractivism and Human Rights in Latin America. The International Journal of Human Rights, 21(4), 387–404. https://doi.org/10.1080/13642987.2017.1301035

Saldarriaga González, Y. S. (2019). Inter-American Human Rights System's Precautionary and Provisional Measures in Cases of Extractive Industries. Revista Navarra Jurídica, 3(1), Article 1.

Schilling-Vacaflor, A. (2017). Who Controls the Territory and the Resources? Free, Prior and Informed Consent (FPIC) as a Contested Human Rights Practice in Bolivia. Third World Quarterly, 38(5), 1058–1074. https://doi.org/10.1080/01436597.2016.1238761

Schmalz, S., Graf, J., Julián-Vejar, D., Sittel, J., & Alister Sanhueza, C. (2023). Challenging the Three Faces of Extractivism: The Mapuche Struggle and the Forestry Industry in Chile. Globalizations, 20(3), 365–383. https://doi.org/10.1080/14747731.2022.2091867

Sena, R. (2020). The Intersection of Human Rights and Climate Change in the Inter-American Human Rights System: What to Hope for? Limits and Potential of Human Rights in Pursuit of Climate Justice. Wisconsin International Law Journal, 38(2), 331–368.

Silva, E., Akchurin, M., & Bebbington, A. (2018). Policy Effects of Resistance against Mega-Projects in Latin America: An Introduction. European Review of Latin American and Caribbean Studies / Revista Europea de Estudios Latinoamericanos y Del Caribe, 106, 25–46.

Spalding, R. J. (2023). Breaking Ground: From Extraction Booms to Mining Bans in Latin America. Oxford University Press.

Svampa, M. (2015). Commodities Consensus: Neoextractivism and Enclosure of the Commons in Latin America. South Atlantic Quarterly, 114(1), 65–82. https://doi.org/10.1215/00382876-2831290

Tetreault, D. (2015). Social Environmental Mining Conflicts in Mexico. Latin American Perspectives, 42(5), 48–66. https://doi.org/10.1177/0022429415585112

Tetreault, D. (2020). The New Extractivism in Mexico: Rent Redistribution and Resistance to Mining and Petroleum Activities. World Development, 126, 104714. https://doi.org/10.1016/j.worlddev.2019.104714

Tigre, M. A., Kasznar, A., Harrington, A., Urzola, N., Bernal, A., Evans, H., & Kleyn, A. V. D. (2021). The Inter-American Responses during COVID-19: Development of Green Human Rights in Indigenous Cases at the Regional and National Levels. Revista de Derecho Ambiental, 15, 7–50. https://doi.org/10.5354/0719-4633.2021.60778

Tigre, M. A., & Urzola, N. (2021). The 2017 Inter-American Court's Advisory Opinion: Changing the Paradigm for International Environmental Law in the Anthropocene. Journal of Human Rights and the Environment, 12(1), 24–50. https://doi.org/10.4337/jhre.2021.01.02

Vidal Parra, S. (2019). The Water Rights-Based Legal Mobilization of the Wayúu against the Cercado Dam: An Effective Avenue for Court-Centered Lawfare from Below? *Antipoda.* Revista de Antropología y Arqueología, 34, 45–68. https://doi.org/10.7440/antipoda34.2019.03

Wright, C., & Tomaselli, A. (2019). From the implementation gap to Indigenous empowerment. In C. Wright & A. Tomaselli, The Prior Consultation of Indigenous Peoples in Latin America (1st ed., pp. 279–290). Routledge. https://doi.org/10.4324/9781351042109-25

Cited legal instruments and case-law by the Inter-American Human Rights System

American Declaration on the Rights of Indigenous Peoples, AG/RES. 2888 (XLVI-O/16) (2016).

Case of Kichwa Indigenous People of Sarayaku v. Ecuador. Merits and Reparations. Series C No. 245. (IACtHR 27 June 2012).

Case of the Community Garifuna of San Juan and Its Members v. Honduras. Preliminary Objections, Merits, Reparations and Costs. Series C No. 496. (IACtHR 29 August 2023).

Case of the Community Garifuna Triunfo de La Cruz and Its Members v. Honduras. Merits, Reparations and Costs. Series C No. 305. (IACtHR 8 October 2015).

Case of the Indigenous Communities of the Lhaka Honhat Association (Our Land) v. Argentina. Merits, Reparations and Costs. Series C No. 400. (IACtHR 6 February 2020).

Case of the Kaliña and Lokono Peoples v. Suriname. Merits, Reparations and Costs. Series C No. 309. (IACtHR 25 November 2015).

Case of the Kuna Indigenous People of Madungandí and the Emberá Indigenous People of Bayano and Their Members v. Panama. Preliminary Objections, Merits, Reparations and Costs. Series C No. 284. (IACtHR 14 October 2014).

Case of the Maya Q'eqchi' Indigenous Community of Agua Caliente v. Guatemala. Merits, Reparations and Costs. Series C No. 488 (IACtHR 16 May 2023).

Case of the Mayagna (Sumo) Awas Tingni Community v. Nicaragua. Merits, Reparations and Costs. Series C. No. 79 (IACtHR 31 August 2001).

Case of the Buzos Miskitos (Lemoth Morris et al.) v. Honduras. Series C No. 432. (IACtHR 31 August 2021)

Case of the Saramaka People v. Suriname. Preliminary Objections, Merits, Reparations, and Costs. Series C No. 172 (IACtHR 28 November 2007).

Case of the Sawhoyamaxa Indigenous Community v. Paraguay. Merits, Reparations and Costs. Series C No. 146. (IACtHR 29 March 2006).
Case of the Xákmok Kásek Indigenous Community. v. Paraguay. Merits, Reparations and Costs. Series C No. 214. (IACtHR 24 August 2010).
Case of the Yakye Axa Indigenous Community v. Paraguay. Merits, Reparations and Costs. Series C No. 125. (IACtHR 17 June 2005).
Case of the Yakye Axa Indigenous Community v. Paraguay. Monitoring Compliance with Judgment. (IACtHR 24 June 2022).
Comunidad de La Oroya vs. Peru, 330/20 (IACHR 2020).
Matter of Four Ngöbe Indigenous Communities and Its Members Regarding Panama. Provisional Measures. (IACtHR 28 May 2010).
Niños, Niñas y Adolescentes de Las Comunidades de Los Municipios de Uribía, Manaure, Riohacha y Maicao Del Pueblo Wayúu En El Departamento de La Guajira, y Otros Respecto de Colombia, 99/2021 ___ (IACHR 2021).
Pueblo Indígena U´wa y Sus Miembros vs. Colombia, 146/19 ___ (IACHR 2019).
Pueblos Indígenas Tagaeri y Taromenane (En Aislamiento Voluntario) vs. Ecuador, 152/19 ___ (IACHR 28 09 19).
The Environment and Human Rights (State Obligations in Relation to the Environment in the Context of the Protection and Guarantee of the Rights to Life and to Personal Integrity – Interpretation and Scope of Articles 4(1) and 5(1) of the American Convention on Human Rights). Advisory Opinion OC-23/17 . Series A No. 23. (IACtHR 15 November 2017).

13 Sustainable development and multilateral development banks

A framework for analyzing sources of norms and decision-making in global governance

Vinícius G. Rodrigues Vieira

Introduction

The diffusion of international norms related to climate change gained momentum in development financing from 2015 onwards, thanks to the implementation of the 2030 Agenda that comprises 17 Sustainable Development Goals (SDGs) defined at the global level by the United Nations (UN). In the meantime, new players entered the universe of multilateral development banks (MDBs) that have either a global or a regional focus on specific groups of states in the world-system. The creation of China-led intergovernmental organizations (IGOs) focused on development finance like the Asian Infrastructure Investment Bank (AIIB) and the New Development Bank (NDB) with clear environmental and social standards (ESS) exemplify that process. Amidst such a context, the World Bank reformed the environmental and social framework (ESF) applied to the loans provided by the International Bank for Reconstruction and Development (IBRD) and the grants offered by the International Development Agency (IDA). Less clear, however, is how each MDB – particularly those focused on certain regions and sub-regions within each continent – foresees the role of subnational actors – including not only provincial and municipal governments, but also specific ethnic groups, like indigenous populations – in applying sustainable development targets and, hence, as sources of the rule of law necessary to tackle climate change.

The goal of the chapter is to map whether and how MDBs operating in Latin America acknowledge subnational spheres of authority (Rosenau 2004) in promoting sustainable development in the light of the 2030 Agenda. For analytical purposes, I conceptualize spheres of authority as having two dimensions – one related to the source of norms, including laws and informal rules under a legal pluralist framework (Davies 2010), and another concerning the source of decision-making. The higher the capacity of a sphere of authority like an IGO, national government, or municipality to be both a source of norms and of decision-making, the more control the same sphere has over the rule of law in a given issue area.

More than any other issue-area in global politics, sustainable development is the one whose provisions depend on multi-level governance (MLG) to be

DOI: 10.4324/9781003519195-13

implemented, thus making it unlikely that any sphere of authority concentrates absolute power in deploying the rule of law by simultaneously exerting the function of source of norms and of decision-making. Hence, the potential conflict around the legitimacy of changes increases. A provincial government, for instance, may manage the resources of a project that is nevertheless implemented under guidelines from an IGO. Likewise, an indigenous community can be allowed to include customary law to manage natural resources, although decision-making eventually remains in the hands of a higher administrative level. In sum, the balance between the source of norms and of decision-making assumes different configurations due to issues of legitimacy vis-à-vis norm-makers and decision-makers that may put under strain the efficiency of targeted changes.

I selected seven MDBs to scrutinize their sustainable development provisions and the acknowledgement of subnational spheres of authority as source of norms and sources of decision-making. Five banks have a regional focus in Latin America and/or its different subregions. They are the US-sponsored Inter-American Development Bank (IADB), the Caribbean Development Bank (CDB) – with partial European sponsorship – and the regionally owned Development Bank of Latin America and the Caribbean (CAF), Plata Basin Development Bank (FONPLATA), and the Central American Bank for Economic Integration (CABEI). The other two MDBs have a global scope – the World Bank, with US sponsorship, and the NDB, which has thus far operated in Brazil, a founding member along with other BRICS Countries (Russia, India, China, and South Africa), and in 2021 accepted Uruguay as a new member.

Through a comparative analysis of each bank's documents after 2015 that provide guidelines for action in sustainable development, I identify the lack of recognition of ethnic and indigenous minorities as subnational actors and sources of norms – either legal or customary – and decision-making by MDBs is often associated with the use of country-systems (UCS) for assessing sustainability targets. Out of the banks scrutinized, the World Bank combines the highest degree of openness to ethnic minorities and subnational actors as sources of norms, but not necessarily as a source of decision-making, thus paving the way for bypassing national governments as the locus for controlling public policy. In such a scenario, empowering ethnic and/or indigenous peoples as actors responsible for spheres of authority in MLG would be a façade for the persistence of top-down approaches on the part of MDBs. That is, while the legal/normative sources are local, the operation of projects ignores sovereignty and, hence, authority is at best shared with foreign stakeholders.

With a focus only on indigenous rights in terms of ESS and without any mention of subnational entities and stakeholders in general, the NDB is open to employing UCS defined at the national level, thus emphasizing sovereignty over sustainable development. The CABEI has analogous positions, not mentioning indigenous populations as potential co-owners of projects and suffering intense scrutiny from civil society for being lenient with authoritarian governments. The

CAF and the IADB stand in between those extremes, with the former being more akin than the latter to the application of national standards in the field, which in turn may reflect their difference in terms of legitimacy and ownership vis-à-vis borrowing members (Rodrigues Vieira 2020, 676). Despite being fully sponsored by its borrowing members in the Southern Cone, FONPLATA has escaped the traditional sovereignty trap and is undoubtedly open to decision-making over operations and normative sources provided by subnational authorities except indigenous ones.

Before proceeding to the analysis, a caveat is worth mentioning: the reliance on MDBs' ESFs, ESS, and other publicly available documents as primary sources leads the paper to focus on a legal-normative analysis instead of exploring the effectiveness of policies those banks engender. The paper first briefly reviews the key works on the interplay between international norms and the subnational level and the role of MDBs as norm diffusers. In doing so, I pay special attention to the distinction between norm localization and norm domestication. I then proceed to the analysis of the selected banks based on a framework that unfolds spheres of authority as a continuum that ranges from the global level to the political-economic organization of indigenous populations as sources of decision-making and sources of authority. The conclusion sketches a classification of the MDBs in terms of valuing the centrality of the national government over subnational units as spheres of authority and, hence, as sources of law – both formally and informally – in defining and implementing sustainable development norms.

International norms, MLG, and the subnational level

While the literature has already addressed whether the subnational level impacts IGOs – as is the case of regions vis-a-vis the European Union (EU) in Brussels (Tatham 2015) – the reverse phenomena still deserve further theoretical and empirical scrutiny. Also based on the EU experience, there is enough evidence to claim that the deepening of regional integration stimulates shifting authority away from national governments to subnational jurisdictions (Schakel, Hooghe, and Marks 2014). It is also well documented that in the fields of sustainable development and climate change, subnational units articulate among themselves to create networks (Happaerts, Van den Brande, and Hans 2010) and even informal IGOs, thus contributing to structuring international regimes (Setzer 2017).

Moreover, the subnational level has led innovation processes in climate-related issues (Jörgensen, Jogesh, and Mishra 2015). as local actors prevail over national ones in adapting policies to general guidelines (Di Gregorio et al. 2019). Hence, it is relevant to explore how such a phenomenon has linkages with national and international sources of policymaking (Jörgensen, Jogesh, and Mishra 2015). I here adopt Marks's (1993: 392) original definition of MLG as "a system of continuous negotiation among nested governments at several territorial tiers." In this vein, I consider that the subnational level does not comprise only states/provinces and municipalities. Nor do I restrict the concept of source of norms to formal legal rules as the recognition of customary law may enhance the legitimacy of projects that rely on foreign resources and expertise, such as those that MDBs sponsor. For instance, under a legal pluralistic framework (Davies 2010, 805), indigenous communities – which are crucial for understanding the limits of sustainable development in Latin America – also integrate de facto MLG systems as native people's rules have primacy over national law in their lands recognized as reserves by national governments. As Benz, Broschek, and Lederer (2021, 10) argue, "[i]ndigenous people and national minorities are considered as actors in MLG."

There is no novelty in integrating those actors into a multi-level framework of analysis. Papillon (2012) identifies that federalism in Canada and the United States went through institutional adaptations to accommodate indigenous claims of self-determination. Yet, based on the Canadian context only, Alcantara and Nelles (2014) claim that not all interactions between indigenous peoples and the state can be understood under an MLG framework. However, when international norms are diffused bypassing the national sphere of authority, ethnic and indigenous communities tend to be empowered through the establishment of transnational linkages with IGOs and non-state actors that as I argue may prevail as sources of decision-making even if customary law is recognized by MDBs' provisions concerning sustainable development.

Specifically in the context of the SDGs, the UN General Assembly resolution "Transforming Our World: the 2030 Agenda for Sustainable Development" (A/RES/70/1) mentions the indigenous peoples six times – "three times in the political declaration; two in the targets under Goal 2 on Zero Hunger (target 2.3) and Goal 4 on education (target 4.5) – and one in the section on follow up and review that calls for indigenous peoples' participation." Yet, there is no requirement that governments gather specific data about them (UN 2024, 1).

In the Western Hemisphere, a proper regime to empower indigenous peoples only emerged in June 2016, when the Organization of American States (OAS) General Assembly adopted the American Declaration on the Rights of Indigenous Peoples after almost 18 years of negotiation. The adoption coincides with the launch of the 2030 Agenda. Article 3 (OAS 2016, 8) recognizes their right to self-determination, including in economic matters, which integrates their collective rights (OAS 2016, 9).

Sustainable development, MDBs, and the localization-domestication dilemma

Policies and practices related to sustainable development must therefore be understood in the context of IGOs and the promotion of specific practices at the global level. For instance, according to Tews' (2005, 64) classification, the diffusion of environmental norms may take place based on cooperation, hierarchy, competition, and communication. In the same vein, Dobbin, Simmons, and Garrett (2007) divide theories of diffusion into constructivist, coercive, communication, and learning ones. As far as IGOs are concerned, their hierarchical/coercive character depends on the so-called structural variables, which are related to their institutional design. They include formal competencies, degree of regime embeddedness, organizational structure, problem of fit (related to whether an IGO can cover a given issue area), availability of resources, and stakeholder involvement (Biermann and Bauer 2004, 192).

Tews (2005, 64) claims that the World Bank, for instance, would represent a hierarchical and, hence, coercive mechanism of diffusion over developing countries. In practice, however, global norms are hardly universal, being instead subject to localization processes. In this vein, norm localization consists of the adaptation of global rules to a specific region that comprises a set of sovereign states or a specific sovereign state (Acharya 2004). In contrast to the original concept of norm diffusion – which assumes a top-down process – norm localization attributes agency to states that are often considered to be mere rule-takers. Yet, in light of the distinction between sources of norms and of decision-making, localizing a global rule may not suffice to empower domestic-level actors vis-à-vis IGOs like MDBs and the foreign interests they represent.

More recently, Restoy and Elbe (2021) put forward the concept of norm domestication, which consists of state and/or non-state actors absorbing and implementing international norms at the subnational level in the case that national governments refrain from adhering to treaties or, in the case they have joined agreements, provisions of those treaties are ignored. The concept was originally developed to explain how global health norms can still be implemented at the domestic level even if national authorities ignore them. Nevertheless, the notion of norm domestication can be applied to other issue areas, including sustainable development, particularly considering that a legal pluralist approach to the topic may emerge insofar as non-state actors and even authorities at the subnational level may rely on informal rules for implementing targets agreed with IGOs like MDBs.

From the beginning, the implementation of the SDGs opened the doors to norm localization and eventually norm domestication, although the latter – in contrast to the former – is hardly acknowledged in MDB documents. The document that outlines the 2030 Agenda, however, opens the door to both localization and domestication by establishing that "governments and public institutions will also work closely on implementation with regional and local authorities, sub-regional institutions, international institutions, *academia, philanthropic organisations, volunteer groups* and others (UN 2015, 15, emphasis ours). In developing the agenda, the UN also committed itself "to fully engage in regular and inclusive reviews of progress at the subnational, national, regional and global levels" (UN 2015, 37), apart from encouraging "[m]ember States to conduct regular and inclusive reviews of progress at the national and subnational levels which are country-led and country-driven," with inputs "from indigenous peoples, civil society, the private sector, and other stakeholders in line with national circumstances, policies, and priorities" (UN 2015, 38). The UN website even dedicates a section to SDG localization, reminding that states declared the commitment to work with local and regional governments to reach the targets of the 2030 Agenda. "Since 2015, metropolises, small cities, regions and their associations alike have been actively localizing the 2030 Agenda, bringing the SDGs closer to the people they serve and using the framework as a tool for planning and execution" (UN Department of Economic and Social Affairs 2024). As of January 2024, there were 159 voluntary reviews by subnational actors.

At their onset, however, MDB's ESS were hardly adaptable to specific contexts at the subnational level. They emerged in the 1980s within the World Bank. They were then officially called "Operational Policies" and "Bank Procedures" (OP/BPs) and aimed at providing "protections against particular risks (e.g., resettlement) and for particular groups (e.g., indigenous people) or resources (e.g., forests, natural habitats)" (Dann and Riegner 2019, 540). The first set of World Bank ESG-related safeguards "largely followed the US model mandated by the federal National Environmental Policy Act (NEPA) of 1969" (Dann and Riegner 2019, 541).

Hence, it is no wonder why safeguards came to be understood as conditionalities analogous to the top-down decisions and rules the US-sponsored financial IGOs imposed on borrowing states' structural-adjustment programmes carried out in the name of diffusing neoliberal ideas (Fourcade-Gourinchas and Babb 2002). Similar processes occurred in MDBs that the US sponsors with its Western allies, focusing on specific regions, as is the case with the IADB, the Asian Development Bank (ASDB), the African Development Bank (AFDB), and the European Bank for Reconstruction and Development (EBRD), all of which adopted "environmental and social standards modeled upon the World Bank's safeguard polices" (Dann and Riegner 2019, 546).

Little, however, has been written on how the World Bank and other MDBs establish linkages with subnational units in Latin America. By analyzing the cases of Argentina, Brazil, and Mexico, Alcañiz and Giraudy (2022) identified that the largest funders of MDBs and other IGOs that finance projects related to climate change direct resources to specific subnational units. These, in turn, tend to receive funds if they display low levels of socio-economic development. Yet beyond describing the distribution of resources, the complex interplay between IGOs and the subnational level in the context of norm diffusion in sustainable development and the interplay among different spheres of authority as sources of norms and decision-making needs further academic scrutiny.

Authority, decision-making, and norms: An analytical framework

The incentives for MDBs to display increasing flexibility in sustainable development-related measures do not only stem from the need to accomplish the 2030 Agenda launched in 2015 but also from developments related to the 2008 Global Financial Crisis. The scenario for norm diffusion, however, shifted not only due to the decline of neoliberalism in the aftermath of that critical juncture for the global order but also because of the United States and the West's relative decline. My main assumption is that MDBs of all feathers – including the US-led World Bank – had their bargaining power vis-à-vis borrowers reduced, thus opening the doors for accepting practices that resemble either localization or domestication processes. However, Washington and her allies still aim to preserve the liberal order (Rodrigues Vieira et al. 2023), thus favouring top-down mechanisms of diffusion. I then posit:

- **Proposition 1**: While US-sponsored MDBs are likely to have sought retaining a top-down approach in diffusing sustainability standards, Non-Western-backed MDBs prefer relying on nation-wide country-systems, thus committing to traditional modes of sovereignty.

Yet, MLG frameworks do not conceive of the domestic level as a single block. Rosneau (2004) claims that governance depends on rule systems that have both formal and informal means of prevailing within a given sphere of authority, which can be broadly understood as a geographical-thematic jurisdiction. Behrend and Whitehead (2016) argue that the rights of citizens vary across subnational units not only in federal countries but also in unitary states. Consequently, when subnational units are understood as spheres of authority, it is necessary to conceive of them in both administrative and legal terms – that is, as sources of decision-making and sources of norms. Provinces and municipalities – plus indigenous nations and ethnic communities – not only implement policies but may have explicit and implicit legislative powers over them. Hence, more than gatekeepers of international norms, governments and the state in various jurisdictions act as co-creators of order through acts of localization (Acharya 2004) and eventually domestication (Rostoy and Elbe 2021). I therefore expect:

- **Proposition 2**: MDBs that recognize subnational actors as sources of norms and/or decision-making tend to disempower the national governments by favouring norm domestication over localization.

Therefore, instead of a binary classification of MLG types between Level I (Hierarchical) and Level II (Diffuse) (as defined by Hooghe and Marks 2004), I opt to place MDBs in a continuum regarding the recognition of international – including global, regional (i.e., Latin American), and subregional (i.e., South

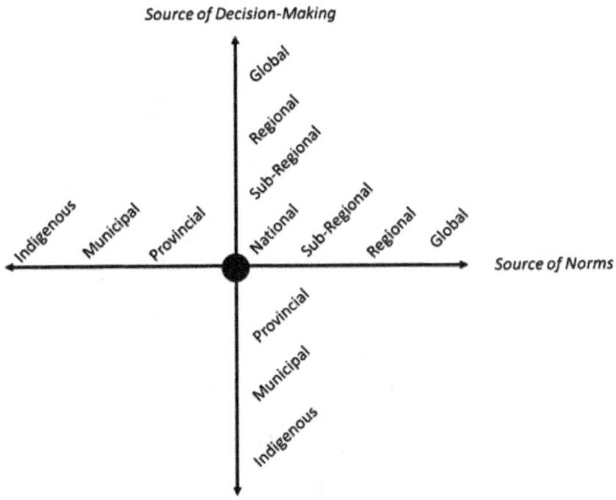

Figure 13.1 Axis of spheres of authority.

American) players – and subnational actors, like provinces/states, municipalities, and even indigenous groups, as sources of decision-making and as sources of norms (Figure 13.1).

With regards to the promotion of sustainable development by MDBs, the combination of propositions 1 and 2 increases the chances that norm domestication in the terms proposed by Rostoy and Elbe (2021) happens. That is the case as the non-recognition of national governments as source of norms and/or decision-making often comes along with acknowledgement that the subnational level has at least one of those competencies at the provincial (state), municipal, and indigenous spheres. Such a scenario not only opens the doors for bypassing the national sphere of authority as the main jurisdiction in charge of gatekeeping foreign influences, but also paves the way for welcoming customary systems of law, including informal rules, in the implementation of development projects.

At the international level, spheres of authority may comprise global IGOs (i.e., the World Bank and the NDB), regionally-focused ones (like the CAF and the IADB), and subregional actors, including the CDB, the CABEI, and the FONPLATA. As shown in figure 13.2, top-down, coercive-like diffusion tends to prevail whenever these spheres of authority are sources of decision-making and also dominate as sources of norms, thus leaving no space for domestic legal-political frameworks, whether formal or informal. By contrast, the legitimation of international action by players like MDBs tends to increase with subnational and indigenous norms prevailing even if decision-making remains in the hands of foreign actors, while resistance to change only happens de facto if both

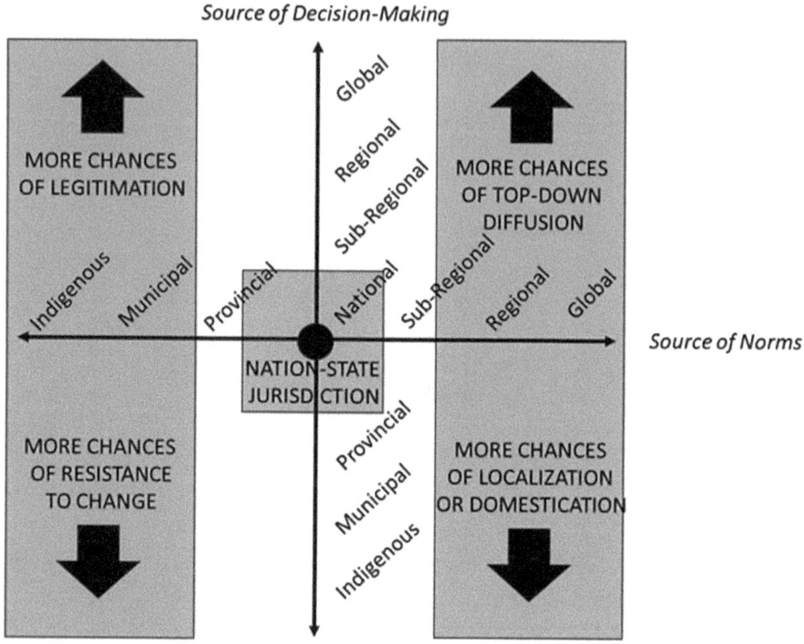

Figure 13.2 Spheres of authority and expectations in processes of norm diffusion.

decision-making and normative frameworks remain exclusively matters pertaining to the domestic level.

Empirical analysis

This section explores the potential combinations of sources of decision-making and sources of norms based on four main cases: two involving regional-focused MDBs in Latin America – the CAF and the IADB – and another comprising MDBs of global scope – the NDB and the World Bank. Three cases – the CDB, the CABEI, and the FONPLATA – are MDBs devoted to actions in specific parts of the Western Hemisphere – namely, the Caribbean, Central America, and Southern Cone, which can be considered subregions. The purpose of conducting separate comparisons considering those different types of MDBs contributes to circumventing the assumption that regional-focused MDBs yield better conditions for borrowers' ownership than MDBs with global scope (Obydenkova and Rodrigues Vieira 2020). The IADB, for example, has meaningful contributions from Latin American borrowing members, including Argentina, Brazil, and

Mexico. Yet, as demonstrated below, the bank has mechanisms to preserve a top-down approach in ESS as much as the World Bank does. Likewise, the fact that the NDB has China as a main sponsor de facto does not oblige other members to fall in line with Beijing's views on environmental and social issues as that bank has provisions for the use of country-systems in sustainable development.

CAF and the IADB: Between a National focus and a thin recognition of the subnational

In September 2016, the CAF launched its first set of ESSs. The goal was to contribute to member states fulfiling the 2030 SDG UN Agenda. The safeguards are as follows: sustainable use of renewable resources, conservation of biological diversity, pollution prevention and management, cultural heritage, ethnic groups and cultural diversity, population resettlement, working conditions and training, and gender equality (CAF 2016). The application of the provisions related to those safeguards is monitored by the Evaluation Program and Environmental and Social Monitoring of Operations (PESASO), "whose purpose is to guarantee the physical, environmental, social and gender equality sustainability of operations financed by the institution" (CAF 2016, 10). Two years later, the CAF launched Green Bonds, targeting the financing of renewable energy projects, which are defined as wind, solar, small-scale hydro (< 20MW installed capacity), biomass, ocean power, and wholly dedicated transmission systems for renewable energy. As a signal of cooperative multilateralism, the bank also has a partnership with the Global Environmental Facility (GEF) for co-financing projects.

The 2016 document mentions the concept of local sensibility (*sensibilidad local*), defined as how local actors perceive the impact of a given action. Perceptions, in turn, would be identified by consultants based on their experience and interactions with locals (CAF 2016, 16–17). Yet, there is no explicit reference to subnational legislation. The adjective national (*nacional*) follows the word legislation 14 times throughout the document. Whenever mentioned, the adjective local qualifies labour legislation only and is mentioned twice as synonymous with national (CAF 2016, 121–122). Therefore, there is no specific provision for adopting subnational rules. Dialogue with communities affected by projects occurs at the implementation level through the Environmental and Social Grievance Redress Mechanism (ESGRM), a channel that receives complaints about violations in projects (CAF 2023). Yet, no reference to indigenous and other types of communities exists as a source of either norms or decision-making.

By contrast, the IADB only approved its new ESF – the Environmental and Social Performance Standards (ESPS) – in 2020, which became effective in 2021. It is officially called the Environmental and Social Policy Framework (ESPF). Yet, the bank's commitment to the promotion of environmental issues can be traced back to four decades earlier. The IADB claims to be the first MDB to pay attention to such topics in 1979, with the adoption of its first environmental policy (IADB 2006, 1). Since 1994, when members completed the eighth replenishment of resources, the environment has become a priority area for the bank along with poverty reduction and social equity (IADB 2006, 1).

The 2006 Environment and Safeguards Compliance Policy stated that "[c] ountry-level environmental analysis will be a principal tool to generate relevant information and to support the development of programming documents" (IADB 2006, 4). Yet, also according to the 2006 document, bank policies came on top of country laws and regulations, which nevertheless had to be considered in addition to the former. The IADB, however, stated that the "appropriate measures" to comply with both would be agreed with the borrowers (IADB 2006, 7). The international-domestic top-down approach could not be clearer than in the following excerpt:

> In the context of individual operations, the Bank will consider the use of the borrowing member countries' existing systems of safeguards for identifying and managing environmental and social impacts. *This will apply when the Bank has determined that the borrowing member country's system is equivalent or superior to the Bank's.*
>
> (IADB 2006, 14, emphasis ours)

That is, if the IADB considers that its legal provisions on sustainable development are superior to any national or subnational rules, there is no space for domestication or even localization. In fact, at least at the rhetorical level, the ESPS focuses more on the improvement of environmental and social governance than on mitigating risks in those fields (Espinoza 2021). The ESPS are the following: assessment and management of environmental and social risks and impacts; labour and working conditions; resource efficiency and pollution prevention; community health, safety, and security; land acquisition and involuntary resettlement; biodiversity conservation and sustainable management of living natural resources; indigenous peoples; cultural heritage; gender equality; and stakeholder engagement and information disclosure (Espinoza 2021).

Table 13.1 compares the CAF and IADB sustainable development-related safeguards as of 2023. The safeguards in bold are those that have a clear equivalent in both banks. Unlike the CAF, the IADB therefore does not consider ethnic groups in general, signalling instead to the protection of indigenous rights. There is, however, a broad mention of cultural heritage, which nevertheless does not encompass the material/economic needs of ethnic minorities. These may be indirectly covered by provisions related to land acquisition and involuntary resettlement. IADB's inclusion of land acquisition signals concerns with individual and property rights, thus reflecting a liberal tradition that disregards customary legal systems. CAF refers to pollution only, whereas IADB employs the broader language of environmental and social risks.

Table 13.1 Safeguards in Latin American-focused MDBs

CAF	*IADB*
Sustainable use of renewable resources	Assessment and management of environmental and social risks and impacts
Conservation of biological diversity	
Pollution prevention and management	Labour and working conditions
Cultural heritage	Resource efficiency and pollution prevention
Ethnic groups and cultural diversity	Community health, safety, and security
Population resettlement	Land acquisition and involuntary resettlement
Working conditions and training	Biodiversity conservation and sustainable management of living natural resources
Gender equality	
	Indigenous peoples
	Cultural heritage
	Gender equality
	Stakeholder engagement and information disclosure

Source: Own elaboration.

In contrast to the CAF, the IADB has, however, made an explicit but discreet signal to welcome provincial and municipal legislation in the implementation and assessment of projects, thus paving the way for norm domestication after the establishment of the 2030 Agenda. In a document issued in 2020, the IADB makes an explicit reference to indigenous peoples, apart from opening the doors for considering borrowers' ESFs as long as they are "likely to address the risks and impacts of the project and will enable the project to achieve objectives and outcomes equivalent to those achieved with the application of the ESPF (functional equivalence)" (IADB 2020, 16). Footnote 27 on the same page of the ESPF document clarifies that borrowers' ESF include "national, subnational, or sectoral implementing institutions and applicable laws, regulations, rules and procedures" in the scope of the project (IADB 2020, 16).

Having said that, openness to subnational norms and rules did not eliminate the 2006 top-down zeitgeist, as the IADB still expresses the ambition of contributing to strengthening borrowers' "national systems" with the purpose of improving their "...capacity to manage environmental and social risks in the medium to long term" (IADB 2020, 11). The bank's due diligence approach, however, seems to seek a better balance between lender and borrower as a source of decision-making.

That is the case as the ESPF states that IADB monitoring/compliance action "will be proportional to risks and impacts that might be associated with it and the prevailing country context for its implementation" (IADB 2020, 12).

NDB, the World Bank, and the contradictions of recognizing country-systems

Founded in 2014, the NDB published its environmental and social guidelines in 2016. The document that details the bank's approach to ESG makes an explicit reference to the use of "country systems," which can be deployed at the operational level "with adequate support … as it also fosters greater accountability and ownership" (NDB 2016, 4). That is, the use of national legislation/frameworks is grounded on the need to provide transparency and a sense of pertaining among those impacted by bank-supported projects.

On the same page, the NDB clarifies that its notion of inclusive and sustainable development entails the "inclusive sharing of development benefits and opportunities including among the traditionally deprived sections such as the poor, disadvantaged, women, children and minorities" (NDB 2016, 4). Thereafter, gender equality is explicitly mentioned as a target to be met (NDB 2016, 5). Specific references to vulnerable groups only come much later, on page 10. They are defined in a broad manner, considering economic and non-economic cleavages alike, then comprising:

> peoples that may be more adversely affected than others by the project and have limited ability to take benefits of the project. It includes, but not limited to, people below poverty line, the landless, the older people, children, women, ethnic minorities, disabled persons etc.
>
> (NDB 2016, 10)

The NDB also signals its intention to operate in alignment with *stricto sensu* international public law – that is, the set of rules, including customary ones that have been agreed upon by sovereign states. Apart from not financing activities deemed illegal in the state where a given project is to be implemented, the bank also rules out supporting "international conventions relating to the protection of biodiversity resources or cultural heritage" (NDB 2016, 13). As far as the latter is concerned, the bank pursues the conservation of "cultural resources and avoid destroying or damaging them by using field-based surveys that employ qualified and experienced experts for the assessment process" (NDB 2016, 18). Finally, the NDB establishes in its sustainable development-related rules that it will seek coordination with other MDBs and IFIs, a signal that the BRICS at least formally refrained from engaging with an extreme form of contested multilateralism vis-à-vis US-sponsored banks (Morse and Keohane 2014).

Safeguards' broadness in the NDB amidst respecting international public law therefore opens the door for state-centric, sovereign-based approaches to sustainable development. Further evidence of this logic lies in the relatively small number of ESS outlined in the NDB policy. There are only three sections, which suggests a relative lack of precision in the bank norms for sustainable development vis-à-vis the provisions of other NDBs. The standards are entitled as environmental and social assessment, involuntary resettlement, and indigenous peoples. A reference to the latter reflects less the recognition of the existence of a strong civil society than the emulation of Western-sponsored banks along with the pressure of the democratic members of the BRICS – namely, Brazil, India, and South Africa – although contributions from Russia, which is home to indigenous Arctic populations, cannot be discarded.

In January 2017, the World Bank's new ESF entered into force. The IBRD/IDA Board of Executive Directors had approved it on 4 August 2016 (World Bank 2023a). As Dann and Riegner (2019, 538) summarize, "[s]afeguards reform epitomizes the changing structures and geopolitical shifts that shape international law in the twenty-first century," thus being the consequence of civil society engagement and a competitive multilateralism exemplified by the creation of the Chinese-led MDBs AIIB and the NDB. The safeguard reform process began in 2012 – that is, before those two IFIs were officially created, yet already under the context in which Beijing had already begun to be perceived as a lender of last resort amidst the West's relative loss of political-economic power in the aftermath of the 2008 Global Financial Crisis.

"The ESF places an emphasis on strengthening national environmental and social management systems and institutions, and supporting Borrower capacity building," the World Bank (2023a) claims. According to Dann and Riegner (2019, 554), the use of country systems (UCS) is the main consequential change of the reform. "In the Safeguards reform negotiations, China, India, Brazil, and South Africa emerged as strong champions of the UCS" (Dann and Riegner 2019, 553). The World Bank 2017 ESF must therefore be understood as the result of a compromise among all member-states and CSOs from the North and the South.

The UCS approach, however, does not consist of a *carte blanche* for borrowers. "If country law is to be applied, it is also necessary to ensure that this is brought on par with the protection levels offered by the ESF before the project begins to be implemented" (Dann and Riegner 2019, 554). As written in its ESF, the World Bank shall "utilize national environmental and social institutions, systems, laws, regulations and procedures in the assessment, development and implementation of projects, whenever appropriate" (World Bank 2017, 16).

Yet, contrary to the NDB country-system approach, the World Bank acknowledged legal pluralism (as defined by Davies 2010) and made clear provisions that open the doors for norm domestication and, hence, the recognition of indigenous peoples as sources of norms and eventually of decision-making. The bank gives "full legal recognition of existing customary land tenure systems of Indigenous Peoples/Sub-Saharan African Historically Underserved Traditional

Local Communities" (World Bank 2017, 80). Moreover, the ESF has set the pursuit of universal access as a goal for World Bank-supported projects once they are implemented (World Bank 2018, 12).

Unlike other banks covered in this paper, the World Bank distinguishes between standards and safeguards. The latter are listed under the following titles: environmental action plans, performance standards for private sector activities, natural habitats, pest management, indigenous peoples, physical cultural resources, involuntary resettlement, forests, safety of dams, projects in disputed areas, and projects on international waterways (World Bank 2023b). There are ten ESS: assessment and management of environmental and social risks and impacts; labour and working conditions; resource efficiency and pollution prevention; community health and safety; land acquisition, restrictions on land use, and involuntary resettlement; biodiversity conservation and sustainable management of living natural resources; indigenous peoples/Sub-Saharan African historically underserved traditional local communities; cultural heritage; financial intermediaries; and stakeholder engagement and information disclosure.

Table 13.2 contrasts the NDB and World Bank ESS. While the former has broad standards, the latter highlights specific concerns by having a specific set of topics to be followed on environmental and social issues. The World Bank reference to the private sector reveals a preference for market-based solutions, which the NDB does not necessarily prioritize given BRICS members' preference for state capitalism. Not only does reference to customary law pave the way to norm domestication, but also stakeholder engagement and information disclosure, as both processes depend on going beyond the supervision of official authorities other than national-level/central/federal governments.

Therefore, the NDB reflects sovereignty concerns in sustainable development. Although the World Bank reformed its ESF policy amidst a strategic context of growing geopolitical competition during which alternative sources of development financing emerged, the oldest financial-focused IGO in the field managed to create a de facto escape clause from biases that may arise from UCS, which relies only on legislation and frameworks at the national level. Not only does customary law from Sub-Saharan Africa apply to the concept of UCS, but also any inputs from stakeholders. With this, projects may increase their legitimacy vis-à-vis domestic constituencies by avoiding the fate of serving first and foremost the purposes of national-level leaders who, regardless of being authoritarian or democratic, do not necessarily express the interests and needs of communities that will suffer most of the impact of IBRD- and/or IDA-sponsored projects.

Other Latin American-focused MDBs and the reinforcement of nation-wide jurisdiction

Like the CAF, the CDB and the CABEI seem to prioritize national decision-makers and norms, while the FONPLATA at least refers to subnational actors

Table 13.2 ESS in global MDBs

NDB	*World Bank*
Environmental and social assessment (including inferred subtopics)	Assessment and management of environmental and social Risks and impacts
Biodiversity resources	Labour and working conditions
Cultural heritage	Resource efficiency and pollution prevention
Gender	Community health and safety
Involuntary resettlement	Land acquisition, restrictions on land use, and involuntary resettlement
Indigenous peoples	Biodiversity conservation and sustainable management of living natural resources
	Indigenous peoples/sub-Saharan African historically underserved traditional local communities
	Cultural heritage
	Financial intermediaries
	Stakeholder engagement and information disclosure

Source: Own elaboration.

at the provincial and municipal levels. The CDB published in 2023 a revision of its energy sector policy and strategy (ESPS). The bank justified the revision on grounds that include the 2030 Agenda, the nationally determined policy contributions of the Paris Agreement of 2016, and the need to improve borrowing member states in the Caribbean, which are suffering increasing vulnerability to extreme climate events (CDB 2022a, 1). In addition, the Covid-19 pandemic hindered the ability of borrowing member states to invest in renewable energy, and the Russian war against Ukraine brought further instability to energy markets, creating further stimuli for investment in renewable sources and reliance on regional hydrocarbon production (CDB 2022a, 3). Energy-related action should consider "the differential and inter-sectional needs of women, the poor, people with disabilities, indigenous peoples, the elderly, and other marginalised groups" (CDB 2022a, 25).

The adaptive social protection framework of 2020 had already signalled the need to consider "intersecting vulnerabilities" associated with social categories, including indigenous status (CDB 2021, 18). Concerns with the indigenous, however, stem less from a principled belief that subnational actors can deliver better policymaking in sustainable development than from the growing evidence on climate change and the natural hazards triggered by extreme weather events (CDB 2021, 10). By contrast, the 2019–2024 Climate Resilience Strategy made no reference to the indigenous population yet had already brought gender issues to the forefront of climate change-related action (CDB 2018, 1).

In parallel to a growing emphasis on SDG/Climate Change, the bank engaged in improving the financial capabilities of cities and villages in borrowing states. Between 2021 and 2023, the CDB "funded the Capacity Building in Municipal Finance programme, which was implemented by the Commonwealth Local Government Forum (CLGF)" (CDB 2022b, 1). The initiative reached officials in six borrowing members: Belize, the Bahamas, Dominica, Guyana, Saint Lucia, and Trinidad and Tobago.

Having a similar size and scope, the CABEI contrasts with the CDB experience as it ignores the subnational level in terms of indigenous-based jurisdictions as sources of decision-making and norms. In the section of the report that seeks to align the bank's ESS with the 2030 Agenda, the municipal level is mentioned in the goal of pursuing energy efficiency and the reduction of greenhouse gas emissions, yet there is no explicit reference to providing direct loans to municipalities. Tackling both challenges would boost cities' competitiveness (CABEI 2020, 20). The same applies to investments in water supply and sewage (CABEI 2020, 60) and infrastructure and sustainable territorial development (CABEI 2020, 36). Also, the bank aimed at supporting municipal-level initiatives that promote gender equality (CABEI 2020, 28).

In fact, the only identity-related cleavage mentioned in its publicly available documents as a target of promotion is gender (CABEI 2024a, 1). Having said that, the CABEI follows the model of other MDBs and has an Environmental and Social Policy that comprises an ESS and a Management System for Environmental and Social Risks divided into a System for Identification, Evaluation, and Mitigation of Environmental and Social Risks (SIEMAS), and an Environmental and Social Corporate Responsibility System (SASC) (CABEI 2024b, 1).

The promotion of welfare is aligned with the SDGs and comprises concerns with "the participation and empowerment of communities and citizens in general is promoted for the joint development of social investment projects, prioritizing issues such as health, education, the environment and community development" (CABEI 2024a, 1). Yet, the CABEI has been criticized for not paying due attention to human rights violations related to the projects it sponsors. Such a bias may arise from the bank's focus on the national level as a sphere of authority. Human Rights Watch points out that during the presidency of Dante Mossi (2018–2023) "the Bank has weakened institutional controls, including by removing the internal auditor, and increased lending to authoritarian governments like those of Nicaragua and El Salvador" (Goebertus Estrada 2023, 1).

For instance, native populations have been ignored in the implementation of the CABEI co-funded sustainable development project Bio-CLMA in Nicaragua under the Ortega regime. The project also relies on sponsorship by the Green Climate Fund, which concluded in 2022 that the project would legitimize the Colonos' invasion of indigenous and Afro-descendent traditional communities' lands. The Colonos "are fellow Nicaraguans, mostly mestizos, who have long been pushing into and invading indigenous lands" (Expediente Publico 2022, 1).

As of January 2024, CABEI was in the process of developing a climate change strategy that may direct 40% of the yearly operations of the bank to projects related to that global challenge (Mainstreaming Climate 2023), but no specific provisions for the indigenous population were reported in the context of sustainable development.

The FONPLATA also ignores the native/ethnic subnational communities. However, in contrast to the CABEI, it has been devoting increasing attention to provinces/states and municipalities in the context of the 2030 Agenda, which dovetails with the pursuit of norm localization and even domestication as there is no proscription to the use of informal rules. The bank 2022–2026 Strategic Plan indicates the pursuit of SDG through projects that address climate change, such as those related to renewable energy, sustainable cities, and integral development (FONPLATA 2022, 5). In addition, there is a clear reference to provincial and municipal governments' role in promoting actions, as the plan mentions that sustainable development projects will be implemented at national, subnational, and city levels (FONPLATA 2022, 5). Moreover, the FONPLATA signalled that it would start providing loans without sovereign guarantees to subnational level actors such as financial institutions, state-owned companies, or any other institution mainly owned by a provincial or municipal jurisdiction (FONPLATA 2022, 5).

Even before the launch of the 2022–2026 Strategic Plan, the bank welcomed the participation of subnational jurisdictions except indigenous/ethnic communities. At least since 2019, there has been the possibility that sovereign loans and technical cooperation are provided to subnational or decentralized jurisdiction and state agencies in general (FONPLATA 2019, 3 and 8). Sovereign guarantees are required though, following a standard common among most MDBs. Specifically, in the case of projects' environmental management, provisions were already implemented according to national and/or subnational norms, without any FONPLATA intervention (FONPLATA 2019, 7).

Conclusion

Figure 13.3 summarizes the findings by placing the MDBs related to the emphasis on the national sphere of authority – understood as the primacy of the central state over other forms of subnational and even non-state authority – in function of the existence of openness to the subnational level and/or stakeholders

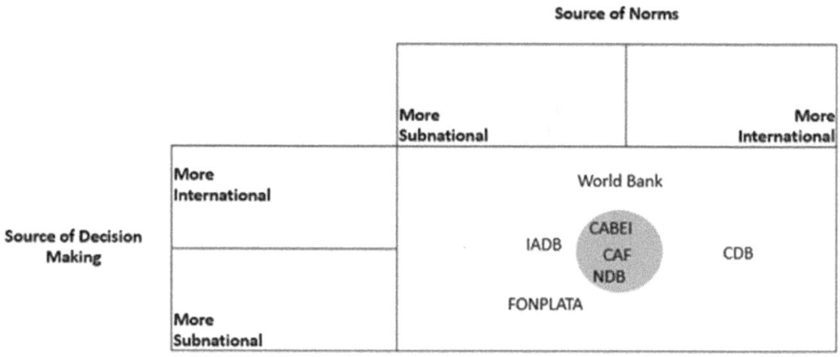

Figure 13.3 Comparison among MDBs.

in general, as well as of specific provisions for indigenous groups as sources of norms and/or decision-making in sustainable development matters. The NDB combines specific provisions for indigenous while not acknowledging the sustainable development frameworks from the subnational level, which implies the primacy of nationally-based country systems. The CAF, in turn, is a step ahead, as minority provisions encompass any ethnic group, yet without any explicit mention of subnational units. The CABEI refers to the municipal level as a source of decision-making, but not in normative terms. These three banks therefore operate mainly in the jurisdiction of the central government of nation-states, represented by the shadowed circle in the figure below, located at the centre of the chart as in the case of Figures 13.1 and 13.2.

The IADB privileges indigenous rights, but at least in a discreet manner, recognizes the role of subnational systems in structuring compliance with ESS. It is, however, distant from FONPLATA due to its emphasis on fostering national-level country-systems. These are not recognized by the CDB, which has only recently begun to acknowledge the role of municipalities. Despite having adhered to the UCS approach in the promotion of sustainable development, the World Bank remains distant from subnational normative frameworks that mostly open doors to domestic-level actors other than the national sovereign state. This is the case as the World Bank has specific provisions for promoting the agency of only traditional groups in Sub-Saharan Africa, which nevertheless points out the recognition of customary rules as part of the rule of law that applies to the implementation of SDGs.

Future research must address whether MDBs and other IGOs and international regimes and institutions in general stimulate or hinder the rise of authoritarian structures of governance, in line with what Behrend and Whitehead (2016) have already discussed in the context of the challenges democracies face in consolidating their rules and practices at the subnational level. Specifically on MDBs, it is also necessary to include other US/Western-sponsored MDBs as well as Non-Western ones focused on regions other than Latin America to build a comprehensive understanding of the tensions that arise from the attrition of different spheres of authority as source of norms and of decision-making in sustainable development and, hence, of the limits of the rule of formal law. This is the case as the recognition of legal pluralism by welcoming the applicability of subnational rules – including customary law – shall enhance the legitimacy of the inevitable changes that the implementation of the 2030 Agenda implies for stakeholders all over the world.

For now, it is plausible to affirm that MDBs with Non-Western sponsorship have a clear alignment with traditional notions of sovereignty whenever sustainable development issues are at stake, which contrasts with the top-down models Northern-based IGOs seem to have historically favoured even whenever. Not necessarily, however, do the MDBs from the Global South lack effectiveness in promoting sustainable development among borrowing states, insofar as UCS may result in an equilibrium between states' thirst for retaining sovereignty and the very much needed legitimacy vis-à-vis stakeholders to make sustainable development more than just cheap talk.

References

Acharya, Amitav. 2004. How Ideas Spread: Whose Norms Matter? Norm Localization and Institutional Change in Asian Regionalism. *International Organization* 58 (2): 239–275. https://doi.org/10.1017/S0020818304582024.

Alcañiz, Isabella, and Agustina Giraudy. 2022. From International Organizations to Local Governments: How Foreign Environmental Aid Reaches Subnational Beneficiaries in Argentina, Brazil, and Mexico. *Environmental Politics*. https://doi.org/10.1080/09644016.2022.2124004.

Alcantara, Christopher, and Jen Nelles. 2014. Indigenous Peoples and the State in Settler Societies: Toward a More Robust Definition of Multilevel Governance. *Publius: The Journal of Federalism* 44 (1): 183–204. https://doi.org/10.1093/publius/pjt013.

Behrend, Jacqueline, and Laurence Whitehead. 2016. The Struggle for Subnational Democracy. *Journal of Democracy* 27 (2): 155–169.

Benz, Arthur, Jörg Broschek, and Markus Lederer. 2021. Introduction: What Is Multilevel Governance? In *A Research Agenda for Multilevel Governance*, edited by Arthur Benz, Jörg Broschek, and Markus Lederer, 1–18. Edward Elgar.

Biermann, Frank, and Steffen Bauer. 2004. Assessing the Effectiveness of Intergovernmental Organizations in International Environmental Politics. *Global Environmental Change* 14: 189–193.

CABEI. 2020. Environmental and Social Strategy 2020–2024. https://bcie2014.sharepoint.com/:b:/s/DocPub/ETvqSgbUCfhIjNMfhAPihMsBlufOQZnHMZZvEJh7Ulg6zg.

CABEI. 2024a. Social Dimension. https://www.bcie.org/en/about-us/environmental-and-social-responsibility/social-dimension.

CABEI. 2024b. Environmental and Social Responsibility: Environmental and Social Corporate Responsibility System. https://www.bcie.org/en/about-us/environmental-and-social-responsibility.

CAF. 2016. Salvaguardas Sociales y Ambientales. https://www.caf.com/media/30035/salvaguardas-ambientales-y-sociales.pdf.

CAF. 2023. Environmental and Social Grievance Redress Mechanism (ESGRM). https://www.caf.com/en/topics/e/environment-and-climate-change/environmental-and-social-grievance-redress-mechanism-esgrm/.

CDB. 2018. Climate Resilience Strategy 2019–2024. https://www.caribank.org/sites/default/files/publication-resources/CDB_ClimateResilienceStrategy_2019-2024.pdf

CDB. 2021. Strategic Plan Update: "Repositioning for Resilience". https://www.caribank.org/sites/default/files/publication-resources/CDBStrategicPlan_2022-2024_Update%28redacted%29.pdf.

CDB. 2022a. Energy Sector Policy and Strategy. https://www.caribank.org/sites/default/files/publication-resources/ENERGY%20SECTOR%20POLICY%20AND%20STRATEGY_%202022_Final.pdf

CDB. 2022b. Local Government Officials Key to Building Forward Better. May 24. https://www.caribank.org/newsroom/news-and-events/local-government-officials-key-building-forward-better.

Dann P., and M. Riegner. 2019. The World Bank's Environmental and Social Safeguards and the Evolution of Global Order. *Leiden Journal of International Law* 32: 537–559. https://doi.org/10.1017/S0922156519000293.

Davies, Margaret. 2010. Legal Pluralism. In *The Oxford Handbook of Empirical Legal Research*, edited by Peter Cane and Herbert M. Kritzer, 805–827. Oxford: Oxford University Press. https://doi.org/10.1093/oxfordhb/9780199542475.013.0034.

Di Gregorio, M., L. Fatorelli, J. Paavola, B. Locatelli, E. Pramova, D. R. Nurrochmat, ... and S. D. Kusumadewi. 2019. Multi-level Governance and Power in Climate Change Policy Networks. *Global Environmental Change*, 54: 64–77.

Dobbin, Frank, Beth Simmons, and Geoffrey Garrett. 2007. The Global Diffusion of Public Policies: Social Construction, Coercion, Competition, or Learning? *Annual Review of Sociology* 33: 449–472.

Espinoza, Joaquin. 2021. The IDB's New Environmental and Social Policy Framework in a Nutshell. November 1. https://blogs.iadb.org/sostenibilidad/en/espf-environmental-and-social-policy-framework-in-a-nutshell/.

Expediente Público. 2022. Through the Bio-CLIMA Project, CABEI Empowers Colonos and Revitalizes Daniel Ortega. November 7. https://www.expedientepublico.org/through-the-bio-clima-project-cabei-empowers-colonos-and-revitalizes-daniel-ortega/#:~:text=On%20August%2031%2C%202022%2C%20the,would%20legitimize%20the%20Colonos'%20invasion.

FONPLATA. 2019. Normas para a elaboração e administração das Operações do FONPLATA. https://www.fonplata.org/sites/default/files/paginas-fonplata/archivos/Normas%20para%20a%20elabora%C3%A7%C3%A3o%20e%20administra%C3%A7%C3%A3o%20das%20Opera%C3%A7%C3%B5es%20do%20FONPLATA.pdf.

FONPLATA. 2022. Plano Estratégico Institucional (PEI) do FONPLATA – Banco de Desenvolvimento: Período 2022–2026. https://www.fonplata.org/sites/default/files/media/documents/PEI%202022-2026%20WEB_PT.pdf.

Fourcade-Gourinchas, M., and Babb, S. L. 2002. The Rebirth of the Liberal Creed: Paths to Neoliberalism in Four Countries. *American Journal of Sociology*, 108 (3): 533–579. https://doi.org/10.1086/367922

Goebertus Estrada, Juanita. 2023. Next Central American Bank President Crucial for Rights in the Region. Human Rights Watch, November 17. https://www.hrw.org/news/2023/11/17/next-central-american-bank-president-crucial-rights-region.

Happaerts, Sande, Karoline Van den Brande, and Hans Bruyninckx. 2010. Governance for Sustainable Development at the Inter-subnational Level: The Case of the Network of Regional Governments for Sustainable Development (nrg4SD). *Regional & Federal Studies* 20 (1): 127–149. https://doi.org/10.1080/13597560903187362.

IADB. 2006. Environment and Safeguards Compliance Policy.

IADB. 2020. Environmental and Social Policy Framework. https://idbdocs.iadb.org/wsdocs/getdocument.aspx?docnum=EZSHARE-110529158-160.

Jörgensen, Kirsten, Anu Jogesh, and Arabinda Mishra. 2015. Multi-Level Climate Governance and the Role of the Subnational Level. *Journal of Integrative Environmental Sciences* 12 (4): 235–245. https://doi.org/10.1080/1943815X.2015.1096797.

Mainstreaming Climate. 2023. Central American Bank for Economic Integration. https://www.mainstreamingclimate.org/organisation/cabei/#:~:text=The%202020%2D2024%20strategy%20comprises,Social%20Inclusion.

Marks, Gary, and Liesbet Hooghe. 2004. Contrasting Visions of Multi-Level Governance. In *Multi-level Governance*, edited by Ian Bache and Matthew Flinders, 15–30. Oxford: Oxford University Press. https://doi.org/10.1093/0199259259.003.0002.

Marks, Gary. 1993. Structural Policy and Multilevel Governance in the EC. In *The State of the European Community*, edited by Alan Cafruny and Glenda Rosenthal, 391–410. New York: Lynne Rienner.

Morse, Julia C., and Robert O. Keohane. 2014. Contested multilateralism. *Review of International Organizations* 9: 385–412. https://doi.org/10.1007/s11558-014-9188-2.

NDB. 2016. New Development Bank Environment and Social Framework, Version 4, March 11. https://www.ndb.int/wp-content/uploads/2017/02/ndb-environment-social-framework-20160330.pdf.

Organization of American States. 2016. American Declaration on the Rights of Indigenous Peoples: AG/RES.2888 (XLVI-O/16). General Assembly. Regular Session (46th, Santo Domingo, Dominican Republic). https://www.oas.org/en/sare/documents/DecAmIND.pdf.

Obydenkova, Anastassia V., and Vinícius G. Rodrigues Vieira. 2020. The Limits of Collective Financial Statecraft: Regional Development Banks and Voting Alignment with the United States at the United Nations General Assembly. *International Studies Quarterly* 64 (1): 13–25. https://doi.org/10.1093/isq/sqz080.

Papillon, Martin. 2012. Adapting Federalism: Indigenous Multilevel Governance in Canada and the United States. *Publius: The Journal of Federalism* 42 (2): 289–312. https://doi.org/10.1093/publius/pjr032.

Restoy, Enrique, and Stefan Elbe. 2021. Drilling Down in Norm Diffusion: Norm Domestication, "Glocal" Power, and Community-Based Organizations in Global Health. *Global Studies Quarterly* 1 (3): ksab025. https://doi.org/10.1093/isagsq/ksab025.

Rodrigues Vieira, Vinícius G. 2020. Hegemonia benevolente e empreendedorismo político como pressuposto para o desenvolvimento regional. In *Desenvolvimento e*

Cooperação na América Latina: A Urgência de uma Estratégia Renovada, edited by Enrique Garcia, 671–686. São Paulo: Edusp.

Rodrigues Vieira, Vinícius G., Krishna Chaitanya Vadlamannati, and Yuanxin Li. 2023. Dispositional Balancing and Hegemonic Order: US Response to China's Financial Statecraft. *The Chinese Journal of International Politics* 16 (1): 1–30. https://doi.org/10.1093/cjip/poac025.

Rosenau, James N. 2004. Strong Demand, Huge Supply: Governance in an Emerging Epoch. In *Multi-level Governance*, edited by Ian Bache and Matthew Flinders, 31–48. Oxford: Oxford University Press. https://doi.org/10.1093/0199259259.003.0003.

Schakel, Arjan H., Liesbet Hooghe, and Gary Marks. 2014. Multilevel Governance and the State. In *The Oxford Handbook of Transformations of the State*, edited by Stephan Leibfried, Evelyne Huber, Matthew Lange, Jonah D. Levy, and John D. Stephens. Oxford: Oxford University Press. https://doi.org/10.1093/oxfordhb/9780199691586.013.14.

Setzer, Joana. 2017. How Subnational Governments are Rescaling Environmental Governance: The Case of the Brazilian State of São Paulo. *Journal of Environmental Policy & Planning* 19 (5): 503–519. https://doi.org/10.1080/1523908X.2014.984669.

Tatham, Michaël. 2015. Regional Voices in the European Union: Subnational Influence in Multilevel Politics. *International Studies Quarterly* 59 (2): 387–400.

Tews, Kerstin. 2005. The Diffusion of Environmental Policy Innovations: Cornerstones of an Analytical Framework. *European Environment* 15 (2): 63–79.

UN Department of Economic and Social Affairs. 2024. SDG Localization and the Voluntary Local Reviews. https://sdgs.un.org/topics/voluntary-local-reviews.

UN. 2015. Transforming Our World: The 2030 Agenda for Sustainable Development (A/RES/70/1). https://sustainabledevelopment.un.org/content/documents/21252030%20Agenda%20for%20Sustainable%20Development%20web.pdf.

UN. 2024. Indigenous Peoples and the 2030 Agenda. https://www.un.org/development/desa/indigenouspeoples/focus-areas/post-2015-agenda/the-sustainable-development-goals-sdgs-and-indigenous.html.

World Bank. 2017. The World Bank Environmental and Social Framework. https://thedocs.worldbank.org/en/doc/837721522762050108-0290022018/original/ESFFramework.pdf.

World Bank. 2018. Good Practice Note: Non-Discrimination and Disability. Environment & Social Framework for IPF Operations. https://documents1.worldbank.org/curated/en/573841530208492785/Environment-and-Social-Framework-ESF-Good-Practice-Note-on-Disability-English.pdf.

World Bank. 2023a. Environmental and Social Framework. https://www.worldbank.org/en/projects-operations/environmental-and-social-framework.

World Bank. 2023b. The Environmental and Social Safeguard Policies: The World Bank's Current Environmental and Social Policies, Consisting of our 11 Operational Policies. https://www.worldbank.org/en/projects-operations/environmental-and-social-policies#safeguards.

14 Unbundling rules of law at the peripheries of Latin American states

Annette Idler and Laurence Whitehead

The standard rule of law model presumes uniformity of law across a given national territory, with consistent enforcement, and reasonable coherence between legal domains. Latin American constitutionalism has operated within this framework over the past two centuries, yet lived experiences of formal and informal adjudication and the reality as opposed to the rhetoric of rights and obligations seldom confirms the accuracy of this model.

Especially on the geographical periphery of most states in Latin America, communities learn to regulate most of their affairs differently. It is not that the national legal order is irrelevant, but rather that it is applied selectively (varying according to type of law, and to segment of society) and that aspirational laws are often disconnected from capacities for enforcement or appeal.

This chapter concerns the Andean republics, paying special attention to the peripheral areas of Colombia. It "unbundles" the governance practices encountered by inhabitants of such locations. In particular, it examines three types of citizenship experiences that fall outside the conventional rule of law framework due to the weakness or absence of state authority. First, citizens can self-organize to maintain their livelihoods and replace the missing state. Second, violent non-state actors can substitute for state structures, while benefiting from a certain degree of local consent (so-called "shadow citizenship"). Or, third, citizens can be left unprotected either by the state or by violent non-state actors, and only able to pursue their livelihoods through illicit means (e.g., illegal cross-border transactions).

Under such conditions, standard concepts of "citizenship" and "governance" require some recasting to reflect the lived realities of affected communities and populations. There are three key features of politics as experienced "from below" in peripheral regions that are particularly consequential for reconsidering conventional mantras concerning "legitimacy" and "rule of law." First, whatever the discourse may be of those holding power and/or exercising authority, in practice they can hardly expect to exercise permanent, exclusive, and unified control over all aspects of public life in the given community. Local non-state actors, such as community associations or illicit actors, also impose rules and exercise practical control. The nation-state cannot reliably provide all the administrative, security, and other services implied by its formal claims to sovereignty, but neither

DOI: 10.4324/9781003519195-14

can violent non-state actors such as guerrillas, or their paramilitary antagonists, or the organized crime contestants for local resources. Instead, these diverse actors engage in some form of hybrid, or complementary, governance with fluid arrangements among each other that can range from competition due to drives for exclusive domination at times, to some formula of tacit coexistence or even explicit cooperation in the form of strategic alliances and sharing of governance functions (Idler and Forest 2015). Second, then, in such a state of fragile equilibrium, ideologically opposed groups do not necessarily fight each other. To the contrary, citizens soon adjust to the realization that enemies can enter pacts, and that apparent allies can prove deceptive and indeed treacherous. Third, and finally, even the most ruthless and criminal of rent-seeking power contenders will find it in their interest to enlist a certain degree of social support. If they are to hold their own against their rivals, they will sometimes need to invest in shoring up their bases. Taken together, these three political imperatives generate a contested and unstable set of rules governing communal resource allocation and dispute resolution, and they fragment the operations of local citizenship. But they do not abolish the exercise of authority or eliminate all sense of underlying rights and duties. They weaken and complexify "rule of law" understandings but leave such principles of compliance – and even empirical legitimacy – intact.

Moreover, at state borders, the national jurisdictions that operate on each side of the border often clash, rather than being coordinated. This gives rise to a space of impunity, especially when crime and other breaches of the law concern border-crossing activities such as smuggling. Given the diversity in governance actors who oversee not only the provision of security, basic services, and certain judicial mechanisms but also the economic domain, a "moral economy" can emerge that provisionally legitimizes illegal transactions in the eyes of the local populations. This is particularly the case where state-provided legal economic opportunities are scarce. Overall, in such contexts, the stark divide between "rule of law" and "unrule of law" principles can be too reductionist to capture the tacit norms and mixed understandings that govern real practice.

The communal view from below can be subject to severe discontinuities. Local power can shift back and forth according to the vagaries of civil conflict and criminal ambition. Consequently, the really existing rule of law in any given community has to be "unbundled" into its variable spatial, temporal, and topical components. For example, national authority may gain traction when there is an election due, with electoral candidates promising more state presence as part of their campaign, or when a police or military presence is temporarily reinforced. But even then, at nighttime or in the more inaccessible zones, effective control may lie elsewhere. After an army offensive or a peace treaty, guerrilla challengers may withdraw or even disarm, but then other violent actors (perhaps with more single-minded criminal intent) may fill the void. Some claimants to power may care about land tenure, whereas others are focused on the recruitment of combatants, or the settling of partisan feuds. Non-violent claimants to local leadership, such as clerics or teachers, may carve out islands of authority on issues of family law or educational practice that the masters of violence are content to delegate to them. Where this is so, legitimacy and governance need to be "unbundled."

This chapter draws on fieldwork from a range of conflictive and differently (non-state) governed regions across Colombia, Ecuador, and Venezuela to "unbundle" practices of governance. They are widespread, entrenched, but also unstable and inconsistent. They may need to be improved but for that to work they first need to be anatomized and taken seriously. We focus on three different types of practices that all coexist with each other and with the selective, albeit deficient, presence of a state-imposed rule of law. The first one concerns the rules and practices imposed by citizens themselves. In this case, where the state does not have the capacity or the will to implement the rule of law, citizens self-organize to make everyday life and people's coexistence orderly. The second type of practices concerns situations where, again, non-state actors replace the state in setting the rules of the game. Yet, in this case, it is violent non-state actors, that is, illicit authorities, who are the agents of this form of governance. To understand how communities are embedded and partake in these dynamics, we draw on the concept of shadow citizenship, which we explain in the next section. Finally, the third type of practices constitutes a grey zone, whereby citizens are caught between the state and state-imposed rules and regulations, yet in absence of fully granted rights and privileges on the one hand and illicit authorities who provide opportunities to citizens in the illicit economy but fall short of providing adequate protection to them, on the other hand. Citizens here benefit from the gap between the state's formal establishment of the law and the shortcomings in its enforcement, yet they are also trapped in this gap as they are not able to resort to protection from either side: neither from the state nor the illicit actors.

While people's self-organization in the first type of practices of rules is relatively self-explanatory, we start by discussing two key concepts that guide our analysis in the second and third types, namely, shadow citizenship and the moral economy.

We then "unbundle" these various practices by providing evidence of their existence in the peripheries of the Andean region, especially in remote regions of Colombia, Ecuador, and Venezuela. We thereby demonstrate that the binary distinction between the rule of law and the unrule of law does not hold in such contexts. Rather, we can conceive of these practices as multiple overlapping rules and norms (including both those that arise from the state and those that arise from non-state actors) that citizens need to navigate.

Shadow citizenship and the moral economy of the Andean borderlands

Shadow citizenship

To understand how rules and practices are shaped in the authoritative presence of illicit armed actors, we draw on the concept of "shadow citizenship" (Idler 2014; 2018). This concept diverges from other frameworks such as "illicit authority" (Hall and Biersteker 2002), which pivots around a state-centric critique of illegality, or "rebel governance," centred on the operations of violent non-state entities (Mampilly 2011). Instead, "shadow citizenship" illuminates the pivotal role of civilian agency, underscoring how individual and collective actions can, to a meaningful extent, sculpt the contours of this unique form of governance.

"Shadow citizenship" comes to the fore in contexts where traditional state–society bonds are frayed or dysfunctional, heralding a paradigm where violent non-state actors step into roles traditionally filled by state entities. In these scenarios, these groups not only stipulate norms and rules of conduct but also provide public goods and services, thus establishing a complex web of mutual reliance with the community. This symbiotic relationship grants these non-state actors a form of "empirical legitimacy," echoing Hall and Biersteker's (2002, 216) notion that such governance mechanisms can indeed garner the Lockean consent of those governed. Consequently, "shadow citizenship" embodies a sophisticated array of unauthorized, yet institutionalized, organizational structures that dictate behaviour within realms governed by these illicit forces.

In a departure from the conventional understanding of illicit authority, the notion of "shadow citizenship" repositions civilians not merely as subjects under an imposed authority but as active participants within their social milieu. This reimagining is predicated on the recognition that citizenship, at its core, is woven into the social fabric and built upon interpersonal trust. Anthropological inquiries into the state-society nexus, especially but not exclusively within conflict settings, have similarly elevated the role of citizens, exploring concepts such as "insurgent citizenship," "alternative citizenship" (Oomen 2004; Holston 2008), and "low-intensity citizenship" (O'Donnell 1993). In scenarios where the state's capacity to fulfil its governance role is found wanting, these frameworks suggest that individuals have the potential to be galvanized, aligning their actions with the principles of democratic legality to forge pathways toward a more inclusive, democratic, and liberal form of citizenship (O'Donnell 1993, 1361).

"Shadow citizenship" diverges from these models by shifting the locus of legitimacy from the state to a violent non-state actor, thereby redefining the traditional social contract. In this recalibrated arrangement, the violent non-state group assumes the roles and responsibilities typically reserved for the state, creating an alternate governance structure where empirical legitimacy and authority are derived from a different source (Idler 2014). This conceptual shift underscores a complex reconfiguration of societal dynamics, where the interplay between authority and citizenship is reimagined against the backdrop of unconventional governance.

In the context of armed conflict, the governance mechanisms exercised by violent non-state entities frequently hinge on the use of violence or coercion to enforce adherence. This dynamic gives rise to what is termed as "shadow citizen security," a phenomenon characterized by a somewhat consensual accord struck between these groups and the communities. Under this pact, communities agree to abide by the rules unilaterally set forth by these actors, in exchange for a semblance of security and justice (Idler 2014). Within the confines of this arrangement, the physical safety of community members largely remains intact, contingent upon their compliance with the established norms. Deviation from these rules, however, invokes severe repercussions, including threats, physical assault, and even death, epitomizing the essence of *shadow* citizen security.

This concept underscores a critical shift wherein the control of violence, a hallmark of Weberian sovereignty, is effectively commandeered by non-state actors, eclipsing the state's own regulatory framework. Despite the rarity of physical violence within the purview of shadow citizen security, its potential application is generally deemed a justified, if not legitimate, form of coercion by the populace, provided it is executed in a discernibly non-arbitrary manner. Instances of rule defiance serve as prime illustrations of this principle, where the measures employed by these non-state entities are viewed not as unwarranted brutality but as a necessary enforcement of order (Idler 2014). Such views can arise from implicit social norms that regulate a given community's understanding of their "moral economy."

The moral economy of the Andean borderlands

Building upon E.P. Thompson's seminal 1971 exploration of eighteenth-century food riots, the notion of a "moral economy" emerges as a nuanced framework for interpreting economic exchanges. This conceptualization transcends the narrow confines of capitalist market dynamics, drawing instead upon the rich tapestry of societal and cultural processes (Polanyi 2001). Through this lens, economic interactions are not merely transactions governed by the invisible hand of the market or analyzed solely through the distribution of wealth and its correlation with societal power structures, as is the case with *political* economy analyses. A moral economy approach delves into the lived experiences and perceptions of individuals enmeshed within these economic exchanges, recognizing the empirical legitimacy bestowed upon certain activities by those involved, particularly in the absence of viable legal alternatives for livelihood (Idler 2021).

The moral economy perspective highlights community perceptions "from below" concerning legitimate principles and procedures for dispute resolution of matters not justly addressed by the ostensible legal authorities (including issues not dealt with at all). As a historian, Thompson was explicitly focused on

English rural life during the industrial revolution, so some care is needed when generalizing from his core case to other settings. For example, whatever moral economy practices may have existed in the Scottish highlands, or among the Catholic peasantry in Ireland under the protestant ascendancy, these local communities were unlike his English villages in that they faced mass dispossession and expulsions (such as the Highland Clearances). In rural England, there was also some judicial harsh treatment (parliamentary acts of land enclosure, Justices of the Peace who were liable to sentence poachers to transportation to Australia for the most minor of property offenses, etc.), but there was some mutual accommodation of interests through local consultations and electoral processes, which over time gave rural workers some stake in the system. Thompson's "moral economy" expressed local claims that stood some chance of a conditional hearing as opposed to outright rejection and indiscriminate repression. Subsequently James Scott (1976) extended the scope of this analysis by turning to the revolutionary conditions faced by peasants in colonial Malaya and later in Myanmar. He makes a distinction between "domination," when the local communities are in direct conflict with the law (as was the case in the 1960s with Colombia's *republiquetas*), and the unstable "hegemony" that mostly concerned Thompson. In the cases he dealt with, peasants:

> were in the throes of being incorporated into both a more implacable state and a larger market. Their reflex was self-protection [...] trying to revivify and enforce certain hard-won understandings of minimal subsistence rights owed to thereby landlords and local elites, and to appeal to an older and more flexible tax system.
>
> (Scott 2005, 397)

This collective reflex should not be seen as an appeal to some romanticized past of earlier goodwill or noblesse oblige, but rather as a reminder to landowners and their allies of the huge potential for theft, arson, and even rebellion if peasant smallholders were pressed too hard (Scott 2005; see also Palomera and Vetta 2016). Such local moral economy reflexes may survive and resurface across generations despite traumatic upheavals, in the absence of a convincing and durable state presence.

In the unique milieu of the Andean borderlands, the intricate web of social life becomes linked with the clandestine currents of cross-border flows, notably those associated with the illicit cocaine trade and the entrenched dynamics of the Colombian armed conflict. To comprehend the moral economy of this region demands an illumination of the complex interplay between the shadowy realms of transnational organized crime and the enduring structures of local social order. This endeavour involves an immersive exploration into the lived experiences of communities as they navigate and shape the economic realities born from this illicit trade. It also requires a critical examination of the stark contrasts between these local perceptions of legitimacy and the external, state-centric perspectives that often prioritize the illegality of the cocaine business above all else.

Through the prism of a moral economy, we gain a nuanced understanding of the interplay between the shadow economies that flourish in the interstices of legality and the overarching structures of legal governance. The lived realities of those dwelling in Latin America's marginalized expanses, such as the Andean borderlands, serve to erode the very bedrock of state legitimacy in their eyes. Such experiences exacerbate the chasm separating these communities, already peripherally situated, from the central authority of the state. In varying locales, the essence of authority – whether wielded by the state or by violent non-state actors – derives from the ability to furnish essential services and public goods, encompassing both security and justice. The dispensation of economic opportunities by these authorities represents merely one facet of the multifaceted strategies deployed to secure the allegiance of the populace. However, the inherent scepticism that violent non-state factions harbour towards local communities renders the attainment of such illicit authority, or shadow citizenship, an arduous endeavour. This scepticism breeds a palpable fear of retribution among the communities for any perceived infractions of the rules, further strained by the arbitrary nature of such punitive measures. Yet these very non-state entities can mitigate such tensions by offering alternative economic opportunities in spaces where the state's legal provisions fall short. These illicit opportunities, emerging in contexts marked by economic precarity, inadvertently cultivate a sense of loyalty towards these non-state actors over the state. This dynamic is bolstered by a proclivity for transgression, a phenomenon borne out of the tacit legitimacy conferred upon these underground economic activities. Such activities estrange the populace from the state, simultaneously drawing them nearer to the sphere of illegal entities (Korf and Raeymaekers 2013, 5).

Consequently, the state, as personified by its customs officials, police, and military personnel, may inadvertently morph into a more formidable adversary to the everyday sustenance of the people than the armed factions themselves (Vorrath 2010, 85–87). This reality is encapsulated in Andreas's (2009, 22) observation that the very definition and viability of smuggling hinge upon the state's monopolistic exertion of its authority to criminalize, coupled with its inconsistent capability or inclination to enforce such laws.

The capacity of armed actors to offer economic opportunities within the realms of the cocaine trade and its ancillary markets not only exacerbates the alienation of communities from the state apparatus but also fosters a closer affinity with these non-state entities in various Andean republics. This dynamic significantly broadens the citizens' tolerance threshold for illicit conduct and the associated risks imposed by these armed groups. Despite potential reservations about embracing such risks, individuals find themselves ensnared in a state of uncertainty. They stand to gain from the chasm between the formal edicts of the state and its erratic enforcement – a phenomenon Holston (2008) terms as "disjunction." Yet, this very disjunction also subjects them to hardship. Given their entanglement in unauthorized activities, these communities are precluded from seeking the state's protection, rendering them vulnerable to exploitation by armed factions without the latter fearing retribution. This precarious balance mutes any appeals for justice, leaving grievances unvoiced and unresolved.

Having set out two concepts central to unbundling the various practices through which multiple forms of rules of law overlap in the peripheries of the Andes, we now turn to discussing three types of practices: those driven by citizens, those by illicit armed actors, and those that take place in the grey zone between the state-imposed rule of law and the illegal, yet perceived as legitimate, opportunities provided by illicit armed actors.

Type one: Citizen practices and the rule of law

Communities self-organizing against the backdrop of an absent state is a widespread practice not just in contexts of marginalized and conflict-affected regions in Latin America but across the globe, especially to replace governance functions that may otherwise be implemented by local state entities. In the Andean borderlands, these functions often include everyday life concerns such as fixing local bridges themselves rather than waiting in vain for the state to come in or charging road tolls to do road work themselves by spanning a cord across a road and making motorists who want to pass pay.

We highlight here one particular practice as it demonstrates that citizens go even further and impose their own rule of law for self-protection where the state's theoretical rule of law does not reach them in practice. What is more, as the following illustration demonstrates, it is sometimes even the citizens' rule of law that protects the supposed rule-of-law-providers of the state. The example concerns so-called peace communities, or peace territories, that emerged in the context of the Colombian armed conflict in various remote, marginalized, war-torn regions. In these territories, communities establish their own manuals of coexistence and make any armed actor – both state actors and non-state actors – abide by them. Our discussion here draws on fieldwork conducted in two of these communities, in Samaniego, a village in the Colombian department of Nariño, and in Las Mercedes, a village in the Catatumbo region of the Colombian department of Norte de Santander.[1]

In the heart of Samaniego, a dramatic event unfolded in 1997 when the left-wing guerrillas National Liberation Army (ELN) abducted Manuel Cuéllar, a mayoral candidate, just on the cusp of his potential election. The spirited response of Samaniego's residents culminated in his release, setting the stage for Cuéllar to advocate for a pioneering initiative: the declaration of Samaniego as a peace territory upon assuming office in 1998 (Rojas 2004, 78; El Tiempo 1997a; 1997c; 1997b; Cadena and Quiñonez 2002). The political landscape of Samaniego saw a notable shift in 2000 with the election of a new mayor, heralding a period of community polarization. While local governance structures, instrumental in the civil resistance narrative, sought to renew dialogues with the guerrilla factions, segments of the civil society, including influential youth leaders and educators, championed the cause of sustaining the peace territory vision, free from guerrilla meddling (Idler, Garrido, and Mouly 2015). Despite these divergences, the resilience of civil society shone through as they navigated these complexities, upholding the principles set forth by local leaders while diligently working at the grassroots level to bridge the emerging divides.

The fabric of Samaniego's society was interwoven with its interactions with armed entities, prominently featuring the ELN as the predominant insurgent force, alongside the Revolutionary Armed Forces of Colombia (FARC), paramilitary groups, their right-wing successors, and national security forces. The communal narrative was enriched by personal connections spanning these armed factions, particularly with the ELN, revealing a deeply entrenched network of affiliations (Idler, Garrido, and Mouly 2015). A notable historical footnote is Montúfar's engagement in the 1980s with a community organization that served as a crucible for future ELN leaders. This legacy of collaboration and shared history empowered Montúfar to forge a peace pact under the auspices of the ELN, embodying a collective aspiration for neutrality and non-violence amidst conflict. The efficacy of these negotiations was bolstered by the existing rapport between the community and the guerrillas, further facilitated by the decentralized command structure of the ELN, allowing for local-level decision-making processes (Idler, Garrido, and Mouly 2015).

State security forces, encompassing both the police and military, were integral participants in discussions aimed at local peace accords. However, the dynamics of these relationships often oscillated between cooperation and tension. Complicating matters, the police station's central location in the city – nestled among the mayor's office, places of worship, and commercial establishments – transformed the area into a potential flashpoint, given its attractiveness as a military target for insurgent groups. The strategic positioning of these state entities, particularly during the implementation of President Uribe's Democratic Security Policy in the late 2000s, further strained the delicate balance of local security. The establishment of a military base, merely a stone's throw from the heart of the community, heightened the risks faced by residents. Guerrilla tactics, including the deployment of landmines to thwart the advance of military personnel towards strategic mountainous terrains in 2008, effectively ensnared the local populace within an invisible siege (Order 284).

Despite these adversities, the community demonstrated resilience and ingenuity in navigating their precarious circumstances. Unable to alter the physical realities of the police station or military base, they nonetheless brokered a tentative truce with the guerrillas. This agreement carved out a semblance of autonomy for the beleaguered residents, granting them specified time windows for safe passage out of the encircled community. A novel aspect of this arrangement was the provision of two mobile phones to the community, serving as lifelines to contact the guerrillas in emergencies, thereby ensuring their unharmed departure from the contested zones (Idler, Garrido, and Mouly 2015).

Las Mercedes, where the ELN once wielded significant influence, constitutes another, albeit less successful, example of citizens establishing their own rule of law. In the wake of paramilitary aggression that marred the rebel-held territories, 2005 witnessed the birth of the "Friends for Peace" initiative in the Las Mercedes community. Spearheaded by a coalition of visionary community leaders, this movement sought to weave a tapestry of reconciliation through informal gatherings, advocating for collective resistance to the corrosive impacts of conflict on communal life. Anchored in a Declaration of Pacific Coexistence, the community's journey towards peace was founded on a delicate balance of neutrality and non-violence, engaging in negotiations with the armed groups that traversed their lands. The initiative persuaded the armed factions to spare the community from warfare.

However, the nascent peace was short-lived. The fragile détente was shattered in 2007 with the assassination of two key peace advocates, exposing the challenges of dialogue with entities such as the FARC, known for their rigid hierarchical command structures that afford little autonomy to local units (Insight Crime 2015). This rigidity complicated any negotiation efforts, as it demanded uniform adherence to the central leadership's edicts. The killings and internal discord led to the dissolution of the "Friends for Peace," plunging Las Mercedes back into acquiescence to the dictates of militarized control.

A turning point emerged in 2013 when, under the auspices of local clergy, the embers of the "Friends for Peace" were rekindled by both its original architects and a new generation of Las Mercedes' youth. This rejuvenated coalition shifted the narrative from direct opposition to armed engagement to a broader vision of social and economic revitalization. By navigating away from the contentious politics of armed resistance, they aimed to foster a unified community ethos that could rally the entire populace. Despite these efforts, deep-seated divisions regarding the community's stance towards the ongoing conflict persisted, casting a shadow over the collective aspiration for a path forward. The quest for consensus on engaging with the complexities of war remained a challenge (focus group with leaders of Las Mercedes, 2014).

By 2014, Las Mercedes found itself under the predominant sway of the FARC, while also serving as a strategic corridor for the ELN, the insurgent Popular Liberation Army (EPL), and various right-wing factions. The labyrinth of negotiating with armed groups was further complicated by the internal rifts within the community itself. Effective negotiation hinges on the establishment of trust-based direct communication channels. Yet, in the absence of mutual trust among community members, these channels are vulnerable to manipulation by individuals seeking to advance personal agendas, malign others, or gatekeep information flow between the guerrillas and the community, potentially skewing the transmission of crucial data (Kaplan 2013, 354). This atmosphere of suspicion coerced residents into compliance with the guerrillas' mandates rather than championing change. These impositions, ranging from weekday alcohol bans to restrictions on nocturnal movement, were ostensibly respected by the guerrillas as long as the community adhered to them, according to insights from civil society representatives in 2014.

Mirroring the situation in Samaniego, the police station in the heart of the city centre became a focal point of tension. Residents in its proximity, wary of becoming collateral damage in guerrilla assaults at night, adopted a routine of seeking refuge with relatives or friends in safer locales, returning only with the dawn's light (based on various interviews from 2014). The community's protracted battle for safety culminated in a legal victory in June 2013, when a national court decreed the police station's relocation. Yet, a year on, this mandate remained unfulfilled (La Opinión 2013), and – as in many other contested locations – not even the national peace accord of 2016 ensured an effective official policing presence. The residents' assertive stance for relocation, perceived as more confrontational towards state authorities than towards the guerrillas, inadvertently cast them in a contentious light. This strategic, yet fraught, positioning led some to label the community as allies of the FARC, complicating the journey towards unity. The quest for impartiality, crucial for the fruition of peace territories, was thus compromised by suspicions of the community's allegiance. In essence, while the people of both Samaniego and Las Mercedes aspired to shield themselves from armed conflict and to forge zones of peace, the latter faced an uphill struggle. The perception of bias in their actions, favouring opposition to state mechanisms over insurgent forces, hindered their ability to establish a consensus-driven peace territory where all armed factions adhered to a unified set of regulations. Overall, as these examples demonstrate, citizens can impose their own rule of law, even amidst competing rules imposed by both the state and violent non-state actors.

Type two: Shadow citizenship and the rule of law

We now unbundle the second type of practices that form part of the multiple rules of law that coexist and overlap in the peripheries of the Andes. These are rules imposed by illicit armed actors, yet respected and consented to by citizens, yielding shadow citizenship. To demonstrate this, we draw on an example of shadow citizenship imposed in the Venezuelan state of Apure in the 2010s.[2] While this vignette concerns Venezuela, it involves Colombia-based guerrilla forces that took shelter across the international border.

In the remote expanse of Venezuelan Alto Apure, a unique détente unfolded in the 2010s, with the Bolivarian Forces of Liberation (Fuerzas Bolivarianas de Liberación – FBL), the FARC, and the ELN engaging in pacific coexistence. This concord stemmed from a collective aspiration for societal acknowledgment, particularly evident in the ELN's endeavours to administer justice within the community, addressing a spectrum of grievances from neighbourly disputes to theft and property damage. Elvira Restrepo (2009), in her examination of the Colombian Justice System, articulates the pivotal role justice systems play in conferring legitimacy, asserting that "the legitimacy of state authority rests on the ability to support and uphold just institutions." This principle of legitimacy extends beyond the confines of state machinery to encompass violent non-state actors as well.

During fieldwork in Apure by one of the authors, a local cleric shared insights that illustrated the community's reliance on these groups for conflict resolution, stating, "If a cow gets lost, people run to the guerrillas. They always run to the guerrillas!" His observations underscored the guerrillas' role in dispensing what he described as "Solomonic solutions" to the community's challenges. The insurgents, in a gesture of measured respect, acknowledged the decisions made by certain segments of the local community. This reciprocity fostered a climate where the directives laid down by the insurgents found a degree of acceptance among the populace. During an interview in 2012, a female farmer from Alto Apure imparted her perspective on the regulations established by the leftist factions, offering a window into the nuanced relationship between the insurgents and the community they influenced.

She recounted that a meeting was convened in the community, attracting many attendees, though she admitted to typically abstaining from such gatherings. This time, however, the invitation seemed to emanate from the communal council, prompting widespread participation, only to reveal upon arrival that the organizers were, in fact, the insurgent group. This group, known to the farmer and not affiliated with the council, aimed to establish certain "rules of coexistence," addressing issues such as the maintenance of clear pathways and the management of livestock. These rules stipulated fines for non-compliance, such as leaving animals unattended on the farm tracks, with penalties designed to enforce cleanliness and order within the community.

The farmer acknowledged the practicality of these regulations, noting their effectiveness in mitigating the overgrowth of farm tracks, a common issue in the area. Despite the imposition of fines, the community had come to accept these measures as part of their collective responsibility, recognizing the necessity of external enforcement to maintain cleanliness. The farmer reflected on the broader issue of community engagement in self-governance, lamenting the lack of initiative among residents to independently upkeep their surroundings, pointing out the perennial neglect of farm tracks as a testament to this apathy.

In this scenario, the regulatory role played by the guerrillas served a dual purpose, reflecting a nuanced approach to governance. The establishment of coexistence rules transcended the pursuit of mere territorial control, aiming instead to garner civic consent through the application of structured, community-oriented regulations. This approach facilitated the management of daily issues faced by farmers, ensuring their autonomy was preserved. The imposition of fines, as opposed to resorting to violence or humiliation, fostered a climate of respect over fear, embodying a strategic shift towards non-coercive methods of compliance.

Such a strategy is particularly effective in scenarios where the objective is to minimize the reliance on violent enforcement while broadening the group's influence within the community. The historical backdrop of violence employed by these groups lays a foundation that obviates the need for its continual use once dominance is established. Instead, a focus on addressing communal concerns and abstaining from violence serves to solidify the group's support base, ensuring a harmonious coexistence.

Reflecting on the period before 2010, the farmer noted a shift in tactics from coercive compliance to seeking social acknowledgement through more peaceful means. This evolution in strategy indicates a deliberate move towards fostering a stable and cooperative environment, prioritizing the well-being and consent of the community over the imposition of control through fear and violence.

The interview with the farmer further unveiled that the guerrillas were perceived as a legitimate authority by the community, highlighting a complex layer of the relationship between armed factions and local populations. When questioned about any disagreeable regulations, the farmer expressed concerns over restrictions on timber harvesting, specifically the prohibition against cutting green wood. This rule, according to the farmer, posed significant challenges for agricultural activities, casting doubt on the community's ability to cultivate crops and sustain themselves. Upon inquiry, it was revealed that the guerrillas had provided some leeway, allowing the felling of up to three hectares of trees, framing any excess as detrimental.

The woman, while critical of the specific regulation against cutting green wood, did not contest the authority of the guerrillas to enforce such rules. Her acceptance of the guerrillas' governance role as a given demonstrates a form of adaptation to shadow citizenship, where the insurgents' authority is normalized within the community. She even adopted the neutral designation "organization" for the guerrillas, a term they themselves use, indicating a degree of legitimacy attributed to their presence. This normalization of the guerrillas' role was evident in their integration into local governance structures, such as communal councils and potentially even the mayor's office in Guasdualito, a town in Apure, signifying their pervasive and accepted influence within the community.

This acceptance extended to broader societal support for violent non-state actors, especially when communities felt abandoned or marginalized by the state. This sentiment was also vividly illustrated by a teacher in the Colombian southern department of Putumayo during a 2012 community meeting, who articulated a collective sense of betrayal by the state, highlighting deficiencies in infrastructure and basic services while the military was the sole state representative. In contrast, the guerrillas, particularly the FARC, were perceived as more dependable, having filled the vacuum left by the state in areas like health care and road construction, thereby earning the community's trust and respect. Their ability to provide security and meet community needs led to a form of shadow citizen security, where the guerrillas, not the state, were seen as the primary guarantors of safety and welfare, further cementing their role as de facto governance providers. This dynamic underscores a complex relationship where, despite the illicit nature of their authority, the guerrillas managed to secure a form of consent and empirical legitimacy through their actions and engagement with the community.

To be sure, not all territories with a ruling armed non-state actor featured such relatively consensual relationships between this actor and the community. In many situations, the armed actor imposed its own rules and order through brutal coercion. Authority was accepted based on fear, not consent. Yet, as this example demonstrates, there are cases of at least some form of consent, problematizing the absence of a state-imposed rule of law as a new order emerges.

Type three: The grey zone space of the rule of law

The third practice that establishes rules and norms overlapping with state-imposed laws and the unrule of law concerns the illegal space that emerges, especially in border areas, where two different economic systems clash, and two jurisdictions come together without necessarily being in sync with each other. The mismatch of two different economic systems provides incentives to engage in illicit cross-border activities at varying scales, ranging from small-scale household goods contraband to serious transnational organized crime such as drug, weapons, or human trafficking. In this context, citizens take advantage of the gap between the existence of laws and the state's inability to enforce them. Yet they also benefit from alternative livelihood options offered by powerful armed non-state actors in this illegal setting. A moral economy perspective shows why these practices are accepted and tolerated, yet it also demonstrates how they put citizens into a limbo situation that is hard to escape as none of the existing rules of law – neither state-provided nor non-state-provided ones – fully protect them.

We illustrate this with the example of gasoline smuggling across the Colombia–Venezuela border, where various forms of gasoline smuggling occur. Despite its illegality, local communities, particularly in Cúcuta, have come to regard the practice of smuggling, especially gasoline from Venezuelan San Antonio, as a legitimate aspect of their livelihood strategy. A high-ranking police official in Cúcuta corroborated this sentiment, noting that for residents, engaging in contraband activities is not merely a choice but a necessity dictated by the unique challenges of living in a border zone. The community's entanglement with guerrilla, paramilitary, and criminal organizations has woven a culture of illegality into the fabric of daily life, normalizing contraband as an economic lifeline and giving rise to shadow economies that, while unofficial, are vital for survival.

This normalization of smuggling as an open secret was evident to anyone traversing the border, where the flux of vehicles and people betrays a bustling contraband trade. The widespread acceptance and participation in smuggling underscore a complex reality where, against a backdrop of limited economic options and persistent conflict, illegal practices morph into a sanctioned part of community life, challenging conventional notions of legality and survival in border regions.

Even when locals partake in what might be considered a relatively benign form of gasoline smuggling, dealing in small quantities, the shadow of a vast, illicit gasoline trade looms large. This larger network involves a diverse array of armed factions, from Colombian insurgents to Venezuelan traffickers, complicating the regional dynamics and inadvertently branding the local populace as complicit. Such associations amplify their exposure to potential exploitation from both state forces and irregular armed groups, embedding them deeper into a cycle of vulnerability and mistrust.

This labelling of locals as collaborators has significant implications for the foundational state–society relationship that underpins notions of citizen security. It directly impacts how citizens perceive their role in maintaining security and how they view the state's obligations towards their protection. The stigma attached to gasoline smuggling exacerbates the risks faced by these individuals and their families, deterring them from seeking redress for injustices for fear of implicating themselves in illicit activities. Extortion, then, becomes a resignedly accepted part of their economic reality, seen as a necessary evil to secure a semblance of protection from both legal authorities and criminal elements. This precarious situation raises questions about the dual roles of law enforcement personnel who may covertly align with the very groups accused of exploiting the community.

In such an environment, where economic desperation prevails, and the pursuit of profit dominates, the blurred lines between oppressor and protector serve to enhance the sway of violent non-state actors over the community. This dynamic fosters a perverse form of allegiance to these groups, driven by a shared interest in circumventing state regulations and maximizing illicit gains. The resulting "tendency toward transgression," as noted by Benedikt Korf and Timothy Raeymakers (2013), not only erodes the empirical legitimacy of state authority but also positions it as a more immediate threat to the community's welfare than the non-state actors themselves. For those living on the margins, the very concept of the state becomes abstract, defined solely by its mechanisms of control and exclusion. As Peter Andreas (2009) observes, the act of smuggling thrives on the state's selective enforcement of its laws, creating a liminal space where individuals navigate the precarity of their existence, simultaneously benefiting from and being harmed by this legal ambiguity.

Gasoline smuggling is just one example of many in which citizens are caught between these two extremes of the (un)rule of law. Similar dilemmas exist in the context of cross-border communities involved in coca cultivation. Communities residing in the Ecuadorian northern border zone, for example, were affected by a situation in which they suffered abuse by the Colombian FARC, whose control reached across the border from Colombia into Ecuador during the 2000s and 2010s up until their demobilization. They were unable to seek protection from the Ecuadorian authorities, however, as they worked in coca cultivation across the border in Colombia and hence engaged in illegal activities themselves. Again, while justified from a moral economy perspective as alternative legal economic opportunities were scarce, this very practice made them extremely vulnerable to abuse.

Conclusion

In concluding this chapter, it's pivotal to reflect on the insights gathered during field trips to Colombia's conflict-ridden border regions. A poignant observation from an interviewee, "Colombia has more territory than state," resonates deeply, underscoring the vast areas under minimal state influence and the consequent vacuum filled by armed groups like the FARC. A visit to Tumaco in 2016, a critical juncture for the FARC as they prepared for demobilization, illuminated the complex dynamics of governance, peace, and the state's role – or its absence – in these territories. The FARC's assertion of being a surrogate state for local communities highlighted a critical gap in the Colombian government's reach and responsibilities.

This sentiment was echoed in 2017, when a local farmer's remark, "War is more than armed conflict," encapsulated the ongoing struggles for basic services, security, and justice, even after the cessation of armed hostilities. These experiences reveal the intricate overlay of legal and extra-legal governance, challenging the binary perception of law and lawlessness. The strategic location of state institutions, such as police stations, often exacerbates the vulnerability of civilians, further complicating the narrative of state protection and lawful order.

In protracted civil wars, some governance functions may be provided by violent non-state groups that are likely to rely on coercion to achieve compliance. So-called shadow citizen security can therefore arise, with a local community complying with illicitly imposed rules in exchange for a certain degree of relative security and even rough justice. In some cases (such as Colombia's early republiquetas), controlling insurgents present themselves as defending the affected population from external threats and impositions (including from unjust government intrusions). Provided these communities comply with such rules, they may indeed retain a degree of physical security, although non-compliance will provoke threats, physical harm, or expulsions. Such is the nature of "shadow" citizen security, where group control over the means of violence supersedes the state's capacity to (in Weberian terms) exercise its "legitimate" monopoly. Where such shadow security becomes well-established, the deployment of physical violence can be quite rare, and sufficiently non-arbitrary to be seen by many as a legitimate use of the means of coercion. But in protracted civil conflicts, this always somewhat precarious sense of security is subject to erosion over time due to the imperatives of survival given the resource and manpower needs of armed groups under challenge. In Colombia, for example, after six decades of intermittent warfare, surviving insurgents are those most effective at controlling recruitment and capturing resources, by whatever means necessary. Initial political idealism or concern for local community goodwill are liable to prove wasting assets given such pressures.

The journey towards re-establishing the state's empirical legitimacy in areas marred by the cocaine economy and armed conflict necessitates a multifaceted approach. It involves not only addressing the immediate economic dependencies of rural communities but also rebuilding trust and credibility. The state's role extends beyond being a mere provider of services; it must embody a source of security, justice, and economic stability, capable of countering the allure and influence of armed groups. By fostering viable legal economic pathways and infrastructure, the government can offer tangible alternatives to the illicit drug trade, thereby reducing community vulnerability and disrupting the power dynamics of criminal organizations.

The distinction between arbitrary coercion and shadow citizen security, and the implications for the state, is particularly revealing in territories with multiple violent non-state groups (as opposed to territories with a single holder of the monopoly of violence). In such cases, shadow citizen security is hard to establish. Quick changes in group constellations and frequent breakdowns of alliances make rules unpredictable and shadow citizen security elusive; punishment, expulsion, or other forms of coercion become more arbitrary and destabilizing. This disseminates constant fear and thereby undermines all constituted sources of authority (Idler 2019, 319). Even in such uncertain conditions, some elements of basic "Law and Order" may still coalesce around local community norms and aspirations, but all such pacts and compromises remain at the mercy of the contending powerholders. The proclamation of a national-level Peace Agreement could seem to provide a great opportunity to crystallize these latent normalization tendencies, and in some settings, that may indeed generate legitimacy and the reaffirmation of full citizenship. Unfortunately, however, the disempowerment of some violent groups may also, in less favoured settings, merely open the way for their equally lawless rivals to fill the resulting authority vacuum. Local geographies are highly diverse in this respect, and violently contested spaces frequently expand or contract without regard for national or subnational boundaries. As some communities emerge from the areas of open conflict, others become new hotspots of violent contention (Idler and Tkacova 2024, see Figure 14.1). In the case of Colombia, the hopes generated by the 2016 Peace Agreement were at least partially negated by the subsequent mass influx of Venezuelan refugees, further destabilizing

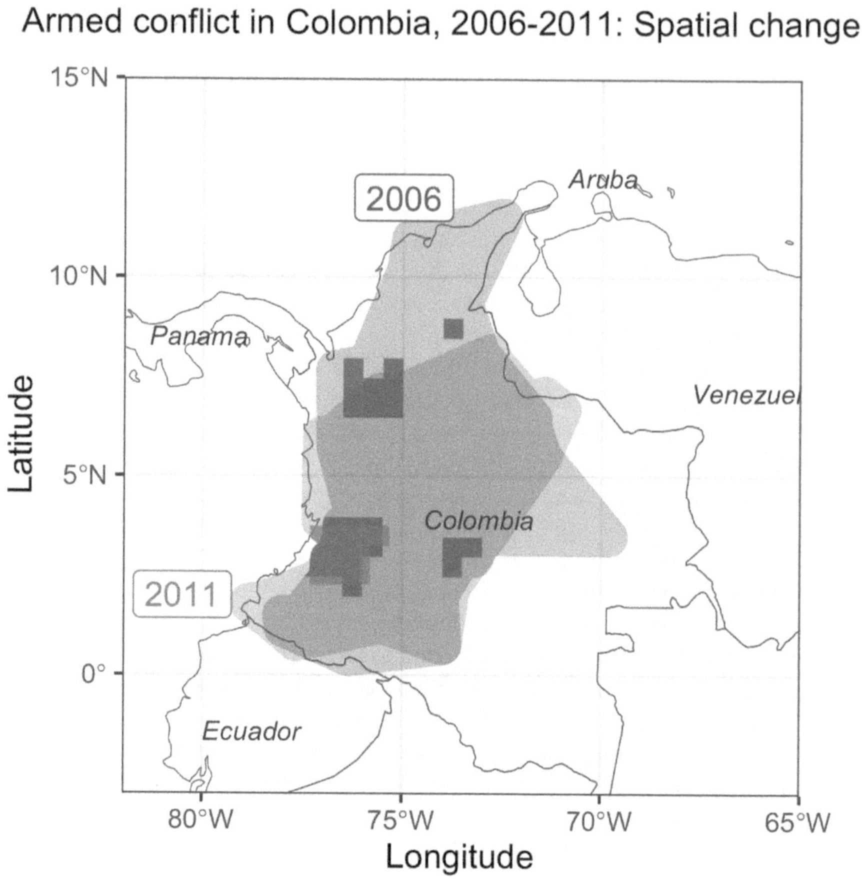

Figure 14.1 Armed conflict in Colombia: spatial change, 2006–2011.

many of the communities that had yet to establish post-conflict legitimate authorities.

Colombia provides an exceptionally durable, complex, and challenging demonstration of the divorce that can arise between rule-of-law idealizations and lived citizenship insecurities. Both the geography and the history of the republic and its neighbours contribute to the depth of this split, which is accentuated by the sophistication and high social standing of its civilian and legal elites.

At the same time, Colombia is also distinguished by the extreme brutality and cyclical recurrence of its chronic internal conflicts. The decade of "*La Violencia*" that followed the assassination of presidential contender Gaitan in 1948 was only briefly curbed by the pacted restoration of legality in 1958, after which communist "republiquetas" initiated a further cycle of rural conflicts that persisted for six decades and generated a massive level of internal displacement. Despite the peace deals of the past decade, at the end of 2022 the UN's Internal Displacement Monitoring Centre (IDMC) still registered 5.1 million persons uprooted by the conflict, making Colombia the fourth worst case in the world (after the Democratic Republic of Congo, Syria, and Ethiopia) with by far the largest number recorded in the western hemisphere.[3] (It could reasonably be objected that Colombia's records are more reliable than most, but even so the IDMC points out that since registration is voluntary, the true total could well be much higher.) The language of "citizenship" is stretched to the limit when at the minimum one in ten of the total population is internally displaced, and there are also at least a million refugees from Venezuela.

But although Colombia may be exemplary in this respect, it is far from unique. Linguistic and ethnic divisions may be greater in Peru; regional divides may be still more intractable in Bolivia and Ecuador; and the racial exclusions derived from slavery are obviously more marked in Brazil. In fact, patchy rule of law coverage has characterized most of South American political development throughout the republican era (and can, indeed, be found to varying degrees throughout the western hemisphere). Colombia's travails with shadow citizenship and the uneven distribution of legitimate authority provide an object lesson both in how these inequitable social realities need to be understood, and in what might serve to mitigate them. "*No se puede opacar el sol con un dedo, pero tampoco hay que resignarse a una noche eterna*" ("We can't ignore overwhelming realities, but nor can we surrender to despair.") In place of absolute or starkly binary disjunctive categories, the pathway to fuller citizenship for more of the population requires patience, careful diagnosis, and above all, attention to the lived experiences of real and diverse local communities.

Ultimately, the transformation of shadow citizenship into recognized and respected state citizenship hinges on the government's ability to assert its presence effectively and benevolently. It's about creating a state that is not only present in name but is actively engaged in the welfare and protection of its citizens, bridging the gap between the governed and the governing. This shift from the periphery to the core of state concern could mark a pivotal step in redefining the relationship between the state in Latin America and its most marginalized communities, setting a foundation for lasting peace and stability.

Notes

1 For a detailed comparative discussion of these two communities see Idler et al. (2015).
2 For a more detailed discussion see Idler (2019).
3 See http://www.internal-displacement.org.

References

Andreas, Peter. 2009. *Border Games: Policing the U.S.-Mexico Divide*. 2nd ed. Ithaca: Cornell University Press.

Cadena, Ingrid, and María Guinness Quiñonez. 2002. "Municipio de Samaniego: Territorio de Paz." In *Experiencias Territoriales de Construcción En Democracia de Paz y Desarrollo*, edited by Escuela Superior de Administración Pública, 95–119. Bogotá: Escuela Superior de Administración Pública.

El Tiempo. 1997a. "Todo Un Pueblo Refrenda Hoy Elección de Sus Autoridades," November 21, 1997.

El Tiempo. 1997b. "Samaniego Le Exige Respeto a La Guerrilla," November 22, 1997.

El Tiempo. 1997c. "Samaniego Quiere Decidir Su Suerte," November 24, 1997.

Hall, Rodney, and Thomas J. Biersteker. 2002. "Private Authority as Global Governance." In *The Emergence of Private Authority in Global Governance*, edited by Rodney Hall and Thomas J. Biersteker, 203–22. Cambridge: Cambridge University Press.

Holston, James. 2008. *Insurgent Citizenship: Disjunctions of Democracy and Modernity in Brazil*. Princeton, NJ: Princeton University Press.

Idler, Annette. 2014. "Espacios Invisibilizados: Actores Violentos No-Estatales y 'Ciudadanía de Sombra' En Las Zonas Fronterizas de Colombia." *Estudios Indiana*.

Idler, Annette. 2018. "Between Shadow Citizenship and Civil Resistance: Shifting Local Orders in a Colombian War-Torn Community." In *Local Peacebuilding and Legitimacy: Interactions between National and Local Levels*, edited by Annette Idler, Cécile Mouly, and María Belén Garrido, 43–62. https://doi.org/10.4324/9781315403182.

Idler, Annette. 2019. *Borderland Battles: Violence, Crime, and Governance at the Edges of Colombia's War*. New York: Oxford University Press.

Idler, Annette. 2021. "Tracing Cocaine Supply Chains from Within: Illicit Flows, Armed Conflict, and the Moral Economy of Andean Borderlands." In *The Governance of the Global Narcotics Trade*, edited by Enrique Desmond Arias and Thomas Grisaffi. Durham, NC: Duke University Press.

Idler, Annette, and James J.F. Forest. 2015. "Behavioral Patterns among (Violent) Non-State Actors: A Study of Complementary Governance." *Stability: International Journal of Security and Development* 4 (1): Art 2.

Idler, Annette, María Belén Garrido, and Cécile Mouly. 2015. "Peace Territories in Colombia: Comparing Civil Resistance In Two War-Torn Communities." *Journal of Peacebuilding & Development* 10 (3): 1–15. https://doi.org/10.1080/15423166.2015.1082437.

Idler, Annette, and Katerina Tkacova. 2024. "Conflict Shapes in Flux: Explaining Spatial Shift in Conflict-Related Violence." *International Political Science Review* 45 (1): 31–52. https://doi.org/10.1177/01925121231177445.

Insight Crime. 2015. "FARC." *InSight Crime – Organized Crime in the Americas* (blog). http://www.insightcrime.org/colombia-organized-crime-news/farc-profile?highlight=WyJmYXJjIiwiZmFyYydzIiwiJ2ZhcmMiLCInZmFyYyciXQ==.

Kaplan, Oliver. 2013. "Nudging Armed Groups: How Civilians Transmit Norms of Protection." *Stability: International Journal of Security & Development* 2 (3): 62. https://doi.org/10.5334/sta.cw.

Korf, Benedikt, and Timothy Raeymaekers. 2013. *Violence on the Margins: States, Conflict, and Borderlands*. New York, NY: Palgrave Macmillan.

La Opinión. 2013. "Los Mercedeños Se Volcaron a Las Calles," November 6, 2013. http://www.laopinion.com.co/demo/index.php?option=com_content&task=view&id=431619&Itemid=28#.VNBLO5U5DIU.

Mampilly, Zachariah. 2011. *Rebel Rulers: Insurgent Governance and Civilian Life during War*. Ithaca, NY: Cornell University Press.

O'Donnell, Guillermo. 1993. "On the State, Democratization and Some Conceptual Problems: A Latin American View with Glances at Some Postcommunist Countries." *World Development*. https://doi.org/10.1016/0305-750X(93)90048-E.

Oomen, Barbara. 2004. "Vigilantism or Alternative Citizenship? The Rise of Mapogo a Mathamaga." *African Studies* 63 (2): 153–71.

Palomera, Jaime, and Theodora Vetta. 2016. "Moral Economy: Rethinking a Radical Concept." *Anthropological Theory* 16 (4): 413–32. https://doi.org/10.1177/1463499616678097.

Polanyi, Karl. 2001. *The Great Transformation: The Political and Economic Origins of Our Time*. 2nd Beacon pbk. ed. Boston, MA: Beacon Press.

Restrepo, Elvira María. 2009. "The Pursuit of Efficiency and the Colombian Criminal Justice System." In *Criminality, Public Security, and the Challenge to Democracy in Latin America*, edited by Marcelo Bergman and Laurence Whitehead, 173–202. Recent Titles from the Helen Kellogg Institute for International Studies. Notre Dame, IN: University of Notre Dame Press.

Rojas, Catalina. 2004. "The People's Peace Processes: Local Resistance Processes and the Development of a 'Zone of Peace' in Colombia." *Reflexión Política* 6 (11): 70–87.

Scott, James C. 1976. *The Moral Economy of the Peasant: Rebellion and Subsistence in Southeast Asia*. New Haven: Yale University Press.

Scott, James C. 2005. "Afterword to 'Moral Economies, State Spaces, and Categorical Violence.'" *American Anthropologist* 107 (3): 395–402.

Vorrath, Judith. 2010. "On the Margin of Statehood? State-Society Relations in African Borderlands." In *Understanding Life in the Borderlands: Boundaries in Depth and in Motion*, edited by I. William Zartman, 85–104. Athens: University of Georgia Press.

15 Latin American state apparatuses and the rule of law

Maxwell A. Cameron

Introduction

The chapters in this book address multiple intersections of the rule of law, development, and democracy in Latin America. In this conclusion, the state apparatus is my specific point of entry into the conversation among the contributors. In a 2023 workshop in Buenos Aires, I was struck by the relevance of Peter Evans' (1989, 1995) powerful and evocative distinction between "developmental," "predatory," and "other apparatuses" to the presentation of several of the draft chapters. It seemed to me that contributors to this book were grappling with problems associated with what Evans called "intermediate states." These are states that do not approximate the ideal type of a Weberian bureaucracy but neither are they merely rent-seeking and corrupt apparatuses. In response, Laurence Whitehead proposed that we think about intermediate state apparatuses with respect to the rule of law. Since this was a topic about which Evans was silent, I agreed to explore the idea. I thought there might be "fruitful convergences" between Evans' work on the state and development and Guillermo O'Donnell's (1999, 2010) work on the rule of law and democracy.

The rule of law concerns the state's ambivalent relationship with the citizen. Behrend and Whitehead in their introduction capture a crucial tension when they write that the rule of law "encompasses more than the application of rules."[1] Formal rules and their application tell us little about the:

> ideas of justice and considerations of what is fair in a given context, how laws are created, contested, and enforced across territory...[or] how societal actors mobilise to defend competing conceptions of justice and how these competing views are negotiated in a given society.
>
> (Behrend and Whitehead, Introduction).

Beyond the view that the law should be administered fairly and impartially lies a "contested terrain" of conflicting concepts of justice, the legal assignment of rights, and democratic citizenship that "only in part is played out on the basis of legal/juristic reasons" (O'Donnell 2010: 111). Understanding the tensions and ambivalences within this contested terrain demands a focus on states, their

DOI: 10.4324/9781003519195-15

legal systems, the social relations they uphold and reproduce, and the patterns of mobilization and resistance they generate.

The following pages explore the implications of the uneven rule of law as an aspect of intermediate state apparatuses for developmental outcomes and the quality of democratic regimes in Latin America. I suggest five ways in which intermediate state apparatuses struggle to uphold the rule of law, all of which are discussed in various chapters of this book. These include (1) subnational variation in effectiveness and enforcement of the law; (2) privileging the legal rights of investors over citizens affected by extractive industries; (3) reliance on informality for social reproduction; (4) the spread of armed non-state actors where the state lacks presence and penetration; and, finally, (5) patterns of democratic delinquency, republican corruption, and other practices that undermine the quality of democracy.

Before proceeding, however, several observations on the state, state apparatuses, and the rule of law are in order. In the next section, I discuss the relevance of Max Weber's theory of the state for our understanding of the rule of law through the work of Evans and, especially, O'Donnell.

State power and the rule of law

In an article written at the height of the Washington Consensus, Peter Evans (1989) took issue with the claim that all Third World states are invariably predatory or rent-seeking. He argued that whether states are developmental or predatory depends on their internal bureaucratic structure and external societal connections. Predatory states possess neither coherent bureaucracies (in the Weberian sense) nor autonomy from private interests. Such states lack the capacity to restrain incumbents from pursuing their own personal goals. Developmental states achieve a high degree of professional and bureaucratic coherence and "embedded autonomy": they are connected with private interests without being captured by them. They more closely approximate the Weberian model (Evans 1995: 12). Developmental states supply public goods by overcoming the collective action problems that would otherwise prevent private interests from contributing to developmental goals. The "other" or "intermediate apparatuses" are neither fully developmental tigers, nor entirely predatory kleptocracies. Despite lacking the internal coherence and embedded autonomy necessary to be powerful engines of development, Latin American states nevertheless perform important developmental functions.[2]

Evans took Weber as his normative baseline for theorizing the state, as did O'Donnell, so that is where we begin. Weber described the state as "a relation of men dominating men, a relation supported by means of legitimate (i.e. considered to be legitimate) violence" (Weber 1958: 78). More concretely, state institutions claim "the *monopoly of legitimate use of physical force* within a given territory" (1958: 78, italics in original). Weber's widely used definition captures the dual meaning of the state as a set of bureaucratic agencies, on the one hand, and a specific monopoly of coercive power, on the other hand. In his reading of Weber, O'Donnell also emphasized this dual nature of the state. "It is a mistake," he argued,

> to conflate the state with the state apparatus, the public sector, or the aggregation of bureaucracies. These, unquestionably, are part of the state but they are not all of it. The state is also, and no less primarily, a set of social relations that establishes a certain order and guarantees over a given territory.
>
> (O'Donnell 1993: 1356)

O'Donnell embraced Weber's analysis of the state, but he sought to further develop an understanding of the law as a constitutive feature of the modern state. This led him to qualify Weber's definition in the following terms: the state monopolizes the legally valid *authorization* of the use of force; whether it does, in fact, monopolize the *use* of force – "legitimate or not but actual" – is contingent (O'Donnell 2010: 51–53). The social relations that establish a certain order are "formalized in a legal system and backed by the state" (O'Donnell 1993: 1356). Indeed, the legal system is a "constitutive dimension of the state and of the order that it establishes and guarantees over a given territory" (1993: 1356). This point cannot be overstated because it informs what can realistically be expected of the rule of law. The order guaranteed by the state and the legal system it formalizes is neither neutral nor impartial: the state "backs, and helps to reproduce, systematically asymmetrical power relationships" (O'Donnell 1993: 1356). This is not to deny that the state, like any association, provides benefits to its members, such as fostering collective action, overcoming free rider problems, and supplying public goods. The lawful state (or *Estado de derecho*) enhances collective power and restrains the arbitrary use of power, but it also creates and reproduces hierarchies that can be oppressive (O'Donnell 2010: 59–62). Behrend and Whitehead capture this ambivalence when they suggest the rule of law creates "arenas of equality for citizens but this formal equality contrasts with multiple inequalities that arise from social and economic relations, territorial variations, and legal agency – i.e. the capacity to make effective use of the law." These inequalities are also sustained by the state.

The ambivalence is inherent in the social relations and legal guarantees associated with capitalist democracy. Inequalities are "intrinsic to the social relations of capitalism" (O'Donnell 2010: 105) and:

> [t]he state, as the guarantor of the capitalist relations of production, is (no less than their economic aspects) a necessary and primordial part of these relations. In addition to guaranteeing their effectiveness and reproduction, the state also organizes relations of production by articulating and buffering

> the relationships among classes and by providing elements necessary to their "normal" unchallenged reproduction.
>
> (O'Donnell 1988: 2)

The state is not a mere instrument of domination of a particular class, class fraction, or alliance, but rather an aspect of the social relations of domination that it co-constitutes, reproduces, and potentially transforms through its legal system (O'Donnell 2010: 105–106). The social inequalities that give rise to relations of domination are not limited to class divisions and relations of production. Michael Hanchard (2018: 177–181) extended O'Donnell's analysis to include racial and ethno-national dimensions of politics. States also guarantee and perpetuate racial, ethnic, colonial, and gender hierarchies, both directly and indirectly through their intersections with other dimensions of inequality. Moreover, the inequalities generated by capitalist social relations are racialized and gendered. The social relations co-constituted and guaranteed by the state are intersectional, and the same logic by which states uphold capitalist social relations applies to the ways in which they reinforce racial, ethnic, colonial, and gender inequalities.

Although states provide unequal social relations with a coercive guarantee, they invariably appeal to general interests like the nation, citizenship, or the people (*pueblo, lo popular*). These general interests are intended to make the use of force "legitimate," as Weber would say, "(i.e., considered to be legitimate)." Such "legitimacy" – always placed by Weber in quotation marks – may have various sources, or "inner justifications," including tradition, charisma, and legal rationality (Weber 1958: 78). Of special interest is the latter, the effectiveness of which, as O'Donnell (1993: 1357) notes:

> consists of innumerable habituated behaviors that (consciously or not) are usually consistent with the prescriptions of the law. That effectiveness is based on the widely held expectation, borne out by exemplary evidence, that the law will be, if necessary, enforced by a central authority endowed with the pertinent powers.

Law provides the "supporting texture of the order established and guaranteed" by the state and, because it is codified and "subject to the interpretations of professionalized knowledge" (that is, the knowledge of lawyers and judges). The formal rationalization of the administrative apparatus of the modern state introduces calculability and specialization into its operation (Weber 1958: 182–183). Only when different agencies possess specific "spheres of competence" can they hold one another accountable within the framework of agreed-upon rules and procedures. O'Donnell called this counterpoint to domination "horizontal accountability," and he argued it was crucial to the rule of law and, ultimately, democracy itself. But if this counterpoint to domination is weak, so is domination itself.

In a pathbreaking article, O'Donnell (1993: 1359) used a cartographic metaphor to think about the state:

> Let us imagine a map of each country in which the areas covered by blue would designate those where there is a high degree of state presence (in terms of a set of reasonably effective bureaucracies and of the effectiveness of properly sanctioned legality), both functionally and territorially; the green color indicates a high degree of territorial penetration and a significantly lower presence in functional/class terms; and the brown color a very low or nil level in both dimensions.

Much of Latin America would be covered by brown areas, he suggested, but there would be important pockets of green and blue. This uneven presence and intermittent effectiveness of the state have highly significant implications. It means that domination is weak, especially on the periphery of states that tend to be highly centralized. But this also limits the possibility of the "legitimation" of domination through law. Thus, the intermediate state apparatus is not only marked by limited accountability and unevenness in the application of the law; it is also a state in which domination itself is precarious. In such a context, the law may provide some supporting texture to the social order, but this is partially offset by unrestrained *de facto* powers, the blurring of boundaries between public and private, gaps in the legal order, and the precarious circumstances of those who most need the benefits of the impartial administration of justice. Domination that must be reinforced at the margins of legality is what gives Latin American politics its distinctly oligarchic flavour (see Boesten and Llanos).

Intermediate state apparatuses and the rule of law: Five issues

In this section, I draw on the chapters from this book to discuss five issues, each closely related to the state and the rule of law. The first, already alluded to above, is subnational variation in effectiveness and enforcement of the law by intermediate state apparatuses. Second, intermediate state apparatuses pursuing resource extraction tend to privilege the legal rights of investors over those of citizens; however, this can be balanced by popular mobilization, both contentious and institutionalized. Third, informality is favoured by intermediate state apparatuses with a low capacity to address the requirements for the social reproduction of the workforce. Fourth, the spread of armed non-state actors reflects the uneven presence and penetration of intermediate state apparatuses. Finally, the tension between formal equality and severe social inequalities results in patterns of democratic delinquency, republican corruption, and other practices that undermine the quality of democracy.

1. *Subnational variation in the rule of law.* Subnational variation is a key source of unevenness in the rule of law in intermediate state apparatuses, and it

is discussed in many of the chapters in this book. What happens when the state does not possess a monopoly of "legitimate" coercion, or when "the effectiveness of the law extends very irregularly (it does not altogether disappear) across the territory and the functional relations (including class, ethnic, and gender relations) it supposedly regulates?" (O'Donnell 1999: 138). The short answer is that states lose their regulatory capacity, local powers, which tend to be less bureaucratic and more patrimonial, are reinforced, crime and unlawful enforcement increase, and democracy suffers (O'Donnell 1999: 138–139).

What O'Donnell called brown areas would include much of the countryside in Colombia, especially those frontier and peripheral areas where non-state armed groups collude with political and economic elites in the struggle for power.[3] State authority tends to be concentrated in major cities, especially their affluent zones. Intermediate state apparatuses rule centrifugally, from the centre outward; thus, as Jan Boesten and Daniel Llanos note, violence tends to be concentrated on the periphery of the national territory. "Behind this apparent core/periphery divide lie subnational institutions that have very little in common with the democratic promises of the country's constitution." An ineffective monopoly of violence at the subnational level encourages the growth of non-state actors who undermine republican institutions and reinforce subnational oligarchic modes of rule.

In Argentina, the brown areas are smaller than in Colombia.[4] Behrend's analysis of Argentina stresses the uncertainties and entanglements of economic elites and informal political dynasties in subnational regimes in which local courts may permit extra-legal activities but where national institutions like the supreme court may still uphold the law and constitution. Behrend notes that there is "enormous variation in political competition, economic development and in the enforcement of the rule of law" at the subnational level in Argentina. There is variation in the degree to which local elites are able to capture subnational state apparatuses, and this has powerful implications for democracy.

By recognizing that formal institutions are not always entirely authoritative, informal and formal institutions are often in tension, and many social structures and practices reinforce non-democratic politics, Behrend offers a more realistic understanding of the functioning of democracy at the subnational level than might be suggested by the ideals of liberal democracy. Indeed, politics at the subnational level – and increasingly at the national level in many countries around the world, not just in Latin America – often appears to be more dynastic than democratic, in the sense that there are often powerful political families in which political succession occurs within the family, and many of these familial dynasties have complex entanglements with economically powerful families. This is about as close a definition of oligarchy as one might imagine.

In her analysis of numerous cases of the politics of succession at the subnational level, Behrend provides us with many examples of struggles over changing the rules to allow re-election, which is a key driver of democratic erosion in Latin America. Efforts by politicians to perpetuate their tenure in power by overriding term limits have led to crises of democracy in Peru, Bolivia, Venezuela, Ecuador, Colombia, El Salvador, Nicaragua, and several other cases. In the Argentine case, provincial governors have had to operate within the context of a powerful national institution: the Supreme Court. This makes Argentina, in Behrend's analysis, a striking laboratory of democratic politics. In this respect, Argentina's provinces have benefited from the strength and integrity of the nation's top court.

2. *Extractivism and the rule of law.* Extractive industries are often associated with conflicts arising from distributive pressures and negative externalities (especially environmental destruction). As Par Engstrom and Edward Pérez note, "Across the Latin America, where extractivism remains the dominant model of development, the surge in socio-environmental conflicts in recent decades constitutes a distinct challenge to the rule of law and basic governability." They add that Indigenous and Afro-descendent communities "are particularly affected, given the significance of land and natural resources for their livelihoods, and in many contexts, their collective survival." Engstrom examines the way in which intermediate state apparatuses supporting extractive projects find themselves caught in the pincers between the Inter-American Human Rights System (IAHRS) and local communities. This fuels governance patterns marked by clientelism and swings between populism and economic orthodoxy, often leading to the state's co-optation by private interests.

Extractivism implies more than the exploitation of natural resources: It is associated with the so-called "resource curse" – the "adverse effects of a country's natural resource wealth on its economic, social, or political well-being" (Ross 2015, cited in Bebbington et al. 2018). A key feature of the resource curse is the way it shapes the underlying pact of domination. The more extractivist an economy, the more states are likely to engage in predatory behaviour. Yet most Latin American states are far from Evans' ideal-type of predatory apparatuses. They may have predatory features, but they also uphold the rule of law, however unevenly. In some areas, Latin American states have been at the vanguard of legal reform and innovation. Of particular interest in this context is the protection of the environment as a result of legislation that guarantees the right to a healthy environment (or, in other cases, the rights of nature itself). Gutiérrez and Christel (2017) have argued that the recognition of environmental rights in amendments to Argentina's constitution has contributed to justice and citizenship rights, but popular participation, both contentious and institutionalized, is necessary to make such rights effective. Through their study of forestry and mining in Argentina, Gutiérrez and Christel show that where local populations have demanded and achieved participation in environmental governance, they have been able to make significant gains against extractive industries.

Argentina's 1994 constitutional reforms introduced new rights into the 1853 Constitution, including the right to a healthy environment. It gave responsibility to the national government to ensure environmental protection throughout the national territory. In Gutiérrez and Christel's account, the constitutionally-enshrined right to a healthy environment, as well as supplementary legislation and administrative measures, empowered social movements seeking to defend the environment both through contentious politics and via institutional channels. They offer an example of how laws can supply the supporting texture of the social and political order in ways that potentially enhance the agency of citizens, creating governance arrangements for participation, and improving the transparency of government agencies. Not only does this reinforce fundamental rights and freedoms, they argue, but it also gives clarity and predictability to the various actors or stakeholders in the policy space. But the law is never enough. Participation and contentious politics are often required to close the gap between what they call formal and substantive law (or law in the material sense, i.e., how it is actually applied and implemented). The law is also a site of contestation because of "contrasting ideas about what is fair and desirable in the relationship between society and nature." The idea of a right to a healthy environment has gained considerable ground globally, and as it does, the working through of the implications is by no means a merely technical matter. The critical issue is whether these matters can be processed in a way that reinforces citizenship. This requires the construction of governance arrangements that are participatory, robust, and transparent, and that enjoy the certainty and flexibility afforded by the rule of law.

In this regard, Yanina Welp's analysis of the use of direct democracy mechanisms (including referendums and citizen initiatives) to manage conflicts arising from natural resource development reveals decidedly mixed results. Although most countries in Latin America have adopted some form of popular consultation, justified in terms of policy legitimation and citizen inclusion, the capacity of these mechanisms to generate these goods depends on conditions most notable for their absence: the rule of law, well-designed decision-making processes, impartial administration, empowered and informed citizens, and responsible politicians.

3. *Informality and social reproduction.* The state is the guarantor not of specific social actors, or even the capitalist economy as a whole, but of the existing social relations within a particular society, including capitalist social relations. Capitalism comes in many varieties, including different modes of production and exchange (O'Donnell 2010: 126). The Latin American variety is aptly captured by Ben Ross Schneider's concept of "hierarchical market economies" (HMEs). A key feature of HMEs is that they are highly unequal (especially at the upper-income end of the wealth and income hierarchy) and involve powerful economic groups, often family businesses (Behrend focuses on this in Argentina). They are also extensively informalized.

Informal economic activity is vital to social reproduction in HMEs. Informal labour is often considered marginal because it reflects the limited capacity for labour absorption by the formal sector in labour-abundant economies. Informal workers are, however, critical to the social reproduction of economic activity. In general, states play a vital role in social reproduction, especially by ensuring a supply of labour. In HMEs, specifically, the fiscal strategy of the state is to withhold the application of the law by limiting regulation and the provision of a wide range of public goods. Critical public goods like housing, food, transportation, caregiving, domestic service, and even security are left to the informal sector. Much of this labour is feminized and undercompensated (see Blofield 2012), and it should be considered a major subsidy to the formal economy. Focusing our attention on social reproduction centres "the forms of provisioning, caregiving, and interaction that produce and sustain human beings and social bonds" (Fraser 2022: 9). This kind of labour is essential for economic development even though it is not accounted for in the official records. The dependence of the formal on the informal economy is reinforced by neoliberalism which "has built an entire accumulation strategy by expelling billions of people from the official economy into informal grey zones" (Fraser 2022: 6). Neoliberal policymakers often implement policies with the ostensible goal of formalizing the informal economy, but their policy solutions to informality actually reproduce informality because they are based on a flawed understanding of its function.

The solution offered by neoliberals is to reduce the size of the state and simplify or eliminate regulations in the formal economy. As a policy to formalize the economy, this recipe has precisely the opposite effect, which is one reason informality has persisted in the neoliberal era even in the context of rapid economic growth. Formalizing the informal sector requires precisely the policy prescriptions most repudiated by neoliberals: namely, to improve the capacity of the state to regulate the workplace, guarantee labour rights, and enforce health and safety standards. These measures need to be coupled with social and infrastructural investments in education, healthcare, public transportation, and communications. Last but not least, given that violence is often concentrated in informal urban settlements and isolated rural locales (Davis 2017), public investments in protecting citizens from violence are necessary to eradicate informality.

In their chapter on informal mining, John Crabtree, Anna Wilson, and Aaron Quiñón Cárdenas note that informality has remained a "conspicuous characteristic of the labour market in Latin America." Since neoliberal policies were adopted in Peru in the 1990s under the Fujimori government (1990–2000), informality has not returned to its previous levels. They therefore reject the view that "the answer to informalisation is to 'deformalise' the formal sector by eliminating labour rights." Nevertheless, they credit Hernando de Soto with calling attention to the role of law and legal regulation. Focusing on gold miners, they highlight the precarity of employment that is outside the scope of legislation, taxation, social protection, and entitlements like sick pay, holidays, and pensions. A major sector of the economy – accounting for over a million workers – is simply outside the scope of public regulation. This is not because the state lacks the financial resources, but rather because informality is integral to the economic model. Formalization, if pursued rigorously, would constitute an attack on the existing system of property relations. The persistence of the informal sector owes less to the costs of formality than to the dependence of the HME model on the presence of a state that does not tax and regulate economic activity outside the formal sector. Informality is the "cushion" of social reproduction that allows for the ongoing extraction of resources without the possibility of transformation into a more inclusive model of development. It is a source of the inequality that the state guarantees.

Crabtree, Wilson, and Quiñón Cárdenas provide an illuminating account of the various (always extremely feeble) efforts that have been made to address informality in Peru over the past two decades. They provide a persuasive case for why it is important to try to formalize the economy from a public policy perspective, yet they note that, despite these compelling reasons, little progress has been made. The explanation is clearly political: there is major political resistance to the kinds of policies that would formalize the economy on the part of elites who benefit from the current neoliberal economic model. Formalizing labour would strengthen the power of workers in a state that has, especially since the Fujimori era, defined its role – enshrined in the 1993 Constitution – as a facilitator of investment, above all in the extractive economy. Crabtree, Wilson, and Quiñón Cárdenas' close analysis of informal miners in Arequipa not only provides an account of the obstacles to informalization; it also shows how important this sector is to the livelihood of local communities (and thus to social reproduction) and how vulnerable the workers are to exploitation by other agents in the market and the state.

Consider the claim by Crabtree, Wilson, and Quiñón Cárdenas that the mercury used by informal miners in Arequipa comes from contraband from Bolivia: "Although we cannot be sure that this is the case," they say,

> some regional official say that the Peruvian police play a significant role in this trade, casting a blind eye to acquisitions in return for payment of bribes, thus (among other things) adding to the costs of production and further undermining the rule of law.

I would add that this means the informal sector subsidizes the efforts of the police to keep the informal economy in a subordinate position, even as it offers a means for survival that is necessary due to the incapacity of the state to provide welfare and the unwillingness of the private sector to pay taxes sufficient to sustain policies that would enhance the economic inclusion of the informal sector. In short, the informal sector is integral to the social relations of domination that are ultimately guaranteed by the state apparatus.

4. *"Legitimate" violence and effectivity.* Intermediate state apparatuses, because they lack internal coherence and external autonomy, are easily penetrated by gangs and criminal mafias. This does not mean that the state does

not provide a guarantee of social order, but rather that legal and illegal activities coexist in the systems of domination states uphold. This explains why Latin America is over-represented in global homicide statistics, and why variation within and across the region reflects the uneven presence of the state. As Deborah Yashar (2018) explains, there are "varied homicide levels in contemporary democracies" in terms of "the geography of illicit political economies, the capacity of state security forces, and organizational competition over territorial enclaves." The variation in violence and the way it spreads in the absence of a state monopoly of legitimate forces is well illustrated by the case of Colombia.

As a rule, the failure to secure a monopoly of legitimately authorized uses of force within a given territory invites other armed non-state actors to enter the territory to supply the basic goods necessary for any social order to function, and they may thereby gain legitimacy in the eyes of local communities in the process. In Colombia, non-state armed groups include communities organized for their own self-defence, guerrilla organizations, or paramilitary organizations; they are often entangled with state agencies or one another in subtle and extraordinarily opaque ways. Ordinary citizens are compelled to operate in the grey zone between the state apparatus's deficient and selective rule of law and the inducements and constraints imposed by non-state actors. Annette Adler and Laurence Whitehead use the term "shadow citizenship" to capture the agency of civilians in these governance structures. The moral economy underpinning shadow citizenship is not a foundation for more liberal democratic forms of citizenship, but it also indicates the weakness of domination when non-state actors perform roles and responsibilities typically assigned to the state. The absence of the state, or its lack of penetration of society, leaves populations vulnerable to predation, weakens the provision of public goods, and corrupts the functioning of state institutions like municipalities, participatory institutions, and political parties in peripheral zones.

Boesten and Llanos seek to explain how "relatively robust democratic institutions" can coexist with "high levels of (political/criminal) violence" in Colombia. Drawing on Jeffrey Winter's (2011) theory of oligarchy, they argue that Colombia possesses the legal institutions and constraints necessary to preserve the material interests of economic elites even as violent non-state actors struggle for control over territory, resources, and power. There is a "functional differentiation" between these two types of oligarchic groups, civil and warring, based on which side of the margin of legality they operate, and yet they interact and are continuously engaged in alliances and struggles. Colombia, they conclude, is characterized by the peculiar "coexistence of warring and civil oligarchies." Although remarkably enduring, this pattern of domination is extraordinarily costly in lives, liberty, and property.

5. *Democratic delinquencies and republican corruption.* Intermediate state apparatuses may contribute to the poor performance of democracy and development. Recent scholarship has called attention to the resilience and persistence

of low-quality democracies in Latin America (Munck 2023, Cameron 2022, Mazzuca & Munck 2021, Whitehead 2021). The region's democracies are at once enduring and stuck in suboptimal equilibria. These equilibria result from deficiencies in democratic regimes and, above all, the states that underpin them. A good example is the widespread phenomena that fall under the rubric of what Laurence Whitehead (2021) has called "democratic delinquency" – i.e., the "severe inadequacies" in the rule of law caused by "social inequalities and political instabilities" (Whitehead 2021: 78). Some democratic delinquencies are high profile, like corruption scandals; others involve everyday insecurities suffered by citizens.

Whitehead and Susana Berruecos' chapter on Mexico's new *Fiscalia General de la República* (FGR) captures a central ambivalence of the intermediate state apparatus. The rule of law demands acceptance of an independent judiciary capable of impartial resolution of disputes among citizens and between the citizen and the state. In highly unequal societies, however, parity of treatment of powerful elites and ordinary citizens is elusive, and this inequity is exacerbated by the spread of criminal violence which threatens to overwhelm the control of the state apparatus. Reinforcing the independence and discretion of top prosecutors, therefore, offers both an appealing solution and a potential problem because it is highly inconvenient to incumbents in office and, moreover, the prosecutors themselves may indulge in arbitrary and abusive power. Since there are both federal and state prosecutors in Mexico, "islands of excellence" in the rule of law emerge in some areas while lawlessness persists in others. Whitehead and Berruecos conclude that progress in addressing Mexico's rule of law failures has been limited despite constitutional and legal reforms aimed at strengthening the independence of the FGR and state prosecutors.

The lack of progress toward the rule of law under the administration of Andrés Manuel López Obrador's Morena party in Mexico is documented by J. Carlos Domínguez Virgen in his study of infrastructural projects. Domínguez uses the term "technopopulism" to capture the politicization of projects that involve both highly technical and socially sensitive issues. Technopopulism is "the selective use of technical arguments in order to justify public policy projects and decisions which also serve political and even ideological interests." Failure to heed technical advice can lead to catastrophic outcomes, and yet technical rationality is insufficient to justify policy decisions. Eager to move forward with infrastructural projects, and seeking to neutralize opposition, politicians can deploy a variety of rhetorical strategies to justify decisions that are, nonetheless, motivated largely by political considerations. Domínguez warns that the harmful consequences of these decisions can create future legal liabilities that it is in the interest of rulers to escape with impunity. Thus, infrastructural projects may provide reasons for politicians to undermine the rule of law.

Often, democratic delinquencies involve failures to uphold republican principles of government. Ordinarily, we think about corruption as the unlawful benefits that public officials attain for themselves or others, but we can also think about corruption, as republicans have done, as a problem of the erosion or corruption of the political regime itself in relation to the general interests it serves. This brings us back to the ideology of the state and its mediations with society. At the substantive core of the republican understanding of democracy is the difficult but essential concept of popular sovereignty. Popular sovereignty – the idea that citizens, through their representatives, are governed by their own consent – is problematic in any diverse, complex, and pluralistic society, but it is also the basis of legitimacy of the modern constitutional democratic state. Popular sovereignty is only meaningful in the context of a legal system (or *Estado de derecho democratico*) that creates a public sphere. In the absence of a legally guaranteed public sphere, the idea of the "consent of the governed" is a chimera. Rule by the consent of the governed demands a set of practices that are constitutive of the democratic state. These include, inter alia, the legal assignment of rights to citizens, legislation by elected officials, the impartial administration of justice, and the presumption that nobody is *de legibus solutus*.

An important recent example of a corrupt practice is electoral denialism – the deceptive allegation of fraud intended to perpetrate fraud. In several countries, judicial procedures have been weaponized to remove duly elected officials from office or block them from running on unproven charges of corruption. In Guatemala, a criminal judge responsible for investigating corruption attempted to block a successful presidential candidate from taking office in order to defend a corrupt mafia in politics. In Brazil, one presidential candidate (Dilma Rousseff) was impeached by Congress on grounds of corruption, in spite of the fact that similar charges could have applied equally to Congress, and another presidential candidate (Luiz Inácio Lula da Silva, "Lula") was imprisoned and blocked from running for office by corruption allegations that were later dropped. In Peru, a president was deposed after attempting a presidential self-coup or *autogolpe* in the face of persistent unconstitutional efforts to impeach him. While some of these leaders no doubt engaged in corruption, malfeasance, or neglect of duties, the legal proceedings against them had political aims that actually served corrupt purposes.

Karabekir Akkoyunlu and José Antonio Lima show how Jair Bolsonaro's attempted *autogolpe* disrupted the political equilibrium in the branches of government and threatened to politicize the military through a process of stealth intervention. In the process, the integrity of the Armed Forces as "guarantor of law and order" was undermined. The breakdown of democracy was largely avoided, however, due to the cohesion of Brazil's otherwise fractured political establishment and by the pragmatism and experience of Bolsonaro's successor, Lula. Akkoyunlu and Lima's account is particularly fascinating because it situates the courts at the heart of the political struggle in Brazil. It was the courts that, through the *Lava Jato* investigations, contributed to the fall of Lula and his successor Dilma, but also held Bolsonaro and senior brass accountable for their roles in seeking to overturn the results of a democratic election, Trump-style. Bolsonaro's criminality and efforts to cover up his crimes and to rule by decree, and spread conspiracy theories and misinformation about fraud, have not been tolerated by Brazil's election authorities or judges. Brazil may be vulnerable to political outsiders who seek to overturn the political establishment, but such outsiders, Akkoyunlu and Lima argue, have rarely succeeded in Brazil. Although Brazil remains highly polarized, and the military retains considerable prerogatives, Lula wisely focused on governance issues rather than seeking revenge.

Conclusion

This concluding chapter has examined five crucial ways in which intermediate state apparatuses have limited democracy and development in Latin America: the unevenness of the rule of law at the subnational level, the imbalance in the rights of affected communities relative to the rights of investors in extractive economies, reliance on informality for social reproduction, the spread of non-state armed actors, and the challenges of democratic delinquency and republican corruption to the quality of democracy. These themes are at the heart of contemporary debates on the state, development, and democracy.

The findings summarized in this book and this chapter suggest important directions for further research. The first is to explore dynamic changes in subnational and transnational variation in the rule of law over time and space. How is the rule of law strengthened or weakened, and under what conditions does strengthening the law in one jurisdiction cause illegal activity to expand into another jurisdiction? A second challenge is the search for alternatives to extractive models of development that place citizenship rights and participation, especially Indigenous communities, on par with the rights of investors. A third theme is the impact of informality on democracy – more specifically, the ways in which informal economic activities are represented in formal and informal governance arrangements – and how informal economies can be formalized. A fourth theme is how to pivot from shadow citizenship to the kind of citizenship supported by a state that guarantees the rights of citizens. Finally, recognizing that the rule of law is a necessary condition for stronger democracies, future research should address the state as a source of both weakness and resilience in suboptimal democratic regimes.

For all these future research agendas, the contributions to this volume provide an indispensable point of departure. They do so, as the editors stress, by addressing the rule of law more expansively, connecting it to developmental challenges, and recognizing the difference between formal rules and how people actually behave. Democracy as a political regime requires a lawful state that backs the rights and freedoms of citizens. This book helps us grapple with the thorny questions that arise when democratic regimes are supported by state apparatuses in which the rule of law is often entangled in formal and informal practices that are undemocratic.

Notes

1 According to Tom Bingham (2011: 8), the rule of law means "that all person and authorities within the state, whether public or private, should be bound by and entitled to the benefit of laws publicly made, taking effect (generally) in the future and publicly administered in the courts."
2 Luis Karamaneff's chapter provides an intriguing example of how a subnational state can achieve industrial transformation without a coherent bureaucracy or embedded autonomy by means of what he calls the strategy of "bureaucratic bypass." In effect, government officials delegate developmental tasks to external agents possessing capabilities the state lacks. Karamaneff examines a province in Argentina that was able to relocate industries within its jurisdiction by hiring surrogates with the necessary information and capabilities.
3 See also Gutiérrez-Sanín (2023).
4 Although fraught (see O'Donnell 2010: fn 4, 94–95), rule of law rankings place Argentina above Colombia. See: https://worldjusticeproject.org/rule-of-law-index/global.

Bibliography

Bebbington, A. et al., 2018. "Resource Extraction and Inclusive Development: Extending the Bases of the Political Settlements Approach," *Governing Extractive Industries: Politics, Histories, Ideas*. Oxford: Oxford University Press.

Bingham, Tom. 2011. *The Rule of Law*. London: Penguin.

Blofield, M. 2012. *Care Work and Class: Domestic Workers' Struggle for Equal Rights in Latin America*. University Park, PA: The Penn State University Press.

Brinks D.M, Levitsky, S., & Murillo, M.V. 2019. *Understanding Institutional Weakness: Power and Design in Latin American Institutions*. Cambridge: Cambridge University Press.

Cameron, M.A. 2022. "Political Regimes: Components, Crises, and Change," in Cameron, M.A. and Jaramillo, G.M., eds. *Challenges to Democracy in the Andes: Strongmen, Broken Constitutions, and Regimes in Crisis*. Boulder, CO: Lynne Rienner Publishers, pp. 23–45.

Christel, L.G., & Gutiérrez, R.A. 2017. "Making Rights Come Alive: Environmental Rights and Modes of Participation in Argentina," *The Journal of Environment & Development*, 26(3): 322–347.

Davis, D. 2017. "Violence, Fragmented Sovereignty, and Declining State Capacity: Rethinking the Legacies of Developmental Statism in Mexico." In Centeno, Miguel A., Kohli, Atul, and Yashar, Deborah J., eds., *States in the Developing World*. Cambridge: Cambridge University Press.

Evans, P.B. 1989. "Predatory, Developmental, and Other Apparatuses: A Comparative Political Economy Perspective on the Third World State," *Sociological Forum*, 4(4): 561–587.

Evans, P.B. 1995. *Embedded Autonomy: States and Industrial Transformation*. Princeton, NJ: Princeton University Press.

Fraser, N. 2022. *Cannibal Capitalism: How Our System Is Devouring Democracy, Care, and the Planet – and What We can Do About It.* London: Verso.
Gutiérrez-Sanín, F. 2023. "Politicians: The Sinews of Counterinsurgent Governance in Colombia," *Third World Quarterly*, 44(6): 1211–1229.
Hanchard, M.G. 2018. *The Spectre of Race: How Discrimination Haunts Western Democracy.* Princeton: Princeton University Press.
Mazzuca, S.L., & Munck, G.L. 2021. *A Middle-Quality Institutional Trap: Democracy and State Capacity in Latin America.* Cambridge: Cambridge University Press.
Munck, G.L. 2023. "The State as a Determinant of Democracy: Durable Poor-Quality Democracies in Contemporary Latin America," *Democratization*, 31(2): 341–365.
O'Donnell, G. 1988. *Bureaucratic Authoritarianism: Argentina, 1966–1973, in Comparative Perspective* [Transl. James McGuire]. Berkeley, CA: University of California Press.
O'Donnell, G. 1993. "On the State, Democratization, and Some Conceptual Problems," *World Development*, 21(8): 1355–1369.
O'Donnell, G. 1999. *Counterpoints: Selected Essays on Authoritarianism and Democracy.* Notre Dame: University of Notre Dame.
O'Donnell, G. 2010. *Democracy, Agency, and the State: Theory with Comparative Intent.* Oxford: Oxford University Press.
Ross, M. 2015. 'What have we learned about the Resource Curse?' *Annual Review of Political Science*, 18: 239–259.
Schneider, B.R. 2013. *Hierarchical Capitalism in Latin America: Business, Labor, and the Challenges of Equitable Development.* New York, NY: Cambridge University Press.
Weber, M. 1958. *From Max Weber: Essays in Sociology*. [Transl. H.H. Gerth and C. Wright Mills]. New York: Oxford University Press.
Weber, M. 1978. *Economy and Society, Volume One: An Outline of Interpretive Sociology*. [Transl. G. Roth and C. Wittich]. Berkeley: University of California Press.
Whitehead, L. 2021. "The Danger of Democratic Delinquency," *Journal of Democracy*, 32(3): 78–93.
Winters, J.A. 2011. *Oligarchy*. New York, NY: Cambridge University Press.
Yashar, D. 2018. *Homicidal Ecologies. Illicit Economies and Complicit States in Latin America.* Cambridge: Cambridge University Press.

Index

Page numbers in *italic* indicate figure and **bold** indicate table respectively

Kolibri 360 GmbH
Ferdinand-Jühlke-Straße 7
99095 Erfurt, Deutschland
produktsicherheit@kolibri360.de